Altogether Fitting and Proper

Altogether Fitting and Proper

Civil War Battlefield Preservation
in History, Memory, and Policy,
1861–2015

Timothy B. Smith

Knoxville / The University of Tennessee Press

LIBRARY OF CONGRESS CATALOGING-IN-PUBLICATION DATA

Names: Smith, Timothy B., 1974–
Title: "Altogether fitting and proper" : Civil War battlefield preservation in history, memory,
and policy, 1861–2015 / Timothy B. Smith.
Description: Knoxville: The University of Tennessee Press, 2017. | Includes bibliographical
references and index.
Identifiers: LCCN 2016033870| ISBN 9781621903116 (hardcover) | ISBN 9781621903130
(kindle)
Subjects: LCSH: United States—History—Civil War, 1861–1865—Battlefields. |
Battlefields—Conservation and restoration—United States—History. | Military
parks—Government policy—United States—History. | National parks and reserves—
Government policy—United States—History. | United States—Cultural policy.
Classification: LCC E641 .S6 2017 | DDC 973.7—dc23
LC record available at https://lccn.loc.gov/2016033870

"We have come to dedicate a portion of that field. . . .
It is altogether fitting and proper that we should do this."

ABRAHAM LINCOLN
Gettysburg Address

In memory of
Mike Ballard

Contents

Illustrations

Shiloh Civilian Conservation Corps Camp
McLean House at Appomattox
Fort Sumter
Harpers Ferry
Ulysses S. Grant III
March on Washington
President Ronald Reagan
Andersonville Stockade after the War
Edwin C. Bearss
African American Civil War Memorial
Corinth Civil War Interpretive Center
O. James Lighthizer

Foreword

Democracy is a fragile thing. If we look back over the history of human existence, we will see that few societies have risen to the challenge of sustaining a democratic political system over a prolonged period of time. In this regard, as in others, the United States of America is exceptional.

Time and again, our greatest leaders have recognized that the success of our experiment in democracy rests upon a knowledgeable citizenry capable of making informed judgments. John Adams wrote, "Liberty cannot be preserved without a general knowledge among the people." Franklin Delano Roosevelt said, "Democracy cannot succeed unless those who express their choice are prepared to choose wisely. The real safeguard of democracy, therefore, is education."

When he was only twenty-three, Abraham Lincoln correctly noted that education was valuable in part because it enables a citizen "to read the histories of his own and other countries, by which he may duly appreciate the value of our free institutions."

In this excellent new book by my good friend Tim Smith, citizens will learn about an important aspect of American history. Readers will discover the fascinating history of the movement to preserve America's Civil War battlefields. It shows how Civil War veterans themselves provided the impetus for early battlefield protection efforts, how the federal government embarked on an ambitious program of preservation in the first half of the twentieth century, and how, in the last three decades, the American people themselves have stepped up and taken action to protect battlefield land from new threats.

Knowledge of the past is indeed essential. To understand who we are, it is essential that we understand where we've been. To appreciate what we have, it is essential that we recognize the sacrifices of our forebearers.

Battlefield preservation is important for this very reason. Preserved battlefields serve as outdoor classrooms where Americans learn important lessons necessary for the preservation of our democracy from generation to generation. Every hour we lose roughly an acre of hallowed ground to suburban sprawl and other kinds of development. Once lost, that land can never be fully recovered. However, while the threats facing Civil War battlefields might be unprecedented, so too is the effort to save those battlefields.

At the Civil War Trust, we are committed to ensuring that the battles that defined who we are as a people are neither forgotten nor destroyed. When it comes to preserving the past I don't think there has ever been a grassroots, bottom-up movement quite like this in our country or even in the world.

From 1861 to 1865, citizen soldiers were the determining factor in the outcome of a struggle that defined who we are as a people. Now, more than a century and a half later, it is ordinary citizens who have come together to preserve that past.

As Abraham Lincoln might say, that is altogether fitting and proper.

JIM LIGHTHIZER
President
Civil War Trust

Preface

In his epic 1990 documentary *The Civil War*, Ken Burns famously declared, "The Civil War was fought in ten thousand places, from Valverde, New Mexico, and Tullahoma, Tennessee, to St. Albans, Vermont, and Fernandina on the Florida Coast." As a result, there are some ten thousand or more Civil War battlefields in America, which when looked at in the context of battlefield preservation creates a massive undertaking. Obviously, not all ten thousand places are worthy of being saved, with many smaller skirmish sites even being lost to history. The 1993 Civil War Sites Advisory Commission narrowed the field of important battles to 384, and narrowing the field further could drop that number to just scores of truly important actions. Still, the mammoth size of actual Civil War battlefield land in America, not to mention battlefields of other wars, is huge and leads to the necessity of some type of overall plan to foster preservation of those priceless sites.'

Fortunately, we now have a national-level entity that is leading the way in battlefield preservation. Inexplicably, that group is not the federal government but a private charitable organization, the Civil War Trust (CWT). The sesquicentennial of the war (2011–15) saw the CWT make large strides forward, primarily with its Campaign 150: Our Time, Our Legacy initiative. Yet the CWT is only the latest, albeit the most successful and comprehensive, entity to attempt to preserve Civil War battlefields. This book is a history of those attempts by various generations over the course of the last 150 years.

There is, however, more to the story than just the actual narrative of battlefield preservation successes resulting in parks. This study weaves together three major themes that have been at work over the years: outright preservation, federal historic preservation policy, and memory. This is not a book on any one of the themes specifically but on all three, woven together in a narrative history built around the people who have carried out the hard work of preservation.

The dominant theme, not surprisingly, is actual battlefield preservation on various levels, namely federal, state, local, and private; this story partly revolves around the mixture of those four levels—the percentages involved—which has varied over the generations. Obviously, federal preservation of battlefields was historically, and still is today, deemed the dominant and best option; local, private, and even state park supporters have long wished for national-level recognition in the form of a national park at their battlefield. State parks constitute the next best level, but unfortunately, dedication and funding among the states has varied widely, obviously being subject to politics and economics. Next below state parks are county and city governments, but they have few resources beyond zoning ordinances and several rural areas where many battlefields are located are not zoned at all. That leaves the private sector, where there is money but, until recently, little collaboration or overall leadership. Fortunately, that has changed in recent decades with the rise of the Civil War Trust.[1]

The various ways to conserve and the resulting fluidity of the process has led to starkly different results on the various battlefields. Consequently, it is necessary to define the word "preservation" as I use it in this book. Is preservation when a park is authorized by a governmental entity such as the U.S. Congress? Is it when land is actually acquired? When property is marked to interpret the history that occurred there? When land is opened to the public? When the land has gained interpretive facilities and staff? As far as tangible preservation at any specific site is concerned, I opt to treat historic battlefield preservation as an evolutionary process, and thus the definition will necessarily vary depending on each battlefield. Basically, I rate each site as preserved when it reaches its highest state of preservation as of 2015 (remembering that it could certainly change in the future). For instance, the battlefields in and around Richmond, Virginia, first had their original cemeteries, then were maintained by a private association, then were a state park, and finally became the Richmond National Battlefield Park. As a result, I treat all the battlefields' history leading up to the climax of its ultimate, present-day preservation status. On the other hand, the Prairie Grove battlefield in Arkansas will not get as much attention, the book simply dealing with the private park that later became a state park. For Richmond, the National Park Service (NPS) era is defined as the ultimate preservation success, while at Prairie Grove, the state park carries the same status.[3]

A more theoretical and academic definition of preservation is just as hard to pin down. Various generations viewed preservation in different ways and those ways changed over time, and while the results have been fairly consistent within the four major areas of preservation (federal, state, local, and private), the reasoning behind the efforts often varied drastically. For instance, veterans of the Civil War had very different views on how and why to preserve in the 1890s than did the centennial preservationists of the 1960s, who themselves had very different motives than do those engaged in present-day preservation efforts. While I will certainly deal with motives within each generation, I have chosen to emphasize the common denominator among all the generations by examining the central factor that transcends every generation: the people behind the preservation. In fact, I have found that battlefield preservation since the Civil War has not particularly hinged on place; most battlefields were located in the South, so that nullified any sectional swaying of the preservation ethic. Nor did the effort necessarily hinge on victory; one would think the federal government in particular would be more interested in Union victories, but Chickamauga, for example, was the first federal park created. Rather, I have found that the key ingredient to successful preservation throughout all generations is the people behind the effort. Whether it was Henry Boynton, David Henderson, or Daniel Sickles early on or innumerable congressmen and senators since, or even today's stalwart preservationists such as Jim Lighthizer, in large part the people behind the respective efforts, and their power, clout, and organization, largely determined which battlefields were preserved and which were not.

This book is a general overview of the preservation process and the people involved, using as many specific examples of battlefield preservation as possible. In that vein, it goes without saying that I cannot treat all ten thousand battlefields in one narrative. Likewise, I cannot document or mention every single episode of land acquisition through the years at any particular site. Therefore, the emphasis in this book (and by extension the aforementioned working definition of battlefield preservation) is on the establishment of the highest level of preservation for each battlefield, not the continual maintenance of preservation since that establishment. Similarly, I cannot treat every single entry at work preserving battlefields, especially in the modern age when numerous sites have their own private associations working hard toward their conservation. The mere listing of many of these in Chapter 7 borders on tedium for the reader, but I did it in order to illustrate the massive influx of private associations in the modern era. Even in that sample listing, however, all entities could not be included, and some readers may be irritated that their local battlefield did not receive much attention or was not even mentioned. The effort here, however, is to provide a broad overview of generations by using as many local examples as possible. Obviously all national and state parks are treated, and many of the secondary county, city, and private efforts are as well. It is virtually impossible to deal with all in the same detail, however, and I have opted to spend the majority of time on the most important parks—parks that have set the standard for preservation in their particular generation.

Choosing what and what not to examine illustrates another major conundrum that has faced preservationists of all generations. Preservationists today, and in each generation since the war, have argued over whether all battlefield land should or even can be preserved. Many preservationists of earlier generations certainly did not think so, and it is therefore necessary to remember that where we find ourselves today was not predestined or foreordained. It is also necessary to remember while reading this book that we look from a vantage point of hindsight, knowing now what many in earlier generations did not.

In dealing with battlefield preservation, I have, as stated, chosen to utilize the generational construct in organizing the chapters, beginning with the Civil War generation itself. While there are many Revolutionary War and War of 1812 sites preserved today (with the Civil War Trust recently moving into that era with its Campaign 1776 project), few of them were conserved prior to the Civil War. One such anomaly was the cornerstone for a monument at Bunker Hill in June 1825, the monument itself not being finished until 1843. The same occurred at Chalmette. Historic preservation during the antebellum period and even many years after the Civil War was tied to important men and houses, and the federal government had little impact on the process, leaving it to private efforts such as at Mount Vernon and Monticello. Historian Richard West Sellars explained that "the new nation lacked the necessary political cohesion and economic strength for a large scale memorialization effort." That mentality stuck for many years; battlefield preservation researchers Georgie Boge and Margie Boge argued, in fact, that this continuing mentality "has been a catastrophe for Civil War battlefield preservation."[4]

Civil War battlefield preservation, or at least the marking of sites, actually began during the war itself. Soldiers erected monuments and signs to denote special places, most often burial grounds, but by the end of the war monuments began to mark historic sites as well. Certainly, national cemeteries on the battlefields did as much. The Reconstruction generation continued this process through numerous new national cemeteries as well as through actual preservation, mostly privately at Gettysburg. Yet in an era of continuing animosity over the war and its causes—namely race and slavery—this generation's work was necessarily one sided, partisan, and limited.

A major change occurred, however, when the federal government became involved. With the establishment of a national military park at Chickamauga and Chattanooga in 1890, battlefield preservation entered its "golden age." Both Union and Confederate soldiers were involved as they reconciled with one another, albeit on a white-supremacy platform that neglected African Americans' role in the war. But aside from those negative social aspects, this reconciliation came at a good time in terms of preservation: the veterans were still around to accurately mark the sites, the battlefields themselves were still almost pristine, and Congress and state legislatures were still full of veterans who were willing to appropriate the needed money. Never again would America have the opportunity to preserve on this level. Yet the veterans of the golden age, golden though it was, performed only limited work, leaving many battlefields untouched and therefore vulnerable to destruction.

The original veterans so limited their work, in fact, that it was only in the next generation, in the 1920s, that a nationwide effort at preserving Civil War battlefields resurfaced. This time it was mostly modern War Department officers who saw a need to comprehensively study the battlefields and determine a fixed policy stating which of them should be preserved and how. This interregnum generation, coming as it did between two towering epochs, the golden age and the New Deal era, nevertheless provided a great deal of preservation thinking as well as much success in actual, tangible preservation. Although routinely left out of the preservation history story, this generation was actually quite important and should not be taken for granted.

The second of the two towering periods of major activity at battlefields came in the 1930s, as the New Deal generation provided much money and labor for work on the parks. Yet there was a significant change that occurred as the New Deal emerged: Congress backed away from actually appropriating money for new parks. With the transfer of the previously established War Department sites to the NPS in 1933, the battlefields were now within a growing bureaucracy that worked through the New Deal to update existing parks as well as create new ones. Significantly, Congress appropriated little money for parks in the 1930s; instead, it depended on New Deal money to make it happen, which occurred in several cases but failed to take place in others. The advent of World War II ended the New Deal and the money used to establish new parks. Thus the federal government began to back away from outright battlefield preservation.

Work restarted in the late 1940s and culminated in the Civil War's centennial celebrations in the early 1960s, but major changes also emerged in this era. The federal government continued to back away from outright preservation, leaving the work to the individual states, which provided a hurry of smaller and more limited parks as a result of the excitement generated by the centennial. A few larger national parks did emerge, but once again it was with little federal money as the individual states were required to obtain the land and donate it to the NPS. At the same time, the centennial reaggravated old racial wounds regarding the causes of the war and destroyed the reconciliationist feeling that had held sway, though continually weakening, since the 1890s.

From the late 1960s to the 1980s, as the centennial passed and the excitement dwindled, the United States entered a period of almost nonexistent preservation work in terms of battlefield preservation. The federal government preserved very little, choosing instead to take an advisory role. The states likewise struggled to preserve their battlefields, and the involvement of private groups became more common. As the nation entered the challenging economic times of the late 1970s and the fiscally conservative 1980s, even less preservation work took place. Compared to other generations, this was a veritable "dark age" in Civil War battlefield preservation.

Yet a new dawn appeared in the 1990s, a seeming Renaissance after the dark ages. It emerged out of the preservation debates at Antietam, Manassas, and other northern Virginia battlefields when historians and preservationists banded together to take action. As a result, numerous organizations were founded, and the federal government reentered the process with a new study of battlefields as well as an office within the NPS, the American Battlefield Protection Program. Still, there were few new congressionally sponsored parks and no leadership for a comprehensive preservation policy. By this time the states and smaller local governments had also given away the mantle of leadership, so the modern generation of preservationists saw the rise of private grass-roots organizations as the key to preservation success. Scores of associations emerged at numerous battlefields large and small, but they could not offer the long-awaited national leadership for the movement. Such an entity appeared when the struggling Association for the Preservation of Civil War Sites combined with the languid Civil War Trust in 1999 to create the Civil War Preservation Trust, now simply called the Civil War Trust. A national standard bearer for Civil War battlefield preservation had finally appeared, although it had taken nearly 140 years to do so.

This narrative takes the reader through the entire cyclical process, which began with the earliest generation's private and state work, moved to large-scale federal efforts, and eventually gave way to state and local government work before returning to the private efforts we see today. And although I will deal with the intricacies of preservation and the people behind the work, I will not deal with two tangential issues. The first is a myth stating that the pattern or the number of horses' hooves on the ground on equestrian statues denotes in some way the fate of a horse's rider. While there may be some coincidental correlation at Gettysburg, where the myth seems to have appeared, there is no evidence that there was any plan behind the system, let alone that it was purposefully carried on to other battlefields. Second, I will not try to differentiate the abundant and various names for the battlefield parks, which include "national military park," "national battlefield," "national battlefield site," "national battlefield park," "national monument," "national historic site," "national historical park," and "national memorial." While there is evidence that the term "national military park" denotes the oldest and most substantial battlefields, there is no real rhyme or reason for naming the parks as they currently are named, and many of them have actually gone through name changes over the years.[5]

Despite recurring myths and definitions, the generational aspect of the historic battlefield preservation movement is clear. Yet other factors also influenced the direction of battlefield preservation. Another issue of concern is the evolution of federal preservation policy, and in particular battlefield preservation policy. Many historians have tackled the larger preservation policy debate through the years, but few have dealt specifically with the battlefield aspect of it. Obviously the two are related, with battlefield strategy coming under the larger umbrella of overall historic preservation. As such, federal legislation such as the Antiquities Act, the Historic Sites Act, and the National Historic Preservation Act deserve discussion in the context of battlefield preservation, but the more specific Civil War battlefield preservation arena's preservation policies deserve greater scrutiny. For instance, developments during the golden age and interregnum eras generated fodder for an overall battlefield preservation policy, yet Congress never took that ultimate step. Likewise, the New Deal efforts as well as limited attempts in the centennial era provided additional opportunities that were never seized. The modern era has seen even more oversight work from the federal government, particularly the 1993 Civil War Sites Advisory Commission report, but again, Congress failed to take the commission's recommendations to create a full policy and the opportunity and enthusiasm evaporated. Now the Civil War Trust is doing what the federal government would not do, but the CWT is obviously limited in what it can accomplish in terms of enforcement, legislation, and statute. Still, the organization provides a national standard to which thousands are rallying.[6]

A third theme is the memory aspect of battlefield preservation. This book is not solely a study of Civil War memory, but it does include the modern aspect of memory study as it has related to and influenced battlefield preservation throughout the decades. Conversely, battlefield preservation has also influenced the memory of the Civil War. Historians have long argued that preservation itself is neutral, telling no story, but that the monumentation on the preserved field is what enumerates sides and is affected by or affects memory. Although I will deal only slightly with the monumentation—one historian has written that battlefields are "like a giant stage set, the play over and the actors gone, but with embellishments of granite and bronze recalling the heroism and tragedy"—I will deal with the changing background of the stage. "Evolution" is therefore a key term, as Americans' memory of the war has shifted over time in large part due to the circumstances in which the various generations lived, which also affected the manner in which battlefields were preserved. Although a primary focus of many of today's historians, memory is really nothing more than historiography writ large, as editors Lawrence A. Kreiser Jr. and Randal Allred demonstrate in *The Civil War in Popular Culture: Memory and Meaning*. Historiography normally judges the ebb and flow of schools of thought among academic publications, and memory does the very same thing, only on a larger canvas that includes much more than just academic writing, including popular sources such as magazines, movies, documentaries, and other nation-swaying media as well as the battlefields themselves. Preservationist and author Mary Munsell Abroe argues that memory and battlefields affect each other: "Interpretation in this sense is fluctuating and ongoing; it reflects the meanings that the Civil War holds for contemporary society as well as the cultural values and social imperatives of those who 'act' upon the fields." Indeed, she adds, "to chart the history of Civil War battlefield preservation is to trace the ways in which Americans have remembered the conflict, reacted to its issues, and use that past to serve the present." Perhaps Edward Linenthal said it best, describing memory as it relates to battlefield preservation as "the process of veneration, defilement, and redefinition."[7] There are numerous examples of this phenomenon. As Civil War Trust president Jim Lighthizer argues, memory influenced what was preserved and what was not, and conversely, preservation or the lack thereof had a lot to do with what was popular and what was not. He cites the Confederate charge at Franklin in November 1864 as proof. Although larger than Pickett's Charge, more deadly, and more crippling to the South, it is yet little known. "And you know why most people haven't heard about Franklin?" he asked. "Because they paved over it."[8]

This book is just that story: of Civil War battlefield preservation over the past 150 years, of how and why, when and where, and, in particular, who. It is also the study of how that process affected, and was affected by, the larger society. Such a study can hopefully illuminate patterns and processes, both good and bad, that can help us learn how to preserve and remember better in the future.

◆ ◆ ◆

An incredible number of people have aided me in writing this book, and while I am tempted to name each and every one, that would run the risk of forgetting some. Suffice it to say that in researching at almost all of the Civil War national parks and many of the state and local parks as well as numerous archival repositories, I was aided by some of the most dedicated public servants in America. Those who work at parks where I could not personally research likewise provided me with much good information via email, mail, or telephone. The search even took me to more bureaucratic administrative officials as well, such as those in federal and state park systems who were not assigned to individual parks. One of the really fun parts of this book was reacquainting myself with old NPS friends and making new friends along the way.

Several historians also aided in this project. John F. Marszalek, as always, read the entire manuscript and made it much better with his careful eye and the plentiful lead from his pencil, noting stylistic and analytical problems. Garry Adelman, historian at the Civil War Trust, also read the manuscript and provided many useful comments. The readers for the University of Tennessee Press, former NPS chief historian Dwight Pitcaithley and Michael Panhorst, also provided welcome recommendations.

Working with the University of Tennessee Press has once more been a delight. Scot Danforth and his wonderful team could not have made the publishing process any easier. Copy editor Karin Kaufmann did a wonderful job on the narrative.

I am especially grateful for a generous faculty research grant provided by the University of Tennessee at Martin. These funds allowed me to conduct research at numerous national parks as well as the National Archives regional branch in Philadelphia.

To my family goes my most heartfelt love. My parents will always be a special part of every book I write. Kelly is the key to everything in my earthly life, and she and Mary Kate and Leah Grace bring such joy and warmth to me everyday. My God is the key to my eternal life, and I thank him for the salvation provided through his Son.

I have dedicated this book to my friend Mike Ballard. Although a very well known and respected historian of the Civil War, Mike is also an archivist, and it was he who first introduced me to battlefield preservation history. Mike had a contract with the Shiloh National Military Park to organize and catalog their administrative records, and he hired me while in graduate school way back in the 1990s to travel to Shiloh and work in the archives there. I jumped at the chance, Shiloh being my favorite battlefield, but little did I know that this initial work would somehow affect nearly every facet of my life. I became so interested in administrative history that I wrote my dissertation on Shiloh's battlefield history, I also hung around until the NPS gave me a job. It was there that a coworker introduced me to Kelly, with whom I have two beautiful daughters. I can not imagine what my life would be like had Mike not asked me to work at Shiloh that summer. Consequently, I am extremely grateful to him for introducing me to the world of archives, Shiloh, and, by extension, everything else that has followed.

Sadly, Mike passed away in October 2016, after the above was written and while this book was in the page proof stage. I was looking forward to sending him a copy when it came out, and letting him know just how much I respected and appreciated him. Now, obviously, I wish the book had come out sooner, but I can only hope that Mike knew how much I thought of him.

Timothy B. Smith
Adamsville, Tennessee

Immediately after the momentous battle at Shiloh in April 1862, Federal soldiers began the process of burying the nearly three thousand men who had died there. It was obviously in their best interest to do so, as their camps had suddenly become a battlefield and were now strewn with thousands of dead men and horses. Not yet ready to move on, the Federals did the next best thing, which was to clear their mangled camps and get them back to some manner of normality. But the gruesome nature of the effort affected all involved; one Federal confided, "Months passed before I recovered from the effects of it."[1]

In burying the dead, the Federals even this early in the war made broad statements concerning how they viewed the conflict in general and what was happening to them in particular. On the broadest level, they showed practical sense in burying all dead soldiers, no matter which side they had fought on. In their remembrance, however, they maintained a drastic separation between friend and foe. Having to bury both Confederate and Federal dead, the soldiers gave much more care to their own Union dead than they did for the enemy. "As I write volley after volley of musketry is being fired over the graves of our men," wrote one Federal. "We dig long holes in the ground, lay them side by side without any coffin, fire a salute over the grave, and then cover their cold bodies with the Tennessee clay." Many of the Federal regiments went so far as to bury their own dead in regimental burial plots, allowing the men who had joined up and fought together to rest together in death. Not so for the Confederates; the same Illinoisan noted, "The secesh we bury with less ceremony, dig a hole roll them in and cover them."[2]

Yet there was a certain memorial quality to the work. Many Federal regiments went so far as to create "a neat fence of wicker work" around their burial plots. At least one regiment went even further. The Eleventh Illinois had seen some of the most brutal fighting at Shiloh, on the Federal right around the Crossroads and its own camp. Illinoisan George Carrington described in his diary the regiment's burial efforts on April 8: "Tommy Newport made a monument of oak five or six feet high, this was set up and the names cut thereon, Co and Regt, letters painted black, the monument painted white. We built a fence with poles around the grave."[3]

This White Post Burial Place, as it is still known today (although the wood shaft is long gone), also signified an emerging trend in Civil War memorialization and by extension preservation. In an effort to mark historic sites with a semipermanent "monument," the Illinoisans were early practitioners of a phenomenon of war-era battlefield marking that would eventually be seen across the expanse of the nation. As these soldiers took it upon themselves to mark significant sites, it was one of the first inklings of an effort to preserve and mark America's Civil War battlefields.[4]

I

As exemplified at Shiloh, the earliest efforts to preserve and mark significant sites took many forms during the war itself, but perhaps the initial major effort to mark specific areas emanated from a surprising development that occurred on many battlefields: tourism. Foreshadowing twenty-first-century tourism, the battlefields saw large numbers of visitors as soon as the fighting stopped. Civilians often came to the fields of battle, but the soldiers themselves had perhaps a greater chance than anyone to see the sites even then growing in fame. As time passed, soldiers began to take the logical step toward marking what tourists saw, beginning an early form of battlefield preservation through interpretation.[5]

Obviously, more people than simply those who had fought at a particular battlefield came to visit it, not so much for the personal reflection as for the novelty and historic appeal. Civilians who were not even connected to the battles often arrived immediately after the fighting had ceased. War chronicler Benson Lossing described the masses who descended on Gettysburg, describing local citizen David M. McConaughy's efforts to care for the tide: "He, like all other patriotic citizens of Gettysburg, had opened his house to the strangers who thronged the town." Lossing was himself one of those visitors, arriving at Gettysburg just a week after the fighting had ended. He described the unearthly battlefield: "Unexploded conical shells were half-buried in the oak-trees, whose branches were cut and bruised by others; and the trunks of nearly all were scarred so thickly with bullet-marks for ten or fifteen feet from the ground, that scarcely an inch together of the untouched bark remained. Over the rocky slope of Culp's Hill, up which the Confederates pressed in front of Slocum's lines, fragments of clothing, accouterments, shells, and fire-arms were strewed among many new-made graves, some in the form of trenches, in which a number of the dead were buried together, with some rude monument to mark the spot."[6]

A similar visitation emerged at Fort Sumter in South Carolina, where a couple of local businessmen began a competition to take visitors near the fort as early as April 15, 1861. Thomas Lockwood's boat, *The Carolina,* ran visitors out near the fort for a dollar a trip. Competition soon emerged from John Magrath's *Patriot,* which undercut Lockwood and carried visitors to the fort for only fifty cents. Later, other boats began to actually land visitors at the fort, even while the war was still going on and Charleston, soon to be enveloped by Union forces, was still a war zone.[7]

At Franklin, Tennessee, where such carnage had taken place late in the war, even greater than at George Pickett's famous charge at Gettysburg, one local attested that after a rain storm he saw "a line of human hands sticking up—some with fingers shut tight, some pointing, and all so ghastly that they were covered hurriedly." It was not uncommon to see the famous Carter family, who lived in a house that sat squarely in the midst of the fighting, out reburying the dead in the days and months after the battle.[8]

Soldiers, having a greater ability to maneuver, also participated in such visitations, especially around still-contested zones of combat. Many commented in letters and diaries about visiting a battlefield from earlier in the war. One Iowa cavalry trooper noted the site of other Iowans' engagement: "The shallow graves had been opened by hogs and other animals, and the skulls and other bones of the dead soldiers were exposed to view, and the marks of that severe conflict were everywhere present." Similarly, a Massachusetts artilleryman engaged in the 1864 Overland campaign recounted in his diary, "At six that evening Malvern Hill was reached. The men examined McClellan's old battle fields with interest."[9]

One of the most visited battlefields in the earliest days of the war was Wilson's Creek, because it sat near major thoroughfares still being used by maneuvering troops. "I was out on the battle grounds on last Thursday," one soldier wrote his uncle, "[and] saw the bodies of men bleaching in the sun that were killed in that battle." Others went into more detail. An Iowan noted that "the marks of that bloody conflict is distinctly visible in-as-much as skulls & human bones lay scattered about the field, and bullets mark nearly every tree. Some as large as my body has been cut off completely by canon shots." Several soldiers described "a huge pit formed by nature which was used for a grave. . . . Bones and hair have been pulled out by wolves &c." Another soldier described the scene: "Saw the sink hole where some 60 or 70 German soldiers were buried. . . . A hot stench was continually escaping and almost suffocating." Some of the soldiers also later visited Pea Ridge, where one described "trees are mown down as though it were done by the Tornado, the winds strong hand, & even the Telegraph polls are cut slick off by the shots."[10]

Obviously, tourism took on a different perspective when soldiers revisited their own battlefields. To a man, they came away moved and stirred emotionally. One Mississippi Confederate on the way to Gettysburg in June 1863 described his feelings when his regiment entered the Antietam battlefield: "Crossed the Potomac by wading and passed through the battle field of Sharpsburg. . . . Much sign of the conflict was visible. The low mounds which cover the bones of those who fell, the furrowed ground, and scarred trees—all speak more plainly than words of that terrible conflict. . . . Sad, sad thoughts are recalled by again reviewing the old battleground." A Federal passing over the Fredericksburg battlefield later in the war similarly described how "we crossed the old battlefield where the regiment had received its baptism of blood, and many now passed over that field in silence with uncovered heads."[11]

The emotion of visiting a former place of fighting is clearly seen in numerous examples of regiments returning to the Chickamauga battlefield after a couple of months. One soldier cut a piece of a cedar tree where he had fought that contained "32 bullets, and, besides, marks of shell-work." The Seventy-Second Indiana visited in December 1863; they were aghast that "their comrades [were] just as we had left them." Similarly, they noted a Confederate hospital, including "scores of dead and decaying bodies, limbs and human bones." The Fifty-Ninth Indiana also visited after chasing the enemy into Georgia. "Colonel Grose asked permission to come by the field and bury the boys that had fallen," one soldier remembered. "It is just two months and eleven days since the battle and the scene is awful." Without proper tools, one soldier admitted, "we had to leave it to some force better prepared for such work."[12]

The most personal of all visitation occurred when soldiers sought and found their specific places of engagement. The same Confederate who described his emotions on returning to Antietam added, "I saw the ground over which we charged on that memorable occasion and the very spot where I was wounded." A South Carolinian went back to the site of the First Battle of Manassas in December 1861 and reported, "I have been again to-day to visit the old battlefield. I never want to see it again. I saw the stump I got behind for a while that day, thinking it might shelter me a little, but if a cannon ball had hit it, it would have torn the stump and me, too, all to pieces, and some of them did not miss it very far. The stump is about ten inches high and nearly rotten. A drowning man will catch at a straw." Similarly, a Federal was consumed with finding his position in the fighting around Atlanta in late September 1864: "On the 28th I went to Atlanta and visited the battle ground where we had charged on the 22nd of July. The long parapets and rifle pits were there and the brick house standing to the left. I walked over the very spot where I led my company against the battery on that fearful day. Desiring some memento to preserve for the future I cut two canes, one a hickory and one of cane."[13]

One of the most poignant episodes of personal visitation came at Wilson's Creek in October 1861. A large group of officers and correspondents returned to the battlefield, and one major described to the group the area where his men had formed and fought. One of the men noted how a bullet had clipped his "chin-whiskers . . . and lodged in the head of his left hand neighbor." Another piped up and reported, "And I believe that I can find the very spot where he fell." Despite the concern over safety from marauding guerillas, the major allowed several men to attempt to find the spot. "Subsequently the party came up," one reporter wrote, "one of them bearing a hat, and imparting the strange information that they had not only found the place where their unfortunate comrade was killed, but his very body, as they well knew from the wound in the skull, and the peculiar hat worn by the deceased, and which they now brought along as a trophy." They then buried their lost brother in arms.[14]

It is little surprise that the growing tourism of the battlefields even during the war began to at least some type of marking, ushering in the first acts of preserving and marking the battlefields for future visitors. But such activity was mostly hasty and largely unplanned. There was, after all, a war still raging. Still, there were examples even during the war of monumentation being thrown together on the spur of the moment. Later in the war, when veterans of Wilson's Creek returned to the battlefield while on campaign, one Federal described a hasty commemoration of Union general Nathaniel Lyon, who had been killed during the battle. "The Third division visited the battle-field of Wilson's Creek on Thanksgiving Day," he noted, "and each man placed a stone on the spot where Lyon fell, so that there now stands a monument some ten feet high, built by eight thousand soldiers, to point out to the visitor of this classic ground the place where the hero died." Another soldier wrote home, "I also added one stone to the pile that marks the spot where Gen. Lyon fell," although another soldier described a more interesting type of remembrance: "Viewed the place where General Lyon fell, looked at the remains of his horse and secured a piece of his hide. A great many have gotten strips for shoe and hame strings." Such commemoration, although commendable, was hastily organized and by definition temporary. Indeed, the pile of stones no longer exists at the Wilson's Creek battlefield, but even the attempt was a marked development in how Americans viewed their battle-fields and their desire to memorialize them.[15]

Perhaps the best example of the wartime marking of a battlefield for visitors came at Chickamauga in October 1863. While Confederate president Jefferson Davis was in the western theater trying to douse the fires of dispute among his army commanders, he took time to tour the Chickamauga battlefield while in Chattanooga. Certainly, this was not the first time a president had toured a battlefield. Davis had done so earlier in the war at Seven Pines, and Lincoln had traveled to the Antietam battlefield and would see the Gettysburg battlefield the next month. Similarly, after the Federals drove the Confederates southward into Georgia after Chattanooga, Ulysses S. Grant rode to the battlefield from Chattanooga in December 1863. George H. Thomas, the "Rock of Chickamauga," conducted Grant on a tour. Still, Davis's visit to Chickamauga was different in that Confederate soldiers, prior to his visit, placed interpretive signs on the battlefield. Although very rudimentary and obviously temporary, this signage was nevertheless the first such effort intended for tourists to appear on a Civil War battlefield.[16]

II

A much more permanent type of battlefield preservation emerged out of necessity. Just as at Shiloh, the side holding the field at the end of the fighting found it also held the responsibility for burying the dead. In many cases, as at Shiloh, the battlefield was the campsite, but in other instances simple humanity dictated that something be done quickly. Practical aspects also existed, and soldiers could not reasonably spend all their time caring for the dead and policing battlefields, especially if active campaigning was under way. Often, commanding generals, such as Ulysses S. Grant at Champion Hill, detailed a small portion of the army, including those units that had suffered the most in the battle, to remain behind to police the field while he pushed on in pursuit of the enemy. In what became standard procedure during and for decades after the war, there was little importance besides basic humanity placed on the enemy dead. Only the bare essentials of getting them covered were performed, whereas more ceremonial care was taken with one's own dead.[17]

Another practical aspect of the burial process, one that most influenced the preservation side of the effort, was the importance of getting the job done as quickly as possible. Disease, morale, and strategic influences all caused commanders to see to the matter immediately, and in that effort to bury the dead as quickly as possible came the principal, if not comprehensive, policy of burying the dead right on the field of battle. Although there were some examples of gathering the dead of units together or burying each side separately, the dead were most often placed in graves on the battlefields, primarily near where they fell. Even at

Shiloh, where Union regiments buried their dead together in regimental plots, those plots were still on the battlefield itself.[18]

As a result, the burial of large numbers of soldiers obviously marked an area as special; the initial efforts at marking sites only added to the pre-existing preservation. One visitor at Gettysburg described how "we passed on to the peach-orchard so prominent in the records of the battle, and then rode back to Gettysburg, observing the fields on our right, over which Pickett swept with his division to the attack of Hancock, thickly strewn with the graves of men and horses, the former marked by small head-boards, and the latter distinguished by large mounds." Yet even the burial of the dead and the marking of their graves with headboards was not totally permanent because the headboards soon rotted or burned. Even the bodies could, and were at times, removed from their battle-field graves and taken to other locations, also illustrating the temporary nature of early battlefield preservation. Sometimes the dead were removed to larger gather-ing sites still on the battlefield, but in many instances the dead of both sides were taken completely off the battlefield. Nevertheless, although not permanent, the original burial of the dead where they fell and the attending wood markers served as necessary first steps toward marking historic sites, even if done for reasons other than preservation.[19]

Fortunately for Civil War battlefield preservation, part of the burial process quickly morphed into a more permanent nature. By early in 1862, Union officials had begun to realize that they needed to implement some type of cemetery sys-tem in which to properly and honorably bury the war's Union dead. The Thirty-Seventh Congress included wording in an omnibus bill that allowed President Abraham Lincoln to establish national cemeteries where he thought necessary. Lincoln signed the bill on July 17, 1862, and that law gave him the "power, when-ever in his opinion it is expedient, to purchase cemetery grounds and cause them to be securely enclosed, to be used as a national cemetery for the soldiers who shall die in the service of the country."[20]

Under this legislation, Lincoln established fourteen national cemeteries in 1862 and sixteen more before the end of the war. These included several sites around Washington, D.C., where large hospitals and camps of instruction were located. Alexandria and Soldiers' Home near the capital and cemeteries at An-napolis, Maryland, Camp Butler, Illinois, and Philadelphia, Pennsylvania, con-tained many soldiers who died in the military but not in battle. Some of the wartime cemeteries, however, were associated with battlefields. A few were estab-lished away from the battlefields, such as at Mill Springs, Kentucky, but several major cemeteries were set up on the battlefields at Chattanooga, Fredericksburg, and Ball's Bluff. Other future national cemeteries, such as the initially state man-aged Antietam and Gettysburg cemeteries, were also right on the fields of battle.

In placing the reinterred bodies in formal national cemeteries on the original battlefields, wartime officials took a major step, again if inadvertently, in securing at least a portion of those battlefields from future development. President Lincoln perhaps said it best in one of the least-quoted portions of his famous Gettysburg Address: "We have come to dedicate a portion of that field as a final resting place for those who here gave their lives." Ironically, even the Northern states were not totally immune from all states' rights issues; many insisted that their soldiers be buried together, not mixed with other states' dead.[21]

The Chattanooga National Cemetery illustrated many of the preservation-related issues concerning the initial national cemeteries. Maj. Gen. George H. Thomas ordered the establishment of a cemetery on December 25, 1863, writing that it be established "in commemoration of the Battles of Chattanooga, November 23–27, 1863." The area itself was battlefield land, one of the overseers remembering that Thomas had himself remarked upon the beauty of the place as a possible cemetery during the battle when "its beautiful undulating surface was made the more apparent by a line of troops which extended over its summit." The ideals of cemetery establishment also illustrated the growing desire to honorably commemorate each individual soldier, which in itself was a growing phenomenon of the nineteenth-century funerary movement. Thomas B. Van Horne, the chaplain in charge of the Chattanooga National Cemetery, reported that extreme care would be taken to "secure a short military history of every officer and soldier interred in the cemetery whose remains have been identified," adding that "it seems eminently fitting that this should be done." He added, "It accords with our intense individualism as a people, and with the value we attach to individual life; and it is demanded by the eminent worth of those for whom historic notice would thus be secured."[22]

Despite the inadvertent progress toward preservation of the original battlefields, the national cemetery effort still had a long way to go to reach even semi-modern standards. Initially, these preservation efforts were done unintentionally through the medium of national cemeteries, placing the main emphasis on the dead rather than on the site. Similarly, the growing nineteenth-century desire for cemeteries to be peaceful and serene places for reflection also affected preservation of the battlefields; the manicured, landscaped cemeteries offered visitors the chance to consider larger issues as they commemorated individual loved ones—at the cost, of course, of altering pristine battlefield land.[23]

In addition to their contextual implications, national cemeteries made several major political statements. The cemeteries were primarily federally funded and operated (Gettysburg and Antietam being two major initial exceptions), which meant that the United States government was now involved in the preservation process. In fact, these cemeteries marked the first large-scale federal involvement in preservation and memorialization. With their involvement, however, government officials made a practical decision that would turn into preservation policy for the next two and a half decades. The federal government only allowed Union soldiers to be buried in these national cemeteries. Confederate dead were either left buried on the field, as at Shiloh, or left for local Southerners to relocate to more proper cemeteries. Although this was a logical policy, some exceptions were made to it; even today there are a few scattered Confederates in national cemeteries, primarily postwar national cemeteries erected around Northern prison camps, which often served initial duty as Northern camps of instruction early in the war. A few Confederates also appear in national cemeteries on battlefields in the South. This distinction between North and South nevertheless continued the United States government's attitude toward Confederates as traitors, and the policy definitely influenced postwar preservation efforts well into the 1880s.[24]

III

Another significant wartime step in the process of marking and preserving battlefields occurred when soldiers moved from their tourism-related or even burial-related markings to more permanent stone monuments. There were several instances of stone markers going up on battlefields, and these effectively denoted significant sites and preserved them for as long as the monument remained on the original site. Those that are still in their original locations are the earliest forms of preservation of Civil War battlefields. Yet the fact that a more durable substance was used to mark the sites did not mean the marking would be permanent, and the battlefield preservation function only continued as long as the monuments remained on site. In fact, only a few such monuments have been left untampered with and are in their original location.[25]

One example is the Bartow monument on the Manassas battlefield. Confederate colonel Francis Bartow was killed in what later became known as the First Battle of Bull Run or First Manassas, on July 21, 1861. As the victorious Confederates held the field, the responsibility fell to them to care for the dead, which also gave them the chance to commemorate. Bartow's brigade did the latter in September 1861, and the Eighth Georgia placed a white marble obelisk at the site where he fell. Hundreds attended the dedication, but unfortunately the monument no longer exists. The Confederates left the area in the spring of 1862 to confront George McClellan's movement to the Virginia Peninsula, and no record of the monument's history endured Federal occupation. Only the base remains today, but it fittingly marks the spot and still performs its act of preservation.[26]

A similar case of even stone monuments' lack of permanency was the Thirty-Second Indiana monument at Rowlett's Station in Kentucky. The regiment was a mostly German unit led by the Marxist August Willich. After the skirmish there in January 1862, a member of the regiment who was a stonecutter by trade fashioned a flat slab to mark the burial place of the regiment's dead. August Bloedner cut the names of the dead on the slab in German and ornamented it with images of the American flag and bald eagle. Although the monument itself still exists, it is not in its original location and consequently has lost the site-specific aspect of its intent.[27]

A similar memorialization occurred at Vicksburg, Mississippi. Garrison troops in the city after the siege and surrender marked the "surrender interview" site where Ulysses S. Grant and John C. Pemberton had met on July 3, 1863, to discuss capitulation. Finding a monument to Vicksburg's Mexican War soldiers already in process in a local stonecutter's shop, Union artisans altered the shaft to reflect the surrender site and erected it at the specific location between the lines. Although different from other contemporary memorials in that it marked the site of a significant event rather than the burial place of the dead, the Vicksburg monument nevertheless no longer resides at its original location. It is now preserved in the Vicksburg National Military Park Visitor Center, and another monument marks the original site.[28]

The oldest intact monument still in its original location is the Hazen Brigade Monument at Stones River in Tennessee. After that battle in December 1862 and January 1863, Col. William B. Hazen's brigade helped garrison the Murfreesboro area. Members of the brigade were also skilled in stone masonry, so they erected an elaborate funerary monument to mark the burial place of the brigade's dead. The soldiers erected a structure similar to an Egyptian mastaba, the monument carrying the names of the dead and inscriptions calling the nation "to greater deeds." In its original location at the Stones River National Battlefield for more than 150 years, the Hazen monument has fully performed its intended purpose of commemoration, remembrance, and preservation.[29]

Two other intact and in-place monuments also went up in June 1865, both at Manassas under the direction of Lt. James M. McCallum. These almost identical sandstone obelisks memorialized the two battles fought there, one monument commemorating the first battle on Henry House Hill and the other memorializing the second battle near the famous railroad cut. These two monuments were the first to mark not just burial places on battlefields or even significant events that occurred there, but the actual battlefields themselves. As such, battlefield preservation as we know it today can be traced back to these two monuments.[30]

IV

Amid all the commemoration and early preservation, Americans on both sides were already forging a memory of the war, even while it still raged. A national memory was still far in the future, but Americans between 1861 and 1865 nevertheless began to view the war through certain prisms. Because they were so close to the event itself, this memory was necessarily fractured, uneven, and personal. The larger issue involved, slavery, was not sufficiently considered in most American minds, certainly not enough for them to construct a coherent reasoning of what it all meant and how it would all play out. Perhaps only the giants of the generation, such as Abraham Lincoln, were gifted enough to see the larger patterns; most Americans' memory of the past as far as the war was concerned dealt with personal loss. Certainly, the embryonic vestiges of preservation and commemoration that took place during the war pointed in that direction, as most wartime monumentation or preservation of sites revolved around memorializing the dead.[31]

Much early war battlefield tourism centered on people desiring to see where heartbreaking events for loved ones had occurred, chiefly for personal satisfaction, whether it was a soldier returning to his area of fighting or wounding or family members venturing to the scene of a loved one's death. Likewise, the vast majority of the initial markings on battlefields revolved around the commemoration of individuals, from the impromptu Lyon monument at Wilson's Creek to the thousands of individual headboards erected to mark the burial places of specific soldiers all across the land. Even many of the earliest monuments were individually oriented. The Shiloh, Barlow, Rowlett's Station, and Hazen monuments, for example, were dedicated to the dead, whose individual names appeared on the monuments. The Vicksburg Surrender Monument, which in itself marked a new avenue of commemoration in that it memorialized a historic site rather than a death or burial site, can also nevertheless be somewhat described as individual in nature, the individuals in this case being Grant and Pemberton. Even the two 1865 monuments at Manassas were dedicated "In Memory of the Patriots Who Fell." Certainly, the country's initial attempts to mark and commemorate, and by extension preserve, were done with individuals in mind, illustrating the mindset of Americans at the time and where they placed their emphasis in terms of memory.[32]

Yet despite the incoherent and embryonic memory of the war at the time, the marking of important sites was already taking place. Although such markings were limited in nature, these early efforts formed the foundation for the preservation movement. The next 150 years would take the conservation effort to heights those early preservationists could not have fathomed.

1

The Reconstruction Era, 1865–1890

The editors of the *Richmond Dispatch* took up exactly where they had left off after their building and equipment were burned in the final days of the Civil War. In its first postwar issue on December 9, 1865, they published a remarkable editorial, "The Past and the Present." Within the argumentative piece, the editors began to implement much of what would become standard Confederate theory, namely, that the South had not been defeated but had been "overwhelmed by superior numbers and resources." It defended the South's right to rebel, stating that the Confederacy had been just and righteous in its actions. The paper let all know that even though overpowered, the South was not broken and would be heard from again. Thus began a period that would continue the Civil War rancor even amid attempts to rebuild.[1]

The Civil War certainly settled many issues, and as such the many deaths that occurred were not in vain. It was to be expected, therefore, that the American public would focus on the loss of so many men during the war. Yet there were larger issues than personal loss at stake. Foremost among the nagging questions answered by the war was the issue of slavery. With the step-by-step process of confiscation acts and other legislation, the way was paved for Lincoln's Emancipation Proclamation. Clearly, major changes were coming. The Thirteenth Amendment to the Constitution, ratified in December 1865, put the final nail into the coffin of slavery, and the entire process, war and all, determined that there would never again be legal, government-allowed bondage in America. In the words of David Blight, slavery was "unmistakably destroyed."[2]

Similarly, the war firmly settled the issue of secession, which had plagued the United States since Thomas Jefferson introduced the idea in 1798. Several states and regions had threatened and talked secession, but it was only in December 1860 that a state actually seceded. The Civil War firmly decided that secession was illegal, and so did the courts. Since then, America has not had to seriously worry about the threat of secession.[3]

Although it decided several major issues, the Civil War also raised other controversies and thereby developed continuing disagreements. Although slavery and secession had been decided, their larger parent issues, racism and states' rights, had not, and both issues became immense problems immediately after the war and in the decades that followed. In fact, racial issues and states' rights are divisive topics even today. And if these larger parent issues are still causing problems today, how much more so were they on everyone's minds immediately after the Civil War? In order to reunite the nation despite these still-divisive issues, Northern leaders embarked on a period of Reconstruction, in which they hoped to deal with the Southern states' return as fully functioning members of the American Union. How to do so was problematic, however, with various theories ranging from leniency to harshness being considered. President Lincoln himself began the process in December 1863 with his annual message to Congress, and he pushed for leniency toward the South. Whether he would have succeeded in his efforts, had he lived, is unknown, but clearly John Wilkes Booth did more harm to the South than he ever could have imagined when he assassinated Lincoln in April 1865. The new president, Andrew Johnson, tried to follow Lincoln's lenient plan and in a period termed Presidential Reconstruction allowed states in the South to return to functioning states. In response, these states sent the Confederate vice president as well as numerous Confederate cabinet officers, congressmen, and generals to Washington to serve as their representatives in Congress.[4]

Those who desired more punishment for the South watched in horror, believing that four years of bloodshed had not changed anything and all those dead had died in vain; the prewar ruling class in the South was still the ruling class after the war. Radical Republicans in Congress, with Charles Sumner declaring that "the rebels must be broken in character as in battle," accordingly began to take over Reconstruction through the passage of legislation over Johnson's vetoes, including such bills as the Civil Rights Act of 1866 and the Military Reconstruction Act of 1867. The latter in particular broke the South into five military districts and basically put the region under military rule because of the violence that had erupted there due to such organizations as the Ku Klux Klan. This period of "Radical Reconstruction" was an attempt to require more punishment of the South for secession and war and to ensure citizenship and rights for former slaves in the midst of a very unequal social atmosphere.[5]

The result was a nation bitterly divided over racial issues, certainly as divided as during the war. One Union veteran wrote that the "only friendship possible was based upon a tacit ignoring of what was deepest in our hearts. And what sort of friendship was that?" The tension, hatred, and animosity among the sections and races not surprisingly caused a divided populace that agreed on little. And that mentality continued for over two decades, despite the formal end of Reconstruction in 1877. With a population tiring of war-related issues and major new factors such as economic catastrophes, political scandals, and westward expansion all vying for the nation's attention, Americans seemingly moved on after 1877, but they saw an attempt at the renewal of Federal oversight of the South, particularly in elections, in the early 1890s. Consequently, the nation endured racial division even after formal Reconstruction ended.[6]

As would be expected, Americans were not bent on reconciliation during Reconstruction. Even newspaper editors took aim at each other, such as the dueling editors in Fredericksburg in 1871 sparring over honoring Federal dead in the city. When the Southern-leaning editor wrote that such recognition was not allowed for the Confederate dead at Gettysburg, the *Fredericksburg Star* retaliated with vitriol, calling the first editor the "Bomb-proof hero" and "cross-grained lunatic." It obviously took time for those feelings of animosity to lessen, so the immediate post-Reconstruction years of the 1880s were not much better than the Reconstruction years.[7]

This divergence was clearly illustrated in the attitudes of veterans and civilians alike as they formed a split national memory of the Civil War. In this heated period from the end of the war to the 1890s, Americans formed a partisan view of the war with little agreement between the two sides. In the South, former Confederates consciously developed the concept of the Lost Cause, with which they attempted to explain their defeat. Former Confederates concentrated on items such as the deaths of major commanders, the problem of Northern-born Confederate generals, and the overwhelming numbers of the enemy to explain their defeat, being careful to note that the defeat was not because of a lack of manhood, bravery, or martial ability on the part of Confederate soldiers. Conversely in the North, partisans waved the "Bloody Shirt" when the need arose to stir the population against the South in support of the Republican Party. Waving the shirt was a reference to the bloodshed the South was still causing in Reconstruction. Obviously, neither side was willing to compromise in full, and the period from the end of the war to the 1890s was an extremely volatile time.[8]

All these various political, economic, and social factors combined to have a major effect on battlefield preservation in the United States. As Americans emerged from war and began to grow into a more conciliatory mood, the ways in which they did so were obviously framed by their experiences in the war and how they viewed the now-past war in their memories. As a result, this veteran generation, which first began the war-era spur-of-the-moment memorialization and commemoration, turned to more permanent and appropriate efforts, and this is clearly seen on the battlefields themselves. Still reeling from the war and enduring Reconstruction-fueled animosity over newly freed slaves, however, Americans were not quite ready to come together. The result was a disjointed and partisan initial attempt at preserving and marking the battlefields of the Civil War.

I

Although work on national cemeteries as well as private cemeteries such as Gettysburg and Antietam (both of which would soon be included in the national system) began even during the war, the vast majority of these federal cemeteries were not established until after the war ended. A very practical reason existed: most battlefields were in the South and the continuing war precluded work on them. The first goal was to win the war; sufficient reinterment of the dead would have to come later. But whether wartime or postwar work, the permanent marking of battlefield sites with graves was a definite step toward preservation of the Civil War's battlefields, saving at least portions of the fields from future development.[9]

Once relative peace came over America, the federal government turned to burying all its war dead. Although the government and local groups had created what would become over thirty national cemeteries by the end of 1865, work restarted at a furious pitch after the war. Unlike most cemeteries established during the conflict, many of these new ones, which would number seventy-three by 1870, were on battlefield land, thereby preserving portions of the historic sites. Although a majority of these later cemeteries were near prisons, instruction camps, or hospital sites, many were in fact on the actual battlefields themselves, including a cluster of cemeteries around the heavily fought-over ground around Richmond and Petersburg, Virginia. Because they were the scenes of heavy fighting both in 1862 and later in the war, these areas required more cemeteries than the relatively spread-out area of the western theater. Cemeteries at such battlefields as Cold Harbor, Glendale, Fort Harrison, Popular Grove, and Seven Pines were established in 1866 to take in the thousands of dead from the area. Other cemeteries in the western theater also came about during this time, including those at Port Hudson, Shiloh, Fort Donelson, Stones River, and Vicksburg.[10]

A few cemeteries were established right on the major battlefields of the war, allowing less logistical effort to move the bodies and thereby preserving at least part of the fields just a year after the end of the war. An example was the Vicksburg National Cemetery, established by Maj. Gen. Thomas J. Wood in 1866. Its forty acres of terraced and landscaped plots sat on the bluffs overlooking the Mississippi River, including where Confederate batteries had engaged the Union navy. More than fifteen thousand Union dead were buried there by 1869, some of them from nearby battlefields such as Champion Hill and Port Gibson, and some even from Meridian and sites in Louisiana. Unfortunately, cemetery officials paid "liberally" for each body of a soldier brought in by civilians, and soon bodies were buried there whether or not they were soldiers.[11]

Shiloh's ten-acre cemetery similarly preserved part of that battlefield, the focal point at Pittsburg Landing on the Tennessee River. George H. Thomas established the cemetery in 1866, and by 1869 it contained some thirty-five hundred mostly Union dead from Shiloh as well as Fort Henry and other areas along the Tennessee River. One visitor in 1867 described Shiloh's cemetery as "the handsomest cemetery in the South," no doubt partly because of the regimental burial plots surrounding the cemetery proper and the magnificent view of the river and its valley.[12]

This same process occurred to the north at Fort Donelson, where in March 1867 the bodies of the Union dead were removed from their battlefield graves and placed atop a hill overlooking the Cumberland River. The exact site had been a postbattle Union fortification during the war and itself had been attacked by Confederates in 1863. The Union fort had been leveled after the war, but the cemetery sat adjacent to the old Confederate fort. The government bought the fifteen acres in April 1867 and distributed the disinterred bodies in a more uniform manner in the new cemetery. Like others, the Fort Donelson cemetery was landscaped, but there was always a tinge of preservation and memorial thought to what was done there. In 1872, the quartermaster general of the United States wrote that the cemetery at Fort Donelson was "a public historical monument of an important battle."[13]

The cemetery at Stone's River likewise sat upon the very battlefield. George Thomas also mandated the establishment of this cemetery, which was done in late 1865, and by the turn of the decade some six thousand dead lay there, relocated from various battlefields in Middle Tennessee. Like the other cemeteries, the twenty-acre Stones River National Cemetery preserved a major portion of the battlefield, where William S. Rosecrans had set up an artillery line at the end of the first day to repel the Confederates. Also like the other cemeteries, the government did not acquire full ownership until 1868, well after the bodies had been moved there. Yet the work at Stones River illustrated the care with which cemetery builders went about their job; Chaplain William Earnshaw reported that his men had been "searching the entire country and tracing obscure byways, feeling it our solemn duty to find every solitary Union soldier's grave that marked the victorious path of our men in pursuit of the enemy."[14]

The cemeteries already in existence on battlefields such as Gettysburg and Antietam also saw additional attention after the war. Union veterans laid a cornerstone for a monument at Antietam's cemetery in 1867, although financial issues prevented completion of the monument until 1880. Most of the initial monumentation at Gettysburg likewise occurred in the cemetery. Former members of the First Minnesota erected a monument in 1867 where their dead were buried in the cemetery. More noticeable was the Soldier's National Monument, placed on or near the spot where Lincoln gave his famous address. It stood sixty feet tall and used human figures to symbolize American history and ideals, including Liberty at the top and a soldier, a recorder, a mechanic, and a gatherer symbolizing War, History, Peace, and Plenty. In 1872, veterans also dedicated a monument to Maj. Gen. John F. Reynolds, a Union general killed in the battle. Although not placed on the spot of Reynolds's death, the monument nevertheless commemorated an event that occurred on the battlefield, foreshadowing future markings on the field.[15]

Because so many new cemeteries were being established, new legislation was added to the 1862 act to legitimize and legalize what was in fact already happening. The dead at battlefields such as Stones River, Shiloh, and Chattanooga had been buried on private land, so in February 1867, Congress passed "An Act to Establish and Protect National Cemeteries." The act took the 1862 legislation further, allowing the secretary of war to "enter upon and appropriate" the land if the owners would not sell, which was a major step in and of itself in the future of battlefield preservation. Now the government could condemn land if necessary. The legislation also required the cemeteries to be enclosed by a wall and possess a lodge and "a meritorious and trustworthy superintendent, who shall be selected from enlisted men of the army disabled in service." The superintendents were also required to keep rolls of the burials, along with each soldier's military information. Because of the 1867 legislation, the War Department condemned the private land at several cemeteries.[16]

In reburying the war dead and creating national cemeteries, however, the government created problems. The emphasis on the dead continued the wartime tunnel vision of memory that focused almost exclusively on the deceased. And the federal government continued to consider only Union troops worthy of reburial, supporting the partisan tone of the veteran generation. During this era, the Confederate dead were either left on the battlefields or moved by civilians or heritage groups to local cemeteries. This lack of equality reflected the bitter animosity of the early postwar years and the realism of Reconstruction.[17]

Southerners felt compelled to act when the federal government would not, although in many cases the Confederate dead could not be located or remained on the fields, as at Shiloh. One searcher at Fort Donelson noted that very few Confederate dead could be found because "the wells and cisterns in the vicinity have, many of them been literally filled with the bodies of rebel soldiers and the apertures covered with rubbish and brush." Still, the Confederate dead were locatable in many areas, as evidenced by the numerous stories of Confederate soldiers' remains being unearthed. Newspapers in the South reported in 1866 that the battlefield at Franklin was "rented by the proprietor to freedmen, and is about to be given to the plow." White Southerners therefore sought to "secure means to remove the bodies before the traces of the graves are trampled out." The result was the Confederate cemetery at the McGavock place, "a fine old plantation," recalled a returning veteran, where John McGavock tendered two acres northwest of his mansion, Carnton, to rebury 1,481 Confederates. As would be expected, the Confederate dead were reburied by state when they could be identified, but only about half were identifiable. Nevertheless, each was given a wooden headboard.[18]

Similar events occurred elsewhere, such as in Fredericksburg, where citizens began burying Confederate dead and caring for their graves as early as 1862. Local citizens chose a plot adjacent to the city cemetery and placed many Confederate dead there, as well as a few Union troops who were later reinterred in the new national cemetery. The local Ladies' Memorial Association cared for the cemetery through the years, being one of the first to memorialize and decorate the graves of the dead in 1865. They later erected a monument on the site, dedicating it in 1884. Other Southerners did likewise. Local citizens cared for the Confederate dead at Perryville, Kentucky; Squire Bottom, who lived along Doctor's Creek, built a Confederate cemetery on a prominent hill on the battlefield and began constructing a stone fence around the site. Similarly, local ladies of Appomattox formed a Ladies' Association in May 1866 and eventually secured land on which several Confederates who had died in the very last stages of the war in Virginia were buried.[19]

This same effort went on all over the South—and not just on the famous battlefields. At Rivers Bridge in South Carolina, where Confederates tried to halt William T. Sherman's advance in February 1865, local citizens went through the same process, illustrating the local nature of the phenomenon as well as its broad extent. Rivers Bridge was obviously a small fight, but it was significant to the residents of Bamberg County, who tried to locate the Confederate bodies for reburial in 1876, reburying those they could find about a mile away at a church that had been burned during the war; they placed a monument above the mass grave in 1878. Illustrating the split mentality typical of the time, the citizens took a different course of action when they dug into Union graves: "We also dug into some other graves by the roadside, but found from the belt buckles and buttons that had U. S. on them they were Union soldiers, and we re-buried them." Significantly, the citizens of the Rivers Bridge battlefield area actually took their efforts one step further. In 1876, several residents created the Rivers Bridge Monumental and Memorial Association, electing R. C. Brabham as its first president. In 1876, the group began to hold annual memorial services at the battlefield, with veterans, governors, and other luminaries attending and speaking. The group was one of the first, if not the first, battlefield association outside Gettysburg, Pennsylvania, and certainly one of the first in the South.[20]

As a result of such activity, the unified nation carried on a non-unified memory of the war based on the treatment of its respective dead. With official federal government partisanship, Southerners chose to take their own stances on the history of the war. This split mentality would unfortunately continue for decades, allowing little in the way of reconciliation prior to the last decade of the nineteenth century. And with that lack of reconciliation came a lack of widespread preservation.

II

Aside from the major work done on battlefields in the form of cemetery construction, which was preservation in and of itself, there was much other activity on numerous Civil War sites during the veteran era. Although these were not necessarily acts of preservation, the battlefields nevertheless saw a major infusion of visitation after the war, largely propelled by the railroad industry, which in the long run was beneficial to preservation efforts in that it kept the focus on the battlefields themselves; one writer remarked that the battlefields were the "surest and saddest prompter of memory." Such a case of visitation occurred at Fort Sumter, where on April 14, 1865, Robert Anderson himself raised the same flag he had lowered four years earlier. As long as Americans remembered the battles and traveled to historic sites such as this, there was a good chance a major preservation effort would emerge. Still, all the tramping was not always welcome, as when Benson Lossing visited the Resaca battlefield in 1866: "We soon left the highway, and took a direct line across the fields for the battle-ground, opening fences for a passage, receiving the curses from a planter because we crossed his cornfield, and laboring a little harder, on the whole, than if we had walked the entire distance."[21]

The initial influx of quartermaster explorers looking for bodies for the national cemeteries obviously brought additional contact with private landowners. Capt. E. B. Whitman, who scoured the western theater searching for the bodies of Federal soldiers, left vivid details about his search. At Fort Donelson in March 1866, Whitman found "the woods . . . studded with the graves," often in varying numbers from "the single grave of the soldier buried where he fell, to the group of one hundred or more buried from the field hospitals or at points where the fiercest assaults were made." In one instance, he found a burial trench at a private residence, the plot now being used as "the site of the family woodpile and chopping yard." At another house he found the burial sites "in the garden and although not actually ploughed over yet there was no external indication of graves." Unfortunately, he also described shallow graves in which parts of bodies were frequently seen above ground. In one instance "portions of the bodies have been dug out by dogs and devoured."[22]

All across America, veterans and civilians alike found that most inhabitants on the battlefields were welcoming. At Franklin, visitors talked with Moscow Carter, owner of the famed Carter House, which sat right in the middle of the fighting. As one veteran noted, "Mr. Carter takes great pleasure in showing any one over the battlefield, and takes great interest in preserving every vestige of the terrible battle." Another veteran remarked how "the old cotton gin has vanished; but the bullet-marked Carter House . . . is still extant." He wrote that the ground was "in about the same condition as during the battle."[23]

A visitor shortly after the war similarly toured the Corinth battlefield and described "the forest trees in all directions rent and torn by shot and shell." He also described the many burial places: "This great battle-ground is dotted—here and there—in some places thick as meadow mole-hills—with the graves of Federal and the exposed remains of Confederate dead." The Confederate veteran went on to describe how the "Federal dead were all neatly interred in the usual way, with head and foot boards in every instance." Conversely, he described "the sights . . . of vast numbers of Confederate 'bones'—whole skeletons and parts of skeletons— lying exposed, and bleaching on the field, in the bushes, and on the hill-sides, under logs, and on stumps."[24]

The battlefields changed dramatically over the decades, however, and in some cases almost immediately. Family members looking for the graves of loved ones at Fort Donelson immediately after the war found that the battlefield and the graves were already being plowed and planted in tobacco. Visitors to Chattanooga in the late 1860s described "Bragg's breastworks still remaining in good preservation" and noted that the Chickamauga battlefield still "looked as if a cyclone had swept through it." Conversely, a Chickamauga visitor in the 1870s described it as already being "all overgrown with trees and underwood." A veteran in the 1880s noted his visit to Chickamauga and admitted, "When we got there, there wasn't a man in the whole crowd that could tell a thing about it. The trees had grown up there as big as my body." A visitor to Franklin in the 1880s noted that the only earthworks still in existence was a three-hundred-yard line west of town, still "much as it was left."[25]

The heavy woods of Shiloh also changed dramatically over time. George B. Davis, a War Department investigator, wrote that the battlefield had "changed much in detail, but little in its general aspect." Veterans were nevertheless grieved at the deterioration, one writing, "You will find the field has grown up to a thick underbrush of black gum and oak." He admitted "a feeling of disappointment, and with it a tinge of regret." The earthworks at nearby Corinth were still visible in the mid-1880s, one visitor declaring that "the old redoubts which encompass the town on every hand, tell of the fearful conflict that once raged over them— on the green slopes beyond the earthworks those who hurled themselves against them in vain lie in unmarked graves—dust and ashes these twenty-odd years." But even those earthworks were in danger of disappearing in just a matter of decades.[26]

A visitor to the Fredericksburg area in 1881 was taken aback at the change in the battlefields, but he also saw some remaining signs of the conflict. In Fredericksburg itself, he noted, "walls of houses that were destroyed during the battle are no uncommon site." At Salem Church, he described how "a few feet in rear of the church is a line of breastworks, now no higher than the knees, and thickly overgrown with weeds." Signs of damage to the church itself nevertheless stood out: "The church walls contain shell-holes and countless bullet marks; while the overhanging oaks show many scars. Indeed, it may be said that as many minie balls have been put into the church as there have been prayers sent out from it." A visit to Chancellorsville on the same trip turned up "the outlines of the old house marked by shrubs, weeds and stray bricks." In some areas, such as in Petersburg, local businesses printed tour guides as early as the late 1860s, obviously desiring to benefit from the economic boost of tourism. William H. Griffith, who owned the site of the famous Crater, certainly did so, charging viewers twenty-five cents for access to a small museum and the site itself.[27]

Such visits became more personal, and emotional, when the tourists were veterans and when they had a personal connection to a particular spot. A veteran's return to Petersburg in 1882 illustrates such emotions:

> Friday I visited the battle fields of Petersburg & spent 4 hours in trying to
> identify the spot where I fell on the 18 of June 64 in leading a charge upon
> the Rebel works. All is changed there now. What was a solid piece of woods
> through which I led my troops is now all cleared field, & the hill side so
> smooth then is now grown up with little clumps of trees—marking some
> spots made more rich perhaps by the bloody struggles enacted on them. At
> last, guided by the railroad cut & the well remembered direction of the church
> spires of the city, I found the spot—or a space of 20 or 30 feet within which I
> must have fallen. It is now a plowed field—too rich, I suppose, since that 18
> of June to be left barren by the owner—& there are in it the remnants of a
> last years cornfield. Standing & musing there remembering how I thought of

mother in that calm ebbing away of life amidst the horrible carnage, I looked
down & saw a bullet, & while stooping to pick it up, another & another
appeared in sight & I took up six within as many feet of each other and of the
spot where I fell. . . . You can not image, I believe, what thoughts came over
me, as I thought of all those who stood there that day—for & against—&
what it was all for, & what would come of it.[28]

That this soldier dwelt on the causes for such carnage fits perfectly with the
era's split memory of the war. And building on that memory was a phenomenon
that drew more veterans and families to the battlefields during this period: veteran reunions. Although Decoration Day quickly took hold in both North and
South and primarily continued the partisan emphasis of sides in the war, unit
reunions were, by definition, completely one-sided. Still, that animosity began
to melt away as this generation matured, and a few joint veteran reunions and
Memorial Day commemorations actually began to take place by the mid-1870s.
One of the earliest occurred in Vicksburg, Mississippi, in 1874. The *New York
Times* reported that veterans of both sides created "an association known as 'The
Order of Blues and Grays,' its avowed purpose being the encouragement of kindly
and frank relations between the survivors of both armies." With Reconstruction
ended in 1877 and the 1876 national centennial celebration helping foster pride in
the Revolutionary generation, joint reunions became more common in the 1880s.
When one took place at Atlanta in 1880, the *Washington Post* proclaimed, "Opening Day of the Reunion of the Boys in Blue and Gray." Another reunion occurred
at Wilson's Creek in 1883. "Throughout the reunion the most cordial feeling has
existed between the old Union and Confederate soldiers," a newspaper reported,
"and the most courteous and generous sentiments have been expressed. Not a
single unpleasant word has been uttered to mar the general harmony and enthusiasm. The men have camped together as though there had never been a difference
between them." Large reunions also took place at Pea Ridge and Gettysburg, including one in 1888 that the *New York Times* described as "the occasion of a reunion both of Northern and Southern veterans." Of course the key feature in the
joint reunions was a total lack of treatment of the causes of the war, mainly race
and slavery, allowing whites of both sections to dwell on features on which they
agreed, primarily the bravery and manliness of the common soldiers (themselves)
they were celebrating.[29]

And as would be expected, the continual visitation to the battlefields led to
some preservation-minded marking. At Chickamauga, a visitor described "little
wooden tablets driven into the ground and . . . shingles nailed to the trees, indicating positions of commands during the battle." Yet much partisanship still
remained, even if presented in comedic fashion. One sign that read "Route of

Baird's and Johnson's Divisions on evening of the 20th" became victim to a prank-ster who scrubbed out the "e" from "Route." The sign then read, "Rout of Baird's and Johnson's Divisions."[30]

Strong views were still held, but they were beginning to thaw as Americans increasingly visited their cherished fields of battle.

III

Many veterans and civilians were fortunate enough to return to the battlefields, but not all had the financial or physical ability to do so. Still, the battlefields called, particularly to the veterans. Francis Shoup, for instance, remarked several years later that spring and the blooms of dogwoods always took him back to the war: "I never see them now that I do not think of Shiloh," he wrote. Fortunately for those who could not return, several artists and publishers sought the next best thing—to bring the battlefields to them.[31]

In the years after the war ended, numerous artists began to paint, draw, or photograph the various battlefields, allowing those who could not travel to them a sight of their historic fields. As a result, the influence of early media productions such as drawings, paintings, panoramas, and cycloramas should not be dismissed in keeping the battlefields in the forefront of America's memory and therefore in eventual preservation efforts. One genre of viewable battlefields came in the most basic and easily disseminated form: book publication. Although the reproduction of still photographs in books and magazines was still far in the future, entre-preneurs such as Benson Lossing scoured the nation and wrote several volumes on his travels to the various fields of battle. Best known was his three-volume *Pictorial History of the Civil War in the United States of America*, which provided vivid hand-drawn illustrations of the fields both during and after the fighting. Veterans who could not actually visit the battlefields no doubt consumed these images, trying to see if anything in their recollection matched the places illus-trated. Another major outlet was the *Philadelphia Weekly Times's Annals of the War*, but perhaps most disseminated were the *Century* magazine articles put out in the 1880s, containing essays written by the war's major participants, including Ulysses S. Grant and P. G. T. Beauregard. These articles eventually were com-piled into the four-volume *Battles and Leaders of the Civil War* and frequently contained wartime and postwar (mid-1880s) images of the fields.[32]

Other media presentations also took veterans back to their battlefields. Gilded Age paintings by artists such as Thure de Thulstrup were remarkable in detail, capturing as best an artist could on canvas what the horror of war must have been like. It was mainly European artists who cashed in on this growing phenomenon, men such as Xanthus Smith with his painting of the battle between the ironclads. Swedish-born Thulstrup was perhaps the best known among them, and his paintings are still regarded as classics, often being used for cover art on published books. In all, he produced numerous paintings of such famous encounters as the Hornet's Nest at Shiloh, Sheridan's ride at Cedar Creek, Grant's assaults at Vicksburg, and Sherman at the Battle of Atlanta, mostly for L. Prang and Company.[33]

Although simple drawings and paintings had their place among America's public, the climax of this phenomenon came with the emergence of panoramas and cycloramas. The very large paintings displayed in great halls in large cities obviously took a long time to create, but they also drew large crowds upon their completion. In an effort to put the visitor almost on the battlefield, they were often accompanied by tangible trees, stumps, fences, and mannequins in the foreground, seeking to make the transition from the physical space to the painting unrealized. One newspaper in Chicago reported, "It is difficult, and in some places impossible to tell where the canvas leaves off and the artificial foreground begins." The effect was that the visitor was almost transported to the battle. These great halls also contracted with famous veterans to lecture in front of the paintings, adding much more reality. Such was the case when Benjamin Prentiss lectured to visitors at the Shiloh Panorama in Chicago in the 1880s.[34]

There was a difference in the styles of the panorama and cyclorama, however. The panorama was not a continuous painting, but rather contained panels that covered only a portion of the surroundings, perhaps like a crescent moon. In other instances, these panoramas consisted of moving scenes on rolls that stationary viewers saw move past them, something of a forerunner to motion pictures. Either way, these paintings offered a remarkable connection to the events depicted, and numerous panoramas were produced in the 1880s. These included portions of surviving panoramas by William Knight of the Andrews's Raid or "Great Locomotive Chase" and another by William Travis of the Army of the Cumberland, the latter a hand-cranked version.[35]

Perhaps the most famous Civil War battlefield panorama was that of Shiloh. Spurred by A. T. Andreas of the Western Art Association, Théophile Poilpot and twelve assistants produced the panorama and displayed it in Chicago in 1885. The panels focused on the Hornet's Nest, with a tangible decorative foreground of trees and artifacts; it even had an accompanying booklet, *Manual of the Panorama of the Battle of Shiloh*. Although later on display in Washington, D.C., the painting was eventually lost. Fortunately, several panels were included in the Shiloh Century magazine articles, and other photographs also exist. The panorama also produced an amusing chromolithograph in 1885. The McCormick Harvester Company produced a scene of Shiloh's Hornet's Nest, complete with a tattered and shot-up building. Yet on the partial front porch sat a shiny, undamaged McCormick reaper with the label, "The McCormick Machines Come Victoriously Out of Every Contest, and Without a Scratch."[36]

Cycloramas, on the other hand, were the capstone of Civil War art. These gigantic paintings made a continuous circuit around the viewers, placing them in the center of the action. Anyone observing the cyclorama could turn a full 360 degrees and see all the battlefield and action as if he were standing on site during the event. Numerous works of this nature existed in their heyday in the 1880s, but sadly only two are still viewable—at Gettysburg and Atlanta. Photographs and scraps of others exist, such as the Lookout Mountain and Second Manassas cycloramas. There was also a *Monitor* and *Merrimack* cyclorama, but all trace of it has been lost.[37]

One of only two cycloramas available for public viewing, the Atlanta painting was a massive 42-by-358-foot canvas that was painted in Milwaukee, Wisconsin, and appeared in Minneapolis, Detroit, and Indianapolis. William Wehner and twelve assistants painted the massive work in the mid-1880s, focusing on the July 22 Battle of Atlanta. The cyclorama first appeared in Atlanta in 1892, with Confederate veteran Charles W. Hubner giving lectures at its presentation. The Lookout Mountain piece, painted by Eugene Bracht, Karl Roechling, and George Koch in Berlin, was transported to America and shown in Atlanta, Chattanooga, and Nashville. Unfortunately, it too was later lost.[38]

Probably the most famous cyclorama was that which depicted the battle at Gettysburg. Although several versions existed, and do even today, the Gettysburg National Military Park has the iconic edition on display. Painted by Paul Philippoteaux and a team of assistants, the enormous paining was 42 by 377 feet. First shown in Boston in 1884, the painting also contained a three-dimensional foreground of trees, bushes, and artifacts. A Boston newspaper declared that "the atmosphere [was] remarkably like nature. . . . It is quite impossible to distinguish a painted cannon from an actual one. . . . The extreme effect of realism is prominent in the painting of the foreground."[39]

These paintings played a major role in commemorating the war's battles, and by extension they were involved in the surge toward embryonic preservation. If not examples of outright preservation, they were nevertheless preserving the scenes and in a sense transported many a veteran back to the battlefields. But they also played a major role in the developing collective memory of the Civil War. Most of the paintings were of Union victories and were presented from a Union perspective. They also spoke volumes to an engrossed and moldable public about what was most important at each battle. There is little coincidence that the Shiloh Panorama depicted the Hornet's Nest, which is seen today as the focal point of the battle. The accompanying manual even went so far as to state, "The Thermopylae of modern times, was the 'Hornet's Nest' at Shiloh," and "for some hours it was the turning point in the battle, and beyond doubt saved what was finally saved of the first day's wreck at Shiloh." A similar reaction took place at

Gettysburg, with the painting of that battle set amid Pickett's famous charge on the third day. It is no coincidence that Pickett's Charge is the focal point of Gettysburg in today's public memory of the war. If these paintings did not actually preserve anything, they played a major role in creating interest in the battlefields and fostering a conception of the war that has remained to the present day.[40]

IV

By far the greatest activity on any battlefield during this period was at Gettysburg, and it was here that outright preservation actually began to take place. Local citizens and officers such as David McConaughy and Maj. Gen. John W. Geary chartered as a corporation, under the auspices of the Pennsylvania legislature, the Gettysburg Battlefield Memorial Association in 1864. The charter stated the association aimed "to commemorate the great deeds of valor, endurance, and noble sacrifice, and to perpetuate the memory of the heroes," but it had pitiful little funding in its early years. The Pennsylvania legislature appropriated three thousand dollars in both 1867 and 1868, and the association bought three small tracts of land on Culp's Hill, Cemetery Hill, and Little Round Top. The state also gave the association authority to condemn land, but because of the continual lack of funding and the Panic of 1873, the association went dormant until the late 1870s.[41]

Despite the problems with the Gettysburg Battlefield Memorial Association, monuments began to go up on the battlefield in the 1870s. In 1878, the Grand Army of the Republic (GAR) post in Erie, Pennsylvania, placed a marker on Little Round Top to show where Col. Strong Vincent fell. The Philadelphia post also placed a marker to note where Col. Fred Taylor died. In 1879, veterans of the Second Massachusetts marked their battle position with a tablet that detailed the unit's actions. All these events were extraordinary for the time. Previously, memorialization had only occurred in cemeteries; now, actual battle sites were being permanently marked. Still, it would be some time before actual monuments went up on the field.[42]

The preservation success at Gettysburg grew in the 1880s, when, with the Gettysburg Battlefield Memorial Association faltering, the Pennsylvania Grand Army of the Republic began to take over. John Vanderslice was a prime mover in this effort, finding at Gettysburg both "scope and possibility" as well as "apparent apathy or inactivity of those controlling it [the association]." Grand Army of the Republic chapters purchased enough association stock and became the majority stockholder by 1880, and they replaced the association's officers with their own. The major shift that resulted fortuitously brought one of the foremost Gettysburg authorities at the time, John B. Bachelder, to the forefront of preservation work there. Although a civilian, Bachelder had gone to Gettysburg immediately after the battle and had been researching the fight ever since. His emergence as the leader at Gettysburg marked a new era for the battlefield, and with it preservation in general.[43]

With a plan in place and the reinvigorated association hard at work buying land, commemorative and memorial efforts soon moved totally out of the cemetery and onto the battlefield. In particular, large monuments began to dot the area, marking a vast change from the mere tablets set up beforehand. The Norristown post of the GAR marked with a marble shaft the place where Brig. Gen. Samuel Zook fell in the Wheatfield. Similarly, veterans of the Ninety-First Pennsylvania placed a monument at their position on Little Round Top.[44]

All the while, Bachelder and the association continued their work, funded by the state of Pennsylvania with a ten-thousand-dollar appropriation in 1881. Bachelder and company used the money to buy land such as the Wheatfield and to build roads. By 1883, the association had title to several hundred acres on both round tops, the Peach Orchard, and Culp's Hill. Various veterans' organizations placed monuments on these lands, including the One hundred and twenty-fourth New York, Seventeenth Connecticut, and Eight-Eighth and Ninetieth Pennsylvania.[45]

Changes in preservation and commemorative mentality also began to emerge once Bachelder and the association began fruitful work at Gettysburg in the 1880s, portending a change of attitude in the future. In 1883, Massachusetts appropriated money to place monuments to its units at Gettysburg, which was the first time a state had done so. This move foreshadowed a flood of monumentation, which in itself was a common hallmark of remembrance in the Victorian age. Prior to 1883, all monumentation was done with private money or through veterans' organizations. Taking Massachusetts's lead, Pennsylvania also gave money in 1884 to mark John Reynolds death site. Meanwhile, the Gettysburg Battlefield Memorial Association bought George Meade's headquarters in 1887 and marked every Union division flank. Bachelder also marked famous places, including his pet project, the Confederate "High Water Mark" and famous "copse of trees." Bachelder's emphasis on the Confederate charge on the third day, like the cyclorama, forever cemented that event in the minds of the American public.[46]

Even the federal government became involved. The War Department had routinely donated obsolete ordnance to various towns, groups, and GAR posts for marking cemeteries and other commemorative areas, but in the late 1870s and 1880s it was almost totally focused on Revolutionary War battlefields, obviously in response to the centennial of that war. The congressional committees overseeing such embryonic work began to consider more comprehensive historic preservation legislation, however, including a national board to oversee the work, a classification system of Revolutionary War battlefields, and a process of matching funds for local preservation work. In the end, little was actually done besides commissioning a survey (performed by Benson J. Lossing) of Revolutionary battlefields and providing money for the erection of eight monuments on Revolutionary War sites. Specifically dealing with the Civil War battlefields, in 1880 Congress appropriated fifty thousand dollars for Bachelder to study the Gettysburg field, survey, and map the area. In the late 1880s, Congress also funded the marking of regular army units at Gettysburg and supported annual veterans' encampments at the battlefield.[47]

The work was not without controversy, however. As the twenty-fifth anniversary of the battle approached in 1888, numerous states asked to dedicate monuments. Bachelder and the association realized it had to provide guidelines for the growing phenomenon and passed a series of regulations to ensure consistency and accuracy. These rules unfortunately caused a series of controversies over monumentation, including a spat between the Twelfth New Jersey and One hundred and eleventh New York veterans and a nasty controversy over the position of the Seventy-Second Pennsylvania monument. The association wanted the monument placed according to its guidelines, but the Pennsylvanians wanted a much more prominent location. The veterans took the association to court, eventually to the Pennsylvania Supreme Court, which ruled in their favor. Egos among aging men with fading memories caused other, similar disputes as well.[48]

Even amid all the work, there was one glaring missing feature at Gettysburg, which illustrated well the divergence of memory in the Reconstruction generation. Just as in the national cemeteries, there was little to no Confederate memorialization at Gettysburg, which was basically at this point a "Union memorial." One association member wrote of an 1882 meeting when "arrangements were made for the reception of a delegation of Confederate soldiers, who visited the field for the purpose of locating the position of several commands." Prior to 1890, however, only two tablets marked any Confederate position. When Southerners asked to be involved, such as in 1884, when veterans of the Second Maryland asked to mark their position on the battlefield, the request met heated opposition. The memorial nevertheless eventually went up two years later. Similarly, Bachelder marked the spot where Brig. Gen. Lewis Armistead fell at the High Water Mark in 1887, but the association allowed few other Confederate monuments. Veterans of George Pickett's division had asked to erect a division monument but were denied, Bachelder compromising with the tablet marking Armistead's death. And even that was not on the Confederate side of the field; it was within Union lines. That was, of course, fine with Bachelder, as it magnified his obsession with the High Water Mark.[49]

As the 1890s neared, however, some saw the dire need to include the Confederates. Bachelder himself grew interested and, because of limited association funding, petitioned Congress to appropriate money to mark the Confederate lines in 1889. He continued to push for recognition for the Confederates, realizing the time was coming when they would no longer be around to help mark the positions. He also realized that the time was soon coming when he, as probably the most knowledgeable man on Gettysburg alive at the time, would not be around either. He sent out a circular letter asking if future visitors to the field would remark, "Was there no opposing army at Gettysburg, where was the enemy?" And in a fitting change of heart for the Gettysburg Battlefield Memorial Association, he intoned that such Confederate inclusion would be done "not for sentiment, but for history."[50]

Ultimately, Bachelder's effort was not successful in such a divisive period. Yet his arguments helped set the stage for a much more successful period in the future.

V

Despite Gettysburg's predominance during this period, other battlefields also began to receive some attention. For instance, in the 1860s the Cantrell family planted a cedar tree at Shiloh where legend held that Albert Sidney Johnston had fallen. At Antietam the Fifty-First Pennsylvania commemorated its effort at Burnside Bridge in October 1887, placing a monument on the end of the bridge across Antietam Creek. Similarly, some marking took place at Franklin in preparation for the Confederate reunion in September 1887. One veteran recalled, "An attempt was made some years ago to mark the spot where Gen. 'Pat' Cleburne fell at the head of his men." He also stated that "a small tablet tells where General Adams died." At Vicksburg, although Ulysses S. Grant did not visit the battlefield while passing through the city in 1880, he did visit the national cemetery. Seven years later, Louisiana placed a monument to its state's troops there.[51]

Monuments also went up on other battlefields. Veterans of the Forty-Third Wisconsin placed a small stone beside the railroad at Stones River, probably marking the spot where some of their men had been buried. Years later, in 1888, a U.S. Regular monument went up in the same area. Several monuments went up near Fredericksburg, including the 1884 memorial in the city's Confederate cemetery. Also on the Fredericksburg battlefield, members of Thomas R. R. Cobb's family erected a monument around 1888 to mark his death site. At Chancellorsville in 1876, Stonewall Jackson's staff officers placed a small quartz rock at the site of his wounding; a larger monument in the vicinity of his wounding appeared in 1888. Veterans of John Sedgwick's corps erected a memorial on the spot of his death at Spotsylvania in 1887. Two monuments also went up in the late 1880s at

Pea Ridge, one in 1887 placed by former Confederates to honor their dead near the Elkhorn Tavern. In 1889 both sides erected a memorial labeled "A Reunited Soldiery."[52]

Ironically, the increased number of markings on other battlefields was at variance with what was occurring in Pennsylvania. These monuments pointed toward the future and the dawn of a new generation. One development included the emergence of other battlefield associations besides the one at Gettysburg. At Antietam, Congressman Louis E. McComas and Rev. C. L. Keedy established the Antietam Memorial Association to create a park. They desired to "make of the Antietam battle-field what was made of the scene of the conflict at Gettysburg." One interested follower noted the association "laid out some avenues along battle lines on that field and encouraged organizations to erect monuments." The association asked for monuments to "perpetuate in lasting and worthy tributes the historic features of that memorable battle." The purchase of land at a battlefield other than Gettysburg was certainly a new idea.[53]

Similarly, thought went into buying land at Chickamauga. In the 1880s, a Chicago post of the Grand Army of the Republic entertained the idea of raising money to buy the battlefield and went so far as to take options on the land for twenty-five dollars an acre. The group ultimately failed in this large venture, but the project certainly influenced others to think more broadly about who could undertake such massive work. The idea also emerged of getting the federal government involved. A bill surfaced in 1887 to that effect, but it was never brought to a vote.[54]

To be sure, federal involvement in outright preservation was a novel idea in the late 1880s. To this point, the only federal monies spent on battlefields had been cemeteries and the acquisition at public auction of about two acres at Stones River in 1875, including the famous Hazen Brigade Monument. Later, the War Department began mapping battlefields in order to teach the lessons of the battles to military officers. This occurred at Gettysburg, of course, but also at Chickamauga. "Shortly after the close of the late civil war," the *Washington Post* reported, the secretary of war appointed a mapping "Commission, consisting of Gens. P. H. Sheridan, George Crook, [and] Jeff C. Davis." Confusion was the result of this haphazard attempt, however, and the officers received reports that were "so conflicting that it seemed impossible to harmonize them." A later attempt also failed due to "personal interests and views so conflicting."[55]

The mapping effort was tried again in the late 1880s, this time spurred on by the Society of the Army of the Cumberland. The War Department sent Maj. Sanford C. Kellogg, a veteran of the battle who had taken part in the famous misunderstanding that had created the gap in the Union lines, and asked other prominent veterans such as William S. Rosecrans, John T. Wilder, Henry V.

Boynton, and Absolem Baird to help as well. In yet another major development different from the efforts at Gettysburg, the attempt included for the first time "many men distinguished on the other side." Several Confederates joined Union veterans as they visited the field with Kellogg in 1888 and 1889, and Kellogg soon completed the maps. The contemporary emergence of a joint Union and Confederate battlefield association at Chickamauga resulted from these early efforts.[56]

The 1880s consequently proved to be a major decade of preservation development throughout the nation. Outside Gettysburg, whose association seemed to be stuck in the old partisan antipathy of the Reconstruction generation, activities were more unifying. Associations lobbying for preserving battlefields were cropping up elsewhere, most notably at Antietam and Chickamauga. That the federal government was beginning to become involved in mapping battlefields was also a good sign. And the inclusion of Confederates in the process of dealing with battlefields was an unheard-of development in this era. Together, these major activities at the end of the 1880s foreshadowed a period that would be much different from the Reconstruction era.[57]

Still, the Reconstruction generation primarily displayed a split memory of the Civil War. Southerners held on to their belief that they were right and could have won had external factors not prevented them. At the same time, Northerners continued their hard line toward the South, whipping up support for partisan policies by hearkening back to the bloody war. The violence perpetrated by the Ku Klux Klan to keep blacks out of society also affected almost all walks of life, and certainly affected battlefield preservation. No better example was the veteran reunion at Pea Ridge in 1889, when in the midst of the reconciliation, including a resolution explaining North-South agreement, one former Confederate "made some remarks that were interpreted by a few northerners as indicating a willingness to start the war anew." A similar instance occurred as Maj. W. A. Wainwright reported about less-than-cooperative landowners in northern Georgia, locals who insisted that the "d——d Yankees shall not be removed, but shall lay where they are, they will not pay taxes to be expended in paying honor to the Yankee Soldiers, will not have their fields torn up to get them out of the ground etc." And it was not just old vitriol from the South that poisoned society; an enormous upheaval occurred in the North when President Grover Cleveland backed a plan to return captured Confederate battle flags to the Southern states. What little preservation that occurred in the years between 1865 and 1890 was thus not surprisingly limited, one-sided in each section, nonfederal, and incomplete. Still, what more could be expected of a generation who endured the harshest war to date in American history and then nearly as grueling a decade of Reconstruction?[58]

But there was a new day dawning in America.

2

The Golden Age,
1890–1912

A sense of festivity hung in the air as what was otherwise a normal Washington summer evening progressed in all its sultry balm. Congress had just spent another regular day in session, but for at least a few congressmen and lobbyists, it was anything but an ordinary night. As soon as Congress passed H.R. 6454, Representative H. Clay Evans of Tennessee, a Union veteran but now representing Chattanooga in the U.S. House, took the bill "the same night" to the White House. President Benjamin Harrison was there waiting, and he signed the seemingly minor measure into law. The process had occurred thousands of times before, and would happen thousands of times in the future, yet this particular law was to have tremendous implications for Civil War battlefield preservation. The bill established the nation's first national military park, and as such it was a watershed moment that fostered a new way of thinking about historic sites, involvement of the federal government in historic preservation, and, perhaps most important, reconciliation between whites in the North and South.[1]

The two and a half decades after the Civil War were so volatile in politics and race that little could be done in terms of reunion. Even with the end of Reconstruction in 1877, animosity still lingered into the 1880s, although tensions between the sections began easing as evidenced by Blue-Gray reunions and a thawing of attitudes toward joint commemoration. Still, the 1880s were primarily partisan and private in terms of commemoration and preservation. Speaking of the slow process of healing from the Civil War, Union veteran Henry V. Boynton spoke volumes when he wrote, "He would indeed be impatient who looked for more speedy progress."[2]

The dynamics of Civil War memory changed drastically with the dawn of the 1890s, however. By that time, Reconstruction was long gone and a bid in Congress to resurrect the old policies failed to take hold amid a surge of government-sponsored (federal and state) segregation. Moreover, an attitude of change was sweeping the nation, with new issues coming to the forefront and replacing the old divisive issues of race and war. Central among them was a shift toward imperialism, in which the United States, by the end of the decade, would find itself with an empire stretching from the Caribbean to the Pacific. Much of that empire was gained as a result of war, which almost always fosters patriotism and cohesion. Northerners and Southerners alike marched off to war under the same banner for the first major time since 1846, and there was even a concerted effort to push reconciliation by bringing old Confederates back into the ranks as general officers who commanded both sections' troops. Joseph Wheeler's interesting experiences in Cuba attested to the desire for Southerners to be brought back into the fold.[3]

Yet it was not just on the political and martial front that change occurred; race relations were transformed as well, and much of the reconciliation among whites was based on a common supremacy felt toward African Americans. In the racial arena, a new day of legalized segregation and white supremacy enveloped the nation. As explained by historian David Blight, the reconciliationist and white supremacist visions of the Civil War overpowered the emancipationist vision: "Southerners found they could transform loss on the battlefield into a reunion on terms largely of their own choosing." Seeking equality for African Americans, Reconstruction was a failure because the gains made in the 1860s with three major amendments to the Constitution were summarily forgotten when Northern politicians and the public seemingly gave up on the difficult and continual fight. White Southerners outlasted Radical Republicans and their Reconstruction, creating a situation in which the South lost the war but won the peace. The white North's backing away from Reconstruction-era policies satisfied the white South, which became much less antagonistic and much more open to reconciliation now that it was on their own terms.[4]

Americans were clearly tired of decades of argument over racial issues, which ultimately brought on the war that claimed more than seven hundred thousand lives and then led to bitter fights in Reconstruction. As Edward Linenthal states, "By the 1890s many Northern veterans had become more sympathetic to Southern views on blacks, and, in consequence, these rituals of reconciliation became rituals of exclusion that ignored the history of black Americans after the Civil War and prevented them from taking part in the healing process." The end of Reconstruction and the rise of imperialism consequently took minds off the past and transported people to the future, a future in which all white Americans could come together in unity and move the nation forward. Of course, this new America came at the expense of African American gains in freedom and equality.[5]

This significant change affected many areas of American life, from economics to politics to society. It also significantly affected the memory of the Civil War: how Americans viewed the conflict and how they now memorialized it. Tiring of years of divisiveness, Americans, and particularly veterans, sought issues on which they could agree, including the honor, bravery, and manhood of the soldiers on both sides. This change in thinking on top of the growing nationalism fostered by the nation's centennial first encouraged preservation and the marking of Revolutionary War sites. The change also affected how Americans viewed and treated their old battlegrounds of the Civil War, where most of that honor and bravery had been tangibly displayed. The birth of the 1890s thus saw a major shift in preservation mentality among Americans, and this shift significantly influenced almost all preservation efforts that have occurred since.[6]

The new preservation ideals were breathtaking. If the period from 1865 to 1890 was racked with partisan, one-sided, bitter, and limited commemoration of the Civil War in general and battlefields in particular, the 1890s were just the opposite in almost every respect. Where most commemoration and preservation had been done by the Union side as at Gettysburg, barely allowing the Confederates to become involved, the 1890s saw a melding of the two sections as they eagerly toiled in the same efforts. If the previous decades had seen struggling private associations with hard-headed and determined leaders trying to keep massive efforts afloat, the 1890s saw the federal government step in and become the leader in battlefield preservation. "It must be done by the National Government or remain undone," the members of one congressional committee argued. If the earlier work had been spotty and limited in scope, the new federal efforts sought to preserve in total, with the emphasis on the details of military movements rather than background causes such as slavery, an idea that fit squarely into the era's emphasis on precision and scientific accuracy. By all accounts, the 1890s were a new dawn in the preservation movement.[7]

At the same time, numerous other factors came together to allow such a golden opportunity for preservation. In the 1890s, many of the veterans were still alive and retained enough of their mental acumen to return to the battlefields and mark them accurately and properly. It would not be long, however, before these aging veterans would pass off the scene, as indeed was already the case with some of the older commanders such as Robert E. Lee and Ulysses S. Grant. Lower-level and younger officers, and even younger men in the ranks, were nevertheless in the late primes of their lives in the 1890s. But they realized they would not live forever; one congressional committee declared that these battlefields would be a "monument to them" before they "left this world." The time to preserve and mark the fields was now, and veterans' organizations such as the powerful Grand Army of the Republic and the newly established (1889) United Confederate Veterans lent their considerable weight to the effort, as did numerous smaller army, brigade, and regimental veterans' groups.[8]

Similarly, U.S. congresses in the 1890s were made up, in large part, of veterans; over half the members of the 1890 Congress were Civil War veterans. That percentage would decline as the decade went on, but in 1890 Civil War veterans held power in Congress to the degree that America would not see again. Accordingly, the time to preserve their fields was now, when veterans dominated the decision-making process as well as the purse strings of the nation. In addition, veterans held sway in the state legislatures, a fact that would also be instrumental in the work of preserving and commemorating the battlefields of the Civil War.[9]

Moreover, it was critical that the battlefields themselves be preserved now, in the 1890s, because they would not be pristine much longer. No one knew it at the time, but America was on the verge of a second industrial revolution, which would see mobilization, urbanization, and massive change alter America's towns and cities. As most battles had been fought around and just outside towns where transportation routes crossed (Gettysburg, Vicksburg, Chattanooga, Atlanta, Fredericksburg, Richmond, Petersburg, Murfreesboro, Nashville, etc.), these towns were set to grow exponentially in the early decades of the twentieth century. The battlefields had to be preserved now, before many of the historic landscapes were tarnished or destroyed.[10]

With all these factors having their effect, America was at a crossroads in terms of its battlefield preservation efforts.[11]

I

Henry Van Ness Boynton dreamed of battlefield preservation and then made it happen. As a veteran of the Thirty-Fifth Ohio, in which he was severely wounded at Chattanooga in November 1863, Boynton went on to become a national newspaper correspondent and political activist. With a national platform, he changed his emphasis from grilling politicians to battlefield preservation. His epiphany arrived one day in the late 1880s while he and his old brigade commander, Ferdinand Van Derveer, were touring the Chickamauga battlefield. Hearing "the voice of solemn song" from a nearby country church on that Sunday, the two old soldiers remembered "the thunder of that hell of battle which had loaded the air with horror through all that earlier and well-remembered Sabbath." It was there that they hit upon a novel idea. They would work to make Chickamauga into "a western Gettysburg," but in a way preservation had never been done before. Unlike the effort at Gettysburg, Boynton wanted both sides honored. He also emphasized total preservation of the field, again unlike what was occurring at Gettysburg. And at that point, he realized yet another first was needed. The main reason Gettysburg was not saved in totality was because of the enormity of the task. It was much more than a struggling private association could handle, and Boynton dreamed of involving the federal government at Chickamauga.[12]

To achieve his goal, Boynton first created an association of veterans "after the general plan of the Gettysburg Memorial Association," he wrote, "only differing from it in any essential feature in its being a joint association of both Union and Confederate veterans." The association met at Chickamauga in 1889, with luminaries such as William S. Rosecrans attending and the reconciliationist air about them expanding. "It is very difficult to find in history an instance where contending parties in after years meet together in perfect amity," Rosecrans told the audience. "It took great men to win that battle, but it takes greater men still, I will say morally greater, to wipe away all the ill feeling which naturally grows out of such a contest." Confederate veteran and Georgia governor John B. Gordon also called on the veterans: "Let us bury the foul spirit of discord so deep that no blast of partisan political trumpet, however wide sounding and penetrating, can ever wake it to service again." With the vast support of the veterans' organizations behind him, Boynton wrote a bill and took it to Congress, where he had Charles Grosvenor, another veteran, introduce it. The bill sped through Congress, and Benjamin Harrison signed it on August 20, 1890. It was a watershed moment for battlefield preservation.[13]

Indeed, Boynton's dream, now reality, embodied many theories that would affect battlefield preservation for the next 120 years. Boynton coined the term "National Military Park," which is still in use today and which signified the fact that these parks were national in scope, not just Union. He also wrote into the bill the complete preservation of Chickamauga, a hallmark of his theory of preservation that he hoped would be copied on other battlefields. Conversely, Boynton also developed a plan of preservation that, in all fairness, should be labeled the "Chattanooga Plan." Urbanization had engulfed much of the Chattanooga battlefield by 1890, and Boynton realized that obtaining the entire area was unrealistic, and the cost of doing so, even if possible, was astronomical. He instead opted for a system in which the battles of Chattanooga were interpreted from roadways and in small, isolated but significant historical areas called "reservations." The government would only buy the latter. Finally, Boynton dictated in his bill that the work would be bipartisan, requiring that one of the three commissioners appointed to oversee the development and maintenance of the park would be a former Confederate. All of this was new and progressive.[14]

Following the now-passed legislation, the secretary of war soon appointed the governing commission. Union veteran Joseph S. Fullerton became the chairman, and the Confederate representative was former general Alexander P. Stewart. The law also required that an active army officer be on the commission, and the secretary appointed Chickamauga veteran Sanford C. Kellogg. Boynton certainly would have had a place on the commission had he desired one, but he opted for a better position in his eyes, that of park historian. An engineer was also appointed, local builder Edward E. Betts, which rounded out the major officials creating the park. Other, lesser clerks and laborers were also a part of the process, but the commission was the major decision-making body.[15]

The commission obviously changed members over time. Fullerton was killed in a railroad accident in 1897, and historian Boynton took his place, serving until his death in 1905. Thereafter Ezra Carmen, who had also worked at Antietam, and bill sponsor Charles Grosvenor served as chairman until 1917, when the Confederate commissioner actually became chairman. The Confederate commissioner slot had changed hands much less. Stewart lived until 1908, and Joseph B. Cumming took his place and lived on into the 1920s, serving as chairman. The active army officer position was a bit more problematic. Kellogg left in 1893 to be replaced by Frank G. Smith, who served until 1908. By that time it was hard to find an active officer who was still a veteran, so that requirement was removed. Thereafter, John Tweedale, Webster J. Colburn, and John T. Wilder served as the third commissioner, although not always harmoniously with the others.[16]

Over the course of the commission's work, the veterans basically built the park visitors see today. In a sweeping change from national cemetery–era construction, the main effort was returning the battlefield to its look in 1863: "The grounds will be a Park only in the sense of being restored to their conditions at the time of the battle. No work will be done for purely decorative purposes." The first task was obtaining the land, but that proved problematic. "The owners of the land on which it is proposed to locate Chickamauga Park evidently intend that it shall cost the Government more than the battle that was fought in that vicinity," one official complained. As a result, most of the battlefield land was condemned in the early 1890s. Then the commission began to mark troop positions. Most of the iron unit-position tablets and cannon, as well as headquarters and mortuary monuments, were erected by the federal government, whereas the vast monuments were mainly state efforts. Each piece of monumentation marked specific sites where units fought on the battlefield. "These tablets are of iron," one newspaper reported, "[and] are so complete and accurate that a perfect stranger, by their aid, will have no trouble in locating the various positions of any body of troops engaged in that great battle."[17]

Meanwhile, a very different work occurred at Chattanooga, where the commission bought only small reservations, opting to place most of the monumentation there. Still, visitors could get a clear sense of the fighting at Chattanooga from these markings, aided by the terrain of Lookout Mountain, Orchard Knob, and Missionary Ridge, which significantly displayed the major fighting areas. Perhaps Prince Henry of Prussia, brother of Germany's Kaiser Wilhelm II and grandson of Queen Victoria of England, best summed up Chattanooga's inspiring potential when he visited. Boynton gave him a tour of Lookout Mountain, at which the prince remarked, "This is magnificent. There is nothing in all Europe that is finer. I have never seen such a battlefield." Boynton obviously liked the accolades, but being American through and through, he remarked several months later when President Theodore Roosevelt toured the same area, "I am glad to welcome an American prince this time."[18]

By 1895, the park was nearing completion, and Congress, again led by Grosvenor, appropriated money for a grand dedication. It occurred on the anniversary of the Chickamauga battle in September 1895, with political luminaries including the vice president and many senators and congressmen as well as thousands of veterans and visitors in attendance. Many states opted to dedicate their monuments during the event. Parades in Chattanooga, speeches, and reunions were commonplace, and an air of festivity and reconciliation filled the days as America dedicated its first venture into national battlefield preservation. "The event proved to be without precedent in the history of wars," the official report of the dedication stated, "and one which would not be possible in any other nation than our own."[19]

The years after 1895 saw the completion of the park's monumentation and markings and a shift toward more maintenance. Remarkable work had been done in a short time, however, and battlefield preservation would never be the same. Henry Boynton was truly the father of the modern national military park idea, and his influence on the battlefield preservation movement has been immense. Few people who today step onto a preserved Civil War battlefield even know the name Henry Van Ness Boynton, but they should. Visitors of today owe him an immense debt of gratitude for his pioneering efforts to preserve battlefields of the Civil War.[20]

The year 1890 saw more than just the preservation of Chickamauga, however. Additional bills were introduced in Congress that year to establish Chickamauga-type parks at Antietam and Gettysburg, but neither passed. Still, Antietam backers, who had gone the same route as Boynton and established an association, succeeded in getting a small appropriation inserted into a larger bill that set up an Antietam "board." This group would mark that battlefield in precisely the limited way that Boynton had at Chattanooga. The secretary of war appointed two veterans to this board, former Confederate general Henry Heth and Union veteran John C. Stearns. With little money and less incentive to do much of anything, these two aged men produced few results in the next three years, although a lot of groundwork was laid. "Had we been placed on the same footing with the Chickamauga Commission," Stearns and Heth wrote, "we would have been able to report greater progress." Part of the hesitance was that Antietam supporters continued to push for an expansion of the effort in Congress, offering legislation for a full military park like that at Chickamauga. That never transpired, and the secretary of war soon had enough: "While fully aware of the difficulties that attend upon undertakings of this kind, at Antietam and elsewhere, I cannot resist the conclusion that the Board as organized under the order of June 17, 1891, is less expeditious in its operations than Congress and the Department have a reasonable right to expect. Over three years have passed since the scheme was undertaken, and the Board has so little to show in the way of accomplished results as to lead to the belief that difficulties have been encountered which are either insurmountable, or cannot be overcome by the Board as at present constituted."[21]

Secretary of War Daniel S. Lamont wanted the work completed, so he reorganized the board, placing active army officer George B. Davis in charge of the work. "By accident," Davis wrote, "I was thrown in charge." Davis was a good choice, having been interested in battlefield preservation as an editor of the *War of the Rebellion*. Davis went to work with a will in 1894 with Heth and Ezra Carmen, who replaced the ailing Stearns. In eleven months the battlefield was completely marked along roadways and small strips of land purchased from the landowners. All marking was done on these strips and roads, unless individual organizations or states desired to erect monuments, in which case they had to buy the land themselves. Davis explained the thinking: "I went up and looked the ground over," he said, "and very shortly reached this conclusion . . . to perpetuate an agricultural community." He added, "I therefore recommended to the Secretary of War that no areas, no tracts of land, be bought at Antietam at all, but that narrow lanes should be obtained along the lines of battle, . . . and monuments and tablets be erected in the lanes that had thus been acquired." Once the work was for the most part done, Davis returned to his War Department work, eventually becoming judge advocate general, but he was never far from battlefield preservation and would often be called on to offer his expertise on the subject. He was proud of his work: "I think the experiment at Antietam was entirely successful, and . . . the will of Congress was fully executed." Meanwhile, another army officer, George W. Davis (no relation), took up the original Davis's work and finished the loose ends by 1898, when the battlefield was placed under the care of a superintendent, sometimes the local national cemetery overseer.[22]

The more limited work at Antietam also had a major effect on preservation, offering what became known as the Antietam Plan. Davis's work there became a model for saving money in preservation and was a competing plan to Boynton's idea of total preservation. Davis's work had been preceded by Boynton's own process at Chattanooga, however, and at a time when Antietam supporters were still trying to get a total battlefield at Antietam. That never happened, and the Antietam Plan developed, although by all rights it should be known as the Chattanooga Plan. The only major difference was that it was performed out of necessity at Chattanooga and by choice at Antietam. The reluctance to appropriate money for a full park at Antietam surprised some, but it nevertheless illustrated the limits on battlefield preservation even amid the excitement of Chickamauga and the beginning of the golden age of battlefield preservation. Significantly, that Gettysburg supporters could only get a similar limited commission for marking that battlefield along the Chattanooga/Antietam Plan in 1893 did not bode well for future preservation.[23]

Despite the reluctance to create huge Boyntonesque battlefields at Antietam and Gettysburg, Congress surprisingly went ahead and established one at Shiloh in 1894. War Department troubleshooter George B. Davis again counseled moderation after a visit to the battlefield, recommending that Congress only preserve a twenty-five-acre site at Pittsburg Landing or, if that was not enough, preserve land along the lines he was working out at Antietam. It certainly should not be a full park like Chickamauga, Davis argued, simply because visitation would be so low. "Indeed," Davis wrote, "you can not buy a ticket to the Shiloh battlefield." Congress did not take his recommendation, and Davis then warned the newly appointed commission that the "present outlook for offices and quarters at Pittsburg Landing is not promising."[24]

Part of the reason Shiloh was funded in full was because of who was behind the effort. Like the other battlefields at Chickamauga, Antietam, and Gettysburg, Shiloh had its own association, created out of a visit by veterans in 1893. They soon had on board a powerful congressman, David B. Henderson, a veteran of the battle who was already a committee chairman and was moving on to even loftier heights. Henderson had a special interest in Shiloh, beside the fact that he had fought there: in Shiloh National Cemetery lay his brother Thomas, killed during the battle. Henderson put his clout behind the bill but nevertheless had some doubts. "Appropriations are unpopular before Congressional elections," he noted. Still, he soon had the legislation passed, although some opposition emerged on monetary grounds. President Grover Cleveland signed the bill into law, and another Boyntonesque park was born.[25]

The secretary of war soon appointed the park's commission, and Henderson was well pleased. Cornelius Cadle of Iowa, Henderson's home state, became chairman, with famed general Don Carlos Buell as the other Union representative. The Confederate commissioner was Robert F. Looney, but both Looney and Buell soon died. The Confederate position went to Josiah Patterson, who likewise died after only a few years. Former Confederate general Basil W. Duke then joined the commission and remained for many years. The other Union position was filled with more stability, as James H. Ashcraft took Buell's position and remained for two decades.[26]

Ironically, others in lesser jobs were perhaps more powerful than even these commissioners, mainly the park's historian, David W. Reed, and its engineer, Atwell Thompson. The latter was an Irish immigrant but had worked as a road engineer under Betts at Chickamauga. Alexander P. Stewart, in fact, recommended him, stating that he was a "high toned, honorable gentleman, capable and educated, and a very competent engineer." Thompson accordingly became the on-site director, while the commissioners, like those at Chickamauga, mostly governed from their homes with only occasional visits. More important, Reed was another Iowan whom Henderson touted (they had served in the same regiment); he wrote Reed to ask for documentation "in making the fight for the Secretaryship of the Shiloh Commission." Thus the threesome of Cadle, Reed, and Thompson soon ran the park; in fact, Buell and Looney fought their dominance early on. Even Henry Boynton, now Chickamauga's chairman, became involved in a nasty Army of the Ohio versus Army of the Tennessee controversy over the one-sided Union markings and Reed's alleged slanted historical work. Boynton even went so far as to write that Reed's errors "tends to cast serious doubt upon the historical methods adopted, and the historical accuracy of the rest of the work."[27]

Despite the controversies and the change in commission members, the work at Shiloh continued and was essentially done by 1905. Engineer Thompson resigned that year and became the engineer for the city of Jackson, Tennessee. Reed himself then moved to Shiloh to oversee the daily operations and eventually became chairman when Cadle defaulted on his work in 1910 and was asked to resign. The secretary of war wrote a terse note: "For some time past the Department has been thoroughly dissatisfied with your method of conducting business. . . . It is therefore requested that you immediately forward to me your resignation as a member of said commission." From then on, Reed was the face of the Shiloh National Military Park and had more of an influence on it than anyone else, first as historian for fifteen years and then as chairman. Reed was instrumental in determining the most significant areas and actions in the battle, and not surprisingly emphasized the area where his regiment had fought: the Hornet's Nest.[28]

As at Chickamauga, the Shiloh commission toiled hard over the years in "the work of converting mere land into a park." Its first effort was gaining title to the land. The process was delayed by a few rogue members of the old association who had options on the land, the leader of which Boynton described as "ignorant, illiterate, and cannot write six lines of decent English." Even the level-headed George B. Davis described him as "that blackmailing humbug . . . who should be disposed of in some way." The options fortunately soon expired and the government went on with land acquisition, mostly through purchase; only a small amount of the land had to be condemned. Once the land was obtained, Thompson worked on roads and facilities, and the commission erected markers, tablets, and artillery to denote specific unit positions during the battle. The states were allowed to place monuments to their soldiers, and they did so in various ways, from larger state memorials to individual regimental monuments—and sometimes both. Thereafter, Shiloh went through the same process that Chickamauga did, although no dedication took place. By 1905, the battlefield was all but completed, and it has changed little since.[29]

Surprisingly, despite its popularity, the Gettysburg National Military Park was only the fourth of five parks created in the 1890s. Obviously, it had seen the most development prior to the 1890s, but when the federal government began to preserve battlefields, three others were already ahead of it. Efforts to get a Gettysburg bill passed through Congress floundered through the early years of the 1890s, when Chickamauga and Shiloh both became realities. The best Gettysburg received was an Antietam-like commission in 1893, tasked only with marking specific points.[30]

Yet that commission was important. The secretary of war appointed old association leader John B. Bachelder to the three-man commission, along with Union veteran John P. Nicholson. For the Confederate representative, the secretary of war appointed former general William H. Forney. The former Confederate remained only a year, to be replaced by William M. Robbins. Robbins remained ten years, to be replaced by Lunsford L. Lomax. Bachelder died shortly into the commission's existence, causing the loss of an amazing amount of knowledge about the battle. Charles Richardson soon took his place and served many years. The commission also hired an engineer, veteran Emmor B. Cope.[31]

The Gettysburg commission inherited much more land than any of the other battlefields, whose commissions had to start their work from scratch. At Gettysburg, the association had already done much preservation work. It took some time for the commission to get acclimated to what was happening, but the change to full park status Congress provided in 1895 only aided preservation at Gettysburg. In that year, at the insistence of Daniel Sickles, who had run for a seat specifically on the issue of creating a major park, Congress moved Gettysburg from an Antietam-style commission to a full-fledged Boyntonesque park. The entire Gettysburg battlefield could never be preserved, due mainly to urbanization and cost, but it was nevertheless more like Chickamauga and Shiloh than Antietam. It was somewhat of a hybrid, although more total than limited.[32]

The Gettysburg commission, now fully at work in 1895, benefited from the association's previous land acquisition and the earlier monumentation process. Still, it bought more land and continued to monument through the years. It also faced a major lawsuit over the Gettysburg Electric Railway Company, which put a trolley railroad through the heart of the battlefield, right where Pickett's famous charge had occurred. The controversy went all the way to the U.S. Supreme Court, which sided with the park. As at the beginning of the national cemetery process, condemnation was verified, making a massive statement that historic site preservation was indeed in the realm of federal government duties.[33]

By the mid-1890s, therefore, four parks had been established, but distinct patterns of opposition had also emerged. While discussing Chickamauga and Chattanooga in 1890, for example, Texas representative and Confederate veteran Constantine B. Kilgore objected: "I am very much inclined to object. . . . I am opposed to this character of legislation. I do not believe Congress ought to indulge in legislation of this kind and appropriating the people's money to buy lands to make parks all over the country." In Shiloh's debate, Confederate veteran Senator Francis M. Cockrell of Missouri argued, "I think it is an entering wedge to an immense mass of business which will entail upon the country an annual expenditure of thousands and hundreds of thousands of dollars. This is only the entering wedge for making every battlefield a national park." Vicksburg proved to be the recipient of such heretofore pent-up opposition, and it would indeed be a rigorous and drawn-out process to get its legislation through Congress. In fact, it would take the Vicksburg association, patterned after the other four, until 1899 to gain success.[34]

Thomas C. Catchings, Vicksburg's representative, initially brought a park bill to the floor of the U.S. House in 1896. The main impediment to the bill was Speaker of the House Thomas B. "Czar" Reed. He simply would not bring the bill up for a vote for economic reasons, despite the Committee on Military Affairs recommending its passage over several sessions. Even David B. Henderson, who by this time was Reed's right-hand man, could not get the Speaker to move: "This simply can't be done. . . . The boys have declared they didn't intend spending another dollar on military park appropriations." On another occasion, Henderson wrote a friend, "I do not feel very hopeful. I have been pushing the Speaker, but much work is needed in that quarter." Henderson was adamant, however: "Depend upon it I will leave nothing undone to help in the Park bill. We have got to take Reed by the throat at this session." Only when Reed decided to resign did he allow the vote on the floor, and it passed quickly. President William McKinley, a Civil War veteran, signed it on February 21, 1899.[35]

Secretary of War Russell Alger quickly appointed the commission, and it would, primarily because of its later establishment, have the least turnover of any of the 1890s park commissions. Alger appointed former Confederate general Stephen D. Lee, Iowan (again with Henderson's help) William T. Rigby, and James G. Everest. They were allowed to elect their own chairman, and the two Union veterans, illustrating some of the reconciliation feeling, voted for Lee. Due to poor health as well as his wife's sickness, Lee soon gave the chairmanship to Rigby temporarily; he handed it over permanently a few years later. He nevertheless remained on the commission until his death in 1908. Confederate veteran Lewis Guion then took Lee's position, the only change in the commission's membership in its history. Vicksburg also had a historian, John S. Kountz, but it did not have an official engineer.[36]

The Vicksburg commission was the most stable of the commissions, but it was also the most controversial. Animosity developed during the major cost-cutting reforms of Elihu Root's tenure in the War Department; the secretary of war wanted the work at Vicksburg done as cheaply as possible. In one instance, the commission had a local Corps of Engineers officer lay out roads, but the War Department sent Chickamauga's engineer Betts to Vicksburg to redo the work much more cheaply. Later, the department saddled the commission with Betts's brother, R. D. Betts. The commission also did not appreciate Henry Boynton's heavy hand over their affairs. Root sent Boynton to Mississippi to find where the War Department could cut expenditures, and the situation developed into a nasty controversy between the secretary and the commission. One member complained, "It looks to me, we are not to have a Park to compare favorably with the others—with the constant restrictions imposed by the secretary." He added, "Our park will be a small affair and not what its friends hoped it to be and not what the survivors of the great armies desire."[37]

Still, the commission was able to do its work of buying land (some of which had to be condemned), building roads, and erecting monumentation. As at Gettysburg, the major portion of the battlefield was bought in totality, with Davis-like wings along roadways extending from the heart of the park to each side. Along these roadways, the commission placed unit-position markers and artillery, and the states erected monuments to their troops. The process was essentially completed by 1908, and then the work settled, just as at the other parks, into maintenance patterns. Significantly, however, part of the Vicksburg commission's work included refurbishing the Shirley House that sat on the lines during the war, illustrating the major thrust of house rehabilitation in Victorian-era preservation.[38]

Even amid the establishment of the five battlefields, there was also important contextual policies and legislation being created in regard to the preservation, commemoration, and use of the national military parks. In 1897, Congress passed sweeping legislation protecting the battlefields. The statute utilized the protection sections in the original bills as patterns and set punishments for anyone committing illegal acts in the parks. Even while establishing legislation to protect the parks, however, the bill did not include an appropriation. An increasingly frugal Congress seemed willing to protect battlefields as long as it cost nothing. At the same time, it was becoming very grudging about creating new parks or providing officials to protect them.[39]

Another significant budgetary aspect in the original parks' legislation was to split federal and state fiscal responsibility for marking them. The federal government administered and protected the parks, but Congress left it to the states to place monuments in honor of the state volunteers who had fought there. As a result, states made large appropriations, actually rivaling if not surpassing federal funds spent on the battlefields. Individual states appointed commissions to erect these monuments "where the representatives of the regiments think the organizations made the most notable record." This dual federal/state responsibility continued over the decades, at varying percentages, with the contributions of local and private organizations eventually added as well.[40]

Perhaps the best example of the larger contextual policy regarding the parks came with the growth of martial activity in the late 1890s. The Spanish-American War began in 1898, and the United States only prevailed because its opponent was even more unready for war. The results were nevertheless a major American victory, including the acquisition of an empire from the Caribbean to the Philippines. War talk consumed Americans, with many volunteering to go to Cuba in state regiments, but the side-effect was that emphasis was removed from Civil War history. With the steam running out of the golden age, the Civil War parks were left somewhat in the rear of public favoritism.[41]

At the same time, Congress saw the need to legislate military use of the already-established parks, which began a very nonpreservationist stance in reference to the parks as the two ideals, preservation and military use, conflicted greatly. Talk of using the parks to train modern officers was rampant in the congressional debates, and in 1896, with Charles Grosvenor again leading the effort, Congress passed legislation that mandated every military park be used for officer training as well as proving grounds for entire units. Grosvenor had originally only intended Chickamauga for this use, but the House Committee on Military Affairs amended the bill to include all of the parks. These would be, one official declared, training grounds "equaled by none." Another wrote that the battlefields themselves "would be worth an entire course in textbooks on the strategy of a campaign and battle tactics." Yet there was some opposition even to this effort, Representative Joseph (Uncle Joe) Cannon of Illinois complaining, "Is this a real necessity, for the benefit of the Army, or is it a power granted which will result in much expense and something of pleasure, without resulting in profit to the Army?" Despite the concerns, the bill passed and many units utilized the parks for maneuvers and drill, especially during the Spanish-American War.[42]

Two of the parks played a role in the Spanish-American War, further diluting their uniqueness and preservation. Whereas only minor numbers of troops camped at Shiloh, that was not the case at Chickamauga. That commission was not ready for the influx of troops, but they did all they could, commission chairman Henry Boynton even receiving a brigadier general's commission. Boynton and the army set up Camp George H. Thomas in the park, and the troops quickly began to fill the quiet expanses. In all, over seventy thousand troops filed through Camp Thomas in 1898, and not surprisingly, they did a lot of damage to the historic battlefield. The troops tore up roads, markers, monuments, and trees, and they left the camp, Boynton reported, in "a most filthy and deplorable condition . . . , so far as unfilled sinks in many camps and unburned refuse of various kinds could defile it." The park had to cover the cost of the cleanup (some $14,224.86) with its own appropriation, and Boynton reported it was "an immense amount of most disagreeable work which did not fall within the sphere of their duties." Despite a major controversy over the quality and quantity of the battlefield's water supply, the War Department chose to keep some troops in the area after the war, establishing Fort Oglethorpe adjacent to the park in 1904. The permanency of Fort Oglethorpe only added to the dilution of Civil War commemoration. Some Spanish American units even went so far as to desire monuments on the Chickamauga battlefield to commemorate where they had camped during the 1898 war. As if monetary concerns were not enough, these added issues of split commemoration and heightened patriotism in another war added to the swell that limited concern for Civil War battlefield preservation in the 1890s.[43]

Still, the 1890s had produced five parks of varying size and scope, and one would be hard pressed to find five more important engagements in the war. And although much more could have been done, these five emerged at just the right time. Because of segregation, they were out from under the engulfing Reconstruction animosity; moreover, the aging veterans were still around, the battlefields themselves were still mostly pristine, and a veteran-dominated Congress was in a willing mood to spend millions of dollars. As a result, these five parks are the best-preserved and best-marked battlefields today because of the era in which they were created.[44]

The establishment of these parks did not happen without problems, however, and other bills to create additional parks were not passed during the decade. Even as patterns developed, including federal involvement, reconciliation (with a Confederate commissioner at times even serving as chairmen), and the totality of the process, monetary concerns limited success, even forcing creation of the Vicksburg park to be delayed several years. Moreover, rumblings of too much money being spent on the parks continued and would soon erupt into open rebellion. With additional events taking the spotlight off the parks as well, the golden age, golden though it was, existed for only a very short period. The window of opportunity was small.

II

Although many factors worked against establishing more battlefields, especially large Chickamauga or Shiloh type parks, the biggest threat to full-scale battlefield preservation came from within the preservation community itself. With the success of the 1890s battlefields, everyone now seemingly wanted a park of their own, and the result was a massive influx of bills to establish additional ones. Therein lay the major causes of the downturn in Civil War battlefield preservation efforts after the 1890s: the desire for so many parks and the desire to establish them cheaply. Ironically, both issues were borne of earlier successes.

Two basic theories on how to proceed had by the mid- to late 1890s emerged amid the hectic spurt of America's major battlefield preservation activity. Henry Boynton, originator and developer of the nation's first park, promoted his theory, what he called a "novel conception on a vast scale." Boynton's idea, implemented at Chickamauga, where he spoke of preserving "the entire field," as well as at Shiloh and partially at Gettysburg and Vicksburg, was to preserve entire battlefields, which necessitated the purchase and marking of large tracts of land. He desired that battlefields be preserved intact, with the vast majority of each battlefield under government control. Unless there was some overarching reason to the contrary, as at Chattanooga, Boynton desired other Civil War battlefields to be preserved along those lines as well. This Boyntonesque theory caught on in Congress, which established the Shiloh battlefield in 1894 along very similar theories as Chickamauga and was also a significant part of the thinking both at Gettysburg and Vicksburg. Urbanization was a factor in each of those, but where it could be done, Boynton desired for fields to be saved in totality.[45]

War Department stalwart George B. Davis offered the opposing view, that of buying as little land as possible, mostly the significant areas, and commemorating the rest of the fighting from existing roadways. This idea, first conceived out of necessity by Boynton at Chattanooga but institutionalized by Davis at Antietam, actually came to be known as the Antietam Plan. It had congealed in Davis's mind during several years of working on battlefield issues as well as in his military background fostering fiscal conservatism.[46]

Forcing the issue between the two plans and deciding future policies was Secretary of War Daniel S. Lamont, who leaned toward his War Department officer. As the desire for preserving almost every major battlefield in totality surged in the mid- and late 1890s, Lamont not surprisingly turned to Davis, his chief preservation thinker, for more advice. In addition to his work at Antietam, Davis had traveled the nation, examining the battlefields and making recommendations to Lamont. He went to nearby Bull Run, for example, to report on the feasibility of making that site a national park. In scouting the battlefield and reporting to the secretary, Davis concluded that most of the extremely significant land of both Bull Run battles lay around Henry House Hill. Immediately, Davis recognized the ability to make a much smaller and cheaper park of only a few acres by conserving only the most historic land of both battles, which conveniently took place on the same ground. The rest of the commemoration could be done along roadways. Davis recommended buying a little land, mostly around Henry House Hill, placing tablets and monuments on a small scale, and even erecting an observation tower so that both entire battlefields could be viewed from the Henry site.[47]

Likewise, Davis traveled to Atlanta to recommend a policy concerning a national park preserving the battlefields between that city and Chattanooga. Once again, he was opposed to preserving large tracts of land as had been done at Chickamauga, because they would cost an enormous amount of money. Rather, Davis opted for something similar to what he had recommended at Bull Run: obtaining key sites and interpreting the events from roadways. Similarly, Lamont sent Davis to Appomattox to report on that site. Unfortunately, despite efforts from private groups, the famous McLean House had been torn down in 1893 for erection elsewhere (the scheme fell through "during the panic which followed"), and the courthouse had also burned the year before. Davis returned with the same idea, preserving only about 150 acres instead of the thousands of acres that had been mentioned. Davis insisted that purchasing thousands of acres "would commemorate nothing, it would perpetuate the memory of nothing." He later stated, "I immediately reported the matter to the Secretary of War, and he approved my recommendation that the place be marked permanently by the erection of tablets." Davis wrote the text for the eleven tablets, which soon went up.[48]

By 1895, with Shiloh and Gettysburg joining Chickamauga and Antietam as preserved battlefields under these two competing plans, and with other veterans pushing for more parks, particularly Vicksburg and Stones River, Lamont called for an overall battlefield preservation strategy. "It is important that Congress should early adopt and consistently pursue a fixed policy in regard to the marking of the battlefields of the Civil War," Lamont reported, and he already knew what he wanted, courtesy of Davis. "I had several conferences with him," Davis remembered, and Lamont reported to Congress that the "policy pursued at Antietam" worked best. "It is earnestly recommended that Congress authorize the marking of the remaining important battlefields in the same manner adopted at Antietam, which can be completed in a few years at moderate cost," Lamont wrote. This was the first formal proposal for a national battlefield preservation policy.[49]

As the calls for more parks began to grow, Davis continued to formalize his policy, explaining his original ideas and his growing concerns about Boynton's theory of total preservation. By the late 1890s, Chickamauga, Shiloh, and a large portion of Gettysburg and Vicksburg had already been largely preserved. Davis argued that those fields were certainly enough, perhaps too much. "My belief was then—it has not been changed—that this was the proper thing for the United States to do for historical purposes, in order that coming generations might see what a battlefield was," Davis argued concerning Chickamauga. "My idea was that it was proper to acquire one large historic field in the West and one in the East, and that there the acquisition of areas should cease." Instead, the Antietam Plan should be utilized elsewhere: "The Government should desist from further acquisition of large tracts of land."[50]

Davis explained why every major battlefield should not be made into a national military park. If each battlefield were saved in total, hundreds of thousands of dollars would be required for land acquisition. Each would also need a governing commission like that at Chickamauga, Gettysburg, Shiloh, and Vicksburg. On top of those costs, there were many supporting the acquisition of Revolutionary War battlefields as well, so the price was potentially enormous. Davis also feared that a day would come when the veteran generation passed away and these large battlefields would not be as important to later generations. He stated that such a park might become a "no man's land" or "a refuge for tramps and all sorts of people." Perhaps worse, Davis feared that "people of competence in the matter of landscape work [would] fall into control, and they make it a [landscaped] park like Central Park."[51]

To Davis, the vast majority of battlefields would best be fitted as historic memorials and teaching tools, with only a couple of large fields that could be used by the military for the "staff ride," in which army officers studied the history of the battle on the grounds themselves. "A battlefield park may be used for two purposes: one, as a site for the encampment of troops; and, as an object lesson in strategy and tactics," he argued. Only a couple were needed. Davis summed up his theories when he wrote, "I think, as a battlefield, Antietam has proved most successful."[52]

Davis's words fell on willing ears as more and more park bills emerged in Congress. With the success of the initial five battlefields, sponsors of other preservation projects, mostly local congressmen from the districts in which the battle-fields lay, sought to fund their pet efforts. Yet few of these later sponsors carried the weight of a Boynton, Henderson, or Sickles, and with a tightening fiscal feeling on Capitol Hill, they were hard pressed to get much support for their efforts. Nevertheless, they began to try.[53]

As time passed, Davis could not keep up with the proposed battlefield preservation efforts; he was the army's judge advocate general, after all, and had other primary duties in addition to being the secretary of war's point man on battlefield preservation. As a result, the many bills began to run together, making more of an impression as a whole in a negative way than individually as important additions to the preservation work already being done. For instance, the other major Civil War battlefield for which a bill was introduced in the mid-1890s was Stones River, which also had a "Stones River Battlefield and Park Association" behind the effort. Representative James D. Richardson offered a bill in December 1895 to create the Stones River National Military Park, which would encompass the national cemetery as well as over a thousand additional acres. The bill went nowhere, but he offered it again in 1897. Again it went nowhere, and the association opted to emplace their own wooden signs, painted white, around the battlefield to mark significant locations.[54]

As the new century neared, a new wave of bills appeared, probably in reaction to Vicksburg's success and the election of a new Speaker of the House to replace the hard-nosed Thomas B. Reed. Even better, that Speaker was Civil War veteran David B. Henderson, who had been so instrumental in getting Shiloh's and Vicksburg's bills passed. It definitely seemed time to move forward despite the opposition, and the flurry of bills that emerged illustrated the possibilities.[55]

These many bills certainly put the preservation mentality forward, and in most cases they were the result of many years of agitation and work. A series of proposed "Fredericksburg and Adjacent National Battlefields Memorial Park" bills were offered in 1899. The Chancellorsville Battlefield Association had developed as early as April 1891, and it gained options to battlefield land but had to give them up by 1894 because the association was, the *New York Times* reported, "unable to meet its obligations." A similar Fredericksburg and Adjacent Battlefields Memorial Park Association appeared later. In 1903, Senator Redfield Proctor (a former secretary of war) offered a bill to fund a total of more than sixty-five hundred acres there, most of the acreage located on the battlefields of the Wilderness, Chancellorsville, and Spotsylvania, with only minor lands in Fredericksburg itself. The various committees were also supportive, stating that at Fredericksburg and its surrounding battlefields, "more great battles were fought, more men engaged, and more execution done, than on any other spot of similar area in the world." Calling the preservation of the battlefields "the duty and privilege of every nation," the committee argued that "the debt of honor must be paid." Despite the committee's support, the bill was never acted on.[56]

At the more rural Perryville battlefield, Representative George G. Gilbert offered a bill at the same time to create the "Perryville National Military Park." The bill carried the standard language of all the 1890s parks, all built on Boynton's Chickamauga legislation, and provided for over a square mile of battlefield to be preserved, certainly most of the field for the smaller battle. The battlefield of about seven hundred acres would be set up and maintained by a commission of three veterans just like the others. Yet despite these efforts, the Perryville park went nowhere.[57]

The same mentality prevailed at Petersburg, when Virginia representative Sydney Parham Epes offered a bill to create a national military park at that battlefield. The legislation was similar in every way to previous successful bills, including a governing commission made up of veterans of both sides. Most notable, however, was the land area encompassed in the proposed park; Epes offered a wide-ranging boundary that came to more than three thousand acres. Like the others, however, the Petersburg bill also failed.[58]

A major effort went forward to create a national military park at Atlanta as well. Numerous battles took place around the city, but Georgia representative Leonidas L. Livingston offered a bill that would make the battlefield of Peachtree Creek north of Atlanta into a park. With detailed boundaries and a similar commission of veterans to oversee the area, the proposed park included some thirteen hundred acres of battlefield land along the creek where the heavy fighting had taken place. The businessmen of Atlanta backed the idea, putting out their own booklet, *The Proposed Atlanta National Military Park*. Although only Peachtree Creek was envisioned as a national military park, the others, already "thickly populated," would receive tablets along the Chattanooga/Antietam Plan. The businessmen called the prospect "a memorial to the historic events and the heroic deeds of the Atlanta campaign," but could not get the legislation passed.[59]

A proposal for a park at Franklin proceeded somewhat differently. Representative Nicholas N. Cox in 1900 offered a bill establishing a "Franklin National Military Park," but it only provided for 150 acres. Still, those acres included the majority of the fighting areas around the Union line: "The lands embracing the grounds along the firing line of the two contending forces . . . and including the graves of the dead there buried." Utilizing the hybrid method at Gettysburg and Vicksburg, the bill also provided for "such approaches and such other lands contiguous to the lands above described." Perhaps Cox saw the fiscal context in which he was working and opted for a smaller Antietam/Chattanooga Plan battlefield from the start. Despite his narrowed vision, that bill still failed to pass, as did other efforts in ensuing years. One Tennessee congressman, former Confederate general George W. Gordon, wrote that the Committee on Military Affairs was "not favorably disposed" to fund any more parks. Senator James B. Frazier of Tennessee similarly wrote that "the Committee on Military Affairs in the House has determined that it will not pass any bill creating additional military parks," adding that "President Taft would likely veto any bill for a military park if one was indeed passed by the Congress."[60]

On and on went the various pieces of legislation during the late 1890s and early 1900s. In all, fourteen different Civil War battlefield parks were slated for preservation in proposed bills: Atlanta, Franklin, Fredericksburg, Bull Run, Petersburg, Perryville, Stones River, Fort Ridgely, Fort Reno, Wilson's Creek, Fort Stevens, Appomattox, Valley of Virginia, and Ball's Bluff. In addition, many Revolutionary War battlefields were also being considered. Simply put, a commission and large land purchases at each site would cost an astronomical figure. Something had to give.[61]

III

Because of so many bills in Congress calling for the creation of numerous big new national military parks, the Civil War preservation movement was quenched altogether. In fact, although an explosion of natural and other history-related parks came as Theodore Roosevelt emphasized conservation in the early 1900s, especially with the passage of the Antiquities Act in 1906 that shifted much of the historic emphasis to aboriginal sites on federal land, there was not a federal military park created between Vicksburg in 1899 and Fort Pulaski in 1924. Although not useful for battlefield preservation in the first two decades of the 1900s, the Antiquities Act was nevertheless an important first effort at a comprehensive national historic preservation policy, and it laid the groundwork for future policies of its kind.[62]

In addition to the Antiquities Act, reasons for the complete halt of new battlefield establishment were numerous. Money obviously had a lot to do with the stall and then the death of preservation initiatives. Controversy over the costs of the battlefields had emerged even in the early and mid-1890s, during the heyday of preservation; some congressmen were bold enough to argue against the appropriations. More notably, Secretary of War Elihu Root in the War Department was at the same time reconfiguring the military to be more efficient and save money. The mood of the nation and Congress was also changing with the emergence of the Progressive movement and the height of the imperialistic age. Governing an empire from the Caribbean to the South Pacific cost money and resulted in reduced attention to battlefield preservation at home. The numbers of veterans in each succeeding Congress in the 1890s was also dwindling, and this too factored into the change. Consequently, money for and interest in creating more battle-fields was increasingly hard to obtain.[63]

The political realities of retrenchment emerged quickly. Vicksburg proved to be the last of the great battlefields preserved primarily by the veterans themselves, and the slow process of getting Vicksburg's enabling legislation even passed illus-trated the difficulty that future bills would have. The initial chief roadblock was Speaker of the House Czar Reed, who refused to bring up the bill for years; he relented only as he was leaving the post. But Reed was not the only obstacle.[64]

There was seemingly an opening that if managed carefully could have signifi-cantly benefited battlefield preservation and all those bills waiting in Congress. When Reed left the House, none other than Civil War veteran and avid battle-field supporter David B. Henderson became Speaker. No doubt preservationists thought the gates would finally be opened and a flood of new parks would be established. Yet one man could not do everything, and there were quite a few po-tential roadblocks, even for Henderson. The Senate had to concur, the president had to sign the bills, and ironically, Henderson even faced opposition within his own House in the form of the Committee on Military Affairs, which had to pass all bills on to the full House. With all the opposition, not a single bill emerged successfully; in reality, Henderson did no better than Reed had done, and he actually had a worse record. Reed had allowed Vicksburg's bill to pass, but not a single battlefield was preserved while Henderson was Speaker.[65]

The battlefield preservation record of Henderson's speakership is clear. A total of ten Civil War park bills (Atlanta, Franklin, Fredericksburg, Bull Run, Petersburg, Perryville, Stones River, Fort Ridgely, Wilson's Creek, and Fort Stevens) were submitted in the two sessions of the Fifty-Sixth Congress (De-cember 1899–March 1901), not including several Revolutionary War battlefield bills. The Committee on Military Affairs sent only three of the ten (Stones River, Fredericksburg, and Atlanta) back to the House. Eleven Civil War battlefield bills (Atlanta, Appomattox, Fredericksburg, Bull Run, Petersburg, Perryville, Stones River, Fort Stevens, Wilson's Creek, Franklin, and Ball's Bluff) came for-ward in the Fifty-Seventh Congress (March 1901–March 1903), but the commit-tee reported to the floor only the Fredericksburg bill.[66]

Opposition was clearly demonstrated in the committee reports that did emerge. Even the positive Fredericksburg report came with an attached mi-nority statement from representatives Richard W. Parker of New Jersey, John H. Ketcham of New York, and Frederick C. Stevens of Minnesota. These three ar-gued that the fourteen bills (including those concerning Revolutionary War bat-tlefields) would cost nearly two million dollars "for beginning the acquisition of the lands alone." They further argued that the committee should not be reporting on one single battlefield, but "should examine and consider all before deciding which exhibits the greatest excellence and which would promise the greatest benefits." They went on: "We further believe it would be wise to consider in this connection the whole system of national parks . . . and then finally determine upon some plan that should harmonize and complete a system of national military parks." Such a plan, the trio argued, would "avoid the haphazard plan of separate commissions, each of which booms its own park, and all of which work at cross purposes." In the end, the three called for a "plan of development that should be uniform, comprehensive, beautiful, and instructive." And in addition to the minority Fredericksburg report, the full committee took the extra step of reporting unfavorably on the Appomattox bill. The legislation called for twenty-five hundred acres of land in the park, but the committee sought the advice of both Secretary of War Root and George B. Davis, both of whom advised that a mere one hundred acres would suffice. Root called the proposed acreage "unnecessarily large" and stated that "no events of any importance occurred upon the tract of 2,500 acres." Perhaps more significantly, Davis responded that "there was no particular area which constituted a battlefield in the sense that there is a definitely marked area which constitutes the battlefield at Gettysburg, Fredericksburg, or Chickamauga." As a result, the committee recommended that the bill "be indefinitely postponed."[67]

A few bills nevertheless managed to trickle through the committee with the potential of passage. But Henderson was surprisingly not any more favorable than Reed had been. Of the three bills referred favorably back to the House in the Fifty-Sixth Congress, none made it to the floor, despite the fact that the Senate had actually passed the Fredericksburg bill. When Fredericksburg supporters went to Henderson for aid, he told them in no uncertain terms there would be no battlefield bills that session. He insisted that he was very much in favor of battlefield preservation, as seen in his work at Shiloh and Vicksburg, but he nevertheless believed that "if he allowed consideration of this bill he would have to allow that of others, and thus he would be greatly embarrassed." Henderson consequently did not bring any of the bills to a vote, not even the Fredericksburg bill. In the Fifty-Seventh Congress, the Senate again passed the Fredericksburg bill, but Henderson once more refused to bring it to the floor of the House.[68]

It is especially curious that Henderson of all people refused to call up the bills. Unfortunately, he never fully explained his reasoning. Perhaps he was having his own doubts, as his "this simply can't be done" statement amid the Vicksburg proceedings illustrated. Perhaps he knew the House would not pass any bills and he did not want to fight a fight he could not win. Perhaps Henderson also feared a presidential veto from Theodore Roosevelt, who some historians have surmised was embarrassed that his father had paid for a substitute during the Civil War.

Another possibility was that Henderson, like many other veterans, was much more interested in his own army's battlefields than those of any others. Henderson had fought long and hard to get bills for Shiloh and Vicksburg passed, but he did not offer the same amount of prodding or even support for battlefields where he, his regiment, or his army had not fought.[69]

The best and last chance to get major battlefield bills through Congress during this golden age of possibility languished because of Henderson's lack of leadership. And Henderson served only two terms as Speaker before retiring to Iowa, leaving the post to Joseph G. Cannon of Illinois, who was even tighter with the purse strings than Henderson and Reed had been. A glorious opportunity passed as a result, and the golden age of battlefield preservation came to a premature end.[70]

IV

Not only did the future preservation movement sputter to an end politically, but assaults on the work already done also emerged after the turn of the century. Due to opposition in Congress, the number of battlefields under consideration, and the prodding of the retrenching Secretary of War Elihu Root, Congress soon held hearings on how money could be saved even in the parks already established. In essence, another round of potential historic preservation policy debates ensued. Root was streamlining the War Department in every aspect, and he wanted it done with the parks as well. He fully realized that the work of park building was ending, and it would take much less oversight to maintain the battlefields than it had to create them. The resulting bills, H.R. 12092, which dealt specifically with Civil War battlefields, and its eventual and more comprehensive replacement, H.R. 14351, which expanded the treatment to all military battlefields of American history, would abolish the four existing commissions at Chickamauga, Shiloh, Gettysburg, and Vicksburg after giving each two years to complete their work. After two years, a national commission would be appointed containing one member of each original commission as well as an active army officer, and it would oversee all four parks as well as a national historic preservation policy. It would also govern the future of battlefield preservation, obviously done along the lines of the Antietam Plan, with "general power to restore, preserve, mark, and maintain." The bill appropriated two hundred thousand dollars in total, the amount each of the four individual military park commissions had requested for that year.[71]

The idea was certainly not new with Root, although his adamancy made the idea go much further than it had before. Assistant Secretary of War Henry Breckinridge had mentioned this idea during the Spanish-American War, and

Col. Charles H. Heyl of the Inspector General's Office had supported such a move too. Later, the tightfisted Joseph Cannon included language in a sundry civil bill asking Root to become involved. Secretary Root accordingly became the prime mover of the idea.[72]

The very same House Committee on Military Affairs that refused to report so many battlefield bills held hearings on this issue in 1902. Not surprisingly, their chief witness was George B. Davis, who was conveniently in Washington as the army's judge advocate general. Congress called on Davis numerous times for advice and counsel in the next several years, Davis testifying several times before congressional committees about the future of battlefield preservation policy.[73]

Most notably, Davis appeared before the Committee on Military Affairs in April 1902. The chairman introduced him with an understatement: "You have taken an interest in this matter." Davis's testimony covered a large range of issues. He recounted his prior efforts and discussed his strongly held ideas on the Antietam Plan. "Those [battlefields] now in possession of the United States are quite enough," he said, adding, "I don't see what would be gained by such an [additional] expenditure." When asked about specifics, the obviously well-traveled and well-prepared Davis had ample answers. At Petersburg, for example, he argued that money should not be spent to preserve "miles of works in which there were never any assaults delivered or sustained. They were simply thrown up to protect troops." At the same time, he did advocate preserving specific sites such as the Crater and Fort Hill, with the rest of the battlefield interpreted from roadways. He gave the same answer when asked about Stones River, Perryville, and numerous other battlefields. "These could be treated on the Antietam plan," he argued, "probably at a very small expense." The committee agreed, the chairman stating, "I think we can frame a bill to suit the situation and send it to General Davis for examination and report."[74]

Davis also endorsed the idea of a central national commission, adding that "it needs some general scheme." But Davis was not for cruel treatment of the old veteran commissioners; he noted that many of the commissioners would be dying soon and favored Congress seeing to the general welfare of all of them.[75]

Not surprisingly, in their report to the full House the committee admitted that "separate commissions were necessary to prepare these great parks," but the "system is too cumbrous to be continued beyond the time necessary." The members also asked that future battlefields be preserved along the Antietam Plan with "plain cannon-ball monuments" and only narrow strips of land being purchased. The committee concluded, "Patriotism demands the preservation of these spots. But it is plain that they will not be preserved if a salaried commission has to be created for every spot."[76]

Opposition to the combination bill quickly emerged, however, primarily from the military park commissioners themselves, most of whom would lose their jobs. Congress's response to the concerned commissions' actions was not altogether positive. The minority members of the House Military Affairs Committee opposing the Fredericksburg bill wrote that "the passage of this bill would add another commission and corps of officeholders to stand in the way of any attempt to unite these commissions and systematize this work into some comprehensive, uniform, and business-like condition." Still, the commissions succeeded in defeating the bill even without a new Fredericksburg commission. Curiously, after his promotion of the idea, Secretary Root did not make it a major priority. Moreover, a jurisdictional fight over the appropriations process in the House caught the bill between the Committee on Appropriations and the Committee on Military Affairs. Most important, Speaker Henderson rose to oppose the bill despite his lack of support for additional battlefield parks. Obviously, his old army allegiance appeared again, and he would not allow his friends, such as Cadle and Reed at Shiloh and Rigby at Vicksburg, to be ousted. Shiloh commission chairman Cornelius Cadle wrote that he had been "advised by one of the powers that be that it will not be permitted to pass." Cadle also wrote David W. Reed, the Shiloh historian, "'Our Friend' said he would simply put a 'spike' in this." Obviously, "Our Friend" was Henderson, who used the same tactics Speaker Reed had used and simply refused to bring the bill, although passed by committee, to the floor.[77]

But the issue would not go away. The same bill reappeared over the next several years, with the committee again occasionally holding hearings. A second hearing took place in 1904, and it seemed to have a much better chance of passage this time. Henderson was gone as Speaker, and Cannon would no doubt support the idea. A new secretary of war, William Howard Taft, was also in office, and he supported the bill. Taft reported to Congress: "The development of the plans contemplated in the establishment of the different national military parks . . . has reached a point where, with a view to economy and uniformity of administration, the four different commissions . . . might well be consolidated into a single commission consisting of three members, or possibly five." He went on: "The conditions heretofore have been such that the Department has not felt called upon to suggest bringing this work into the hands of a general commission, a step against which no valid objection can lie if only public interests are to be considered." Taft was not able to make much headway, however, and the bill continued to languish.[78]

Yet another attempt occurred two years later, in 1906, as the House Committee on Military Affairs dealt with a similar bill. Taft again pushed the idea, but he had no better luck. The committee did agree, however, that "with a view to more economical administration . . . the conditions that now prevail result in salary rolls out of all proportion to the total expenditures for improvement [at the parks]." This bill's death did not keep the same bill from being offered in succeeding Congresses, although apparently Congress never again held hearings on it. The net result was a stalling of the preservation effort, especially regarding Civil War battlefields. Over the next several decades, only minor marking occurred, such as a monument funded at King's Mountain in 1906, money to finish the monument at Chalmette, Louisiana, in 1907, and legislation to create a small park at Guilford Courthouse, North Carolina, in 1911 and 1917. Significantly, all were pre–Civil War sites.[79]

Success came six years later, when Taft was president of the United States. Enough support for reform existed in 1912 for Congress to pass a small section in an appropriations bill that stopped the appointment of new commissioners to fill vacancies. The language read: "Hereafter vacancies occurring by death or resignation in the membership of the several commissions in charge of national military parks shall not be filled, and the duties of the offices thus vacated shall devolve upon the remaining commissioners or commissioner for each of said parks." Although it was not a combining of the commissions, it was the death knell to the existing bodies. The aging veterans would obviously begin to thin out soon, and with them would go the three-man commissions. It was not all Root and Taft had wanted, but it got the job done. The nation still spent hundreds of thousands of dollars each year on the battlefields, but it was nevertheless the beginning of the end of the golden age's vaunted veteran commissions.[80]

V

Although the big federal parks of the 1890s received most of the attention during this period, and rightly so, there were other preservation efforts on other battlefields. Most of these were early efforts at private preservation in places other than Gettysburg, and most preservationists struggled just as Gettysburg's association had. Logically, if Gettysburg of all places could not be funded through private effort, other battlefields could not either.

The most basic form of preservation was marking significant sites on privately owned property. In some cases, these sites were generally considered significant, but in others, they were significant only in the minds of the people erecting the monuments. Either way, quite a few monuments began to go up on battlefields that as yet had no federal preservation. At Stones River, Union veterans placed a monument on the battlefield near McFadden's Ford to mark the line of Federal artillery that helped repel the January 2, 1863, Confederate attack. Called the Artillery Monument, this tall obelisk went up in 1906. Similarly, the United

Daughters of the Confederacy (UDC) erected a monument to the Confederate dead on the Perryville battlefield in 1902. In larger scope, veterans and family members of soldiers placed some twenty-six different monuments around the Fredericksburg and vicinity battlefields between 1890 and 1912, several of them being dedicated by veterans to their regiments, including the Twenty-Seventh Indiana, One hundred and twenty-seventh Pennsylvania, and Forty-Ninth New York. The state of New Jersey itself began to erect monuments for its troops, placing one to the Twenty-Third New Jersey and two different ones to the Fifteenth New Jersey, one at Salem Church and the other at Spotsylvania. Different entities erected nine monuments around Petersburg, in addition to numerous smaller markers, including Confederate monuments placed in the 1890s by the Ladies' Memorial Association. Veterans of both sides also placed monuments to regiments or leaders who died, and the states of Pennsylvania and Massachusetts erected monuments to their troops who fought at Petersburg. The state of North Carolina erected a monument and tablets to its troops at Appomattox in 1905, and New York placed monuments to three of its regiments, the Fifth New York, Tenth New York, and Fourteenth Brooklyn, in 1906 at Manassas. Veterans of the Seventh Georgia placed seven small markers at Manassas in 1905, and a marker to Fletcher Webster, the son of Daniel Webster who was killed in the fighting, went up at the same battlefield in 1914. Veterans also placed a monument to the Confederate dead at Bentonville in 1895.[81]

This nonfederal commemoration and preservation of battlefields that were not deemed worthy of government preservation illustrated in embryonic form a hallmark of future preservation: an individual state taking the initiative. And in a major step forward, these states at times began to preserve their own land. Although state parks systems were decades in the future, most not appearing until the 1920s or 1930s, several states began to make some effort at preservation, and these battlefield parks were incorporated into state systems later when the larger entities were established. These were nevertheless state ventures, which added yet another layer of effort in the fractured early preservation movement.[82]

Perhaps the earliest modern state effort to commemorate and preserve a nonfederal battlefield occurred in the first decade of the 1900s, in North Dakota of all places. The battle of Whitestone Hill had been fought there in September 1863 as a continuation of the Union army's conflict with Native Americans. The major disruption had come in 1862 in Minnesota, but units of the Federal army took the campaign westward all the way to North Dakota. Efforts to preserve this battlefield began as early as 1901, with North Dakota congressman Thomas F. Marshall leading the way. The local Grand Army of the Republic post became involved as well, and the North Dakota legislature passed a bill organizing a three-veteran commission, strikingly similar to the national park commissions, to study and preserve the battlefield park outlined in the legislation. Marshall also succeeded in getting a federal bill passed to erect a monument on the battlefield, a tall shaft with a bugler on the top. Veterans and local citizens dedicated the monument on October 13, 1909, with Congressman Marshall giving the dedication address. He reminded his hearers that they were "standing on soil made sacred by the blood of the soldiers of 1863." Although a system of North Dakota state parks had not yet been established, this land eventually became one of the units of that system, preserving seventy-six acres of the battlefield.[83]

A similar process, commemorating a similar occurrence, developed in Minnesota about the same time. As in North Dakota, there was no Minnesota state park system until 1935, but that did not stop the state legislature from preserving one of its major Civil War battlefields. The Minnesota legislature had been involved in several historic efforts prior to 1900, including marking the site of the release of Native American prisoners at Camp Release in 1889 and dedicating a monument there in 1894, as well as providing funds for preserving the small battlefield at Birch Coulee in 1893. The process of preservation at Birch Coulee was long and drawn out, however; the commission tasked with acquiring the battlefield and erecting a monument chose to do so over a mile from the actual site to be near a road. Nevertheless, under the leadership of veterans Charles E. Flandrau and Charles H. Hokins, the state funded the preservation of the more important Fort Ridgely site in 1895. Desiring to preserve the site of two significant battles with the Sioux in August 1862, the state acquired some ten acres and erected a major monument in 1896. Although the site was preserved, the backers of the Fort Ridgely idea soon also netted a major first in the process of battlefield preservation, that of propelling the site into an actual state park. This occurred in 1911, when the Fort Ridgely State Park was approved and larger land acquisition took place—some fifty acres initially. Other acreage was also added through the years, and the park was incorporated into the new state system upon its founding in 1935.[84]

There was also state movement in Florida at the Olustee battlefield. The February 1864 battle was the largest in the state, and preservation took place in 1909 when Florida obtained title to two acres donated by Austin B. Fletcher and another acre donated by John and Eliza Brown. The state erected a monument on the site of the battlefield, dedicating it on October 23, 1912. Florida did not yet have a state park system, so the United Daughters of the Confederacy cared for the small site until 1949, when it was incorporated into Florida's state park system as the Olustee Battlefield Historic State Park.[85]

Although most of these early efforts were state related, a couple of private enterprises also succeeded, although success was a relative term. Most of such work came from the United Daughters of the Confederacy, including in 1911 when battlefield owner J. R. French donated six acres of Florida's Natural Bridge battle-field to the women's group. The battle at Natural Bridge occurred in March 1865 as a Federal force was turned back from an inland excursion, failing to drive away a defending Confederate force and being unable to cross the St. Marks River at the natural bridge. Confederate veterans lobbied for a monument, which was eventually dedicated in April 1922 in the form of a memorial arch.[86]

Backers of the effort to preserve the Prairie Grove battlefield in Arkansas sought help from both state and national officials, but neither was forthcoming so the local people had to do it themselves. Fortunately, there was a great deal of interest in the battlefield, with veterans holding reunions on site as early as 1886. Eventually, the local chapter of the United Daughters of the Confederacy, led by their president, M. L. Hilderbrand, took up the task, creating an association much like those at many other battlefields. This association, actually headed by the UDC, succeeded in buying nine acres in 1908 from Kibble and Hattie Cummings, with additional land acquired in 1914. The women named their park the Prairie Grove Confederate Memorial Park, and although the association was chartered by the state, the legislature refused funds to maintain the site. Still, the park was dedicated in 1910, and the town of Prairie Grove annexed it in 1917 for purposes of law enforcement. The state's reluctance to get involved continued for decades, however, and Prairie Grove did not become a state park until 1971.[87]

Illinois veterans also took it upon themselves to preserve a portion of the Kennesaw Mountain battlefield near Atlanta. There, Col. Dan McCook's brigade fought in an area known as Cheatham Hill, and McCook fell in the fighting. After the war, veterans of the brigade formed an association to perpetuate the memory of their beloved leader, and by the 1890s they had decided to buy the land in Georgia where McCook had fallen. One of the members, Lansing J. Dawdy, bought sixty acres from owner Virgil Channell and donated it to the Kennesaw Mountain Battlefield Association, which unlike most battlefield groups was actually chartered in Illinois rather than the state in which the battlefield lay; the association then deeded the land to the McCook association in 1904.[88]

Thus, although Shiloh, Gettysburg, and other 1890s parks received all the acclaim, there was much successful work being done elsewhere, and even more work that would never see success. Still, a significant turn in preservation mentality had taken place during this period, when states, in addition to adding monuments to the national parks, stepped in to acquire and preserve sites that federal officials would not. These actions ushered in a path for the future, when federal acquisition would nearly halt and state work would far eclipse that done by the United States government. Battlefield preservation roles were already beginning to develop this early in the process.

VI

Despite the limited success of the golden age of Civil War battlefield preservation and the emerging challenge to the commission system it had set up, the era was indeed the golden age; never before had the opportunity been so ripe to establish battlefields of this nature. The fierce Reconstruction debates over race had muted much of the potential in the earlier decades, but the sweeping reconciliation of the period, fueled by the patriotism of the Spanish-American War, fully offered a time in which whites of both sides came together in near equality and preserved together. Likewise, never before had the opportunity to act on so grand a scale been so real. Only struggling associations had done any work prior to 1890, and that was mostly at Gettysburg. The size of the task required an overseeing entity that was big enough to handle the situation, and only the federal government possessed that ability.[89]

The opportunity would never come again. The veterans would soon pass from the scene, taking with them knowledge of the battlefields and what had happened there. Similarly, other veterans would be leaving Congress in droves over the next few years, and that body would certainly be less and less interested in spending huge amounts of money on their fathers' battlefields. Although no one knew it at the time, a massive wave of urbanization was also just around the corner, during which time many of the battlefields left unpreserved during the 1890s and 1900s would fall to progress. The result was a critical window in which major work could be done, and fortunately five parks were established. These remain today the most complete and well-marked fields of battle. Yet this generation left its task incomplete, and preservationists have been working against the current ever since to rectify the situation.[90]

But perhaps the selective memory of the war that developed around these battlefields during this generation was as important as the parks themselves. The golden age generation certainly had its own view of the Civil War, and in many ways, especially militarily, their influence has been enormous. If the immediate postwar generation's memory of the war was divided and controversial, this generation primarily saw reconciliation instead of divisiveness. Such white reconciliation was seen in many of their efforts from the lack of congressional action on restarting Reconstruction to the reunions of the veterans. Yet nowhere was the feeling of mutual support shown more than on the battlefields these veterans created, and speeches at monument dedications were filled with reconciliation rather than animosity. And it was all done in a larger context, illustrating the joint white comradeship of bravery, honor, and courage of American soldiers, as exemplified by the many wondrous monuments containing statuary of brave soldiers in battle. The House Committee on Military Affairs rightly noted that the work at Chickamauga "is in all its aspects a purely military one," and in selectively pointing to the martial prowess of the soldiers of both sides instead of the causes for the battles themselves, battlefield preservationists also spoke volumes in the imperialistic era about America's military might as compared to the vaunted European armies and soldiers.[91]

Obviously, it is important to note that not all old soldiers bought fully into the reconciliation of the times; many still harbored resentment over losing the war or losing loved ones. Historians such as Caroline Janney have focused our attention on this minority. One Northern newspaperman, commenting on the possibilities of battlefield preservation, wrote, "It makes a true soldier's blood boil to think of having those battle fields covered with Rebel Monuments." The South had its own reservations, one United Confederate Veteran organization declining William McKinley's offer to care for Confederate dead: "The South has not ever, does not now, nor ever will ask for the care of their dead by general government." Similarly, Mississippi governor James K. Vardaman told Illinois veterans that he was glad they were praising their boys in blue but wanted them to understand that Southerners were similarly going to praise their boys in gray: "It matters not whether it pleases anybody excepting us." Even Mississippi senator (and former Confederate general) Edward C. Walthall's spoke of needing to utilize "Blue and Gray *gush*," indicating he was not wholeheartedly behind reconciliation. Still, he was one of the major movers of the Chickamauga bill in the U.S. Senate.[92]

Nevertheless, the images of reconciliation, particularly as evidenced on the battlefields, far outweighed the fairly isolated negative retorts to unity. Speeches, joint reunions, and even the establishment of battlefield parks themselves, with both sides involved, illustrated the degree of reconciliation. Early Manassas park pusher George Carr Round organized the Manassas National Jubilee of Peace on the fiftieth anniversary of First Manassas, for example, with president William Howard Taft offering the main speech at the event. At Chickamauga, during Pennsylvania's dedication in 1897, Governor Daniel H. Hastings stated that "time has cooled the ardor; has tempered the judgment; has healed the wounds and has mellowed—aye, obliterated all sectional animosities." Former Confederate general Basil W. Duke spoke at the Shiloh Illinois monument dedication in May 1904: "We, who once confronted each other on this field in 'stubborn opposition,' now meet with friendly intercourse—meet with no thought of the past conflict, save to wish to honor its heroes on both sides." Monuments also exemplified the times, including Chattanooga's New York Peace Monument, the later Vicksburg Memorial Arch, and other monuments denoting reunion, which were vastly different from the one-sided monuments of the earlier generation. In fact, former Gettysburg superintendent John Latschar recently noted that "the

majority of the monuments [at Gettysburg] call particular attention to the bravery, the courage, the valor, and the manliness of the soldiers. A few commemorate
the preservation of the Union. Not one commemorates the [divisive issue of the]
ending of slavery."[93]

On a more tactical level, these veterans, mostly the historians, also created a
certain image of each battle that has influenced historiography and memory to
the present time. Henry Boynton at Chickamauga massaged the story of that
battle and the placement of monuments to make his regiment's action central
to the climactic fighting at Snodgrass Hill. Others argued that he repositioned
his place of assault up Missionary Ridge at Chattanooga to place his monument
on one of the more prominent reservations owned by the government. Similarly
at Shiloh, David W. Reed took great pains to emphasize his regiment's area of
fighting, and the centrality of the Hornet's Nest dominates Shiloh historiography to the present day. Until recently, visitors to Shiloh were bombarded with the
importance of the Hornet's Nest, including in the official brochure and the park's
introductory film. A century of popular memory buildup is hard to break, but a
more contextual presentation of the battle has recently been put forward both at
the park itself and in more academic genres.[94]

A similar story emerged at Gettysburg, where John Bachelder promoted his
High Water Mark thesis, which was dependent on the importance of Pickett's
Charge on the third day. Even non–Civil War buffs know of Gettysburg and the
climactic charge at the end of the battle, and a century of that thesis holding sway
has created a permanent grip on popular memory. There are, however, others who
argue that different aspects of the battle were just as, if not more, important than
Pickett's Charge. At the forefront of these alternate theses are the supporters of
Joshua Lawrence Chamberlain and his stand on Little Round Top on the second
day. Hence, a more contextual approach is also beginning to be taken at Gettysburg and in the literature on the battle.[95]

This golden age generation achieved significant progress in both the preservation of battlefields and the stories told of the battles fought on them—stories that
in many ways are still dominating these site's histories. It was a time when endless
possibilities existed and when significant battlefield parks were produced. It was
truly a golden age.

3

The Interregnum,
1912–1933

Babe Ruth, of all people, was the center attraction at the Chickamauga and Chattanooga National Military Park in April 1930. In town with the New York Yankees to play an exhibition baseball game, Ruth went atop Lookout Mountain and, to great fanfare, placed a wreath at the base of the New York monument. The combination of two very American symbols was especially poignant; this was a peace monument, and baseball symbolized perhaps the best of America as the nation's pastime. Ruth then, according to a newspaper account, "hammered a baseball off the crest of the mountain for a distance of half a mile, thereby setting a new world's outdoor record." It was an oddity to be sure, but the entire event symbolized much more. America had entered a new era in which the old veterans were no longer the primary stars at the battlefields. The military parks were now in the hands of a younger generation, and Civil War tactics and movements were not the public attractions they once were.[1]

To be sure, the United States was going through a massive transformation in the 1910s and 1920s: urbanization, modernization, and global warfare. The second industrial revolution was changing American society, as more and more mechanization and stiffer regulations birthed by the Progressive movement en-abled more leisure time and increased mobility. The number of automobiles had grown significantly, making travel easier and faster. Although aviation was still in its infancy, it had an effect as well. America's involvement in what became World War I in 1917 also created a massive social change. Rural Americans began moving to towns and cities to work in the war effort, and the massive exodus of African Americans out of the South to cities in the North changed the dynamics of race relations even in this Jim Crow era. A postwar movement toward isolation and domestic projects also changed American interests.[2]

As a result of so much social upheaval, change also came to the preservation community. Historian Charles Hosmer has remarked that the age prior to 1926 and the major work at Williamsburg, Virginia, was "largely disorganized and lacked any professional guidance." Such was certainly the case with Civil War battlefield preservation. With so many new and alluring entities to catch people's attention, the Civil War parks seemed to slowly fade into oblivion, especially their management within the War Department. For example, at Chickamauga and Gettysburg, the soldiers of World War I took some of the limelight away from veterans of two wars back. In the 1890s, the Civil War veterans were the last American soldiers who had fought a major war. By 1920, however, veterans of two additional major wars were in the limelight, especially the returning soldiers of World War I. Notably, the years 1917 and 1918 saw many longstanding yearly Civil War veteran reunions cancelled for the first time in decades. Newer monuments also gained more attention; one prime example of modern commemorative efforts was the emergence of the American Battle Monuments Commission in 1923 to commemorate American actions in foreign lands. Ironically, a historic preservation policy was possible for activity in nations abroad, but Congress would not provide one for work inside the United States.[3]

At the same time, the Civil War veteran generation was also beginning to rapidly pass off the scene. This demise logically came in waves, with the most famous higher-level officers such as Lee and Grant dying prior to the major work of preservation in the 1890s. The torch then passed to the younger, midlevel officers of the 1860s, but that wave too began to pass away, even in the 1890s and the early 1900s. Numerous lower-level privates who were just boys in the 1860s were the last wave, but even they were growing old in the 1910s and 1920s, and the vast majority would depart during this interregnum. Consequently, focus quickly shifted to newer veterans of more recent wars. The change in commission status in 1912 illustrated the obvious. Some sitting commissioners would live almost to the end of this era of change in 1933, but most would die much earlier, phasing out the commissions. Their replacements were by and large of the new generation of sons of veterans who became superintendents at the various parks. These descendents of veterans would as a group still adhere to what they learned from their fathers and hold them and their parks in high esteem, but they were not veterans themselves and accordingly brought in new ways of thinking and acting.[4]

The change in power from Civil War veterans to nonveteran descendents was vividly seen in the increasing call for a different government agency to handle battlefield preservation. Always a War Department mission, by the 1920s maintenance of the old battlefields and preservation of new ones was increasingly a bother to the new, modern War Department. Having moved past the Civil War to newer wars, the War Department became less and less concerned with the Civil War parks and by the mid-1920s was openly advocating transferring them away so that it could concentrate on fighting future wars, not remembering past conflicts.[5]

Ready to inherit the military parks was the National Park Service (NPS), which emerged in 1916. Established to oversee the massive growth of parks during Theodore Roosevelt's conservation era, the NPS was a natural choice to oversee the battlefields; leaders such as Stephen Mather and Horace Albright quickly began to lobby for their transfer. This proposed transfer, essentially the switch to a more bureaucratic and professional, although less personal, oversight of the parks, symbolized the decline of the veterans' influence.[6]

The growth of the National Park Service and its desire to administer the battlefields illustrated the wider interest in historic preservation as a whole that grew during this era. In addition to the Antiquities Act of 1906, a number of other preservation efforts began to emerge, emphasizing historic houses such as Mount Vernon or the creation of Colonial Williamsburg, lauded by historians as a major turning point in American preservation theory. The growing conservation of battlefields was similar in nature to the idea behind preserving the natural parks: both offered glimpses of America's greatness, fostering a nationalism born of natural wonder in the nature parks and martial prowess in the historic parks.[7]

Additionally, the concurrent modernization and urbanization affected future preservation. The golden age generation, for all it did, still mostly missed the narrow window that would close with the urbanization of America's cities and towns. As even the smaller towns grew, they began to engulf nearby battlefields. Rarely did battles take place right in town; for the most part, they raged just outside town limits as the armies fought over the crossroads of transportation routes. As a result, when the preservation movement that was muted altogether in 1899 restarted in the mid-1920s, it had much less to work with and as a result had to devise new methods.[8]

Amid all the change, this newer generation of preservationists soon set to work. One military official later described how the time was right "following the settlement and readjustment of things after the World War." Members of

Congress also chimed in that "we feel the sentiment in our community now is peculiarly ripe for the memorialization of those events." As a result, members of Congress were mindful of the past as well as the future; one congressmen saw the danger of not acting now: "And 25 years from now, probably, the subcommittee and Congress itself, no doubt, will be severely condemned for their shortsightedness in not making provision for [battlefield preservation]." The result was a new wave of park establishment that later led to the major work of the 1930s and the New Deal era. This interregnum sat squarely between two major epochs of battlefield preservation history, the golden age and the New Deal, but it would be a mistake to dismiss the importance of this period in the overall battlefield preservation process.[9]

I

Despite the 1912 legislation ending the battlefield commissions as they had been known, this new generation began with a flurry of activity. The year 1912 was exactly in the middle of the nation's commemoration of the fiftieth anniversary of the Civil War, and being so close to the age of reconciliation, it is no surprise that such a feeling of togetherness and harmony among white Americans infused the activities. Numerous reunions and ceremonies were held at many battlefields, the Grand Army of the Republic events at Chattanooga and Chickamauga carrying the theme "One People, One Nation, One Flag." Alfred B. Beers, commanding the Grand Army of the Republic, told the veterans, "Between Northern and Southern States everlasting peace abides. . . . This gathering touches the heart more than any other, because the Union veterans feel the sympathy and cooperation of the Confederate veterans. It is a privilege to note that the Confederates, who were once against us, are now first and foremost with us and hand, heart, and soul for the Union." The Grand Army of the Republic even asked the old Confederates to wear their uniforms, although one newspaper noted they "wear the gray forever on their proud old heads." Perhaps President Woodrow Wilson said the most when he spoke at Gettysburg's fiftieth anniversary, which historian David Blight has termed "an extraordinary festival of reconciliation": "How wholesome and healing the peace has been! We have found one another again as brothers and comrades, in arms, enemies no longer, generous friends rather, our battles long past, the quarrel forgotten—except we shall not forget the splendid valor, the manly devotion of the men then arrayed against one another, now grasping hands and smiling into each other's eyes."[10]

But even with the emphasis on the golden anniversary, federal activity regarding battlefield preservation continued to be almost nonexistent for the first decade or more of this new generation and actually took some steps backward during this period. Following the 1912 commission legislation, aging commissioners began to die at a rapid rate. They had died prior to 1912, of course, but other commissioners were always appointed to take their place, maintaining the continuity. The legislation put an end to commissioners being replaced, however, and thus came the end of the commissions themselves. By the end of this era, in 1933, the commissions were gone.[11]

The transition from the commissions of veterans to nonveteran superintendents became an obvious metaphor for the general dwindling of the veteran generation itself and its power in politics and society. Still, this transfer came with some modicum of continuity in that many of the new nonveteran superintendents who began to take over the parks were able to utilize the old soldiers' knowledge and advice for several years prior to being left on their own to manage the parks. The result was that these superintendents, who were often literally sons of veterans rather than veterans themselves, largely carried on the maintenance of the parks with the same love and devotion as had the veterans. The fact that the parks remained amid their old bureaucracy in the War Department added to the continuity.[12]

Nevertheless, change was a fact. At Chickamauga, the three sitting commissioners in 1912, Chairman Charles H. Grosvenor, John T. Wilder, and Confederate Joseph B. Cumming, had all died by 1922. Both Grosvenor and Wilder died in 1917, leaving Cumming as the sole commissioner and chairman. He was the only other Confederate commission chairman, in addition to Stephen D. Lee at Vicksburg, although Cumming's ascension was out of necessity rather than by choice. Cumming carried on meetings of the commission anyway, one entry in the minutes stating, "The Chickamauga and Chattanooga National Park Commission met this day at its office in Chatt., Major Jos. B. Cumming, Chairman, being present." Cumming himself died in 1922.[13]

Fortunately, Chickamauga and Chattanooga had a capable superintendent by this time, who had learned from the commission and carried on its work. Richard B. Randolph had been a clerk for the commission in Washington, D.C., but was chosen as the new superintendent of the park when on-site engineer Edward E. Betts retired in 1911. Since the commissioners did not generally live near the park (Grosvenor lived in Ohio and Cumming on the other side of Georgia), they were not able physically to oversee the battlefield and more help was needed when the active engineering phase ended. The War Department settled on on-site superintendents to work under the commissions but to be the everyday administrators. Randolph accordingly moved to the park. With Cumming's death in 1922, Randolph became the park's "chief executive officer" and would remain so through the rest of this generation and into the next.[14]

A similar transfer occurred at Shiloh. The three sitting commissioners in 1912, Chairman David W. Reed, James H. Ashcraft, and Confederate Basil W. Duke, were likewise all gone by 1920. Both Reed and Duke died in 1916, and Ashcraft died in 1920. The War Department had already settled on a superintendent at Shiloh after Reed, who lived on site, had to move back to Iowa for health reasons. DeLong Rice had been appointed as commission secretary in 1913, whereupon the ailing Reed advised him of his work, "I have been for two weeks laid up with a broken thigh, and Major Ashcraft's wife is very sick and General Duke is in such poor health as to prevent his presence on the Park." Rice accordingly oversaw the work as "Secretary and Superintendent," starting in 1914.[15]

Rice continued his work as head of the Shiloh park, especially after Ashcraft's death in 1920, when he became the sole administrator. Rice was something of a Renaissance man; he was an avid writer and poet who spent long hours in seclusion atop one of the Indian mounds in the park, looking out over the Tennessee River for inspiration. He also wrote history, including *The Story of Shiloh*, in which he continued emphasizing the Hornet's Nest—something he had learned well at the feet of his mentor, David W. Reed. Unfortunately, tragedy ended Rice's tenure at Shiloh in 1929, when he and his son were fatally injured by a gas explosion in their house on the battlefield. Even in tragedy, however, yet another son of a veteran who was actually raised on the park amid the commission's work became the new superintendent. Robert A. Livingston had been the park's clerk since 1916, and he remained superintendent through the rest of the generation and into the next.[16]

Gettysburg saw a similar decline of commissioners. Confederate Lunsford L. Lomax died early in 1913, and Union representative Charles Richardson died in 1917. Chairman John P. Nicholson, who had always been a major driving force behind the association as well as the park, having been one of the original commissioners and chairman since 1893, lived until 1922. Even after Nicholson's death, however, veterans still had a say because the new superintendent was the aged but still very active park engineer, veteran Emmor B. Cope. He continued to oversee the park until his death in 1927, at which time a series of army officers took charge. Although not Civil War veterans, Col. E. E. Davis and Col. J. F. Barber continued the militaristic ideals of the park, and then civilian landscape architect James R. McConaghie took control until 1933.[17]

Vicksburg retained a commissioner longer than any of the other parks, nearly through the entire 1920s. Confederate Lewis Guion died in 1920 and James G. Everest passed away in 1924, leaving chairman William T. Rigby to govern the park alone. He did so until his death in 1929. To help Rigby in his final year, the War Department brought in L. C. Swett, who served much as Randolph and

Rice did prior to the commission's passing at Chickamauga and Shiloh. Upon Rigby's death, Swett became "Overseer in Charge of the Park" until 1931, when army officer Maj. John B. Holt became superintendent through the remainder of the generation.[18]

Only Antietam was any different, not falling under the 1912 guidelines because it had no commission. In the years after George W. Davis finished the work in 1898, the park bounced around various entities of the War Department. Not knowing what to do with it when it was completed, the secretary of war gave Antietam to the regional quartermaster, who could think of nothing other than placing it under the Antietam National Cemetery superintendent. That quickly became more than the cemetery superintendent could handle, so Elihu Root, in one of his few expansions of authority, hired Charles W. Adams as superintendent in 1900. Unfortunately, Adams was murdered in 1912 by a local resident upset over land issues with the park. George W. Graham then became superintendent but had to be fired for drunkenness and other offenses in 1913. Thereafter, a series of superintendents ran the park in a much calmer manner until 1915, including John L. Cook, the cemetery superintendent. Jacob Manath then became the park superintendent until his death in 1925. C. H. Bender took over and remained in charge until 1928, when George B. Alexander became superintendent and held the position until 1933.[19]

By 1929, then, all aspects of the original commissions were gone, except the legacy they left behind on the five battlefields and in the minds of their followers. Significantly, these second-generation stewards saw battlefield preservation and maintenance primarily as their mentors did. Randolph at Chickamauga, Rice and Livingston at Shiloh, and certainly Cope at Gettysburg all kept an eye trained more rearward than forward. That said, there was some modernization. Rice, Randolph, and others realized that the visiting cliental was changing in the early years of the twentieth century. With visitation originally made up substantially of veterans, now descendents were appearing at the parks in droves, with fewer and fewer veterans visiting, especially by the mid- to late 1920s and early 1930s. The result was a shift from primarily militaristic commemoration to more education and interpretation for a populace lacking knowledge of the Civil War.[20]

II

Although the original 1890 commissions were literally passing away right before America's eyes, a new wave of battlefield preservation developed in the 1920s. With America's involvement in World War I at an end and a period of isolationism developing, as well as the martial spirit of a victorious people enthused by their war efforts in the late 1910s, America saw a resurgence of emphasis on the Civil War as well as other wars. In an almost mirror image of the first decade of the 1900s, many congressmen wanted a national military park made out of their local battlefield. As a result, numerous bills emerged in the mid-1920s, even more than in the lockdown in the early 1900s, and the House and Senate military affairs committees held numerous hearings throughout the decade and into the 1930s to somehow formulate a response.[21]

With so many bills in the legislative hoppers, federal officials in both the legislative and executive branches were wringing their hands over what to do. In the first session of the Sixty-ninth Congress alone, for example, some twenty-eight different preservation bills were submitted, with fourteen of them calling for the creation of huge national military parks. The total appropriations, if passed, would have been about six million dollars. This was similar to the body of bills offered in the early 1900s, and Congress had, as a result, refused to do anything for nearly twenty-five more years. Certainly, that was not the needed response now, but funding every one of the bills would take more money than the government could afford. Obviously, a new plan was required, something more than that instituted by Secretary Lamont back in 1895. This time, a concerted, comprehensive, and total historic preservation plan of action was needed to deal with this growing and important issue. Unfortunately, it had been nearly twenty years since a concerted effort had been made to organize the preservation process, and most of the participants, such as George B. Davis and Henry V. Boynton, were no longer alive. The secretary of war and House and Senate military affairs committees consequently had to begin again almost from scratch, or as one official noted, the "policies had to be evolved from the ground up."[22]

Meanwhile, many members of Congress were becoming anxious about all the park bills. Senator James W. Wadsworth, chairman of the Committee on Military Affairs, was even described as being "perturbed as to the number of those bills and did not know what to do." After Wadsworth and several other members of Congress approached him, Secretary of War John W. Weeks tasked his Army War College in 1925 to make a study of the battlefields and determine exactly how preservation should be done. It was a significant step, because the study became the first systematic survey of historic properties in American history. Weeks correctly surmised that "the atmosphere would be cleared if a study and classification of battle fields were made." Lt. Col. C. A. Bach, who was the chief of the historical section of the Army War College, submitted his report dated May 28, 1925, and it was quickly approved by the secretary of war. The war college officers described the two major types of preservation to this point, Boynton's total policy seen at the big national military parks and Davis's (actually Boynton's as well) limited Antietam Plan approach. They then recommended instituting a third level, even below the limited Antietam Plan, that of simply placing a marker or monument on an extremely small area of land, perhaps one acre, to denote the site of a battlefield. This approach had been used to this point to mark Revolutionary and War of 1812 sites, including Saratoga, Princeton, Monmouth Court House, Bennington, Moore's Creek, New Orleans, Tippecanoe, King's Mountain, Yorktown, and Horseshoe Bend. A few Civil War battlefields had received similar treatment. The War College officers saw no reason to change this unplanned historic policy, so they set up a series of classes of importance (based on this previous work) in which to place the battles, which would hopefully lead Congress in its attempt to preserve.[23]

The War College recommended three classes of battlefields, which was not altogether different from the older generation's actions, but then also began to formulate a policy by placing certain battlefields in those categories, which was an entirely new step. The first category was Class I, which consisted of the big national military parks. The War College defined these as "battles of exceptional political and military importance and interest, whose effects were far-reaching, whose fields are worthy of preservation for detailed military and historical study, and which are suitable to serve as memorials to the armies engaged." Pointing out that the nation already had four of these Civil War sites (Chickamauga, Shiloh, Gettysburg, and Vicksburg) and one Revolutionary site, Guilford Courthouse established in 1917, it recommended no new Civil War battlefields be established along these lines. In fact, it surprisingly differed with Congress, stating that Shiloh should not even be considered a Class I battlefield and have a national military park. Since Shiloh had already been established, however, it did not need changing now. The report placed importance on the year 1863 with the other three parks, writing that it "may well be considered the critical or decisive year" and that "at the end of 1863 the outcome of the war was no longer doubtful." The only battlefields recommended by the War College to be turned into major national military parks were the Revolutionary battlefields at Saratoga and Yorktown.[24]

The next group, Class II, consisted of battlefields that were of lesser importance and would be termed national monuments and preserved in varying degrees. The officers explained that these battles, some two thousand in total, were so extremely different in scope that they felt the need to divide them into two subclasses. Subclass IIa included battlefields that, although still important, were less significant than the major battles and were to be preserved along the old Antietam Plan idea. The college defined these as "battles of such great military and historic interest as to warrant locating and indicating the battle lines of the forces engaged by a series of markers or tablets, but not necessarily by memorial monuments." The officers recommended only New Orleans from the War of 1812 and fifteen Civil War battlefields be included in this subclass, including the Bull Run battlefields, Fort Donelson, Richmond's many sites, Fredericksburg and nearby battlefields such as Chancellorsville, Spotsylvania, and the Wilderness, battles around Atlanta, Petersburg, and the Shenandoah Valley, as well as Nashville and Bentonville.[25]

Subclass IIb consisted of the remaining battles, and these were to be commemorated simply by a marker or small monument on as little ground as possible. These were "battles of sufficient historic interest to be worthy of some form of monument, tablet, or marker to indicate the location of the battlefield." Obviously, some of these battles were more important than others, and the college offered a ranking system in which larger engagements such as Franklin, Cedar Creek, Kennesaw Mountain, Champion Hill, Perryville, and Pea Ridge would be given larger monuments or markers than would smaller battles. Basically, the War College recommended the importance of the battles "might fittingly be indicated by the size of the monument."[26]

While the War College officers were at work, Congress also became involved in the planning and formulated a bill that would hopefully take care of the crisis. H.R. 9765 took preservation mentality in a somewhat different direction, and not necessarily the way the War Department's War College thought it should go. Instead, the legislation called for creation of a "National Military Park Commission," consisting of seven members appointed by the president, to study the issue and create "a comprehensive plan for the marking and the commemorating of every battle field." To make sure proper studies were done, the bill also prohibited any purchase of land to create parks until the commission researched and approved the plan. When the chairman of the Committee on Military Affairs, Noble J. Johnson of Indiana, shared the draft bill with Secretary of War Dwight F. Davis in March 1926, however, Davis objected and urged the committee to turn back toward the existing bureaucracy in the War Department rather than create a new one. Davis argued that the legislation was "objectionable and unnecessary," writing that his department could do it easier and cheaper, and that a calculated effort was needed rather than an overall "omnibus" act. Davis obviously persuaded the chairman and the committee, which then sought new legislation from Davis. He wrote a new bill, which simply gave his department the power to perform "studies and investigations and, where necessary, surveys" in order to provide "a general plan," obviously based on the War College study. The committee reported the new bill favorably in May 1926, and it became law in June without any change. America now had a concerted battlefield preservation process, if not a full policy, in the War College plan.[27]

With passage of the bill giving the War Department oversight, but significantly not necessarily institutionalizing the War College's class system itself, the department realized what a task it had before it. Secretary of War Davis soon issued a "preliminary plan . . . by which the investigation and survey of American battlefields for commemorative purposes, can, in his opinion, be most economically carried out." But the process proved slow. Although the War Department was required to submit a report each year, its major work did not begin until late in 1927. Nevertheless, as warranted in the plan, the secretary appointed a three-member commission of officers to oversee the study, logically including Col. William R. Gibson of the Quartermaster Corps, who would oversee the parks when established, Maj. Dwight F. Johns of the engineering corps, who was to perform the scientific study and provide cost estimates, and eventually Lt. Col. Howard L. Landers of the historical section of the Army War College to provide historic guidance. Secretary Davis tasked these three to "consider the general subject from a broad national standpoint and to propose policies for my consideration." Davis stated in his initial report in November 1926 that these three would study the history of each site, make personal visits, and survey the areas at battlefields for which congressmen indicated they would submit legislation.[28]

Preliminary work soon began, but considerable time elapsed before the real activity started. The effort really got underway with the addition in September 1927 of Lieutenant Colonel Landers as the historical expert to the three-member body. Landers over time became almost obsessed with preserving battlefields and put the next several years of his life fully into the work. He made such progress that the House Committee on Military Affairs asked the War Department to extend his tour from the standard four years so his work could progress. He became this generation's George B. Davis.[29]

The Landers/Gibson/Johns team devised policy for the War Department and was able to provide its first report in December 1928. By that time, the commission had visited thirty-four battlefields of the Class IIb group, including Appomattox, Ball's Bluff, Brices Cross Roads, Cassville, Dalton, Eastport, Iuka, Fort Fisher, the Atlanta Campaign, Monocacy, Ox Hill, Pea Ridge, Fort Stevens, Tupelo, Westport, and Wilson's Creek. In their report, the commission recommended monuments costing as little as twenty-five hundred or five thousand dollars for small engagements such as Tupelo, Fort Stevens, Ox Hill, Monocacy, Iuka, Eastport, Brice's Crossroads, and Ball's Bluff. Larger monuments in the range of twenty-five thousand dollars were recommended for bigger battles such as Dalton, Fort Fisher, New Hope Church, Pea Ridge, Resaca, Westport, and Wilson's Creek. Interestingly, the meager appropriation for Monocacy got Landers in trouble with his local neighbors, because he lived near the battlefield and had to try to explain to them why he supported a smaller monument. Other larger battlefields, such as Franklin, would receive a forty-thousand-dollar memorial, and Appomattox would receive the largest at one hundred thousand dollars. On all of these sites, the land area recommended was only one acre, since any more would necessitate law enforcement and maintenance or even a superintendent, all of which would increase the cost. Landers's work continued the next year, with the December 1929 report adding twenty-three more battlefields, including Citronelle, Fort Blakely, Spanish Fort, Helena, Philippi, Rich Mountain, and Ringold.[30]

Landers continued his work into the 1930s. For instance, he visited Kennesaw Mountain and proposed that a monument go up at Pigeon Hill to commemorate the entire battle, although some believed Big Kennesaw would have been the better place; Landers was too worried about accessibility there. He also visited Richmond, where, as was his custom, he spent several weeks on site, holding public hearings and working in office space set up specifically for his use. Landers also worked with contemporary congressionally established commissions at Stones River, Fort Donelson, Petersburg, and Fredericksburg. He spent four days with the Stones River commission in 1928. "I frequently brought up the subject of expediting this work," Landers wrote the quartermaster general.[31]

And more than just historical investigation and engineering surveys were taking place. By 1929, several studies had reached the point where Congress was ready to act. Landers and company had investigated those battlefields that congressmen brought to their attention with the intention of introducing appropriate legislation. The process began to bear fruit in 1929, when Congress negatively considered an omnibus bill to fund several monuments but nevertheless passed legislation for two one-acre plots and monuments in Mississippi at Brices Cross Roads and Tupelo. The president signed the act to establish both sites on February 1, 1929. One acre at each was acquired by 1930, and the monuments went up in 1931. The acre at Brices Cross Roads was perfectly situated at the original crossroads, but the Tupelo site was to the east of the main battlefield, behind Union lines. Unfortunately, over the next few decades bureaucratic chaos ensued in regard to oversight of these monuments, to the extent that there was even thought of turning the sites over to the state of Mississippi in the 1950s. That state had formed its own commission to study adding more land, but little occurred for many decades while governance of the plots bounced between the Shiloh National Military Park superintendent and the Natchez Trace Parkway's overseer. Nevertheless, the process, especially the third option of small monuments on tiny plots of land, was beginning to work as envisioned.[32]

Landers and Congress also worked on the monument for Appomattox, where the effort brought fewer dividends. In 1929, Congress passed legislation to appoint a three-man commission to study the marking of Appomattox with the one-hundred-thousand-dollar monument recommended in the earlier War Department study. The commission, made up of Lt. Col. L. C. Pope of the army engineers, Northerner Robert Baxter, and Southerner Robert A. O'Brien from Appomattox itself, voted two to one to build the monument. O'Brien was the dissenting vote, proposing instead that Appomattox be turned into a park instead. He had ample local backing, one War Department official writing that the people were "very anxious for the establishment of a national military park." Nevertheless, the majority ruled and reported to Congress: Appomattox was "not of sufficient historical and professional military interest to justify the expense of preserving and marking . . . by the national government." Accordingly, Representative Harry St. George Tucker offered a successful bill in 1930, appropriating $150,000 for the monument, but Secretary of War Patrick J. Hurley disapproved and had Congress change it to a $100,000 monument on one acre of land in accordance with the earlier War College survey. Eventually, a five-man commission was established under the legislation to oversee the monument's placement, and they even held a national contest, but there was still so much support for O'Brien's viewpoint that nothing further was done.[33]

Landers also worked on an additional park in 1930, although it was not primarily Civil War in nature. The 1925 report had recommended that Yorktown be made a national military park, primarily because of its Revolutionary War value. Yet there had been fighting there during the Civil War too, and some of the existing trenches dated from the 1860s rather than the 1780s. Consequently, any preservation of Yorktown had to include Civil War preservation as well, although probably by extension rather than directly intended. Congress passed enabling legislation in July 1930, and President Herbert Hoover used his executive order powers to declare the boundaries of the national monument on December 30, 1930. A few monuments already existed on the battlefield, some dating to 1884, but now an outright park existed. Six years later, in 1936, Congress designated the park a national historical park, known today as Colonial National Historical Park. Although it was not its main focus, Colonial nonetheless preserved a Civil War battlefield.[34]

With progress being made in both the investigations and the beginning trickle of implementation on the actual battlefields, the Committee on Military Affairs held a hearing in 1930 on the state of battlefield preservation. Landers was its key witness. The members debated H.R. 11489, which was an omnibus bill "covering all places on which action has been taken by the War Department." It appropriated $624,000 for the work and an annual maintenance appropriation, but only for the sites Congress was dealing with at the time, not all battlefields. Landers said that costs for total preservation would be even higher, including some ten million dollars for marking the Class IIa sites and another ten million for marking all two thousand Class IIb sites. There was understandably opposition because of the huge numbers. Representative John C. Speaks of Ohio did not like the idea of a War Department board of officers making decisions and continually returned to the idea of a commission, to which Representative Percy E. Quin of Mississippi humorously responded, "Oh, don't talk about any more commissions." The hearing room burst out in laughter, but Speaks continued, arguing that it was fine for the military to do the research "but, when it comes to the great memorial feature, I think somebody closer to the people of the United States ought to have part in whatever is done." Others objected to it being an all-military affair, asking if civilians were involved. Landers responded that "each of us has a civilian employee working with us." There was even some questioning about the lack of peer review, Representative Jonathan M. Wainwright of New York asking Landers, "As I understand the program you have, this scheme for commemoration carries with it your suggestion as to which points should be memorialized and the expense that should be incurred in so doing?" Landers reminded the committee that there were three members on the commission, and though he was the historical expert, he had at times changed his mind after consultation with the others: "We play the game with each other." Committee members also questioned the one-acre policy, deflecting Landers's concern about lawlessness; Representative John J. McSwain of South Carolina cajoled Landers about "lawlessness, bootleggers, blind tigers, and so forth."[35]

Despite the possible costs, the committee sent the bill on to the House with a favorable report, explaining correctly that "if the battle fields and historic places in the country are to be marked and commemorated it is necessary that action to this end be taken without further delay. The corroding hand of time is rapidly removing forever the landmarks, the old parapets, the old bastions, the old trenches and other relics and parts of the original field or place. The monuments to be erected to commemorate the battle fields of the War Between the States will stand as testimonials to the heroism, the fortitude, the courage and the valor of the brave men of both armies and will testify to the greatness and the glory of our common country."[36]

Despite the supreme effort in the committee, Acting Secretary of War F. Trubee Davison recommended that the bill not pass. It was a purely financial decision, Davison writing that it was "contrary to the efforts being made to curtail Government expenditures by the War Department." Of course, the Great Depression had hit just seven months earlier and the government was in a period of retrenchment. The appropriations for fiscal year 1933 were as a result cut, forcing the Landers group to slow down its work "owing to the present conditions of the national budget," Secretary of War Patrick J. Hurley explained. Travel funds were also severely curtailed "until funds for mileage are appropriated by Congress." Congress consequently returned to its battlefield-by-battlefield piecemeal process rather than an overall directing policy for the time being, and although no one knew it at the time, the death of the omnibus bill signaled the last chance for major work along the War College guidelines because another idea was at the same time becoming a major issue—transfer of battlefield oversight and preservation policy away from the War Department and its War College study.[37]

III

Despite the retrenchment in the early 1930s, Congress managed to preserve four additional major battlefields in this interregnum era. But there were several differences in these newly preserved parks as compared to their predecessors from the 1890s. Policy makers of the 1920s had examined old reports and files, but there nevertheless was a feeling of starting over from scratch in the 1920s. Indeed, there was little carryover from the earlier golden age generation except for the commissions, which soon died out and even in their latter stages wielded little actual power or influence over new preservation efforts. For example, prime movers Henry V. Boynton and George B. Davis had died in 1905 and 1915, respectively. Few if any of the officers tasked with the work in the mid- to late 1920s had worked with either, and a significant amount of theory and knowledge vanished with Boynton, Davis, and other early preservationists. Likewise, once formed, these new parks were totally different from most of the 1890s parks, the new ones being patterned after the Antietam Plan. Because of money, urbanization, and policy decisions, each of the parks formed in the 1920s and 1930s were mere shells of the original battlefields, containing just a few hundred acres. Although the preservation process was more organized in the 1920s, the parks were still much thinner than the golden age battlefields.[38]

The 1920s preservation effort actually began in a subtle fashion, with President Calvin Coolidge using the declaration power of the 1906 Antiquities Act to pronounce several Civil War–era forts as national monuments in October 1924. This power had been used for such purposes as far back as 1910, when Big Hole battlefield in Montana and Sitka in Alaska were declared national monuments, but not for Civil War sites. Although the War Department did not desire military parks at these locations, Coolidge declared Castle Pinckney in South Carolina and Fort Pulaski outside of Savannah, Georgia, as national monuments. Pinckney had been used as a prison, but Fort Pulaski was a legitimate battlefield, having been bombarded by the Federal navy in 1862, its walls pocked with holes from the Union attack. Several efforts to make the site a local or national memorial had failed through the years, and the War Department had done only minimal upkeep before the declaration. Since the area was already under the War Department's care, however, no land changed hands until later in the site's history.

Without the need for land acquisition, the switch went off easily and cheaply. Unfortunately, the War Department had little money to spend on the fort, and only minimal upkeep and repairs took place throughout the 1920s and early 1930s, despite the numerous efforts of local congressman Charles G. Edwards.[39]

A similarly lackluster effort occurred at Fort Stevens in Washington, D.C., site of the small battle that ended the 1864 Confederate approach to the Union capital and most famous as the place where Abraham Lincoln himself came under fire. Although today a part of Rock Creek Park, established in 1890, Fort Stevens was not acquired until later. A dramatic attempt to connect various Washington, D.C., forts emerged in 1902 but also saw little success. Fortunately, the first tract at Fort Stevens was preserved in 1925. The government, under the National Capital Parks Commission, obtained additional tracts at Fort Stevens through 1933.[40]

More formal national military parks also appeared during this era, including two small Revolutionary War sites at Moore's Creek (1926) and King's Mountain (1931), as well as the more complex actions that assured Yorktown's preservation as part of Colonial National Historical Park in 1930. Concerning Civil War sites, a much more normal process occurred with the preservation of the Petersburg battlefield. Although discussed during the golden age, this project, like all the others, had faced many challenges. The Petersburg National Battlefield Park Association had emerged in 1898, but it did not succeed in the effort to establish a park. Most of the supporters realized they could not get a big park like Chickamauga or Shiloh, so they eventually opted for a "smaller plan of a national battlefield at Petersburg." They also devised a "Gettysburg to Petersburg Memorial Road," symbolically covering the height of the Confederacy and the downfall. Even the city of Petersburg became involved, forming a Battlefield Park Committee and putting money behind the project. Still, none of these early efforts succeeded, despite the state of Virginia and the city itself acquiring small tracts of land over the years. Even some private enterprise took place as the owners of the Crater maintained a small museum and charged visitors to see the site.[41]

Petersburg fortunately received a lot more attention in the post–World War I era of patriotism, isolationism, and generally good economic times. As another wave of battlefield bills again began to flood Congress, the bill concerning Petersburg was actually the first to be acted upon. Congress initially passed legislation in February 1925 for a commission to survey the battlefield, and Secretary of War Weeks appointed Union veteran James Anderson, Confederate veteran Carter R. Bishop, and military engineer Lt. Col. Francis A. Pope to the commission. The men met in April at the Petersburg City Hall to begin their work, electing Anderson as chairman and Pope as secretary. The members met several times that spring and surveyed the battlefield in order to "decide just what was wanted for the proposed park." They found that most of the earthworks and the breastworks between the major forts were still "in very good condition." By the fall, the com-mission made its report, recommending a small park and construction of a road along the lines of the earthworks.[42]

Upon the original commission's recommendation, Congress provided enabling legislation in 1926. In accordance with the War Department study placing Peters-burg in the IIa class, Congressman Patrick H. Drewry's H.R. 7817 provided for a small park along the Antietam Plan, about 185 acres in total area, even as the orig-inal appropriation was cut from a hundred thousand to a mere fifteen thousand dollars. Drewry's idea was to establish the park and then later get additional appro-priations for actual land purchases. Since this was the first actual movement toward restarting the program left dormant since 1899, he thought it was perhaps best to move slowly and incrementally. Yet Drewry met opposition. Samuel J. Montgomery of Oklahoma argued that with so many bills before them, they needed a significant study of the site and a "comprehensive report from the Committee on Military Affairs." He continued, "I think they should take up these matters comprehen-sively and study them all and then select the ones they really prefer to establish as military parks and not take them up piecemeal." Perhaps Montgomery was not aware that such a study was already being processed in the War Department, but he objected and stalled the bill until later in the session. Both houses eventually passed the bill, however, with both houses' committees offering their full support. President Calvin Coolidge signed the act on July 2, 1926.[43]

The new secretary of war, Dwight F. Davis, appointed a new commission to build the park, although Carter Bishop was in this group as well. Added was Henry W. Comey for the Federals, as Anderson had died in April 1926, and Lt. Col. Henry C. Jewett of the Army engineers as secretary. Local supporters also established the Petersburg Battlefield Park Association to aid the commission in acquiring land. This commission worked with Landers and the others to study battlefield preservation, and by the summer of 1928 it was able to recommend a plan for the park. The commission desired two roads, one along each line of earth-works (Union and Confederate), as well as larger tracts containing forts or the Crater itself, portions of which had by then unfortunately been turned into a golf course. Because of the length of the roads and the need to acquire larger tracts for forts, the commission recommended that 396 acres be in the park, including a couple of portions of adjacent Fort Lee. The proposed battlefield would cover the majority of the major fighting areas east of Petersburg as well as a few areas to the west. Although not as comprehensive as the earlier national military parks, the recommended area at Petersburg still contained the battlefield's major sites.[44]

Despite a continual change among the military officers from Jewett to Lt. Col. James Blyth, Col. Tenney Ross, and then Maj. Arthur E. Wilbourn, the commis-sion worked over the next few years to put their approved plan into action. The members began acquiring land at a steady pace, eventually holding more than four hundred acres. Periodic trouble emerged, however, especially with the onset of the Great Depression in late 1929. The local association also had problems with the commission. They thought, for example, that Bishop was "too old for useful activity in this work." Others thought the commission was too slow and suggested "that we speed up our work on the park" to provide more jobs for the unemployed. Work steadily continued nonetheless, and the 440-acre park was finally ready for dedication on June 20, 1932. Representative Drewry presided over the ceremony, with Assistant Secretary of War F. H. Payne delivering an address. Local citizens also presented a pageant titled "The Siege of Petersburg." Additional land, including the Crater, was added in 1936.[45]

The battlefields around Fredericksburg went through a similar process about the same time. Like Petersburg, supporters of a Fredericksburg park had long wished for federal action but were never quite able to make it happen. The Fredericksburg and Adjacent National Battlefields Memorial Park Association worked hard to secure federal aid, and even some private groups placed monuments on the fields as early as the 1880s. As at Petersburg, the first success came when an initial commission was established in June 1924 to investigate the possibility of creating a park. Famous veteran John L. Clem and Confederate veteran John T. Goolrick (who was sick and missed most of the meetings and died in September 1925, to be replaced by Vivian M. Fleming), along with Maj. J. A. O'Connor of the army engineers, recommended creating the park along the "Antietam system." Congress soon debated H.R. 9045 in 1927. Creating this park also met opposition, namely from Representative Fiorello H. La Guardia of New York, who objected to bills for parks at Fredericksburg, Fort Donelson, and Stones River, delaying each. LaGuardia wanted to wait until War Department inspections were completed before creating parks, but his opposition failed. Both houses passed the bill, and President Coolidge signed it on February 14, 1927. The legislation created a Class IIa park out of the Fredericksburg, Spotsylvania, Wilderness, and Chancellorsville battlefields.[46]

Secretary of War Davis again appointed a new commission consisting of Clem, Fleming, and Capt. George F. Hobson. A constant transfer of the army officers affected this work as well, with a series of officers serving as secretary of the commission and doing most of the work. Col. Tenney Ross replaced Hobson, and Major Wilbourn, who was also overseeing the work at Petersburg, served after Ross's tenure and throughout the remainder of the park's creation process. Confederate veteran Vivian M. Fleming also died during the work, in November 1930, and former congressman R. Walton Moore replaced him. Still, the process of acquiring land, fencing, and marking went on over the next few years. Portions of the park were dedicated at different times, with a major dedication of the entire park taking place in October 1928; President Coolidge was the main speaker. Other dedications of specific parts occurred later, with the Fredericksburg dedication taking place on November 11, 1931. Representative Schuyler O. Bland, the bill's sponsor, made the dedicatory speech, although portions of land were added in the years to come and additional dedications took place on the other battlefields. By 1932, the park contained more than two thousand acres.[47]

That same year, 1927, saw another park established, this time in the western theater. Stones River supporters had been calling for a park since 1895 but had not been successful in their effort. By 1927, the War Department was already working on a comprehensive study of the battlefields, so Stone's River did not get a preliminary study or commission like Petersburg and Fredericksburg; its legislation went straight toward a commission to build the park under the 1925 War Department study. Representative Edwin L. Davis's H.R. 6246 was passed in February 1927, and President Coolidge signed the bill on March 2, just days after he approved the Fredericksburg bill.[48]

The secretary of war appointed a Stones River commission, consisting of John D. Hanson as the Union representative, Sam H. Mitchell as the Confederate commissioner, and Maj. John F. Conklin, the army engineer member, as secretary. The commission met in March 1928 to begin its work, electing Hanson as chairman. The commissioners then scoured the field of battle, noting what plots were already in government possession, mostly having been acquired in April 1928, and also noting the lack of any extant earthworks or signs of the battle. After a thorough study, the members recommended a park of just 325 acres, it also being styled on the Antietam Plan as a Class IIa battlefield. In addition, the commission recommended opening lanes to give access to the park and to mark certain sites on and off the battlefield, including the headquarters sites of both William S. Rosecrans and Braxton Bragg.[49]

The secretary of war approved the plan "in principle" and the commission began its work. Most of the actual work fell on Major Conklin, because the aging veterans were very limited in their activities. Conklin wrote Howard Landers, then working on the army study of battlefields, that "the veteran members of the Commission are very fine gentlemen of whom I am very fond, but after all is said and done, they have been of absolutely no assistance to me in the preparation of the Stones River Report. Little can be expected of a man eighty-five years old." Despite his hard work, Conklin was later moved to additional duties and Capt. H. J. Connor replaced him at Stones River.[50]

Work nevertheless went on, the commission overseeing the building of roads, walkways, and paths. The major item of work was land acquisition. Much of the area, some twenty-five out of fifty-five tracts by November 1931, had to be condemned. Still, the park was virtually completed by 1932, and it contained some sixty tablets marking significant areas. With virtual completion, the park was dedicated at the cemetery rostrum on July 15. Connor then turned over his duties supervising the park to the Army's Fourth Corps Area, which placed it under a superintendent, Melroe Tarter.[51]

An almost identical process occurred just to the north at the Fort Donelson battlefield. Although the local process of creating a park had long been envisioned, like at Stones River, the major move to preserve Fort Donelson came after the War Department began studying the battlefields, so there was no early commission such as those at Petersburg or Fredericksburg. Representative Joseph W. Byrns offered legislation in the Seventieth Congress, H.R. 5500. Earlier efforts by Byrns had passed the House but had failed in the Senate. Representative La Guardia objected again, asking "if it is the intention to bring in a string of these park bills at this session." The House eventually passed the bill anyway, as did the Senate, and Coolidge signed the enabling legislation on March 26, 1928. Interestingly, the legislation, unlike at other parks, stipulated that the national cemetery at Fort Donelson be made a part of the park itself.[52]

The secretary of war appointed a commission made up of Confederate member E. P. Martin, Union veteran Charles G. Mathews, and Maj. John F. Conklin, who was at the same time serving on the Stones River commission in nearby Murfreesboro. The commission met at the courthouse in Dover in September 1928 and elected Martin as chairman. The commissioners met again in October and thoroughly scouted the battlefield, finding most of the earthworks "in a remarkable state of preservation." They then formulated a plan within the constraints of Fort Donelson being a Class IIa battlefield, desiring to acquire only the fort proper as well as a strip of land along the Confederate outer works—some eighty acres. They unfortunately decided against acquiring the major battlefield of February 15, 1862, because of "the present inaccessibility of the scene of this severe fighting, and due to the lack of funds at hand with which to build roads to make the scene of this fighting accessible." The members also decided to emplace some seventy tablets and "pointers," as well as obsolete cannon, mostly inside the park itself along the Confederate outer works.[53]

With approval of the report, Conklin began work on the park, although he asked to be relieved of his work at Stones River. Eventually, he was relieved of both. Maj. F. S. Besson took over in September 1929 and H. J. Connor, also in charge at Stones River, succeeding him in August 1930. Union commissioner Charles Matthews died in 1931, but he was not replaced on the commission. By 1932, the park had some ninety-three acres, seven tracts having been condemned, with fifty tablets to mark significant locations. The majority of the earthworks were in good condition, but some of them had to be rebuilt and refurbished. With the dedication of the park on July 4, 1932, including speeches by Senator Cordell

Hull and Representative Byrns, Connor gave control of the park over to a super-intendent, Walter T. Murray. Unlike many of the 1920s parks, Fort Donelson received an elaborate monument to the Confederate soldiers who had fought there, placed by the United Daughters of the Confederacy in June 1933.[54]

By the end of the 1920s, then, Civil War battlefield preservation had been restarted. Congress and the War Department used the War College's guidelines, and four major parks were established while other significant Civil War sites were also marked. Yet these parks were substantially smaller than the 1890s parks, all established along the Antietam Plan rather than Boynton's plan. The lack of full preservation at these sites has resulted in continued attempts, to this day, to remedy the lack of totality. The ghost of George B. Davis lived in the 1920s—and still does in the twenty-first century.

IV

Besides the promulgation of the Army War College plan and the preservation of several sites, there were also other notable efforts occurring during the 1920s and 1930s that significantly affected battlefield preservation. A major one was the removal of military parks from the War Department to the newly created National Park Service of the Department of the Interior. The NPS was already governing most of America's scenic parklands in the West, and the idea seemed logical that the military parks would be better served under that agency rather than under the War Department, which was tasked with fighting wars and protecting the United States. The change from veteran to nonveteran clientele for the parks also played a role in altering the battlefields' purposes. In addition, there was a political aspect to the desire to transfer the parks. The NPS, a fairly small agency mainly important in the West, sought to add the large and popular eastern parks to their control in order to gain more status and funding. The NPS also believed that they could run the parks better than the War Department did; on one visit to Gettysburg and Antietam, Stephen Mather and Horace Albright were appalled at the lack of land held in each park and were similarly not impressed with the interpretation. "We were also unhappy about the quality of the guide service," Albright wrote. And it was true; as Charles Hosmer has written, "It appears that the only full-time historian working on the problems of interpreting these parks was Landers himself."[55]

Yet the idea of transfer was not new in the 1930s. It had surfaced as early as 1923 with the appointment of the Joint Committee on the Reorganization of the Executive Departments. Secretary of War Weeks supported the idea, as did Interior Secretary Albert Fall, with Weeks's successor Dwight F. Davis even appearing before the committee in 1927. Somehow, the War Department parks failed to make it into the joint report and nothing was done, perhaps because Weeks had problems with Congress. Few congressmen took him seriously, one representative saying, "Oh Secretary of War Weeks was in favor of giving away almost everything the War Department had," adding that in one case he gave away so much to the navy that all the army "had left . . . [was] the flag pole." Still, Davis continued to push the idea, and a board of officers studied the matter in 1927, recommending the change. Other government bureaucrats agreed, including those from the Interior Department and the Bureau of Efficiency, which had suggested the move in the first place. The main thrust of the argument was that all parks needed to be under the control of one agency and that the secretary of war desired to be out from under the monetary obligations of the task. In larger reality, the parks were old news now, even the newer ones. They were no longer the queens of remembrance. Now they were bothersome entities that were shuffled from bureau to bureau in the army, with no one quite wanting them and no one knowing what to do with them. War Department officials readily admitted that the only reason they remained in the department was for "sentimental reason."[56]

As various bills to transfer the parks came and went with each Congress in the late 1920s, with one even passing the Senate committee and Senate in 1928 but failing in the House, the House Committee on Military Affairs finally held a hearing on the issue on January 31, 1929. The bill in question was S. 4173, which would put the parks under the NPS, also transferring civilian personnel at the same classification as well as any remaining money from that year's budget. The legislation also stipulated that any remaining commissioners, namely William T. Rigby, would be continued in office and that the secretary of the interior would continue the military park work under the 1925 War College study. Many congressmen were supportive, the corresponding Senate committee recommending passage, as did Secretary of War Davis and Secretary of the Interior Hubert Work. For his part, Vicksburg commissioner Rigby, the only commissioner left, cried at the thought of switching the battlefields to the National Park Service. For the record, Lieutenant Colonel Landers was not in favor of transferring the parks either.[57]

The hearing did not go well for the supporters of the transfer, partly because the key bureaucrats involved, secretaries Davis and West, did not bother to attend. Another part of the problem was the War Department's key witness: Assistant Secretary of War Charles B. Robbins. Albright, the director of the NPS, thought Robbins "seemed to feel intimidated by the questions asked him, and in my judgment he could have pressed our point of view harder." Robbins worked himself into a corner on several occasions but continually repeated the mantra that the secretary, who was out of town, desired all parks be under one head. Beyond that, he could not provide any real reason why the parks should be transferred. And then he blundered into disparaging the NPS by remarking, when asked why War Department national cemeteries at these parks would not be transferred as well, "We do not want military cemeteries to be playgrounds." Members quickly jumped on that statement, William F. James of Michigan asking him, "You do not want the Gettysburg Park to be a playground, do you?" Others chimed in, Hubert F. Fisher of Tennessee agitating the issue by remarking, "If the experience of the Interior Department, and their purpose, is along the line of making playgrounds, I do not see any point in the War Department transferring the parks." Robbins also slipped up and told the committee, which was concerned about the NPS getting War Department records, that the department would gladly copy the records. The committee piled on again, Robbins having to admit that making copies of their orders and files to send to the NPS would cost the government money. Those congressmen who believed that no funds would be saved or services improved by a transfer now had hard facts to support them.[58]

With the damage done, brand-new NPS director Albright, who had taken over for the ill Stephen Mather just days earlier, knew there was little he could do besides repair the damage. He began by stating, "I realize that there is not really very much use in discussing our phase of this matter." Still, Albright was much more professional and quicker on his feet than Robbins, and he did repair much of the damage. Albright firmly told the committee, "The point is not that the men in charge of the parks are not all right." He went on to explain how the War Department was in the same shape the national parks had been in prior to the NPS's establishment: parks had been all over the Interior Department and the result was "chaotic." The establishment of the NPS had brought all Interior Department parks under one agency, however, and the system was running smoothly now. Albright also fought the idea of parks being playgrounds, stating that the chief goal was "inspiration and for education." He even hit the popular hotdog stand notion: "Those are the things that we are more opposed to than anything else in the world, and we do not permit them at all in the national parks." He reminded the committee that the NPS had other historic parks established under the 1906 Antiquities Act under its care and the agency was competently administering them. Albright assured the committee that the NPS's goal was "absolutely 100 per cent conservation."[59]

Albright also took the offensive, arguing that sentiment "means most to us in this connection," reminding the committee that the NPS had been called "silly sentimentalists." He noted that although the War Department was doing a fine job, "we are the people who can probably handle these areas just as well and probably better along certain lines than the War Department." The emphasis on education and preservation was key, and Albright's argument seemed to resonate with some of the committee. In fact, Albright had the congressmen admitting over and over by the end of his testimony that the NPS was doing a stellar job, although the members still stated that they thought the battlefields should remain in a military setting.[60]

In the end, there was just too much opposition within the committee for Albright to make any headway. Representative James began the hearing by asking, "I was wondering whether it was a case of the Department of the Interior trying to grab off a few more things, or the War Department trying to get rid of something." He later added bitingly that the NPS "do[es] not know what they [the battlefields] are or what they mean." Representative Speaks agreed, stating, "I can not see the slightest justification for the Interior Department having supervision and control of anything in the nature of a military park." Another noted, "Never in my opinion has a bill been sent up here by the War Department that is worse than this one, and I am surprised that they would advocate it."[61]

Overwhelmingly, the main objection was military in nature. Otis S. Bland, a congressman from the Fredericksburg, Virginia, area, argued, "I wish I could bring myself to the thought that war is at an end. I can not." Hence, the military needed places to train the army. Transferring the battlefields was about the same as "putting military instruction under a medical school." The congressman from the Chickamauga area, S. D. McReynolds, likewise wrote that if done, "I imagine that I can see yellow busses and [hotdog] stands throughout, marring the beauty and usefulness of this park."[62]

There was perhaps more to the congressional committee's denial of the secretary of war than mere sentiment and military training, however. In fact, a rift had developed between Secretary Davis and Representative Speaks of the House Committee on Military Affairs. The committee was cool to several ideas of preservation, including Nashville's battlefield, especially so when connected with the secretary. At a hearing in 1928 on the Nashville battlefield's preservation, Speaks let his animosity out when he asked a witness from Nashville, a Mrs. Gillentine, what had brought her to Washington to begin with. She was in town for a meeting of representatives of several women's organizations who promoted military preparedness in the United States. Representative Speaks noted that he was "awfully sorry to see all you folks down here." A recent civilian meeting had asked the secretary of war, the secretary of the navy, the army chief of staff, and "all the Army authorities" to speak, but they did not allow Speaks to address the crowd "on the other side of the question." Speaks later described the cabal in the military as the "War Department machine" and said that "the greatest propaganda machine in the world is right down in the War Department. They have got the men, the money, and everything." Another congressman was similarly angry that one of his bills in 1928 to require superintendents of the parks to be former service men had received a cold response from the War Department, which stated that the bill had been "introduced for political reasons."[63]

Despite the defeat of transfer opponent John M. Morin of Pennsylvania in the 1928 election, which made Albright think there might be an opening, the issue still so rankled the Committee on Military Affairs that when it was again brought up in 1930, and Landers testified about the historic work, it was easily defeated. Landers was candid enough to answer that he was sure both secretaries approved of the idea to transfer the parks to the Interior Department, the secretary of war mainly "to get rid of them as a charge against the War Department's funds." Congressman after congressman once again went on record against the idea, William H. Stafford of Wisconsin stating that the NPS had "no concern or interest in them as military or strategic historical points of interest," and later adding that the NPS was a "civilian organization that is not in sympathy at all with them as military points of vantage or study." Others gloated that the proponents of transfer had "met with a complete and I think unanimous reversal here on the day it was proposed." Landers could only agree that it was well known in the War Department "how strongly opposed the committee was to any change."[64]

As Congress made it clear that they would not pass legislation to transfer the parks any time soon, the NPS sought other means to accomplish the change. Albright himself began to work to add significant new federal historical parks in the East to his NPS, culminating in the establishment of the Colonial and Morristown parks, which strengthened his hand in terms of his agency's ability to govern historic sites. In 1929, President Herbert Hoover also looked into the idea of transferring the parks by executive order. He asked Attorney General William D. Mitchell to look into the legality of such a move, and Mitchell unequivocally responded that it was "not within executive authority" to do so. At issue were fourteen NPS sites as well as fifteen Department of Agriculture sites that rested in national forests. Delving into the wording of the Antiquities Act, under which most of the agricultural areas had been established, and the various pieces of individual enabling legislation for the military parks, Mitchell argued that Congress had not provided enough leeway in the bills to allow such transfer and cited several precedents that likewise opposed the move. As a result, Hoover began to seek authority from Congress to reorganize his executive branch, but the deepening Depression soon took away all attention and the matter died.[65]

Franklin D. Roosevelt entered office in March 1933, and he also sought the authority of Congress for the same reorganization. The matter of the military parks was specifically called to his attention through a Sunday automobile drive that Albright was amazingly able to take with Roosevelt. Albright did not miss this once-in-a-lifetime opportunity and talked feely with the president about history, subtly bringing up the idea of transfer. Roosevelt told Albright to begin work on it, and sure enough, after congressional authorization to do so (Roosevelt's Democrats having taken over Congress in the 1932 election), Roosevelt issued executive orders on June 10 and July 28 (effective August 10) reorganizing the executive branch and specifically placing several parks currently in the War Department and the Forestry Service under the NPS. A few additional but undesirable changes caught Albright off guard, however, including changing the name of the NPS to the Office of National Parks, Buildings and Reservations; fortunately, the name was quickly changed back to National Park Service. Although the NPS already had leveraged its way into controlling newly established historic sites at Yorktown and Morristown, and although the NPS had recently beefed up its historical office staff, Albright wrote that he was "stunned by its scope. It not only gave us the War Department historic sites of all kinds—battlefields, parks, monuments, and cemeteries, including Arlington National Cemetery—but the District of Columbia parks and public buildings." The transfer therefore accomplished with one quick signature what Congress would not do. The political and legal ramifications were huge, but the consequences were just as enormous for the battlefield preservation movement. No longer would preservation be a military-centric idea; now the relatively new National Park Service, previously a western-oriented natural agency, would have authority over the existing battlefields as well as any new ones developed in the future. The NPS thus emerged at the front of the historic preservation process. The implications were enormous.[66]

V

Amid all the federal-level debate over how to preserve, what to preserve, and who should be in charge of what, there were also nonfederal entities at work. As during the golden age of preservation, these were state efforts that were precursors to the development of the various state park systems. Although a few organized state park agencies appeared in the 1920s, such as in Tennessee (1925), most did not develop until the next generation in the 1930s. Still, states established individual parks much like the federal government had done at Yosemite and Yellowstone and the battlefields long before the National Park Service.[67]

The unsure period between the golden age and the New Deal era on the state front was much like the limbo in which the movement found itself on the federal level: disorganized, widespread, and uncoordinated. With the demise of the commissions, the rise of the congressional studies, and the ultimate transfer of the parks to the National Park Service, the private and state actions were limited, but there were state, city, and even non-intended federal actions that preserved battlefields throughout the period. One example of the widespread reach of the preservationists during this era came at what was not even technically a battlefield but was nevertheless an important site associated with the Civil War. When Jefferson Davis fled Richmond in April 1865, he traveled westward in Virginia and through North and South Carolina into Georgia, pursued the entire way by Federals. They caught up with him near Irwinville, Georgia, where he was captured in May 1865. A local legislator, J. B. Clements, offered a resolution in the Georgia legislature in 1915 to donate four acres where Davis had been captured, and the formal deed was signed in 1920. Additional land was added in later years, and the site ultimately became a part of the Georgia system of state parks.[68]

A similarly odd transaction occurred in 1924 at Fort Macon, North Carolina. Having been fought over in 1862 as part of Ambrose Burnside's North Carolina actions, the fort was captured after a naval bombardment and remained in Union hands throughout the war. As part of America's coastal defense network, the fort remained under the War Department until 1924, the same year President Coolidge declared Fort Pulaski to be a national monument. No such declaration came for Fort Macon, however, and it was ultimately sold to the state of North Carolina for a dollar. Similarly, at Fort Morgan on Mobile Bay in 1927, the state of Alabama purchased the fort and created a state park. As with many of the other forts, Morgan had been altered by that time, with numerous outer batteries having been established and with the concrete Battery Duportail built within the fort itself during the Spanish-American War era. A similar change at an older fortification now no longer in use occurred at Fort Pike near New Orleans, Louisiana. Although technically not a battlefield, it did change hands when Federal forces captured New Orleans in 1862. The government abandoned the fort in the late nineteenth century, and the state of Louisiana acquired it in 1928 and made it into one of the state's first parks, certainly the state's first historic park.[69]

Another oddity was the preservation of Fort Negley in Nashville, Tennessee. Although not technically a battlefield, the fort was a major bastion in the defenses of Nashville, and the Battle of Nashville itself had been fought in December 1864 just to its south. The area had been used for various purposes through the years, including as the site of Ku Klux Klan meetings. With the city's acquisition of the fort in 1928, it was now preserved, and later New Deal workers restored the fortification in the 1930s. Additional work has been done more recently, and it is now a thriving city park.[70]

Another effort at preservation came when Tennessee established the Nathan Bedford Forrest State Park on the Tennessee River. Despite Forrest's antiblack activities, there was no popular outcry at the naming, there being an obvious lack of what David Blight described as the emancipationist vision of Civil War memory. Across the river from the site of the battle at Johnsonville, in which Forrest defeated several gunboats, the park preserved several landmarks such as

Pilot Knob, used by river boat pilots to guide them and where Forrest had located artillery. H. B. Pafford offered to donate the land where Pilot Knob lay, and the state gave a modest appropriation. Benton County, Tennessee, administered the park for several decades until the state took complete control in 1963.[71]

While such tangential efforts took place, more and more states established park systems during this period, and a few major battlefields deemed unworthy of national parks were quickly taken in by state agencies. Such was the case with the many battlefields around Richmond, Virginia. Leaders of the Richmond Rotary Club and Richmond Chamber of Commerce, including historian Douglas Southall Freeman, banded together to form the Battlefield Markers Association, which erected sixty-nine stone and metal markers at various sites around the city in 1925. Dedicated in November of that year, the featured speaker was Robert E. Lee's grandson, George Bolling Lee. Turning from marking battlefields to preserving them, the group, now incorporated as the Richmond Battlefield Parks Corporation, bought two hundred acres at Fort Harrison in 1927 and a tract at Cold Harbor soon thereafter. Ultimately, the group raised fifty thousand dollars in private funds and bought eight different Richmond locales, including Gaines's Mill, Cold Harbor, Malvern Hill, Fort Harrison, and Chickahominy Bluff. The local governments also donated part of the gasoline tax to fund a road to connect them, which was dedicated in September 1930. By 1932, the group had purchased 684 acres, which they turned over to the state of Virginia as its first state park. The Richmond Battlefield State Park was formally dedicated on June 22, 1932.[72]

Other state parks also came into being during this era, including two in West Virginia. There the state legislature established Droop Mountain Battlefield State Park in 1927. A battle had occurred there in November 1863, the largest engagement in the state during the war. West Virginia officials had proposed a state park system as early as 1925, but Droop Mountain was its first park. Much of the push for establishment of this park came from a local legislator, John D. Sutton, who had served as a Union soldier in the battle. His 1927 bill created the five-man Droop Mountain Battlefield Commission, which was to survey the land, take options on the tracts, and locate battle lines. The governor quickly appointed the commission, with Sutton as the chairman. The commission recommended buying 125 acres on the battlefield, which the state did, and the commission marked battle lines with twenty-nine interpretive signs and several monuments. The state dedicated the park on July 4, 1929, and additional land has been added over the years.[73]

In March 1931 the legislature also established the Carnifex Ferry Battlefield State Park, site of the September 1861 fight between William S. Rosecrans and John B. Floyd. Senator P. N. Vaughan pushed the effort in the legislature, and the bill established a commission and the purchase of one hundred acres of land.

The commission, made up of nonveterans, soon went to work. In just a few years, the park had acquired 156 acres and the commission began to mark the battlefield "for the benefit of the public and West Virginia history." Lack of money prevented a desired amphitheater and ball field, but the core of the battlefield had been preserved.[74]

Another major state park developed during this period on the Mississippi River at Columbus, Kentucky. The idea emerged out of the 1927 river flood, when Red Cross representative Marion Rust was so enthralled with the area that he pushed for a park. Viewing the earthworks, he said, "If such a magnificent ruin were anywhere north of the Ohio River . . . it would long ago have been memorialized." Adding to the uniqueness of the site were cannon and cannonballs still lying around the area. Rust was amazed that the local population took no more interest in the locale than they did but he soon had them inspired with thoughts of a national park, or at the least a state park: "National if it proved out right but, at least, a state park." As at Carnifex Ferry, Rust also demonstrated the changed feeling toward the reasons for parks. History continued to play a major role, but he also wanted "education, recreation, and aesthetical improvement." He added that "lustrous growth and bird life abounds." The Columbus-Belmont Battlefield Park Association soon emerged under president Phil Porter Jr., and it succeeded in 1928 in getting an establishment bill passed in the state legislature by local representative J. D. Via. The original bill required the association to raise twenty thousand dollars before the state would act, but a 1930 amendment rescinded that requirement. Over time, local citizens gave money, school children saved pennies, and a substantial amount was raised only to be lost when the local bank failed during the Depression. The association persevered nevertheless, and owned some 330 acres by February 1934, a few acres having been condemned. The total eventually grew to 461 acres under park director Emma Guy Cromwell.[75]

Another state park that emerged during this period was at Arkansas Post. It was established as a state area in 1929, when local representative Ballard Deane offered legislation to create the Arkansas Post State Park. Governor Harvey Parnell signed the legislation and appointed a commission to oversee the work, with J. W. Burnett as chairman. The commission accepted a donation of twenty-five acres and then acquired additional land in ensuing years for a total of forty-five acres. The park included the area where the former French settlement had been as well as the former site of the Confederate Fort Hindman, which had been attacked and captured in January 1863 (both had by that time been washed away by the bend of the Arkansas River). Yet the reasoning behind creating first a state park and then a national park was primarily other than Civil War related, as the post had served as the first French settlement in the area and then as the first capital of Arkansas. The Civil War activities there only added another layer of importance to what was already a major Arkansas site. As a result, backers of the project received much more enthusiasm from state officials than they did from national preservationists.[76]

There were also a couple of incidental federal preservation initiatives during this era. For instance, the War Department's establishment of Fort Bragg in North Carolina in 1918 inadvertently took in the site of the March 1865 battle of Monroe's Crossroads, situated in a part of the fort near the Longstreet Presbyterian Church. Several Civil War graves dotted the area, as they still do today, although visitors are restricted due to the area being an active Army military training firing range and drop zone. Similarly, the War Department established Fort Lee in 1917 near Petersburg, Virginia, and the site contained much of the Dimmock Line, where the initial fighting for Petersburg had taken place. Earthworks were abundant on the site.[77]

Work also continued at Kennesaw Mountain, and it eventually took on a federal flavor as well. Although sixty acres had been purchased at Cheatham Hill, little had been done for more than a decade while the association continued to raise money. The funds were in hand by 1914, when the association dedicated a large monument on the fiftieth anniversary of the battle. Contingents of both Northern and Southern heritage groups attended, as did the governor of Illinois. Other smaller monuments also went up, and the entrance to a tunnel used to dig under the Confederate lines was marked.[78]

Eventually, the association realized that a massive amount of work and money was needed to care for the area and decided to donate the land to the federal government. The secretary of war would not accept it without congressional approval, however, and Illinois representative Joseph Cannon offered a bill that passed in 1916 to accept the sixty acres to be known as the Kennesaw Mountain National Battlefield Site. Unfortunately, problems with the land title dragged the effort out, and it was only in 1928 that the federal government actually took control of the site for a fee of ten dollars. Later legislation appointed a commission consisting of an active army officer and a Union and a Confederate veteran to survey the site and report on the feasibility of making Kennesaw Mountain a full-fledged national military park. The resulting bill was one of many that appeared in the mid- to late 1920s, but like most of the others, it went nowhere, despite the fact that it was continually offered in new Congresses throughout the late 1920s and early 1930s. Meanwhile, the site went through a number of overseers, including a local resident, Reverend J. A. Jones. Eventually, the site came to be administered by the superintendent of the nearby Marietta National Cemetery.[79]

Some local enterprises also took place in this era, including the 1929 donation to the Ohio Historical Society of Buffington Island, where John Hunt Morgan had been captured in July 1863. Likewise, another old coastal fortification was also preserved during this period, when, in 1926, the army donated Fort Gaines, on Alabama's Dauphin Island, to the city of Mobile. Fort Gaines, along with Fort Morgan on the opposite side of Mobile Bay, had battled David Farragut's fleet in August 1864 but could not repel the advance. The fort changed hands eventually as the city gave it to the Alabama Department of Conservation, which in turn donated the fort to the Dauphin Island Park and Beach Board, where it is preserved today.[80]

A private movement to preserve the battlefield at Mansfield, Louisiana, also surfaced during this time. The Mansfield Battle Park Association had emerged in 1907, intending to preserve the site where Nathaniel Banks's Red River campaign was turned back in April 1864. Little came of the idea for several years, but in 1924 the local United Daughters of the Confederacy chapter acquired four acres of the battlefield. The next year, on April 8, 1925, the anniversary of the battle, relatives of Prince Camille de Polignac dedicated a monument to him and Alfred Mouton, who had been killed there. At the same time, Richard Taylor's daughter and grandson dedicated a smaller monument to the Confederate commander at the battle. Other, smaller monuments to lesser officers also went up in the late 1920s.[81]

A much larger private effort occurred at Manassas, where the only real commemoration besides the wartime monuments was a small museum run by the Henry family in the reconstructed house on Henry House Hill. In 1922 a group of local citizens preserved part of the battlefield near the Henry site and called it the Manassas Battlefield Confederate Park. Led by board president E. W. R. Ewing, the group purchased 130 more acres that year. They did so strictly for Confederate and Lost Cause memorialization, however, some loudly denying any chance of the battlefield being a national affair. "I wish to register my most ardent protest against this movement," one person wrote his congressman in 1927, "for the reason that the fewer 'Damedyankee' monuments I see in Virginia the better." He went on to say there were already some in Virginia "decidedly objectionable to Southerners who know anything about the history of the period of the war between the States." He later argued that "when I was still a boy and to this day Yankee monuments could be seen on every hand in the form of lone chimneys and crumbling and charred walls of mills, colleges, churches and private homes that had been reduced by the torch of vandalism. The North, particularly New England, does not know that the war is over. I still hear them yapping about John Brown, Abe Lincoln and negro slavery in sermons and speeches that I hear over the radio." The unreconstructed Rebel particularly advised against Northerners and "some of the business interests of Manassas—who may have been the descendents of Carpet-baggers or scallywags—who were willing to sell their birthright for a few paltry dollars that they might gather from the sale of souvenirs and the sale of real estate." Other proponents were much more supportive, however, with one Sons of Confederate Veterans organizer noting that the Confederate park was a place "for both the 'Gray' and the 'Blue'—but with an emphasis on Confederate achievements and history." Coupled with similar opposition that emerged elsewhere, particularly in Richmond, it seemed that the old reconciliationist ideals of the 1890s were beginning to crumble.[82]

Despite the varied manner of conserving on the state and local levels, preservation continued to occur, illustrating the wide appeal of Civil War battlefields not only to the old soldiers who had fought on them but also to the newer generation, some of them descendents of veterans. They too hoped to preserve these historic sites and often took matters into their own hands when the overworked federal preservation machine could not reach their isolated areas. It is fortunate that they did so, because today the parks they created are some of the war's best-protected nonfederal battlefields.

VI

The period between 1912, when the golden age commission system was abolished, and 1933, when the National Park Service took over the battlefield parks, was truly an interregnum. Two towering periods flanked this era, illustrating two very different preservation approaches. Yet this middle period was by no means a backwater era when nothing of use occurred. To the contrary, battlefield preservation made significant headway at this time, with new parks as well as the first concerted attempt at dealing with a serious preservation policy. Had the War Department's system not been cut short less than a decade after it was enacted, there is reason to believe that the system would have continued to work well.

Unfortunately, there were also less-beneficial aspects to this period, such as the clear realization that many of the battlefields had already become too urbanized to preserve. Furthermore, the continual reliance on the Antietam Plan style of preservation, by necessity or choice, assured that many of the battlefields were barely preserved, leaving to future generations much work that could have been better accomplished in the 1920s, or even better in the 1890s. As with every period, fiscal concern arose and limited what could be done.

Another negative aspect was the lack of continuity from one generation to another. When Bach, Landers, and others began their investigations and work on behalf of preservation, they literally had to begin anew. It is doubtful that Landers, who was a low-level artillery officer in the early 1900s, ever met, much less personally knew, George B. Davis or, even more remotely, Henry Boynton. A new generation had to start almost from scratch, but they made a good account of themselves. Unfortunately, the same problem was present when the NPS took over. The service quickly shed most of the old War Department stewards and brought in its own bureaucrats.[83]

And significantly, the shift from War Department to Interior Department, from the Quartermaster Corps to the National Park Service, symbolized a larger shift elsewhere that had a tremendous effect on preservation mentality. The shift cogently illustrated the change from veteran stewardship and visitation to nonveteran operation and clientele. It also emphasized the change from veterans to nonveterans in Congress. Perhaps most significantly, the shift from War Department to National Park Service illustrated the change in America's memory of the war. Whereas veterans of the golden age generation performed their work out of a deep sense of connection and love for the battlefields and their friends who had fought and died there, the newer generation had no such personal connection and began to view the war very differently. Whereas the old veterans used the parks as tangible pieces of reconciliation, the newer generation had no such personal stakes involved. As Ed Bearss has noted, the "Park Service owes something to those people. No Park Service employee ever was shot at on those grounds unless they were shot at by an irate tourist. Those people that made those parks fought—died there—and their contribution should count far more than anybody that's had anything to do with the Park Service or in the War Department years after."[84]

Although a heavy emphasis on reconciliation continued to be seen in speeches and rhetoric even during this new era, additional memory themes illustrating the new generation's disconnection with the war also crept in. As the congressional committees poured over plans and seethed with reconciliation, they also began to include more modern approaches to the need for preservation. For those who had not lived through these battles or the war, one committee declared, a park "makes alive these matters of history which unless they are commemorated are going to die out." Although a few of the old War Department stewards, such as DeLong Rice at Shiloh, perceived the need to educate and interpret to these new visitors in the coming style of the NPS, and the War Department even issued regulations in 1931 calling for guides services to cater to the newer generations, that mentality was vastly muted prior to 1933. It would surface in full form only after the NPS took control of the parks. The desire to balance preservation with the military and public use was also lacking prior to 1933 as the War Department and Congress sought to justify its large expenditures on the parks with tangible returns, most notably in the form of military maneuvers and training.[85]

The House Committee on Military Affairs that recommended Petersburg be a park provided a prime example of these shifting ideals. It gushed the standard reconciliationist sentiment, stating the park would "commemorate the highest ideals and exploits of American valor and strategy, without the taint of bitterness or shame to either side," but it also added to the reasons for preservation—"military as well as historical value"—and noted that the park "will serve very practical, educational, historical, military, and patriotic purposes." Similarly, the

Senate committee recommending the Fredericksburg park noted it would be used for "patriotic and educational purposes and for historical and professional study," again later commenting on the "very practical, educational, military, and patriotic purposes."[86]

Others had distinctively more modern ideas when dealing with the obvious military advantages the parks allowed. With World War I behind them and, unknown to them, another looming ahead, this generation was leery of more fighting and looked to the past to learn how to stay out of war or, when confronted by such killing, how to fight it with the fewest number of casualties. At the dedication of the Stones River park, for example, Maj. Gen. Edward L. King remarked, "It is fitting today that we consider this problem of war from the serious angle and be prepared so that there will be fewer of these graveyards in the future." The House committee recommending the Petersburg park similarly noted that "the trench warfare of the Great War in Europe was based very largely upon studies made by military students of the works around Petersburg."[87]

Others had additional reasons for creating the parks, with the growing tourist industry brought about by more leisure time and mobility adding a significant amount of money to any area with a park. A local Petersburg newspaper related that visitors spent "an average of five dollars each" at similar parks, and creating one at Petersburg would not only bring in flocks of tourists but also business conventions and greater employment opportunity. Land would also "enhance in value many, many times its present worth." Nature and recreation were additional drivers to establish parks, particularly state parks, with founders openly advocating the need for recreational ball fields and amphitheaters and touting the flora, fauna, and bird watching venues. The obvious desire for increased visitation and tourist dollars also affected the desire to continue to make the story visitors heard one of heroism rather than of the war's grisly and uncomfortable causes. The pattern of keeping race out of the story and out of Americans' memory of the war continued.[88]

Consequently, the period between the two great epochs of battlefield preservation clearly was a significant time in and of itself. It hearkened back to the old veterans' attitudes of reconciliation and sacrifice, yet it brought about new ideas of tourism, modern military study, and historic education. But the major result coming from the 1920s was a growing disconnection with the war itself. The Civil War became an aspect of one's ancestors' lives rather than one's own, of history rather than personal connection, and future preservation mentality followed suit.

The Vicksburg Surrender Monument was the first major Civil War commemoration of an event rather than a burial site. The shaft marked the site of the meeting between Ulysses S. Grant and John C. Pemberton on July 3, 1863, at Vicksburg, Mississippi. Courtesy of Library of Congress.

The 1863 Hazen Brigade Monument at Stones River National Cemetery is the oldest Civil War monument still in its original position. It marks the burial site of members of the brigade who died in the battle. Courtesy of Library of Congress.

One of two Manassas (Bull Run) monuments at Manassas National Battlefield Park. Federal soldiers dedicated two almost identical monuments at Manassas, one for each battle, in June 1865. They still stand in their original places. Courtesy of Library of Congress.

View of Main Entrance to
Shiloh National Cemetery

Shiloh National Cemetery was established in 1866 at Pittsburg Landing on the Tennessee River. This hand-drawn image is one of the earliest views of the cemetery, showing the entrance and original keeper's lodge. Courtesy of National Archives.

One of only two cycloramas still viewable today, the Atlanta Cyclorama gives vivid detail to the July 20, 1864, battle. Note the actual railroad track in the foreground and how it blends into the painting itself. Courtesy of Library of Congress.

John B. Bachelder was the foremost expert on Gettysburg after the war. He worked with the Gettysburg Battlefield Memorial Association and then was appointed to the Gettysburg National Military Park Commission. Unfortunately for the work at Gettysburg, he died shortly thereafter. Courtesy of Gettysburg National Military Park.

The Chickamauga Memorial Association held a grand barbeque in 1889, whipping up support for a park. Henry V. Boynton was the instigator, and he and his effort proved imminently successful. Courtesy of *Society of the Army of the Cumberland.*

As the father of the national military park, Henry Van Ness Boynton was the instigator of the Chickamauga and Chattanooga National Military Park. His idea for total preservation of battlefields became the accepted theory in the 1890s. Courtesy of *Confederate Veteran.*

Secretary of War Daniel S. Lamont oversaw a massive expansion of the national military park effort during his tenure. With several proposed parks and their enormous cost, Lamont called for the first systematic policy on battlefield preservation. Courtesy of Department of Defense.

Secretary of War Elihu Root oversaw a rigorous streamlining of the War Department among his major reforms, and the battlefield parks were no exception. With numerous park bills flooding Congress, Root called for a battlefield preservation policy as well as legislation to combine the various park commissions. Courtesy of Department of Defense.

Brig. Gen. George B. Davis is normally considered the father of the Antietam Plan, by which battlefields were preserved on a much more limited and cost-efficient manner than with Boynton's total theory. Although Boynton used the more limited method at Chattanooga prior to Davis at Antietam, Davis's plan became the government-preferred process and would be used extensively for decades. Courtesy of Library of Congress.

Speaker of the House David B. Henderson was an avid supporter of parks at Shiloh and Vicksburg prior to his tenure as Speaker, but his assumption of that office amazingly ushered in a period of no activity on the battlefield preservation front. Courtesy of House of Representatives.

This view shows a typical scene on one of the 1890s battlefields. Here park historian David W. Reed and his family visit Shiloh's Hornet's Nest, where he had fought and which he emphasized in the literature on the battle. Note the 1890s-era tablets placed on the field. Courtesy of Shiloh National Military Park.

While the federal government established the 1890s-era parks, the states funded most of the monuments. Here the Illinois state memorial is being built at Vicksburg. Courtesy of Vicksburg National Military Park.

Illustrating the reconciliation of the times, the Vicksburg Peace Jubilee was a massive event that saw thousands of veterans reunited at one of their most important battlefields. Here the large logistical effort of tents and meal tables can be seen. Courtesy of Vicksburg National Military Park.

As the original park commissions began to fade into the past, younger, second-generation superintendents began to oversee the parks. DeLong Rice was the son of a Confederate veteran and ran Shiloh much as the veterans had. Courtesy of *Michigan at Shiloh*.

4

The New Deal Era,
1933–1945

The scene was solemn as the old veterans made their way toward one another, white beards and feeble legs reenacting Pickett's famous charge. Reflecting national unity and remembrance, the occasion was complete with numerous commemorative events and even the participation of the president of the United States. Franklin D. Roosevelt himself had come to Gettysburg to commemorate the seventy-fifth anniversary of the battle in July 1938, lighting an "eternal" peace memorial and playing up the reconciliation that by that time was heartily accepted. Indeed, it had been rooted in nearly fifty years of racial segregation, allowing the old divisive issues of race to be all but forgotten, left to the nation's past. Although reconciliation remained a tenet of battlefield preservation from then on, illustrated by the shaking of hands across the stone wall by Union and Confederate veterans, perhaps Roosevelt's presence was the truly significant fact that pointed toward the reality of the present. Reconciliation was an accepted fact now, and had been for decades, but the president's presence highlighted a new dynamic in battlefield preservation and commemoration—that of the mushrooming federal government's role, especially during Roosevelt's New Deal. With new ways of thinking, new money to spend, and new leaders in charge, the New Deal and the National Park Service drastically altered the way current battlefields were managed and the way new ones were developed.[1]

In his early years in the White House, President Roosevelt took a special interest in national parks in general and Civil War battlefields in particular. Aside from the fact that much of his New Deal took place in the parks, Roosevelt was personally interested in the history of the battlefields and in their care. Indeed, he often visited them, as he did on the anniversary of Gettysburg. There is also an iconic photograph of him sitting in a car atop Lookout Mountain, cigarette in mouth, seemingly overshadowing the entire panorama on which the battles for Chattanooga played out. As a result, when Horace Albright mentioned to him the desire to transfer the military parks to the National Park Service, Roosevelt listened carefully.[2]

But Roosevelt's interest and participation in events at the battlefields can perhaps be looked at as a metaphor for what was happening on a larger scale. Into office had swept this new president who inspired the nation's people in extremely bleak times. He also oversaw a growing fascination with the Civil War, which would be played out in anniversaries throughout the latter half of the 1930s as well as in hundreds of the most popular battle histories and biographies written during the period, some of them still standards of the literature today. Perhaps, however, Roosevelt sitting high atop the mountain at Chattanooga provided the most metaphorical illustration; he seemingly sat above it all as a great chess master who was able to move the much smaller entities below him around at will, as he had done with the parks themselves in transferring them. At the same time, the episode also illustrated a certain detachment from the intricacies of the battlefields, as Roosevelt and his federal government, high above the grounds, utilized them in a much less personal manner than had the veterans of the previous generations.[3]

The transfer of the battlefields to the National Park Service and the emergence of the mushrooming bureaucracy that oversaw them indeed resulted in a major change of focus. For most of the battlefields' histories, the War Department had had an intimate relationship with the veterans, especially with the commissions on which they sat. But the passing of the veteran generation left America to forge ahead without any real and personal connection to the war. Now the battlefields rested within a much larger bureaucracy that ushered out most of the old War Department personal influence; NPS bureaucrats brought in to replace the old veterans and their successors now primarily governed the parks. These NPS officials were usually less interested in the battlefields themselves, certainly less so than the former commissioners, and saw their status as temporary duty stations in the continual advancement process within the bureaucracy. One superintendent even referred to his battlefield as "the thing," as in "purposes for which the thing exists." Certainly, no veteran would have referred to a battlefield so callously. Another NPS official openly declared, "We are in the tourist business, and we are interested in attracting as great a number of visitors here as possible." As a result, much more turnover occurred among staff and managers within the NPS than had occurred within the War Department or, certainly, the commissions. Now, officials with no special personal affinity for the battlefields came and went and governed the parks more as a business than as a labor of love.[4]

That is not to say that some NPS officials did not gain a special appreciation and even love for the battlefields at which they served. There was, in fact, some effort to continue the desires of the commissions, especially the later ones, by trying to fashion the fields into how they looked during the war. NPS official Branch Spaulding met with the Petersburg commission in 1933 immediately after the transfer and reported, "I have made it my purpose in these meetings to determine the desires of the commission as to the manner in which the park should be developed." Still, the NPS had its own way of doing things that was obviously at odds with the old veterans or military personnel. Spaulding remarked in the same report that "an able landscape architect can still do a great deal toward beauty and erosion control in these tracts." In speaking of Fort Stedman, Spaulding added, "It is in this area that the landscape architect has his best opportunity for improvement of the scene." Ed Bearss summed up the change in speaking of the old commissions: "Thank God the War Department had em [originally]. I hate to think what some of our planners would have thought of them."[5]

Consequently, when the NPS arrived it began a new way of working with a new visiting clientele, those not necessarily immersed in Civil War tactics and strategy. One Stones River official wrote that the parks were now "for the benefit and enjoyment of the people." Superintendent McConaghie at Gettysburg remarked how the more rapid lifestyle affected visitors: "They do not want to spend the time here to fully understand the field." In a vivid illustration of the change in mentality, landscape architect–turned–superintendent McConaghie even promoted planting trees to block the views of the troop-position monuments on the battlefield: "Carefully plant so that the numerous monuments will appear to fit and be screened so as not to unduly affect the landscape."[6]

One of the most important new areas of emphasis for the new clientele was an avid educational program, which the newly revived NPS struggled to organize amid the breathtaking changes wrought by the Depression, New Deal, and the transfer. Realizing the change offered a golden opportunity to get into the historic preservation and education business in a huge way, the NPS began to organize a history branch, appointing a chief historian, Verne Chatelain. He significantly placed his stamp on historic and educational efforts at the historic sites. One Stones River report stated that "in taking over control of the historical areas, the National Park Service immediately began the development of an educational policy applicable to these places." The NPS also developed a historical program intended to "provide the maximum of reliable information to the visitor." The parks accordingly began to produce guide books and pamphlets as well as offer lectures and talks, something the War Department never fully embraced.[7]

The NPS also brought in its own managers, some very quickly and others over time. The change was immediate at two of the newest parks, which were governed by army officers at the time of the transfer. At Petersburg, NPS official B. Floyd Flickinger took control on August 10, the date of transfer. Philip R. Hough took control of Fredericksburg and Spotsylvania on August 12, just two days into the NPS rule. The change was also swift in some of the older parks. John K. Beckenbaugh took over for George B. Alexander at Antietam on September 30, 1933, and on the same day John B. Holt turned over Vicksburg to Lewis G. Heider. Within a month or a little thereafter, new NPS superintendents were in control of four of the nine Civil War military parks in existence at the time of the transfer.[8]

The others were also changed over time. Robert Livingston at Shiloh, although born and bred on the park and a member of the staff since the 1910s, was shifted from his position by 1936, although his transfer also had a great deal to do with a spat he had with one of Tennessee's senators, Kenneth McKellar. NPS bureaucrat Charles S. Dunn followed, but the direct connection with both the site as well as the old commission was broken with Livingston's departure. Similarly, Richard Randolph did not remain long at Chickamauga, although it was health reasons that forced him out in 1937. Walter T. Murray at Fort Donelson was technically the national cemetery superintendent, but he oversaw the park as well until his departure in 1938. Thus within five years, NPS personnel had replaced seven of the nine War Department managers at the battlefields. In the remaining ones, James R. McConaghie lasted only until 1941 at Gettysburg and Melroe Tarter remained at Stones River until 1942. In total, all War Department leaders were gone from their original positions within the first decade.[9]

Little else could be expected, however, because the veterans themselves were dying in huge numbers, and more and more battlefields were continually being added to the NPS system under professional NPS leaders. And in those additions, the 1930s New Deal parks stand out as perhaps the climax in federal preservation of battlefields, certainly in quantity if not in quality.

I

Along with the many changes in the early 1930s regarding the administration of Civil War battlefields, the U.S. government took a step forward and created a larger policy of preservation in 1935. Obviously reacting to the broad influx of historic sites into the previously nature-dominated NPS, Congress established legislation that would provide a national level of historic preservation consciousness. Such efforts had been attempted earlier, as with the legislation that provided for the condemnation of land for national cemeteries and later national military parks as well as the passage of the 1906 Antiquities Act. Although both were stepping-stones to a future preservation policy, neither was broad enough to qualify for national-level policy. The 1935 Historic Sites Act tried to remedy that, although it too was not nearly as comprehensive as was needed or that would emerge in later decades. Yet it was a start.[10]

The Historic Sites Act served as the first modern attempt to give to the NPS the process of documenting, declaring historic, and overseeing the various historic sites. Although several future-minded individuals associated with the NPS had already begun to look at expanding into historic realms in previous years, in particular John C. Merriam (whose committee work later became the basis for the NPS's historic branch), there was little the agency could do until it possessed the statutory rights to move forward. In fact, the NPS's chief historian, Verne Chatelain, noted that "we simply couldn't do anything more than we were doing for the time being until we had created the kind of organization that was needed." The 1935 act provided those territorial rights to history within the federal government, but as Boge and Boge stated, "Its impact was limited because federal ownership was not promoted as the primary preservation tool." For the most part the act affected the more limited theoretical level, providing a way of describing historic sites and documenting them for future generations.[11]

One of the major tangible results was the perpetuation of the New Deal's temporary Historic American Buildings Survey (HABS) within the NPS. Although begun several years earlier to provide work for unemployed Americans, the program documented numerous historic buildings with photography. In fact, the documentation is still relevant today, much of it available from the Library of Congress website. Fortunately, the HABS files provide documentation of many sites that no longer exist. The Historic American Buildings Survey has since been joined by the Historic American Engineering Record (HAER) and the Historic American Landscape Survey (HALS), all today under the NPS's Heritage Documentation Programs Office. Unfortunately, the act established no penalty for destroying historic sites; indeed, many of the buildings documented by the Historic American Buildings Survey are no longer standing.[12]

The Historic Sites Act likewise authorized an extensive survey and declaration process for significant sites, the National Survey of Historical Sites and Buildings. Still in its embryonic stage in the 1930s, this process eventually developed into the modern National Historic Landmark program, with the first declarations of National Historic Landmarks coming in 1960. In addition, the act created the National Park System Advisory Board, which was intended to aid the secretary of the interior in deciding what and what not to preserve. In actuality, this board would serve as somewhat of a detriment to Civil War battlefield preservation in that it often recommended against creating new battlefield parks. Yet for all it did or did not do, the Historic Sites Act was an important step toward a national policy of historic preservation, building on the earlier efforts of the Antiquities Act, the NPS establishment, and even the 1925 War College battlefield survey.[13]

Still, despite the change in departments and agencies governing the military parks and the larger context of historic preservation, Congress could not keep itself from dealing with pet projects in a piecemeal fashion. One of the major results of the transfer from the War Department to the NPS was that the 1925 army preservation plan, which was beginning to work well, was dropped by the NPS and the service offered no replacement. Thus another clean break with the past occurred. The NPS seemed to think it knew better than the nonprofessional historians of the army; in reality, the NPS would have done well to continue its work along the lines of the War College survey. As there was no guiding plan after 1933, Congress continued to pass more and more individual legislation creating additional military parks, including the Revolutionary War's Saratoga National Historical Park in 1938. Other non–Civil War preservation activity went on at Chalmette and Little Big Horn. Similar additions were mostly nature parks that had some aspect of Civil War history attached to them. An example was the Cape Hatteras National Seashore Recreation Area, which included those portions of the North Carolina Outer Banks that had seen combat in Ambrose Burnside's 1862 campaign. Congress established the area in 1937, although it would take many more years to actually turn it into a park. Likewise, the Cumberland Gap National Historical Park, which obviously had to do with expansion and frontier history as well as scenic beauty, was nevertheless instrumental in transportation realms during the Civil War and at times saw armies move through. President Lincoln, in fact, was a firm believer in operations around the gap. Congress passed legislation authorizing the park in 1940, although like Cape Hatteras it would be years before work actually began on it and a park emerged. A different battlefield preservation approach likewise came with the acquisition of the Chesapeake and Ohio Canal in September 1938. Many crossings and some fighting had occurred along the banks of the canal, river, and its general area, including at Shepherdstown, West Virginia, and battle sites at Folck's Mill, Hancock, and Williamsport, Maryland. Almost as an afterthought, the Appalachian Trail, which opened in 1937, also preserved portions of the South Mountain battlefields where it crossed Turner's Gap, Fox's Gap, and Crampton's Gap in Maryland, and the battle site at Cool Spring in Virginia.[14]

A similarly stunted effort during the New Deal era came at Monocacy in Maryland. Veterans had placed monuments there starting in 1907, with the New Jersey monument, and 1908, when a Pennsylvania monument went up, and over the years a memorial to Vermont troops (1915) had also been erected, as was a UDC monument (1914) to Confederate troops at the battle. The local population desired more than just monumentation, however, so the Monocacy Battlefield Association continuously called for a national military park. One War Department official, in fact, wrote the quartermaster of a meeting of the association, noting that "the local people are determined that a monumental monument, in the shape of a small park with roads, landscaping, and other activity be created, at a cost of several hundred thousand dollars probably. They were firmly convinced that Monocacy was one of the most important and significant battles of the Civil War. What they want is a Gettysburg Park on a much smaller scale." Backing their claim was a report written earlier in the 1930s in which Colonel Landers stated, "In all of the battlefields and military monuments I studied, and they amounted to three or four hundred in all during the 5 years, there were but two wherein I felt a classification change should be made; one was King's Mountain and the other was Monocacy."[15]

Several bills appeared in Congress to create the park, but nothing happened until 1934. Both the House and Senate committees on military affairs, despite the transfer of battlefields to the NPS, recommended passage of H.R. 7982. This bill called for a small park of fifty acres and set forth the reason as historical in nature while adding a note on the budding tourist industry. "During more than 6 months of the year," the committee wrote of the main highway through the battlefield, "from 2,000 to 3,000 automobiles travel the boulevard daily." The committee also noted that Monocacy was very close to Gettysburg, where "700,000 tourists" visited annually, many of whom would "pass alongside of the Monocacy battlefield." Congress ultimately passed the bill in 1934, creating the Monocacy National Military Park, but the legislation significantly stated that the battlefield would be declared a park "whenever the title to the lands deemed necessary by the Secretary of the Interior shall have been acquired by the United States and the usual jurisdiction over the lands and roads of the same shall have been granted to the United States by the State of Maryland." It was park establishment that hedged on the financial aspects, obviously hoping for donation of land. Unfortunately for backers of the Monocacy battlefield, the expected land donation never occurred, and it would be decades before the NPS acted on this authorization. Meanwhile, the battlefield continued on in private hands.[16]

In addition to the stunted and limited efforts at Monocacy and elsewhere, there was also a flurry of major preservation successes during this era. One successful federal endeavor built on the earlier work at Kennesaw Mountain.

Although veterans had begun the preservation process at Cheatham Hill and had even erected a few monuments, the private veterans' group could not financially see to the continuing operation of the site and ultimately donated the land to the War Department. Even that took a decade to accomplish as land titles were sorted out to the government's satisfaction. Little else occurred until Congress created a national park in 1935. The legislation was basically the same as that for previous parks, except this time the battlefield was placed under a superintendent of the NPS instead of the War Department. There was opposition to the action, however, one congressman asking why they were passing such a bill "in face of the $4,880,000,000 public-works program in the balance" and "when millions are looking for jobs, out of work, and many of them starving." Still, most supported the bill, significantly adding additional uses than just historic or commemorative. House sponsor Malcolm C. Tarver of Georgia noted that it would be "alongside the Dixie Highway, traveled annually by many thousands of tourists." The change in visiting clientele was obvious.[17]

The NPS soon began its work at Kennesaw Mountain, sending engineer Olinus Smith to Georgia to begin the process of additional land acquisition. Unfortunately, word soon got out that the government was going to buy land and a cartel emerged with the hopes of getting rich quick. The two sides battled each other in the courts, but eventually condemnation proceedings took place and the park began to grow with the acquisition of some twenty-two hundred acres. Additional land was added under future appropriations. The park was first placed under the care of Chickamauga superintendent Richard Randolph, and it did not receive a specific superintendent itself until 1937, when Bowling C. Yates took the helm.[18]

A similarly staggered start occurred at Appomattox. Despite the 1890 marking, the 1920s commission, and the 1930 monument legislation, nothing else had been done there until the NPS took over planning for the site. The monument plan never got off the ground despite the authorization of one hundred thousand dollars, and although a design was chosen, enough opposition arose that nothing was done. The NPS breathed new life into the project, however, with new ideas of not just marking but also of restoring and reconstructing key buildings such as the McLean House and the courthouse. Local supporters of the idea of a park instead of a monument banded together and formed the Appomattox Historic Park Association. It persuaded Congressman Patrick Dewey to offer the bill authorizing the park in 1935. The legislation stated the park was "for the benefit and enjoyment of the people" and argued that Appomattox should have "a memorial park instead of a memorial monument." The bill carried over the unused authorization of one hundred thousand dollars from the monument legislation.[19]

Like other efforts in Richmond and elsewhere, it was several years before the actual park took form. The NPS first placed the effort under the Colonial park superintendent but transferred it in 1936, along with other Civil War parks in Virginia, to a place under Branch Spaulding, superintendent of the older Fredericksburg and Spotsylvania park. Funds from Congress were eventually forthcoming, and New Deal agencies were used to finish the effort. In fact, in another round of fiscal hesitation, Resettlement Administration funds were used to buy the land and laborers from the Civilian Conservation Corps (CCC) helped do much of the work at the park, such as beginning reconstruction of the McLean House and building a bypass that would take traffic away from the heart of the site.[20]

Like Kennesaw Mountain and Appomattox, the Richmond National Battlefield also had its beginning in private and state efforts, although a federal park came to fruition in 1936. Douglas Southall Freeman and a host of other Richmond luminaries had begun marking the battlefields around Richmond in 1925 and then began to preserve the sites, eventually creating a state park. The state soon found it did not have the financial wherewithal to maintain it, and a serious effort to make Richmond's battlefields a national park soon emerged. The first step was congressional action that funded a War Department survey of the Richmond battlefields, which Landers made in 1929. Representative Andrew Jackson Montague of Virginia eventually offered a bill to create the park, and the Virginia legislature officially deeded the land, again saving money, although as at Manassas there was opposition from some who feared "the grounds might not be properly marked by Federal historians." One Virginian stated, "Northern historians might destroy the value of the area as a great Confederate memorial park by markers out of harmony with southern convictions." Despite such Lost Cause rhetoric, which seemed to be increasing, many opposed the move out of "sentiment rather than distrust." Still, most supported the donation, mainly because of finances, and Montague soon pushed H.R. 1415 through Congress with limited debate and with President Roosevelt's approval. NPS officials then descended on the newly formed park and with the help of the New Deal agencies had the battlefields prepared for visitors by 1944. The park was administered by superintendents at other sites in Virginia, namely Fredericksburg and Spotsylvania, until that date, after which Floyd Taylor became Richmond's first resident superintendent.[21]

Another federal adventure began at Manassas, despite the heated opposition of a few private die-hard Confederate supporters. A portion of the land had been preserved as the Confederate park, and Congress gave the NPS authority to establish a federal battlefield at Manassas in August 1935. With no appropriation to actually acquire the land, the Roosevelt administration had to maneuver to fund the acquisition, and the New Deal came through to provide that opportunity. Land acquisition began under the Resettlement Administration, as at Appomattox, and Roosevelt declared nearly fifteen hundred acres as the Bull Run Recreational Development Demonstration Area, which was intended to offer city dwellers near the nation's capital opportunity for recreation. The historic nature of the site made it that much more appealing and was a major factor in preserving it. Funds for the work came from the Civilian Conservation Corps, which built roads and cleared the grounds.[22]

As the climax to the Manassas process, the secretary of the interior formally designated the battlefield, under the auspices of the Historic Sites Act, a national park in May 1940. Two major projects soon began. One was the placement of a monument, funded by the Virginia state legislature, to Stonewall Jackson on Henry House Hill, where the general had gained his famous nickname. This effort was not without controversy, however, as the winning sculptor of the contest, Joseph P. Pollia, built a massive statue of a herculean Jackson on a herculean horse. Confederate veterans argued that "neither figure resembles the subject it supposedly depicts," with one even saying the horse looked more like "a lion or a buffalo." One newspaper reported that "more smoke has been raised regarding the choice of the statue to grace Manassas Battlefield since the project was started in Richmond than Jackson ever stirred." Still, the monument was eventually dedicated in August 1940, with the unveiling by Jackson's great-great granddaughter and the principal speaker being Douglas Southall Freeman. Other parts of the monument caused additional confusion as well, some viewers noting an already developing (and largely unintentional) pattern of the horse's feet telling whether the human commemorated was killed, wounded, or unhurt. The pattern did not fit at Manassas, and one park employee took a humorous approach to the matter, stating to the superintendent at Gettysburg (where much of the mythical pattern developed) that "in this case the creator of the Henry Hill statue may not have fully imbibed the tradition; Joseph Pollia, I believe, is of Italian extraction." The other, and less controversial, project was construction of a major visitor center that would house a museum and administrative offices. The building, costing fifty-four thousand dollars, was begun in 1941 and finished the next year. Inexplicably, it was placed on Henry House Hill, on the focal areas of both battles.[23]

Despite the establishment of several new federal parks, money issues were definitely beginning to take a toll. The funds being spent on the New Deal severely cramped the government, and many fiscal conservatives opposed creating any new government entities outside that effort. The congressman's rant over funding new items "in face of the $4,880,000,000 public—works program" illustrated the concern. And there were those inside the NPS who were also opposed to creating new parks. In a June 1935 memo to Verne Chatelain, the service's chief historian, Assistant Director H. C. Bryant wrote, "Where, oh where, is money coming from to maintain every house once occupied by a notable and every patch of ground fought upon? I have grave fears over the tendency to be willing to take over so many sites. Bull Run makes how many battlefields of the Civil War to be maintained by the Government?" He went on to declare that "the whole historical park system will soon be cluttered with so many minor areas that no one will be able to search out the significant ones. This is another appeal for caution instead of acquisition!" The result of all the concern was a new federal preservation process in which Congress first authorized a site without actually funding it, often stipulating that once the land was acquired it would be formally declared a park. That is exactly what happened at Appomattox, Richmond, and Manassas. And that is the formula that caused Monocacy to never be developed in the 1930s, or for decades afterward, for that matter. Moreover, the massive spending on World War II was right around the corner, and it would not prove helpful to federal preservationists. In fact, there would not be a single national, or state for that matter, battlefield preserved during World War II (Harpers Ferry was only authorized). Modern economic concerns certainly factored into the battlefield preservation movement.[24]

II

Just as federal preservationists were making progress at multiple sites in this New Deal era, so too were state and local governments. Perhaps they were inspired by the revival of interest among federal officials, or perhaps they realized there was New Deal money available from the federal government to aid in building state-run sites. Many states were establishing their own park systems at the time as well, and they were gaining much acclaim. As a result of these factors, the various states began to preserve far and wide, establishing the best-known battlefield state parks in the nation. At the same time, however, the growth of these state parks illustrated the subjective nature of battlefield preservation in determining which battlefields were important enough for national distinction and which had to be preserved by lesser entities such as individual states. In large part, as had always been the case, it fell to the respective power of a battlefield's local congressman or senators to get a federal bill passed; those who could not were left with the option of a state or local park.[25]

One of the first state parks created during the New Deal era was Sailor's Creek in Virginia, site of a major battle along the retreat route of the Army of Northern Virginia in April 1865. Robert E. Lee lost a major portion of his army there, but it was not until 1934 that serious efforts were taken to preserve the site. Some talk of making the site a national park surfaced, but the NPS soon squashed that idea, arguing that it was not important enough to be saved as part of the federal system. It consequently fell to the Commonwealth of Virginia, whose legislature passed a bill in 1934 appropriating money to buy the most significant resource on the battlefield, the Hillsman House and ten acres of adjoining land. The legislation placed the battlefield under the Virginia Conservation Commission, although it would later be placed under the auspices of the state parks and actually managed by a nearby state park's administrative team. A 1940 piece of legislation expanded the site to two hundred acres and provided for the restoration of the farm house.[26]

The year 1936 saw the emergence of several other state parks around the nation, including perhaps the largest and most important battlefield that would never reach the level of a federal military park. Perryville warranted a national military park, but the backers were never able to get one passed through Congress. It was not for a lack of effort, however, with the initial bills offered to Congress appearing as early as 1903. Through the years, monuments went up at the battlefield, such as the 1902 Confederate monument and a corresponding Union monument in 1931 under the auspices of the Perryville Battlefield Commission. Still, the site was never preserved until the state included the creation of a state park at Perryville in a government reorganization bill in 1936. The legislation allowed for the state park, although it would be two more decades before the battlefield was opened to the public.[27]

Another eventual state park came to fruition at Rivers Bridge in South Carolina, where in February 1865 a small fight occurred as Confederates tried to stall William T. Sherman's advance through the Carolinas. Local citizens began the effort to rebury the Confederate dead after the war and, in 1876, organized one of the first battlefield memorial associations in the nation. Little preservation occurred until 1939, however, when local owner John D. Jenney donated the battlefield to the Rivers Bridge Monumental and Memorial Association. Although Jenney was not a veteran he had been present as a boy, watching the fighting from a nearby tree. Jenney donated additional land later, and the association bought even more. It was able to open the battlefield and its extensive earthworks to the public as the John D. Jenney Park in 1941, but that was not the extent of the preservation or administration of the site. Just four years later, in 1945, the association donated the 286-acre park to the state of South Carolina, when Rivers Bridge became the first historic park in the state's park group. Significantly, however, Rivers Bridge, small though it was, signaled the changing process of battlefield preservation. As evidenced elsewhere, particularly at Manassas and Richmond, a fondness for the old Confederacy was again growing out of the reconciliationist era, with one publication noting that not only was the park the first historic park in South Carolina but it was also "the only one to commemorate the Confederacy." More ominously, the South Carolina state park system, part of the Forestry Commission, immediately began to implement recreational activities, including "a play field, facilities for picnickers and possibly a swimming pool." All were eventually put in place, illustrating the change in emphasis from strictly historic commemoration to tourism and recreation.[28]

A different and unique type of preservation, although one that would eventually develop into a state park, occurred at the same time at Fort McAllister near Savannah, Georgia. The site of Confederate efforts to defend Savannah from Sherman's approaching columns at the end of the March to the Sea, Fort McAllister was privately owned through the 1930s, but that owner fortunately and somewhat surprisingly acquired a deep interest in the fort and had it preserved. By this time a rich Henry Ford had bought thousands of acres in south Georgia, including the site of the fort. Hearing that there was a Civil War citadel on his land, Ford eventually went himself in search of it and managed to find the walls amid the thick undergrowth and trees. He spent about fifteen thousand dollars, hiring laborers and workers to clear the fort's grounds and restore it. The workers unearthed bombproofs, replaced rotten beams and wood, and made the site accessible, although it was not opened to the public. Ford also obtained authentic cannon to be put in place, although his interest in the fort waned as he grew older and business interests took his attention; he also began to experience health issues.[29]

Although nowhere nearly as well funded, operated, or beloved as the national parks established during this era, such as Manassas, Richmond, and Appomattox, the state parks that emerged were nevertheless very important in the preservation process. Many preserved portions of famous battlefields, providing a basis for future work, and supplemented federal efforts by providing an additional outlet for preservation efforts, primarily those that the federal government had rejected but were important nonetheless. As with many state parks, the rise of these parks enhanced the newer generation's ideas of moving away from a tactical emphasis as provided by the veterans. As was the case on a limited level with the NPS, where one superintendent even implored visitors to look beyond history and enjoy "another side to the notable Battlefield," in this case redbuds and dogwoods, the state parks took the new emphasis to a much broader level, even providing ample recreational areas right on the battlefields. The old veterans would certainly have objected to swimming pools and ball fields on their old battle sites, but by this time only a very few veterans were still around and the parks had to change to meet the wishes and desires of the newer visiting generation. As attitudes changed, many battlefield preservationists tried to keep pace.[30]

III

The New Deal also had a profound effect on those battlefields already established and the development of those just coming into being. Little money was appropriated outright for battlefield preservation, but the New Deal offered a significant amount of money for park projects, with agencies such as the Civilian Conservation Corps, Public Works Administration (PWA), Civil Works Administration (CWA), and numerous other alphabet-soup agencies with high-sounding acronyms providing unprecedented numbers of workers and funding. Park managers who were at all familiar with the histories of the military parks no doubt realized the boon of the influx of laborers to their sites that only a decade or two before had struggled to even have a superintendent in charge, much less a large, permanent workforce. With the need to put Americans to work during the Great Depression, however, it mattered little what that labor was as long as it was work that could provide paychecks to workers. The immediate hope was relief for the millions of Americans who were unemployed, with the more long-term desire being recovery from the massive Depression then rocking the world.[31]

Yet the New Deal had a larger impact on the battlefields than just relief and recovery. Although the influx of labor was beneficial to park managers, it nevertheless symbolized in clear form the switch that had taken place in terms of the purposes of the battlefields. The veterans had desired their battlefield parks to reflect the way the ground looked on the specific days of battle decades ago, and even the War Department administrators kept a certain military mentality when managing the parks after the commissions went out of existence, but the National Park Service was never oriented toward the old veterans' desires. The massive change wrought by the New Deal workers completely transformed the parks from anything the old veterans could have ever envisioned. Specifically, there was the twofold emphasis on restoration and accessibility, each of which altered the original battlefields and was geared toward the general public. Whereas the veterans and even the War Department officers had viewed the parks as memorials to the war generation and even study grounds for current military officers, the National Park Service viewed the parks as the people's battlefields and geared them toward the general public. One Civilian Conservation Corps official at Petersburg tellingly wrote that the main intent of the work on that battlefield was to "make the area more beautiful and interesting to the public."[32]

Changes, therefore, quickly occurred that forever altered the battlefields, one Gettysburg official declaring the work remedying the "accumulation of years of needed clean-up work." Restoration of various park properties included everything from restoring earthen and masonry fortifications to revitalizing buildings. The similar idea of public convenience ushered in a massive building program as well, including constructing new public contact stations and visitor centers, altering, widening, or significantly changing historic roadways, increasing hiking trails through battlefield forests, and increasing attention to public interpretation and education, or what the veterans and military officers would have considered dumbing down the story. One NPS official, in fact, wrote of "present[ing] to the casual layman certain outline facts." The results were vastly different battlefields coming out of the New Deal.[33]

Examples abound as to the negative tangible and physical results of New Deal agencies. At Shiloh, for example, the Tennessee Valley Authority (TVA), one of Franklin D. Roosevelt's 1933 "hundred days" achievements, proved a great boon to the area but adversely affected the battlefield. With the water level much higher and the addition of year-round navigation, water submerged a large portion of Pittsburg Landing and caused erosion along the great bend of the river, leading to damage on the park roadways and the famous Indian mounds on the bluffs south of the landing. Unwise tree cutting along the banks did not help either. In addition, the TVA's flooding of the river basin affected other battlefields as well, including Johnsonville, site of Nathan Bedford Forrest's defeat of several gunboats. Most notably, the rising waters behind Kentucky Dam completely flooded Fort Henry, which has not been seen since the 1940s, although the TVA acquired (and later transferred to the Forestry Service) some of the outer works in its Land Between the Lakes refuge.[34]

Other New Deal agencies also worked at the battlefields. One of the initial New Deal efforts was the Civil Works Administration, which was a temporary agency intended to provide relief during the hard winter of 1933–34. As did the state-run Federal Emergency Relief Administration, the CWA began in December 1933 and lasted only through April 1934. Yet it was an early employer of historians from which the NPS benefited as it began to grow into a historic-minded agency. At Fort Donelson from December 15, 1933, to April 25, 1934, for example, the CWA employed hundreds of men and three women to plant trees, work on erosion control, apply gravel to roads, and perform a cleanup. In all, the total cost of labor and materials came to $29,287.14. Historical work was also carried out with the assistance of seven historians, guides, and a stenographer. This historical work was divided into two parts: research and public relations. Obviously the historians did the research and the guides performed tours and school talks and advertised in local media. Similar work went on at Gettysburg and Antietam, where the labor was divided between historical research and cleaning the Philadelphia Brigade monument area. At Kennesaw Mountain, CWA workers built dams to control erosion, planted grass and trees, and built hiking trails.[35]

The Civil Works Administration laborers at Shiloh primarily worked for Smithsonian Institution archeologist Frank H. H. Roberts Jr. and his assistant, Moreau B. C. Chambers. The archeologists directed digs at the Indian mounds within the park, and the CWA personnel performed the work. Unfortunately, the workers were not trained in archeology and were not that careful about their labor. Records noted "skull smashed in finding" or "skull when found was in good condition but was damaged by visitors during our absence." Other CWA workers labored on erosion control, road construction, and general cleaning, as well as historical work in which local writers turned out 106 "Historical Reports."[36]

One of the best-known agencies of the New Deal, the Civilian Conservation Corps also affected the battlefields' physical makeup. Initially known as Emergency Conservation Work, the CCC employed young men in national and state parks to perform reforestation, erosion control, and fire maintenance work. World War I veterans asked to be included, and thousands were, including African American veterans of the war. At Petersburg, for example, an influx of staff and workers drastically aided that park in its development. A camp superintendent, foremen, engineers, historians, technicians, mechanics, blacksmiths, and clerks were all part of the CCC company in addition to the actual work force, which normally numbered over a hundred men. Company 1364 made its camp at Fort Stedman, and the location included barracks, mess halls, an infirmary, recreation halls, and even an athletic field, all of which transformed the original landscape. The men worked to "clean up the dense undergrowth from the earthworks so as to make them visible from park drives." They then seeded "wire grass" to keep down erosion. Later, they planted trees and sodded roadways, and the park "gradually emerged from its wild state," one official noted. The camp itself was perfectly maintained, with stone pillars marking the entrance and "spacious lawns . . . , fish pond, and flower boxes."[37]

Civilian Conservation Corps restoration efforts changed the appearance of the battlefields and at times historic earthworks and buildings elsewhere as well. At Fort Pulaski, Company 460 restored "decayed casemate floors," brickwork, and leaks in lead roof sheeting. They also wired the fort for electricity and telephones and created a new drainage system. "Sally-port doors [were] made to operate," read one report. Similarly at Vicksburg, the workers battled the loose soil by filling in washes and gullies and reconstructing the vast earthworks. One historian has surmised, "To a considerable extent, the Vicksburg battleground today is the product of CCC landscaping." The same occurred at Fort Donelson, where laborers restored the Confederate powder magazine and "contributed to the beautification about the Confederate Memorial erected by the United Daughters of the Confederacy." The workers also quarried rock, built a road to the top of Big Kennesaw Mountain at that battlefield, and built the Adolph Ochs Observatory Museum at Point Park at Chattanooga. Fredericksburg and Spotsylvania saw CCC camps at its Chancellorsville, Spotsylvania, and Wilderness units.[38]

Some battlefields produced a different sort of Civilian Conservation Corps history because some camps were made up of African American enrollees. African American veterans of World War I worked in the camp at Richmond, where they cleared land, improved roads, and built a visitor center. Another camp was transferred to Appomattox, where they worked on the bypass and restored or rebuilt historic houses. Two African American companies were at Gettysburg, one camp at Pitzer's Woods and another at McMillan's Woods, where they provided fire prevention, erosion control, sodding, and cleaning. One of the camps was actually officered and staffed entirely by blacks, an anomaly in itself in the Civilian Conservation Corps.[39]

Few racial problems developed in Pennsylvania, but Shiloh was different. It also received two African American camps, one on the battlefield itself and one stationed at nearby Corinth, Mississippi, to work on the "general beautification of [the] highway" that connected the two. The result was nevertheless the same in terms of changing the landscape. Workers at the Shiloh camp engaged in road work, erosion control, landscaping, forestry management, and fire prevention. At times they channeled creeks to allow better flow and built check dams to ease erosion. Unfortunately, segregation and racism reared their ugly heads, and the enrollees faced segregation even regarding where they could picnic with their families. "Complete segregation of white and colored enrollees" was the official CCC language. Politicians battled over the issue, with Senator Kenneth McKellar of Tennessee writing that "colored camps are problems, and the only way they can be managed is to take them up with the local authorities before making a recommendation." African Americans fought back. "We are advised," the National Association for the Advancement of Colored People leadership informed the Civilian Conservation Corps, "that a gang of outsiders working around the [Shiloh] camp steal the clothing and shoes of the enrollees for which the enrollees have to pay; that no serious effort is made by the officers to patrol the camp so that the property of the enrollees can be protected; that there is a further complaint about food." Despite the racial problems, the CCC workers transformed Shiloh and many other parks, but the racial episodes only underscored that in terms of battlefield preservation and Civil War memory, the parks were still solidly in the throes of the reconciliationist memory that completely ignored racial issues.[40]

Other New Deal agencies were also at work on the battlefields. The Public Works Administration, part of the National Industrial Recovery Act, provided schools, courthouses, and hospitals all across the nation, as well as railroads, tunnels, bridges, and even the aircraft carriers *Yorktown* and *Enterprise*. It also heavily influenced the battlefields. At Shiloh, PWA funds provided upgrades in the sewage, water, and electrical systems and allowed the building of two entrance stations, four houses for staff members, a concessions building, and a large administration building that is still being used as the visitor center today. It also provided for a new visitor center at Chickamauga. Public Works Administration funds at Fort Donelson "constructed roads which enable[d] the visitor to travel by automobile or bus to many of the major points of interest." Workers used PWA funds at Stones River to grade road banks and seed grass as well as create a sight barrier between the Hazen Monument and "objectionable views." At Gettysburg, the PWA funded repair of historic farm buildings and trails and provided new contact stations, and at Antietam the funds were used to repoint monuments.[41]

Smaller agencies also provided funds and workers for the battlefields. The Federal Emergency Relief Administration and its later designation, the Works Progress Administration (WPA), provided guides at Stones River for visitors to utilize when touring the park and funded the restoration of Fort Negley at Nashville. The WPA likewise fostered fencing, cleaning, and removal of dead trees at Antietam, and it provided visitor and traffic studies at Gettysburg and "outdoor" maps at Richmond. At the same time, the National Youth Administration provided workers for cleaning bronze tablets there. Although not officially New Deal entities, other government agencies also transformed battlefields during this time. At Shiloh, the Bureau of Public Roads and U.S. Geological Survey concreted and surfaced roadways, at times changing their historic routes and cutting 1862-era trees. "The principal obstacles were trees," one report read, "especially those old enough to have existed at the time of the Battle of Shiloh." The writer reported, "It was of course impossible to avoid cutting some trees." The road bureau also worked heavily at Gettysburg.[42]

The New Deal agencies were busy at nonfederal sites as well. At Columbus-Belmont in Kentucky, a Civilian Conservation Corps camp built a curved roadway and parking area, a picnic area with concrete ovens, and trails, and restored one of the earthen redoubts and the Confederate dispensary. Workers also mounted a thirty-two-pound cannon and the famous sixteen-foot anchor used to hold the chain that stretched across the river during the war. The CCC also completely revolutionized Fort Macon into a state park and worked hard at Fort Morgan on Mobile Bay, refurbishing the part of the fort that had fallen into disarray. Many of the post–Civil War structures there were removed with Works Progress Administration and Civilian Conservation Corps funds and workers, and the laborers also built a road from nearby Gulf Shores, Alabama, while repairing some of the brick work and other Civil War–era facilities. Works Progress Administration work also helped the Arkansas Post State Park build camping cabins.[43]

There remained opposition to the work of these New Deal agencies, however, and portions of their efforts continued to illustrate the growing fracture in the reconciliationist viewpoint and the renewal of newer animosities between the sections. At Chickamauga and Chattanooga National Military Park, for example, a dispute arose over the park's new entrance road. Director Arno B. Cammerer of the NPS sent Conrad Wirth down to foster an agreement, which he did. He quickly held a groundbreaking, but at the event he was introduced to the animosity some Southerners still felt over the war. Two older ladies carrying Confederate flags refused to be seen in the picture with Wirth, who was born in Connecticut. "It seems they were unwilling to have a Yankee in the picture with them," Wirth noted.[44]

Although time did not stand still and progress was inevitable, the New Deal had a huge impact on the battlefields, just as it did on the nation's entire landscape. Battlefields by definition are more affected by physical transformation than most state or federal parks, and they were certainly more so given the early veteran care for their landscapes as historic fabrics. The New Deal work had a drastic effect on the battlefield landscapes, including everything from erosion control to water and fire management to placing new buildings on the battlefields at Shiloh, Chickamauga, Vicksburg, and a host of newer sites. Perhaps most transformative were the restoration projects at battlefields, specifically with earthworks or some other type of fortifications. The efforts at Fort Pulaski, Petersburg, and Vicksburg were highly questionable in terms of preservation, and much of what visitors see today dates back to the 1930s and the New Deal work instead of the Civil War. All in all, the New Deal was a major effort to relieve and recover, and it was paradoxically successful only in the former. For battlefields, the New Deal was a contradiction of massive progress in terms of modernization and visitor accommodations for the modern public, but it was often done at the expense of the historic fabric the veterans had cared for so dearly.[45]

IV

If the 1930s were ample years both for the establishment of new parks and the revitalization of already existing battlefields, the 1940s were the exact opposite. World affairs had an important impact of preservation efforts. Labor and money were easily attainable during the 1930s, but those funds and workers dried up in the 1940s as the United States went to war. The battlefields themselves were affected as cutbacks occurred and staffs went off to war, but the establishment of parks was also curtailed. Congress was focused on the war effort, and the state legislatures were largely involved with caring for their own citizens. As a result, little except a small authorization for Harpers Ferry and a designation of a few small sites connected to the Atlanta campaign emerged between Manassas's establishment in 1940 and the end of World War II. Congress passed the Harpers Ferry authorization in 1944, but like Monocacy it was not to be an actual park until the land was donated. Similarly, in October 1944, Acting Secretary of the

Interior Abe Fortas declared under the Historic Sites Act five separate Atlanta campaign areas (Ringgold, Rocky Face Ridge, Resaca, Cassville, and New Hope Church) of only fifteen acres total to be collectively the Atlanta Campaign National Historic Site. The land was federally owned, having been acquired in the late 1930s under the Historic Sites Act, and was thus eligible for park status by declaration. Still, it was not a major park, and the land had already been acquired. As a result, not a single battlefield park of any kind was preserved while new battlefields abroad were being fashioned in a new war.[46]

World War II also affected the existing parks in one way or another, whether it was through a lack of staffing, lack of funding, or lack of visitors. Some parks were more affected than others, with isolated battlefields such as Antietam or Shiloh suffering far less impact. Although larger parks along major travel routes would see more changes, it fell to those battlefields that were near military installations to see the most change. As was the case with Gettysburg and Chickamauga in World War I, these parks were again affected, although to a lesser degree than in the earlier worldwide conflict. Still, the results were felt, primarily on the land itself. At Petersburg, for example, a reinvigorated Fort Lee saw battlefield land used for a variety of purposes. A hundred-acre portion of the park was set aside as a hospital, and a much larger section provided for a quartermaster training school. The quartermaster students often used the park for training, particularly studying the problems faced in supplying the armies during the Civil War around Petersburg. The park staff, most notably the historians, were active in working with the army in training these officers. Heavy traffic by the army also caused concern over physical harm to the parks, and roads were heavily damaged until a compromise was worked out in which the army took over maintenance. The army effort at Fort Lee also necessitated additional progress in terms of modern aids such as power lines and water reservoirs, which were built on the park. As troops came and went not only to Fort Lee but also to the numerous military installations along the Eastern Seaboard, the Petersburg battlefield likewise became a popular place to bivouac overnight for large caravans of troops on trucks. Obviously, government land could be more effectively used than private acreage, so Petersburg became a haven for transient troops. Despite the damage to the resource and the additional support required, the park staff accomplished its task despite having to close public contact stations due to the lack of personnel.[47]

A similar phenomenon played out at Gettysburg. Although not on major transportation corridors, Gettysburg was nevertheless involved due to its status as well as its history of housing army instillations, particularly during World War I. This time, the army also used part of the field, although not nearly to the extent of twenty years before. Some troops' arrival caused more concern than others, with a particularly invasive issue being quartermaster troops who moved into museum workers' already cramped offices; space was now even more at a premium. On the battlefield, the army set up the small Camp George H. Sharpe at one of the old Civilian Conservation Corps camps. Although an army instillation, it was not a primary base and had only a few soldiers garrisoning it at any time. Perhaps most problematic were two German prisoner of war camps established right on the battlefield. The camps, which at times housed over nine hundred prisoners, contained captured German soldiers who were let out on work details. A few escapes occurred, but the fugitives were quickly apprehended and the camps did not seem to cause much adverse reaction from the local public.[48]

Chickamauga was the battlefield with the most history of housing army troops. It was extensively used both in the Spanish-American War and World War I. The proximity of Fort Oglethorpe adjacent to the park ensured military activity there, although like Gettysburg it was this time much muted and in no way as intrusive as during the two previous wars. Most of the military activity was confined to the fort itself, although the army at times could not help but utilize the thousands of acres of government land nearby. The army nevertheless established a Provost Marshal General's School at McDonald Field, although the school did not remain in service long. In its most important and famous contribution, the battlefield then hosted, in the buildings of the old provost school, a Women's Army Auxiliary Corps (WAAC) training center. The center gained much local and national attention as large numbers of women came through the park throughout the war, even netting a visit from President Roosevelt himself. The park superintendent described the effect as the female soldiers were drawn up in formation: "[The WAACs] did not know what was in the offing. They had been told to prepare for inspection." They soon learned better, however, when a twenty-one-gun salute occurred and the presidential motorcade came to a stop in front of their formation. It was "a day memorable in the lives of every WAAC at Chickamauga Park," the superintendent wrote. In addition, like the other battlefields, Chickamauga also had quite a large number of transient troops moving through the area and camping at Wilder Field.[49]

Other battlefields were also affected, with some, particularly the coastal fortifications that had been let go by the War Department, being called back into service. The CCC had restored Fort Pulaski between 1933 and 1942, but with war the fort suddenly became a logical defensive attribute. It was closed to the public, and although the chances of an attack were slim, the military utilized the fort and the surrounding area for military purposes. A nearby island that had been added to the national monument in 1936 also became the site of a naval base. Similarly, Fort Macon was also brought back into military service. The CCC had converted it into one of North Carolina's premier state parks, but the war created a need for defense and so the War Department leased it from the state during the war.

Like Fort Pulaski, Fort Macon was also closed to the public and a coastal artillery garrison was based there. The same thing happened at Alabama's Fort Morgan, although there was less of a threat to the Gulf Coast than to the Atlantic Seaboard. Still, the military reoccupied Fort Morgan, even though it was a state park, and equipped it with modern weaponry. It served as a training ground for coastal artillery.[50]

In addition to the use of the parks by military personnel, the loss of large amounts of manpower significantly affected the sites. For example, many Civilian Conservation Corps camps went out of existence, and NPS employees were cut at the various parks as well. Speaking of completing Appomattox's restoration, one NPS official wrote that "the outbreak of World War II and then the Korean War made it impossible to achieve this goal." One Richmond official admitted that by the time the war came, the work was "simply a problem of maintenance," and many CCC camps were moved or severely downsized to side camps at the battlefields; most closed by 1942. The removal of all that manpower left the NPS with a shortage of labor, Floyd Taylor at Richmond writing during the war that "meanwhile much of the fine development of previous years had become a total loss, and, to the writer, it is as though he left the Park in 1940 and returned about 1935." At Manassas, visitation was anemic, although many military personnel came from nearby Quantico and Fort Belvoir; Superintendent Joseph M. Hanson was at times the only staff person on site. Similarly, Superintendent James R. McConaghie at Vicksburg had to patrol the park himself and even at times take the entrance fees at the visitor center. In order to gain more visitation and thus money for staff, McConaghie hit on a major public relations campaign when he organized a July 4 celebration at the park, that day also being Vicksburg's surrender date. He falsely called it the first celebration of the date since the Civil War. His effort was a success, at the cost of igniting a major false rumor that has been hard to kill.[51]

In perhaps the most noticeable damage done to the battlefields, many lost some of their tablets and monumentation as commemorative objects were put into scrap metal drives. At Perryville, anniversary activities stopped during the war and a few of the commemorative cannon were included in the drive and melted down for the World War II effort. At Vicksburg, many of the original park commission tablets and signs were hauled off for scrap during the war effort, some twenty-five tons. The same thing occurred at Chickamauga, netting primarily broken tablets and unused cannon balls. Fortunately, an idea to remove the metal portions of the park's monuments did not come to fruition. At Gettysburg, the park provided some eighteen tons of scrap metal, including signs and actual Civil War cannon. The park even developed plans to rate levels of scrapping, even including the metallic portions of monuments. Fortunately, that never came about.[52]

Although the major need was to win the war and all assets were utilized to attain that goal, the preserved battlefields were nevertheless damaged due to increased activity. Large numbers of marching soldiers and heavier use damaged both roads and fields, but other activities such as drilling and the establishment of rifle ranges, buildings, and even recreational locations such as theaters took their toll. But the major impact on the battlefield preservation movement was the quick halt made to the establishment of additional preserved battlefields, both federal and state. A flurry of activity had begun in the mid-1920s and continued to 1940, but there it stopped. And although no one knew it at the time, the United States would emerge from World War II in 1945 a changed nation, with very different ideals and perspectives. As a result, the battlefield preservation movement which had progressed so quickly in the last decade and a half was never really restarted, causing a clear break with the preservation generations that came afterward.[53]

V

The United States of America was indeed a very different nation in 1945 than it had been in 1933. Having emerged from the Great Depression, World War II, and the massive spending on both, the nation's infrastructure was now stabilized. The era also ushered in what historians call the "welfare state," which would become more permanent in future decades. The world war transformed American culture, society, politics, and economics, and sparked the Cold War. Americans accordingly emerged from the whirlwind years of the New Deal and World War II a changed people.[54]

Civil War battlefield preservation also changed during this period. Federal preservation of major battlefields had continued with Appomattox, Richmond, Kennesaw Mountain, and Manassas, but these were very different sites from their predecessors. Several of these battlefields, most notably Monocacy, had merely been authorized but had no appropriation to carry the desire into effect. Only through funding by New Deal agencies did others such as Appomattox and Manassas come into being, and the state of Virginia donated Richmond's battlefields. While spending massive amounts of money on the New Deal, Congress was loathe to spend any additional funds on specific battlefield appropriations, and had the New Deal not existed many of the fields would never have been established. As a case in point, Monocacy never received any New Deal funds and was destined to wallow for decades until an appropriation restarted the effort. In addition, there was an almost complete lack of any initial preservation action, such as the establishment of enabling legislation, federal or state, during World War II.[55]

Part of the change in preservation activities was tied to the corresponding change in American ideals toward the parks themselves and, specifically, toward battlefields. Although there was still plenty of reconciliation on display, as evidenced by Roosevelt's speech in 1938 at the peace flame at Gettysburg and the patriotism-rich war years when North and South again fought together as one, the reconciliationist movement was beginning to wear away in the face of newer ideals and attitudes. The insistence that Virginia battlefields should be preserved by Southerners as state and local parks rather than by Northerners with their "yankee historians" was a prominent if not widespread crack in the armor of reconciliation. And it grew over time. Animosity between "certain unreconstructed factions in the South, and . . . irreconcilable forces in the North" almost derailed the famous 1938 Gettysburg reunion.[56]

Perhaps the larger defining reason behind the shift in ideals had to do with the passage of time. As the nation moved further from the 1860s, and particularly with the passing of the veteran generation, most immediate connections with the war passed as well. Additional wars and millions of newer veterans also had an effect. Now references to the Civil War no longer carried the connotation of "our" war, "our" battlefields, or honoring "our" brothers in arms; increasingly, references to the Civil War took on more historic phrases. The detachment of the people from the war itself and the emergence of new wars drastically altered the way Americans viewed the Civil War. The effect was seen in what the War Department and National Park Service spent money on in building the parks. At a time when veterans were the chief clientele, the War Department placed monuments, tablets, cannon, and markers to cater to a war-familiar public. The NPS, on the other hand, strove to educate and assist a much less martial public in the 1930s and 1940s, providing parking areas, restrooms, and visitor contact areas. One NPS official at Vicksburg described the new type of visitors as "out for a good time" and basically of two classes: "Garden Club people—high class; Mardi Gras people—not so high."[57]

Above all, the manner in which Americans used battlefields also changed as the nation's collective memory shifted. In the Reconstruction generation after the war, the battlefields were used as partisan memorials to each side as the flames of animosity still raged. Then, in the golden age, those flames died down as the battlefields were used as reconciliation devices to bring the sections together, obviously being used as a tool to cement white Northerners and Southerners at the expense of African Americans. Next, as the veteran generation passed away in the 1910s and 1920s, the battlefield parks still under the War Department were used primarily as larger-than-life lessons of America's martial and political prowess. Employed physically during World War I, the battlefields embodied the spirit of a nation that saved the world for democracy by almost superhuman military efforts half a world away. Such a view only reinforced earlier generations of Americans who had fought first to create and then to sustain this widely acclaimed best government. Americans' views of battlefields changed again in the 1930s and 1940s, however, although they were still within the broader constructs of the reconciliation theme. Amid the throes of the Great Depression, Americans needed assurance of their ability to wade through problems, and the battlefields of the Civil War were part of a larger context of Americanism that assured modern Americans that previous generations had conquered much larger problems than they now faced, and so could they. As World War II rolled around, the same spirit drove Americans once again to see themselves as the world's rescuer, all the while taking lessons from previous generations who had met large threats victoriously. And many of the fields were themselves used to mobilize and train men and women for this new effort. The battlefields, as part of the larger celebration of the United States, gave comfort, stability, and inspiration in hard times. And the NPS was active in providing this lesson, as evidenced by one regional office memo requiring that "all types of historical park literature should place greater emphasis upon the principles of freedom, democracy, and self rule that underlie the basic political philosophy of the American people and our constitution. . . . Patriotism and appreciation of American traditions should be emphasized."[58]

The reasons given for establishing battlefields also changed. Whereas veterans in the 1890s and even the 1920s spoke of honoring their armies, their dead, and their bravery, now park establishers spoke of new ideals—such as preserving history. One official said of Stones River, "It's aim is not to glorify war, but to pass on to future generations an example of the idealism of men—Americans, both Confederate and Union—who fought for great principles." Preservationists also began to see battlefields in the light of natural resources and providing the public with beautiful landscapes and wildlife to view. In some instances, recreation became a major plus for park establishment, and some even began to talk of the tourism benefits of establishing national parks. Perhaps one NPS official at Richmond described the new mentality best when he spoke of the park's "threefold purpose." It still intended to honor "heroic sacrifice" and "to make readily comprehensible to the public the military activities," but it also created "a place where people may go to find natural beauty and recreation, as well as instruction." Added to that was the effort "to preserve and develop the charm of scenery and animal life now extant in the area, and to develop sources of pleasure which are deemed desirable." Although all these reasons were valid, they diluted the original purpose behind the veterans' establishment of battlefields, and continued to ignore the centrality of slavery as a major cause of the Civil War.[59]

A corresponding change occurred when visitors came to parks for reasons other than Civil War commemoration. Government officials admitted in 1933 that "in the National Park Service a close relationship exists and must continue to exist between recreational and educational features. While a historical park is rightly regarded as hallowed ground, and while a dignity in keeping with its nature will continue to be maintained, the visitor is not actuated by a desire to weep for departed heroes, he wished primarily to enjoy his visit, and it is certainly to that extent a recreational visit." While later NPS officials sought to redefine recreation as "refreshment of body or mind," newer generations of Americans began to use the parks for a variety of activities. The continuance of golf courses inside the parks at Petersburg and Chickamauga even into NPS years was telling, as was the establishment of horse trails at those parks as well as at Fredericksburg. Historical pageants were numerous, but perhaps the Miss Antietam pageant in the 1930s was the low point of that park's anniversary events.[60]

Obviously, the changing times and ideals spurred a similar change in the memory of the war. Where the reconciliationist view had been dominant since the 1890s, fostered by the veterans themselves and to a certain extent by the military officers who ran the parks thereafter, the new NPS governance created an atmosphere in which a new memory began to develop: "Modern 'tourists' are looking for a park as well as a battlefield." Reconciliation was still a large part of Americans' memory of the war, but they also increasingly viewed the war through other lenses. The key here too was the passing of the veteran generation, which by 1945 was all but gone. Those who were still alive were not able to travel to the battlefields or attend reunions and celebrations, much less promote their veteran-inspired memory of the war; certainly, they had little if any effect on the preservation process. Accordingly, the American people came to view the war as a historic event rather than as a personal experience, but that in itself was a necessary and important change for the American public. It provided separation from the older reconciliationist memory, firmly ending the conscious thought of "our" war. The result allowed a newer interpretation of the war to emerge in the next era, one that would once again be distinctly tied to the larger cultural and social events of the nation and the causes of the Civil War.[61]

That new interpretation included a contextual awareness of the war, as one NPS official at Vicksburg noted: "The story imparted to the visitor [by the guides] is not simply a recital of events connected with the siege, but an interpretive account of the siege, conveying the importance of this engagement in relation to the war as a whole and the significance of Vicksburg in the development of American life and institutions." Greater emphasis was placed on context, civilians, and other nontactical history, but no mention was yet made regarding slavery and race as causes for the war. While the battlefields were expanding their interpretive scope, they were still mostly tied to the old reconciliationist milieu in an effort to steer clear of these divisive issues. And in that realm, the parks of this New Deal and war generation continued to serve well—as white uniters, not dividers.[62]

5

The Centennial Era,
1945–1965

A distinctly new type of battlefield emerged as the B-29 bomber *Enola Gay* sped
away from its harrowing work over the skies of Hiroshima, Japan. August 6, 1945,
obviously had a profound effect on the world; it not only began the end of World
War II but also portended a much more dangerous type of warfare. In the realm
of battlefield preservation, the use and transportation of nuclear weapons by air
also portended a major change in how war was fought, leaving obsolete the fortifications that had been the staple of America's defense for nearly two centuries.
As a result, the future of Civil War battlefield preservation, no less than human
history itself, would evolve in concert as the nation turned to preserving the historic and now-obsolete fortifications. If World War II had a drastic effect on the
United States as a whole and on battlefield preservation in particular, the ensuing
decade and a half illustrated those changes and their effects. Changing attitudes
and ideals, and the memory of the Civil War, all combined to alter the very face
of battlefield preservation during the 1950s and early 1960s, creating an entirely
different movement that was all but disconnected from the former eras. Added
to that was the excitement over the centennial of the Civil War, which produced
a much wider yet drastically different preservation movement.[1]

During the postwar years, it was as if the preservation movement had to be
restarted after the lack of almost any work during World War II, and the only

entity that was in any position to call for or provide for continuity was itself changing. The NPS had become so dependent on New Deal funding in the 1930s that it was only able to establish and preserve new battlefields and then transform them into actual parks with the help of the various New Deal agencies that provided purchase money, laborers, and rehabilitation funds. That source dried up during the war, however, and the NPS in the late 1940s and 1950s was a much leaner agency that would not see a major Civil War park created until just before the centennial. The Civil War–related parks that were established in the meantime were either forts that were no longer needed by the military or tangential parks that were primarily focused on other history or even nature but by happenstance contained some historic Civil War resources.[2]

A primary reason the NPS gained former forts was because so many were decommissioned soon after World War II. With the birth of aviation and, later, the development of rocketry that could carry nuclear payloads, the United States had to shift its longstanding first line of defense, no longer focusing on the navy and coastal fortifications. The ability to fly over coastal defenses, with either airplanes or rockets, made these forts obsolete as America's first line of defense. That duty shifted to nuclear deterrence and massive retaliation. Thus the War Department and, after 1947, the newly named Department of Defense began to let them go, and the logical place to send them was to the various park systems.[3]

Another factor, as always, was money. The Great Depression and World War II had plunged America deep into debt, and the 1950s saw a cut in spending on discretionary items. The Korean War also cost billions, as did the change in the "American Way of War" from mobilization and demobilization during wartime to keeping a large standing army. Veteran programs such as the new GI bill also cost millions. In regard to the NPS specifically, the agency turned from outright preservation toward consolidating what it already had. Its Mission 66 plan, implemented in the mid-1950s to rebuild the parks' infrastructures, was intended to revitalize the federal park system by 1966, the fiftieth anniversary of the NPS. The result was that money went to existing parks rather than to the creation of new ones.[4]

Other factors were also involved in the change in preservation focus. By the end of World War II in 1945, America had three brand new generations of veterans from the three newest wars to consider and honor. The 1950s saw the last living Civil War veterans replaced with veterans of the Korean War, although many of those soldiers were also World War II veterans. The emphasis was on the living and returning veterans of the newest wars and the aging veterans of World War I—even the Spanish-American War. By 1960, the last of the living veterans of the Civil War had died, and the United States concluded its tangible connection with the conflict and moved it fully into the realm of history.[5]

Another factor changing American attitudes during this era was the growing civil rights movement. Due in part to the changes wrought by World War II, African Americans made slow gains throughout the 1940s and 1950s, including desegregation of the military and, via the courts, an end to government-sponsored segregation in schools. Although the movement would not burst into full bloom until the 1960s, during the Civil War centennial, the changing attitudes toward race in America nevertheless resulted in some rethinking of the causes of the war, African American participation in it, and the broader resulting accomplishments. It took a hundred years before the possibilities the Civil War had produced bore fruit in terms of full equality, and it would be a few more decades before the African American role in the war fully integrated itself into the battlefield preservation movement. Yet the foundations laid in this era enabled broader thinking on the subject.[6]

As a result of these economic and social factors, along with the simple fact that many of the more famous Civil War battlefields had already been preserved in some fashion prior to this era, a definite slowdown occurred in terms of federal preservation efforts. A small spike in federal work occurred for the centennial itself as the 1960s came nearer, but the larger effect was a transfer of preservation activity primarily to the state level, with numerous states taking the lead to preserve smaller battlefields and make them state parks. Some private efforts also took place, but the net result was a change from primarily federal preservation, as seen through the golden age, interregnum, and New Deal eras, to state and local preservation. And although no one could foresee it at the time, this change would be permanent. Never again would the federal government lead a massive movement to preserve Civil War battlefields. The result was a host of new sponsors of battlefield preservation, which were almost totally disconnected to the former movements and which did not bring to the process the expertise or resources that the federal government had provided.

I

The slowdown in federal Civil War battlefield preservation after World War II was evident in both the number of sites established by Congress and the type of parks preserved. In all, only two sites closely connected to the Civil War were saved during the 1940s and early 1950s. Two more were established in the years immediately prior to the centennial, but the 1950s plainly illustrated the reduction that would slow even more in the decades to come. Likewise, the types of battlefields established were mostly non–Civil War primary sites and were cost effective in that they were already owned by the government and required no transfer of money or appropriations. An example of the former was the Army Corps of Engineers' purchase of much of the land that would eventually surround the proposed Allatoona Lake in Georgia. Part of the land bought contained the October 1864 Allatoona battlefield, but the purchase was made for recreational purposes around the eventual lake. As another example, the Fort Caroline National Memorial in Florida emerged in 1953 and contained portions of the Saint John's Bluff battlefield, but it was largely preserved because of its sixteenth-century colonial history.[7]

The changing theory of preservation during this era included work that was in large part on historic forts still used in the 1940s for national defense but now unarguably outdated, a direct result of the United States' changing first line of defense. Fort Sumter in Charleston Harbor, for example, was deactivated in 1947. Being one of the most famous of all Civil War sites, the fort was obviously ripe for inclusion in the NPS but in actuality was already a major tourist attraction, even prior to World War II. Abandoned by the War Department, the fort nevertheless received visitors aboard vessels of several tourist operations as well as private boaters. There was also some interpretation of the site, including markers remembering Robert Anderson and the Federal garrison, both placed in the 1930s. Because of the regular tourist visitation to the somewhat dilapidated and dangerous ruins, the NPS had been involved in inspecting the fort since 1936, even then desiring ownership of the site. The city of Charleston's Historical Commission also pushed for preservation, but the War Department wanted to hold on to the fort and did so through World War II, until it became obvious it was worthless to national defense. The war had caused a regarrisoning of the fort with antiaircraft guns, and as a result it was closed to the public, but the end of the fighting brought its eventual decommissioning. The movement to make Fort Sumter a national memorial and part of the NPS began soon thereafter and quickly reaped vast benefits because of its government ownership. The Charleston commission, led by chairman Daniel Ravenel, began agitating for the fort and pushed for the inclusion of Fort Moultrie and Fort Johnson as well.[8]

The War Department made preservation a reality in 1947 when it decided to offer the fort as surplus material. South Carolina officials quickly jumped at the chance. Senator Burnet R. Maybank argued that it would be heresy to let it go to private hands: "You might as well offer the Statue of Liberty for sale." He and others quickly formalized legislation to transfer the fort from the War Department to the NPS, creating the Fort Sumter National Monument, although the simultaneous change in military organization required amending the bill to allow the Department of the Army under the Department of Defense to transfer it instead of the War Department. The Senate passed the bill in July 1947 and the House in April 1948, whereupon President Harry S. Truman signed it, completing the transfer.[9]

The NPS found major challenges in taking over Fort Sumter, however. Echoing the growing Southern heritage stance already seen so vividly at Richmond and Manassas, South Carolinians not surprisingly styled the fort as a shrine to the Confederacy. One local newspaper reported, "An historic site has been saved from a fate worse than Yankee cannon fire" and went on to argue that "the unbowed pride of the Confederacy, the grand old fort which never surrendered under the Confederate flag, stands ready to rise now to even greater heights." The newspaper also recommended which sources NPS historians should use, stating that "the Federal government, in its guide book, should not be permitted to use the description given in the *Encyclopedia Americana*, which is punk." One NPS official later declared, "Thus, the National Park Service received its baptism of fire in Charleston, South Carolina."[10]

Fort Sumter was indeed a dilapidated fort, one official calling it "a confused combination of century old ruins with newly obsolescent modern defense." The modern was not really that modern, however. Battery Huger, which had been built inside the fort in the late 1890s during the Spanish-American War era, provided a conundrum for Superintendent William W. Luckett, who found it difficult enough just to get to the site. Luckett and other NPS officials ultimately settled on leaving Battery Huger intact, as well as the fill that stabilized the new portion, despite it covering the eastern half of the original fort. They decided to interpret the Civil War actions in the unaltered ruins of the western side and use the newer battery facilities, to be interpreted as part of the "evolution of coastal fortification," as administration and public service areas.[11]

Luckett and a team of NPS personnel soon went to work, cleaning and renovating what had been transferred. It was a difficult task, Luckett writing in 1950 that "the superintendent found that he had inherited a buried fort, which was covered with weeds, debris of every description, and a series of old dilapidated buildings." Eventually the site was cleaned, renovated, stabilized, and opened to the public. Luckett placed eleven historical tablets around the fort, educating and interpreting its history to the public. He also emplaced cannon and an original flag that had flown over the fort, donated by the State Historical Society of Colorado of all people. More land on shore was eventually added as well, including a similarly deactivated Fort Moultrie in 1960.[12]

The only other major Civil War park established prior to the mid-1950s buildup to the centennial was Harpers Ferry, although it had a much broader history than strictly the Civil War. In fact, the House committee overseeing the bill noted that "the historic interest was not limited just to a period of 1861 and 1865" and required several amendments to broaden the outlook. Tinges of George Washington and Thomas Jefferson as well as slavery, early frontier settlement, and transportation loomed large in Harpers Ferry's history, in addition to the relatively minor Civil War action there in 1862. Indeed, the critical subject of slavery in the site's history resulted in Harpers Ferry's inclusion of the slavery issue at the site and foreshadowed the change in the NPS's treatment of the Civil War that would flower in the 1990s. One newspaper in 1951 illustrated that change, remarking, "John Brown's body lies a-mouldering in the grave at North Elba, New York. His soul goes marching on at Harper's Ferry, W. Va. West Virginia would like to keep the old fire eater's soul marching in a National Park near the site of his famous stand in 1859."[13]

The first attempts to create a park at Harpers Ferry dated back to the mid-1930s, when local citizens began to promote the idea and the NPS studied the potential of such a move. The plan had major supporters, including Storer College president Henry T. McDonald and Congressman Jennings Randolph. The two finalized the idea after touring the flood-devastated town in 1936. McDonald soon became head of the Harpers Ferry National Monument Committee and Randolph began action on the federal level. Illustrating the newer mindset of preserving history and earning tourist money, McDonald noted that "thousands of tourists will visit the section, which will benefit not only Harpers Ferry but the entire Eastern Panhandle of West Virginia." He also described "a continuous golden wave of wealth to this whole general section" and spoke of its "supreme interest to students of history, students of scenic beauty, and students of nature's surprising riches." Grand ideas emerged, including extending the Skyline Drive to Harpers Ferry and connecting it with another proposed parkway, the Lincoln Memorial Highway, which was to run from Washington to Gettysburg. The backers proposed to get Maryland and Virginia involved too, so that land in each of those states could be part of the proposed park.[14]

Randolph and McDonald worked tirelessly for the next several years, and it was critical that the process move quickly. At one time in the 1940s there was a feasibility study on creating a huge reservoir on the Potomac River, which would submerge the old town as well as many parts of the old Chesapeake and Ohio Canal. NPS officials argued against the move and were supportive of acquiring such a historic site. With little money, however, they had to wait. Congress was also "impressed with the importance of the project," one committee declared, but felt "this was a case in which Congress itself should fix the boundaries and with certain limitations." The money situation was on every mind, with the Department of the Interior even opposing an earlier 1943 bill that required the federal government to pay for the land. Acting Secretary Abe Fortas supported a replacement bill that required donation of the land, stating significantly in 1944 that "this [new] bill will not require any funds during the present war." Congress passed the new bill in 1944, requiring that the land be donated, another example illustrating how the federal government was getting out of large-scale battlefield acquisition and purchase. It would continue to accept historic sites, but others would have to pay for them. Nevertheless, wanting to move on with the process, NPS official Conrad L. Wirth wrote McDonald in 1944 that "Congressman Randolph had done an excellent job in getting the legislation through. The second step, to get the land, is yours; and the third, to properly develop and administer the Harpers Ferry National Monument, is ours." That success did come, once West Virginia acquired and donated to the federal government the lower town and certain higher ground tracts in the state in July 1953. At that time, the Harpers Ferry National Monument, later changed to "Historical Park," became official. Unfortunately, McDonald had died in 1951, before he saw his dream come true.[15]

The NPS quickly moved in, federal officials finding, as at Fort Sumter, a dilapidated, boarded-up old town. The NPS crews went to work and soon stabilized buildings, cleaned streets, removed nonhistoric buildings, established museums and parking lots, and set in place new water and drainage efforts. The NPS also thoroughly marked the park with hiking trails, signs, and maps. Over time, additional acreage came into the park, including land in Maryland and Virginia around the prongs of the Shenandoah and Potomac, which joined there.[16]

Despite Fort Sumter and Harpers Ferry joining the NPS in the late 1940s and early 1950s, federal preservation was obviously growing weaker. That only two permanent sites were created in the time prior to the growing centennial fever was telling, as was the fact that neither acquisition was funded primarily by the federal government. Seemingly gone were the days when congressmen could get standalone bills establishing their pet parks passed through Congress.

II

Although little funding emerged after World War II for new parks, there was money to be had for the NPS and its battlefields. Yet this new NPS funding was part of a backward-looking policy rather than a forward-looking effort to preserve additional sites as rehabilitation of the old parks rather than the creation of new ones became the approach. Accordingly, the Mission 66 program, intending to modernize the parks by the fiftieth anniversary of the NPS in 1966, took all the money the NPS had. Many Civil War battlefields consequently received upgrades during this time, despite the fact that many of them had gone through a massive overhaul and refurbishment less than twenty years before under the auspices of the New Deal.[17]

The plans and accomplishments of Mission 66 for existing Civil War battlefields were all aimed at the coming centennial celebrations. Projects ran the gamut from unique and site-specific work such as new docks and a wharf at Fort Sumter to more traditional infrastructure projects such as sewage and utility work at several parks, including Shiloh, Richmond, Chickamauga, Fort Pulaski, Fort Sumter, Kennesaw Mountain, and Vicksburg. Park housing for employees was proposed at Richmond, Petersburg, and Fort Donelson, and Richmond and Petersburg received comfort or entrance stations. Trail work and landscaping went on at Manassas, Shiloh, Stones River, and Kennesaw Mountain.[18]

Other improvements included the addition of historic jobs that helped the NPS interpret for and educate the public better. For instance, Petersburg and Fort Sumter received cannon with project funds, and Petersburg, Fort Pulaski, Fredericksburg, and Vicksburg all received revamped interpretive exhibits and signage. Other sites, including Appomattox, Kennesaw Mountain, and Vicksburg, desired work on important historic structures. Fort Pulaski also received funds for fort stabilization.[19]

Two areas of concentration seemed to be the focal points for Mission 66, however. Many parks received road and parking work. Manassas, Richmond, Shiloh, Stones River, Appomattox, Vicksburg, Chickamauga, Fort Donelson, Fredericksburg, and Kennesaw Mountain received funds for newer and better roads. Obviously, many of the parks contained multiple units or had disconnected sites, such as Richmond, Chickamauga and Chattanooga, and Fredericksburg and Spotsylvania, which created the need for good roads to move travelers to and from each site. Others, such as Fort Donelson, were still lacking a major tour route as of the 1950s, and Shiloh received the Highway 22 bypass, which unfortunately was not a bypass at all but did redirect traffic onto a fast-flowing alternative route outside the heart of the park.[20]

The major effort of Mission 66 was to provide adequate visitor centers so that the staff could greet the public and showcase historical exhibits, maps, and slideshows or films. In fact, Shiloh led the way regarding the latter in 1956 with the NPS's first motion picture interpretive film, *Shiloh: Portrait of a Battle*, which was shown at the park for the next fifty-six years and was only replaced in 2012, during the sesquicentennial of the battle. These new visitor centers also contained adequate staff offices, libraries, and other staff locations. And the centers played another significant if not obvious role, in that they helped expand the stories told at the individual sites. In the larger contextual thinking of the newer generations, these visitor centers contained much more thematic contexts of the Civil War, although the social changes of the 1960s were not sufficiently in force yet to cause a total examination of the causes of the war as they related to racial issues.[21]

At least twelve major battlefields received new visitor centers or expansions of older centers. For instance, the New Deal–era visitor centers at Shiloh, Chickamauga, and Manassas received expansions. Others received brand-new visitor centers even though their New Deal–era buildings were relatively new: Petersburg, Cold Harbor, Stones River, Chattanooga (Lookout Mountain's Point Park), Fort

Donelson, Gettysburg, Fort Sumter, Chancellorsville, Kennesaw Mountain, and Vicksburg. Most visitor centers looked very similar, being primarily one story at least at the front (some had lower levels on sloping ground). The centers were at times built to blend with the story being told at the park, such as Vicksburg's visitor center, which was created in association with replica earthworks leading to and from the building. Although these buildings have proved worthwhile ever since, and most are still in use today, they came at a time when NPS officials amazingly believed they should be put at the center of the most famous areas of fighting. The visitor center and cyclorama at Gettysburg emerged right on Cemetery Ridge, Antietam's developed right at the Dunker Church, and on and on went the placement of visitor centers right on some of the most significant areas of each battlefield.[22]

Despite the good work done in Mission 66, the plan nevertheless leveled two attacks on traditional preservation. The construction and building further removed what pureness these battlefields contained, although progress by that time was such that it had to be done. Indeed, Mission 66 took a great deal of criticism from traditional conservationists that it was geared more toward public conveniences than actual preservation of resources. Likewise, the money put into Mission 66 and the rehabilitation program likely kept some new preservation efforts off the table. The lack of preservation at any solely Civil War battlegrounds immediately prior to the centennial attested to the lack of willingness on the part of the NPS and Congress to preserve any more battlefields.[23]

In addition, a split was developing between the sections and eroding the reconciliationist memory of the war. As congressional committees held hearings on appropriating money for Mission 66, for example, Southern senators continually asked for appropriations for parks in their states, causing NPS director Conrad Wirth to notice that "the hearings took a great deal longer" when they were there. Senate committee chairman Carl T. Hayden of Arizona also noticed, and he joked, "Off the record, Connie, I thought the South lost the war between the states." Wirth shot back, "Yes, Senator they did, but they didn't lose a battle."[24]

Moreover, this period even witnessed the regression of preservation. The 1944 Atlanta Campaign National Historic Site was never really launched, and in September 1950, Congress rescinded the acting secretary of the interior's declaration of the site. The bill removed its national park status and instead vested the land to the state of Georgia for its governance and upkeep. Similarly at Vicksburg National Military Park, certain land, a total of nearly two hundred acres of siege lines complete with monuments and markers, was deemed unnecessary for continual inclusion in the park. The city of Vicksburg, which was effectively ringed by the park and whose expansion was for this reason thwarted, sought to control the lands east of town and began to talk about the idea of regaining the land even in the 1950s. A public outcry resulted, but the plan was formally established in 1963, ironically the hundredth anniversary of the siege. The NPS traded nearly two hundred acres on the south end of the park to the city and county in return for several hundred acres that joined the park farther to the north. The question then arose of what to do with all the monuments along the recently released roadways, and there soon emerged a plan to move them to the current site of the USS *Cairo* (there was no *Cairo* then, although that in and of itself is a unique preservation story) and create what Ed Bearss described as "a big monument marble orchard." He also noted that the only thing that kept the move from happening was that "too many of them [monuments] said 'happened here.'" Still, the deed was done, a morose Bearss declaring that "they gave away an invaluable part of the park that was protected to the City of Vicksburg under the understanding that the City of Vicksburg would maintain the land in a park-like character, but within a year, they'd bulldozed almost everything in there."[25]

Instead of preserving additional battlefields, it seemed Uncle Sam was having a hard time just keeping up with what he already had.

III

Because of the lack of NPS and federal government preservation throughout the late 1940s and early 1950s, the task of preserving new battlefields largely fell to state and private efforts. This venture took many forms, from simple historic markers being placed at various sites, such as by the Georgia Historical Commission, to the climax of state work, the state park. In the latter category, an early centennial-era state park came to be in Maryland along South Mountain, where severe fighting had raged prior to Antietam. Established in 1949, Gathland State Park carried with it a significant set of parameters, including the continual rise of recreation as a cause for preservation. Gathland sat astride the Appalachian Trail and providing a wider preserved area was the major impetus for creating the park. The fact that it contained portions of the severe fighting area at Crampton's Gap was a plus, but since the rest of the battlefield was not preserved, it seemed recreation was the key factor. Gathland also contained the 1896 War Correspondent's Memorial Arch, set in place by George Alfred Townsend when the land was his personal estate. Other state parks eventually also preserved locations of the widespread South Mountain battlefields, including George Washington State Park and the newer South Mountain State Battlefield, which also helped preserve Turner's Gap and Fox's Gap.[26]

A smaller effort at preservation occurred in 1955 at Staunton River Bridge in southern Virginia. The site of a small action where local home defense soldiers turned away a Federal cavalry raid during the Petersburg campaign, the battlefield of six and a half acres had once been donated to a couple of Confederate veterans. Still privately owned, the battlefield saw no preservation or commemoration until the local United Daughters of the Confederacy chapter placed a monument at the site in 1955 and asked the state to acquire the land. The Virginia legislature did so, taking the battlefield in donation and assigning it to a nearby state park. Unfortunately, little if any commemoration occurred thereafter.[27]

A similar small effort took place in North Dakota at the Killdeer Mountain battlefield in 1955. There, the July 1864 engagement against the Sioux continued the Federal pursuit of the Native Americans, ending in their rout at Killdeer Mountain. Little conservation took place prior to the 1950s, but in 1955 the state acquired a one-acre site. The site did, however, eventually contain a small monument erected in 1957 and the graves of two Federal soldiers who died in the battle.[28]

Even as smaller, tangential state parks emerged, a few major sites also developed. A major state park became a reality in 1954 at Mansfield, Louisiana. Earlier work by the United Daughters of the Confederacy had resulted in four acres being preserved, with numerous monuments going up in the 1920s. The UDC managed to acquire forty more acres by 1934, while at the same time several New Deal organizations worked at the park. State park status had to wait until the centennial fever hit, however, and it was only in 1954 that the state legislature authorized the state park system to accept the forty-four acres. The official deeding took place in February 1955, and the legislature passed two appropriations totaling seventy-five thousand dollars for improvements. That appropriation resulted in a new museum and visitor center opening on the anniversary of the battle, April 8, 1957. Since then, additional acreage as well as monumentation has also been added to the park.[29]

One of the most important Civil War battlefields not in the NPS system is Bentonville, site of one of the last major battles of the war as Joseph E. Johnston tried to stop Sherman's advance through North Carolina. Like Perryville, Bentonville was one of the only set-piece battles between major Civil War armies that was not included in the NPS. Little preservation or even commemoration had been done at Bentonville since the war—only the 1895 Confederate monument and a later 1927 UDC monument marking a Confederate line. North Carolina began the process of preservation in 1957, when the state legislature appropriated twenty-five thousand dollars to purchase fifty-one acres of land and the famous Harper House, which had served as a hospital during the battle. About the same time, local citizens formed the Bentonville Battleground Association and raised money to restore the house. That group later morphed into the larger Bentonville Battleground Advisory Committee, set up by the state archives, and it was tasked with raising money for a visitor center. It did so, and the legislature chipped in a large amount as well. The visitor center was dedicated on the one hundredth anniversary of the battle, March 21, 1965.[30]

A similar state operation was established at Grand Gulf in Mississippi. Site of the longtime Mississippi River town just south of Vicksburg, Grand Gulf was not a traditional battlefield in the Vicksburg campaign but the site of a naval bombardment as Ulysses S. Grant sought a place to land his army on the east side of the river. The town was destroyed and the earthworks became overgrown over the decades, along with being partially flooded at times by the river's rises and falls. The Mississippi legislature created the Grand Gulf Military Monument Commission in 1958 to acquire land for the park, and it did so over the next few years. The commission ultimately acquired two major sites, Fort Wade and Fort Coburn, and Governor Ross Barnett dedicated the park on May 6, 1962. The state also built a visitor center and museum, which was dedicated later in the decade when the park was officially opened to the public. Archaeological excavations likewise came along, but the entire work at Grand Gulf continued the redivergence between the sections over Civil War history. One report during this time period stated that "the cruel reconstruction policy forced upon Mississippi after the war all but killed off any hope of revival for devastated towns such as Grand Gulf." A later report illustrated an additional developing theme, especially at state parks: "The magnificent earthworks, made impregnable by [John] Bowen and his engineers, are relegated to a low priority in favor of non-related structures and picnic facilities."[31]

A similar effort took place at Lexington, Missouri, site of the September 1861 battle and surrender. After having various owners through the years, the battlefield finally gained some federal attention in the 1930s as the Works Progress Administration worked to stabilize the Anderson House, which had been a hospital during the battle and was heavily damaged. The county continued some upkeep into the 1950s, until the Anderson House Foundation was established in 1955. Full state preservation success came in 1959, however, when the state acquired the house as well as seventy-five acres of the battlefield, naming it the Civil War Battle of Lexington State Park. More rehabilitation of the house took place through the years, as well as archeological excavations, and today the park is known as the Battle of Lexington State Historic Site.[32]

The small battlefield at Natural Bridge in Florida likewise became a state park during this era. The United Daughters of the Confederacy had managed the six acres until 1950, when they donated the site to the Florida state park system. In the ensuing years, Florida added additional land, first leasing property and then decades later acquiring much of the original battlefield in its current 135-acre state park.[33]

Unfortunately, aside from state preservation efforts that took up the slacking federal work, other sites did not manage even that level of preservation. Conservationists at these sites consequently found nontraditional ways to preserve their battlefields. Some were aided by the creation in 1949 of a major private preservation entity, the National Trust for Historic Preservation. A private group chartered by Congress, the organization had little power yet in large measure became the face of the preservation movement and nongovernmental policy for decades; numerous preservationists followed the trust's example and used privatization of historic preservation to save their local fields of battle. One such private venture, which later developed into a first-rate state park, was at Port Hudson, on the Mississippi River in Louisiana. Site of the summer 1863 siege that was the last Confederate bastion on the river, surrendering a few days after the fall of Vicksburg, Port Hudson's preservation history dated back to 1930, when the local UDC chapter placed a Confederate monument on the battlefield. Real preservation activity dated to the centennial era. It was then that a group of local Baton Rouge leaders formed the Committee for the Preservation of the Port Hudson Battlefield, led by chairman Fred G. Benton Jr. A notable member of the board was T. Harry Williams, history professor at Louisiana State University. The group met initial success and even formed a larger entity known as the Port Hudson Campaign Committee, which contained additional civic leaders and historians such as Charles Elliott, Lawrence Hewitt, and Arthur Bergeron. The group successfully urged the state to acquire the Port Hudson battlefield and make it into a state park. The state responded, and by December 1965, the Louisiana State Parks and Recreation Commission had acquired over 640 acres from the Mills family estate. Although it would be years before the site was opened to the public, a large portion of it was nevertheless preserved during the centennial era, and more land was added later.[34]

With the lack of success in lobbying for a park, Franklin residents likewise began a grass-roots effort to preserve their sites. Much of the initial work occurred because of Southern heritage groups' efforts, such as the local United Daughters of the Confederacy chapter that preserved Winstead Hill in 1948; they teamed with the local Sons of Confederate Veterans, who maintained the site. It consisted of fewer than ten acres and was clearly pro-Confederate, but it was preservation nonetheless.[35]

A more bipartisan effort occurred in the early 1950s, when local residents convinced the state of Tennessee to buy the Carter House, which sat right on the battle lines and saw some of the worst fighting in the Franklin area; numerous buildings on the site were marked with bullet holes and other damage. Led by author Stanley F. Horn, the group of citizens achieved their goal in July 1951, the legislature appropriating twenty thousand dollars for purchase and more money for restoration. The Tennessee Historical Commission was tasked with overseeing the expenditure, but the state made clear it would not run the site. A private corporation, the Carter House Association, resulted, its purpose being "maintaining and preserving as a shrine and memorial to the Battle of Franklin the Carter House on Columbia Avenue in the Town of Franklin." The association returned the house to its original condition and opened it to the public in 1953. With little hope of receiving more state money, the association charged for membership and tours. Over time, it also built a visitor center, museum, and parking lot.[36]

Unquestionably, Franklin was a major Civil War battlefield, and it was unfortunate that federal or state authorities did not preserve it. Still, the effort by the community illustrated what could be done even on the most local level. It also foreshadowed the future of Civil War preservation work, when federal and state funding would almost completely dry up.

IV

If there was ever a time when Civil War battlefield preservation should have been front and center, it was during the war's centennial from 1961 to 1965. In fact, there was somewhat of a resurgence of preservation at the time, but it was unfortunately not totally on the federal front. The federal government, led by its chief historic preservation agency, the NPS, should have been heavily involved in the centennial in terms of preservation, but that was not the case. As a result, only two major federal parks were established prior to the centennial, and not a single national park establishment bill was passed during the commemoration period itself. Instead, the federal government seemed to concern itself mostly with oversight, which would become more and more common in the ensuing decades.[37]

Due to vast local and regional lobbying, particularly by the relatively new urban Civil War roundtables, Congress created the Civil War Centennial Commission in 1957 to oversee the celebrations and commemorations. Led initially by Karl S. Betts as executive director and Ulysses S. Grant III as chairman of the board, the centennial unfortunately had a rocky beginning. The commission planned a vast Cold War celebration of patriotism and sectional unity, one publication alerting readers that "the Centennial is no time for finding fault or placing blame or fighting the issues all over again." Chairman Grant himself called for "a better popular understanding of America's days of greatness, a more unified country." Working on the national level with the commission and through state-level commissions in most states, the commemoration pushed the continuation of the old reconciliationist heroism of both sides and talked up unity. The result was massive interest.[38]

That unity quickly faded, however, and shattered the reconciliation that had been so dominant since the 1890s. The buildup was more impressive than the result, in large part because of a disaster in the initial commemoration at Fort Sumter when government-appointed leaders failed to recognize and confront segregation in Charleston's hotels. Thereafter, many Americans lost interest in the centennial; issues such as the civil rights movement, Cold War tensions, Cuba, the Kennedy assassination, Vietnam, and even the growing space program received more attention. In fact, the centennial's major historian, Robert J. Cook, has argued that Southerners hijacked the centennial after 1961, even holding their own segregated "Confederate State Convention" at the same time that the national commission held events in Charleston. Southerners also formed the Southern Conference of Centennial Commissions. Such efforts quickly made the centennial in the South into a forum for anti-integration and states' rights. Northern state-level commemorations were mostly educational and patriotic, but as John Bodnar has noted, "The South celebrated a regional more than a national past." At perhaps the climax of Southern non-unity of commemoration, Alabama governor George Wallace gave an extremely partisan states' rights speech at the Alabama monument during Gettysburg's celebrations, and Northern governors quickly took him to task in their own divided rhetoric. What started out as a promising event consequently ended in failure, with numerous events such as commemoration of the explosion of the Crater and the United States Colored Troops massacre at Petersburg being muted, each side reverting to its own rendition of history and choosing not to partake in national events.[39]

Still, there were many fitting events connected with the centennial. Movies galore on the Civil War came from Hollywood, and historians turned out many significant books, such as Bruce Catton's and Shelby Foote's three-volume histories. Large papers-compiling and publication projects such as those for Ulysses S. Grant and Jefferson Davis also emerged. Other professionals participated as well, with historians such as Allen Nevins and James I. Robertson taking over the helm of the centennial after the debacle that ousted Betts and Grant. As another example on the more local level, Stanley F. Horn, biographer of the Army of Tennessee, was deeply interested in Shiloh's centennial events.[40]

The centennial also saw the birth of a major American pastime: reenacting. As part of a growing "distinct Civil War subculture," as Edward Linenthal describes it, consisting of urban roundtables, war gamers, relic hunters, and collectors, reenactors took the war's remembrance to a higher level. Most "sham battles" had previously been performed by veterans or the military, or both, and when Shiloh attempted to create the NPS's first introductory film in 1954 and 1955, they could not find a major pool of reenactors. A small contingent had done some reenacting at Brices Cross Roads, but Shiloh park officials had to turn to national guard troops and school kids to find the large numbers of men they needed. Event reenacting took a major step forward during the centennial, however, with many sites holding some type of reenactment. The first major land battle, as opposed to reenacting the firing on Fort Sumter, was at Manassas on July 22–23, 1961.[41]

The battlefields also conducted memorial and commemorative services, in large part to keep Southern society from segregating events, although at times they had to work around weather and timing. Winter was a bad season, as were holidays. This was especially so at Stones River, fought December 31–January 2. Superintendent Lawrence W. Quist worried that the festivities at Stones River "would perhaps turn into a celebration, for some, rather than a commemoration." Quist wanted to delay the events until the spring and the dedication of the new Mission 66 visitor center. Still, the NPS seemingly did no more than other groups in commemorating the war. A list of activities in the Washington, D.C., area showed no preservation and no major building efforts, although there was a two-million-dollar effort to repair Ford's Theatre in 1964. Small crowds at only a few programs over the four years marked the events. Efforts at non-NPS battlefields sometimes attracted larger crowds, such as the commemoration at Rivers Bridge in South Carolina, which brought five thousand visitors in 1965.[42]

Unfortunately, the entire process took on a circus atmosphere at times. It was well known that the states milked the events for every dime they could get, and many private companies expected great profits from tourism, publications, and even fireworks sales. Some of the events were especially bizarre, beginning with the first and largest reenactment at Manassas in the summer of 1961. The centennial of the Chickamauga and Chattanooga battles even included sack races, log sawing, and horseshoe competitions. Many cringed at the tourist-trap attractions set up around the battlefields, and Allen Nevins even talked of the "carnival atmosphere," thereafter downplaying plans for reenactments and focusing more on educational and interpretive efforts: "We feel that reenactments possess too much celebrative spirit and too little commemorative reverence. This soldier playing mocks the dead." One writer went so far as to recommend reenactors use real bullets, whereby America would "be free of one of the sicker elements" of its population.[43]

There was also a distinct lack of involvement of top-level federal officials in the centennial commemorations. Shiloh tried without success to get President John F. Kennedy, Vice President Lyndon B. Johnson, and even Harry Truman to speak at its commemoration. In hopes of not alienating Southern voters, Kennedy did not attend other events, such as the commemoration of Lincoln's Emancipation Proclamation, which was held in Washington on the steps of the Lincoln Memorial. He likewise did not attend the centennial of Lincoln's Gettysburg Address in November 1963; instead, the president chose to go on a political trip to Texas that month, and it cost him his life. That said, there were high-level attendees at some events. Organizers for the 1965 Bennett Place commemoration tried to get

President Johnson and noted historian Allen Nevins, but they settled for Vice President Hubert H. Humphrey, who gave a spirited address connecting the 1860s with the 1960s: "We should always remember this lesson from the past. For the radicalism that dominated the Reconstruction era is a vivid example of the mindless, vengeful kind of extremism that even today, if left unchecked, could bring our great democracy to its knees. We must never permit vengeful radicals to dominate the American scene. We must never permit the spirit of radicalism to poison the minds and hearts of the American people. This is the real lesson we can learn from the Bennett Place." Predictably, not all of North Carolina's populace took the speech to heart, and there were Ku Klux Klan demonstrations the day Humphrey arrived. Moreover, the crowd at the event was well leavened with Confederate uniforms and numerous known Klan members. The commemoration went off safely nevertheless, with the Eighty-Second Airborne Band providing the music.[44]

By the end of the centennial, a certain recognition had emerged that the effort at national unity based on the heroism of both sides had failed. America was more deeply divided on racial issues, and military and social issues as well, in 1965 than it had been in 1961. An illustration of that division came in the closing program of the centennial commission in 1965 at Appomattox. Southerners attended, but they only cheered on two occasions during the program: when Robert E. Lee's great grandson was introduced and when the U.S. Marine Corps Band played "Dixie."[45]

V

Although the Civil War centennial was celebrated over the course of four years, it spurred little activity in terms of federal preservation. In fact, only two major Civil War battlefield parks were established (Horseshoe Bend would also be created in 1956) in connection with the coming centennial in the late 1950s, and none were established during the centennial. One other tangential Civil War park would emerge in 1960, but its primary history was colonial. Nevertheless, the centennial-era federal parks provided more preservation, but they probably would not have been established were it not for the excitement generated by the coming centennial. Still, the establishment of these parks turned two major precedents on their heads, removing from the process what little overall preservation policy the nation still retained. One was the use of the Antietam Plan, which would be scrapped as entire battlefields along the Boynton theory were once again preserved. The other was the process set up by the 1925 army study, wherein each of the fields actually preserved were intended to be originally marked by simple one-acre plots and a monument. Both became full national parks.[46]

As the largest Civil War battle west of the Mississippi River, Pea Ridge had been fought early in the war, in March 1862, when Earl Van Dorn and Sterling

Price tried to turn back a Federal offensive into Arkansas. Unfortunately for them, their bid ended in defeat. Through the ensuing years, Pea Ridge had seen a lot of preservation support but none of it achieved success until the centennial excitement swept over America. There was even a citizen petition calling on Congress to create a park in 1890, the same year major federal preservation efforts began at Chickamauga and Antietam. Nothing came of it, or the many bills that also emerged from local congressman through the ensuing decades, although Pea Ridge did garner a War Department inspection in 1926. The legislation appointed a three-man commission, which included Confederate veteran C. L. Pickens, Union soldier Evans S. Morgan, and army officer Donald H. Connolly of the Corps of Engineers. Few in Washington backed the idea of a park, however, with one secretary of war reporting on a possible bill, "The battles in and around Pea Ridge are not considered of sufficient historical importance for commemoration by the establishment of a national military park and approval of this Bill is not recommended."[47]

Other studies emerged as the government money–rich 1930s passed on. The Works Progress Administration funded another study of the potential park, only to meet defeat again. There was even a joint federal-state effort to preserve the field in the 1930s, Arkansas governor Charles H. Brough trying unsuccessfully to garner matching funds from surrounding states. One NPS history noted that "everyone praised the idea but no one praised it enough to pledge monetary support." The only positive outcome of all this effort was the formation of the Pea Ridge National Park Association, headed by veteran Pickens, which continued to lobby for a federal park but was repeatedly met by a determined NPS and even some local congressmen. One Interior Department official wrote Representative Clyde T. Ellis that the NPS thought "the site was not relatively as important as other areas" and would not pursue making Pea Ridge a park. Ellis in turn wrote Arkansas officials that they had better settle for a simple monument along the lines of the 1925 War Department recommendation, and to look toward state, county, or perhaps even private sponsorship of the monument.[48]

Efforts to create a park at Pea Ridge became serious again in the mid-1950s, when Orval E. Faubus became governor. Best known for his opposition to integrating Little Rock's Central High School, Faubus was also a major supporter of the Pea Ridge plan. He reconstituted the association, and a monumental appointment came when Faubus named George Benjamin to the group. The car salesman soon became chairman and quickly used his clout with the Automobile Dealers Association to secure national support for Pea Ridge. Fortunately for him, Secretary of the Interior Douglas McKay was a car dealer from Oregon. Benjamin still had a hard sale, however, because the Interior Department's National Park Advisory Board was against making Pea Ridge a park and even Secretary McKay recommended that no funds be spent studying a potential park because the likelihood of it getting congressional approval was remote. Benjamin would not give up, however, and enlisted the support of other famous Americans, including Harry S. Truman and Douglas MacArthur, who was a native of Arkansas. A turning point came when someone realized that Idaho representative Gracie Pfost, chairman of the House Interior and Insular Affairs Subcommittee, was also a native of Arkansas. Federal officials still recommended that Arkansas make Pea Ridge a state park, but the state's congressional delegation would not budge and pushed for passage, one committee presuming its importance by calling the battle the "Gettysburg of the West."[49]

The Arkansas congressmen turned out to be a major force; Ed Bearss wondered how "for a state with only six representatives and two senators, [it] had the most powerful delegation in Congress." The delegation convinced the key Senate and House committees, both of which recommended passage, by arguing that "it does not appear that such [startup] costs would be substantial," mainly because the land would be donated, Elkhorn Tavern could serve as a museum, local citizens would donate artifacts, and few roads would be needed. The committees also produced their own report from a Library of Congress historian claiming that the Department of the Interior's own negative report contradicted itself. It even argued that "if the Battle of Pea Ridge had been fought in the well-populated East, the main theater of the Civil War activity, it would have been given much attention and memorialized as a military park long ago." As a result, the establishment bill passed through both houses in the summer of 1956, and Benjamin pulled more strings, this time masonic strings, to get a word in with President Dwight D. Eisenhower's personal assistant. Eisenhower signed the bill in July.[50]

Opposition still emerged, however, illustrating federal unwillingness to continue costly preservation of battlefields. There was official opposition from the Bureau of the Budget as well as the NPS, based upon a negative recommendation from the advisory board, which declared "the results and significance of the battle were principally regional in character." The proposed park was even derided in Washington; NPS director Conrad Wirth joked of it and another proposed park, "Well, I'm afraid we may be getting two new parks—Piss Ridge and Horses**t Bend." Moreover, like the developments in the 1930s parks, part of the bill required that no federal money be spent acquiring the land; the legislation placed the major land acquisition costs on the state of Arkansas, which would then have to donate the acres to the NPS. Ed Bearss noted that the thinking was that "maybe the State of Arkansas might not acquire the land, maybe it will not become a park."[51]

Bearss himself had a lot of power to determine the nature of the new park. As a historian at Vicksburg, he was on the team sent to Pea Ridge to develop boundaries for the new reserve. Most thought it would be only a modest park of a few hundred acres, but Bearss and NPS stalwart Roy Appleman began working on the significance of the battlefield and boundaries while other NPS personnel on the team worked on issues such as land and administration. Although most thought in terms of a seventy-five-acre park, Bearss and Appleman successfully argued for a forty-two-hundred-acre area, which was eventually what went forward. Bearss later lamented not getting everything he wanted, but he was satisfied: "We didn't get a chicken farm that we wanted—Appleman and I. They argued over easement for it and we lost that argument. But we basically got what we wanted." Ironically, the very land that everyone thought would be donated had to be condemned.[52]

Arkansas responded quickly. State legislation established the Pea Ridge Park Commission, which was tasked with buying the battlefield and transferring it to the federal government. The legislature appropriated $250,000 in 1957 and approved that much more two years later. In a few years the state turned over to the NPS more than four thousand acres, which included practically the entire battlefield. A ceremony took place at the high school gym in Pea Ridge on March 7, 1960, the anniversary of the battle, in which the state officially turned over title to NPS director Conrad Wirth.[53]

The NPS moved on site in 1961 and began readying the new park for an eventual dedication in May 1963. The legislation had allowed some owners to move modern buildings from the land, but others were obviously retained, such as the famous Elkhorn Tavern. The NPS used prior studies as well as onsite efforts by historians such as Bearss to establish a procedure for preservation and interpretation, including the famed tavern. The house had been destroyed in 1862 but was rebuilt in 1885. The new structure still contained the original foundation and chimney, and it was restored again in 1965. The NPS also began acquiring through donation or purchase artifacts and museum items to interpret the battlefield. Included in the acquisitions were a Sixth Missouri Cavalry battle flag, two Napoleon cannons, and a copy of the *Official Records* for research. All this work being done in the midst of Mission 66, the battlefield also received a new visitor center. Unfortunately, Pea Ridge witnessed more controversy when Texas erected a monument in conjunction with its nationwide commemoration of Texas troops. Superintendent Raymond L. Nelson declined the offer of the monument, fearing it would only be the first of a wave of what he considered intrusions on the historic landscape. Public clamor was against the park's decision, however, and the monument eventually went up in a nearby town. Later, when President

Lyndon B. Johnson, himself a Texan, became involved and allowed the monument to be erected in the park, the local citizens decided they liked it so much in town that they asked to have it left alone, which it was. But the damage between the park and community from this controversy, and others, had been done.[54]

A similar occurrence took place just a few miles to the north, at Wilson's Creek in Missouri. There, Sterling Price had repelled a vicious attack from Nathaniel Lyon, which cost the latter his life. As was the case with most other battlefields, there had been many attempts through the years to establish a park at the site, but backers had settled for minor victories. The Springfield University Club, for example, placed a marker on the presumed spot of Lyon's death in 1928; the original stone pile was by that time long gone, and the actual site was officially lost to history. Also promising some future success was a late-1920s War Department study based on the 1925 report, in which the battle, not even listed originally, had been bumped up a category in importance. Wilson's Creek was even included in the catch-all omnibus bill in 1930 but did not make it through. In 1938, a bill in the Missouri legislature to purchase the battlefield passed through both state houses, but Governor Lloyd C. Stark vetoed the measure, despite public backing and a seventy-seventh anniversary program in August 1938. It was, as a result, only when the centennial began that sufficient force gathered behind the idea to create a federal park. In fact, local efforts such as the 1950 establishment of the Wilson's Creek Foundation by the Springfield Chamber of Commerce began the process, with foundation president L. E. Meador leading the effort to raise money to purchase part of the site. School kids also raised funds, and the foundation was able to purchase thirty-seven acres at Bloody Hill in October 1951 from Robert and Myrtle McClure. Meador did not stop there and continually worked through the 1950s to gain support for a national park.[55]

The effort to establish a federal battlefield continued to meet many difficulties. One was the same reluctance on the part of the NPS to create another park, especially so close to Pea Ridge. One committee report recited a letter from an assistant secretary of the interior stating its view that "the Civil War has been adequately commemorated in the series of battlefield parks already established and does not favor the establishment of additional areas for this purpose." The NPS was evidently basing its stance on its advisory board's recommendation, in which "the Board voted unanimously in the negative." Another obstruction was lack of support in Congress; both Senator Thomas C. Hennings and Representative Dewey Short repeatedly offered bills to create the park, but the closest the effort came to success was a series of on-site hearings held at Springfield in 1959, during which one of the present congressmen remarked to John K. Hulston, one of the local organizers, "John, if you can come up with an old sword or belt buckle from out there on the battlefield with the initials 'L.B.J.' it would be mighty helpful to our cause." Obviously, LBJ was Lyndon Baines Johnson, then the majority leader in the Senate and the future president.[56]

Meador and local congressmen continued pushing the idea until eventually it caught on in the form of H.R. 725. The House and Senate interior and insular affairs committees soon held hearings and reported on the bill favorably, the Senate committee arguing somewhat exorbitantly that "some historians contend that the War Between the States was won in the West and the turning point in these victories was the loss to the South of the State of Missouri at Wilson's Creek." With such high rhetoric, Congress passed the legislation in April 1960, creating the battlefield "as a public park for the benefit and enjoyment of the people of the United States," but again with the stipulation that Missouri provide the funds to acquire the land, another clear indication that the federal government was distancing itself from large-scale and costly battlefield preservation. President Dwight D. Eisenhower signed the bill into law, and a grand dedication of the new park took place on August 10, 1961, the centennial of the battle; the Navy's Blue Angels were even in Springfield to perform. Missouri senator Stuart Symington was the featured speaker, and the main event was the transfer of the thirty-seven acres to the NPS.[57]

Obviously, the work at Wilson's Creek was far from over, and the foundation then turned its attention to gathering more money for land acquisition. As had become standard, the stipulation was that the NPS or the federal government would not pay for the land, so the foundation turned to the state, which responded by creating the Wilson's Creek Battlefield National Park Commission. Eventually, the commission oversaw a $351,800 appropriation from the state for land at the park, which would then be turned over to the NPS.[58]

Work progressed as more land came into the park. The NPS moved in and began work, creating a water and sewage system, surfacing roads, placing aluminum interpretive signs, and building infrastructual buildings such as staff quarters and maintenance facilities. The historical work on boundaries and site history was again done by NPS historian Ed Bearss, who once more pushed for total preservation. This time Appleman was not on the team and his considerable weight was not present to keep the proposal intact, resulting in the regional director cutting the proposed fifteen hundred acres by about a third. The NPS nevertheless took full control and opened the park to the public in September 1972.[59]

While Pea Ridge and Wilson's Creek were major Civil War parks, another tangential area also became federal in 1960: Arkansas Post National Memorial. It had been established as a state park in 1929 and functioned as such through the decades thereafter, even as calls for making it a national park continued to emerge. The NPS was loathe to include it in their system, Conrad L. Wirth writing in 1948 that the NPS had done "an extensive study" of the site in 1939 and that it was the opinion of NPS officials that "the historical associations of the park as it exists are purely local and entirely separate from those of the now obliterated site of the original settlement." He concluded, "In the circumstances I can see no logical reason why the area should not continue under the administration of the State of Arkansas." That the primary purpose for the park was not related to the Civil War was an additional factor, despite its centennial birth. The 1972 superintendent's report said as much: "The Memorial commemorates primarily the first permanent European settlement west of the Mississippi River.[60]

Nevertheless, calls for national preservation of the site continued, especially from the powerful Arkansas congressional delegation, and a new round of studies in 1956 and 1957 found the same result—that Arkansas Post had no national importance. The Arkansans would not give up, however, and a compromise was struck in which the area would be made a national memorial instead of a larger national monument or even national park. The Senate committee argued that "designation as a national monument or a national park would appear to be inappropriate because the area will memorialize events which took place some distances away for the most part, at locations which are today unknown." This compromise legislation quickly went through Congress, creating the Arkansas Post National Memorial in July 1960. The bill appropriated $125,000, of which no more than $25,000 could be used for land acquisition. Although that maximum was later raised, the state of Arkansas donated their state park land and acquired additional acreage within a boundary designated by the secretary of the interior. Various park service resources were then provided, and the area was soon converted from a state park to a national site, although infrastructure lagged behind as only temporary housing and visitor contact services were immediately established. The NPS also built an entrance road and hiking trails and placed interpretive signage around the park. To stabilize the continual flow of the river and to mitigate any effects of a reservoir being built by the Army Corps of Engineers, the NPS also worked with the corps to construct a "rock dike" along important points of the park. Administratively too small to be an independent park at this point, Arkansas Post was put under the authority of the Hot Springs National Park superintendent when the NPS formally took control in June 1964.[61]

Although the centennial saw a slight upsurge in the creation of Civil War battlefield parks, with an even better twist of preservation of almost the entire battlegrounds at both Pea Ridge and Wilson's Creek, the period of centennial preservation was a much-muted era that securely fit into the mold of lessening federal efforts to preserve Civil War sites. The NPS did not desire any of the late 1950s or 1960s battlefields, and they were only added to the system because of determined local congressional support. Moreover, when Congress agreed to pass those bills, they did so without any major financial appropriations. Land acquisition at all three federal sites established during the lead-up to the centennial years was carried out entirely on the state level, with the federal government only accepting donation of the land once it had been acquired by the states. The combination of leaner fiscal times due to greater worldwide commitments and the lessening perceived need of (and availability of) major Civil War sites certainly fed into the lessening federal preservation effort in the 1950s and 1960s.

VI

Despite the work on the federal level, the centennial celebrations saw perhaps their biggest embodiment in battlefield preservation on the nonfederal level. Although some private and local community efforts came about during this period, the vast majority of the nonfederal action came on the state level as the various states combined the centennial celebration with expanding state park systems. The result was a flurry of activity between 1961 and 1965.

A few states initiated preservation efforts as early as 1960 and 1961. In an ongoing effort to preserve Fort McAllister near Savannah, Georgia, the state ultimately took control of the fort in 1960. The earliest efforts had been entirely private at the behest of and funded by Henry Ford. Once he died, the estate managers began to sell off many of his lands, including Fort McAllister. The state of Georgia stepped in and acquired the old fort, now beginning to corrode once again because of neglect, and made it into the Fort McAllister State Park. Over time, the site nevertheless developed into a major recreational camping and enjoyment park, but it also preserved the fort itself and the story of the events in December 1864.[62]

Another state that sped up preservation was Arkansas, which created a flurry of parks, primarily the three that commemorated the Camden Expedition of 1864. Although Marks Mill and Poison Springs were established in 1961, they were merely roadside parks with no facilities or staff, though they did contain some monuments and interpretive signage telling visitors what had happened at the sites. Jenkins Ferry was the largest of the three, containing a pavilion and other recreational enticements. The first effort to purchase battlefield land there had come in 1928, when local masons bought three or four acres and the local United Daughters of the Confederacy erected a small monument. Little else occurred for the next three decades, except some visitation to what was locally becoming known as a small park. Then in 1961, local organizers convinced their representative in the legislature to offer a bill to create a state park. The state consequently bought nearly forty additional acres and took out a century-long lease on the masonic property. More land was added in the succeeding decades.[63]

North Carolina was very active in its centennial-era preservation as well. One site that gained a state park was Fort Fisher, just outside Wilmington. It was the last major Confederate port open to trade in late 1864, although the Federals attempted unsuccessfully to bombard the fort and assault it into submission in December. They failed, but Sherman's Carolinas campaign soon outflanked the area and the Confederates had to withdraw anyway. The state began development of the site as early as 1960, when it took charge of the property, and work on the site continued throughout the centennial years. A major step took place in 1965, when a new visitor center opened. Ultimately, the site contained 264 acres either owned by the state or leased from the federal government.[64]

North Carolina also created a state park at one of its most important Civil War sites. The Bennett Farm, where Johnston surrendered to Sherman in the closing days of the war, had been touted for preservation for years, but neither federal nor state officials had paid much attention to it. As a result, the farmhouse itself began to collapse and decay over the years and became a haven for thugs. In fact, the house burned in 1921 after "a night of occupation by hobos." The chimney still stood, however, and local lawyer Reuben Oscar Everett began a lifelong mission to save the site. He succeeded in getting the state to create a commission and provide funding in 1923 to keep up the area. The biggest early advance in preservation also came in 1923, when the landowners unveiled a "unity" monument at the site. The commission had big ideas for the dedication, even inviting President Coolidge. When he did not accept, they turned to Secretary of War Weeks, but he declined when complaints arose that he was speaking at a "Confederate Memorial." Eventually, a senator and Johnston's nephew and Sherman's grandson spoke. Later, the landowners donated the three acres of the homestead and even later an additional twenty-seven acres to the Bennett Place Memorial Commission.[65]

Thereafter, little preservation or even marking was done at Bennett Place. Even a roadside historical marker was not put up at first because Everett and the state official in charge of markers could not agree on the text for the sign. By the late 1950s, however, centennial fever was sweeping the nation and the commission arranged for a similar-sized and -shaped log structure to be moved to the site to stand in for the no-longer-extant farmhouse. At the same time, the commission knew it could no longer care for the area financially, so calls again went out for the state to take over the site. The legislature agreed, and Bennett Place became a state park in 1961. Locals planned an elaborate dedication in April 1962, even inviting John and Jacqueline Kennedy, who declined. The services were nevertheless held, and the long-awaited highway historical marker went up that same year as well.[66]

The state park movement even affected battlefields in the far West. A seemingly inconsequential effort in Arizona began in the late 1950s and actually achieved the establishment of a state park at Picacho Peak in 1965. Although not in the realm of a Gettysburg or a Shiloh, or even other state parks such as Bentonville or Perryville, Picacho Peak was established in remembrance of a small skirmish in the Arizona Territory in April 1862, often touted as the state's largest Civil War engagement. Picacho Peak's beginnings, as with so many other parks, were in the local community. By 1958, Arizona state park system officials had studied the potential of its inclusion in state ranks, not just because of its history but also, and perhaps even more so, because of its geological and natural wonders; the historic aspect only made a stronger case for inclusion in the state park system. Park officials then began to seriously consider the idea, conducting a feasibility study and negotiating a land transfer with the federal Bureau of Land Management. Local support continued to be strong, and the state legislature finally passed a bill creating the Picacho Peak State Park in 1965. The state eventually acquired 640 acres, and the initial park manager, Don Clow, went to work creating visitor services, roads, and parking areas. The park opened to the public in 1968, and more land was acquired in the ensuing decades, ultimately resulting in a park of nearly four thousand acres.[67]

There were also more private efforts to preserve historic battlefield sites during the centennial. Failing to gain national or even state attention to their local battlefields, citizens went forward on their own, and often their projects became successful over the decades. One such local effort was at Honey Springs in Oklahoma, site of an unsuccessful July 1863 attempt by Confederates to secure control of the Indian Territory. The battlefield lay unprotected until 1963, when local groups such as the Oklahoma Civil War Roundtable and the state's centennial commission began to encourage the idea of preserving it. That year they established the Honey Springs Battlefield Commission, sponsored by the Oklahoma Historical Society. Plans called for a park, perhaps even on the national level, but unfortunately a couple more decades passed before any firm action toward preservation took place.[68]

In southern Louisiana, local efforts succeeded in getting Fort Jackson on the Mississippi River donated to Plaquemines Parish in 1962. Adm. David Farragut's fleet passed it and Fort St. Phillip in April 1862, but the fort had been deactivated after the Spanish-American War, during which time it had received the customary development and modern guns inside a new addition in the center of the fort. It was also used as a training area in World War I but was thereafter turned over to private owners. The fort unfortunately deteriorated over the decades, filling with mud, water, snakes, and a variety of other animals. In 1961, the local parish government stepped in and acquired the fort and eighty-two acres. They built a retaining wall to protect the site from water, cleaned the brush and mud that had overwhelmed the historic area, and built roads and a parking lot. They also revamped the original woodwork, brick, and gun emplacements, and even put artifacts on display.[69]

More isolated local efforts also occurred during the centennial, such as Atlanta citizens marking the various battlefields of Peachtree Creek, Atlanta, and Ezra Church. Tellingly, although individual states and even lesser bodies were far less able to preserve on the scale of the NPS, the reality was that the federal government was growing less interested in major battlefield preservation and had long since stopped putting major funding into the effort. The lack of federal work left the states to carry the load, and with inadequate resources they did an incomplete job. Still, the states and even local and private government and citizens were able to preserve at least a portion of their historic sites, and their contribution to the cause of battlefield preservation should not be overlooked.[70]

VII

The World War II–era preservationists hailed the coming Civil War centennial as a harbinger of preservation. They got preservation, just not in the way they envisioned and not to the degree it could have been. Such a momentous time seemed perfect for a revitalization of historic battlefield preservation on the federal level, but it fell flat in terms of NPS and congressional participation. Only three primary battlefields were preserved, along with two additional sites that had at least some connection to the war. Moreover, none of the major land acquisition at any of the five was funded by the federal government; it was mostly left to the states to acquire land and donate it to the NPS. The preservation process of the 1950s and early 1960s therefore continued the dwindling federal involvement, especially in funding, that had begun in the 1930s.

Still, a significant amount of preservation was begun and at places concluded during the centennial era. Tellingly, the most significant work was at the state level, which in itself posed problems for preservation. Almost everyone associated with a local battlefield ultimately wished for that site to be made into a national park; even backers of small and seemingly insignificant battlefields dreamed big dreams and desired inclusion in the NPS. Obviously, that was not to be, so many local organizers settled for state preservation. In itself this was deemed less satisfactory due to the ensuing local instead of national status and the inconsistent and less-than-total resources on the state level. If it was the best they could get, however, many local groups settled for it.[71]

A significant part of the reasoning for the lack of federal funding came as a result of the changing manner in which Americans viewed the Civil War. The initial split memories of the war in the Reconstruction generation were significantly blended in the golden age and its attendant reconciliation, but that brotherhood began to crack, even as reconciliation remained dominant through the 1920s, 1930s, and 1940s. Some partisan and sectional avarice had begun to creep back in by then, especially at Richmond, Manassas, and Fort Sumter, but by the 1950s it was much deeper and in the 1960s it became dominant. A large reason for this development proved to be the missteps of the original leadership of the national centennial, which allowed white Southerners the opportunity to use the platform of centennial celebration as a forum for states' rights and the old Confederacy in a backlash against the growing civil rights movement. White Southerners cannot bear all the blame, however. Historians have also castigated President Kennedy's mediocre reaction to segregation during the earliest months of the civil rights movement, during the centennial, as an effort to keep from alienating white voters in the South in the upcoming elections of 1962 and 1964.[72]

Other issues that severely refocused Americans' attention included Vietnam and the Cold War, although many saw in their battlefields, and in the generation who had fought on them, examples of stalwart and brave Americans who had endured grueling troubles and come out stronger. As one Georgia centennial report stated, the "greatness displayed by our forefathers a century ago . . . enables us to look forward with calm confidence to the crises which confront us in the world today. Because our forefathers endured, we know that we must strive to endure and to carry on as they would expect us to do. Their strength is our strength. Their example is our example. And their standard—God fearing, devoted, patriotic, brave, statesmanlike and enduring—is our standard."[73]

Of greatest significance, however, was the civil rights movement, which caused a major change regarding America's memory of the Civil War. The North certainly won the war, but the South won the peace for the next hundred years. John Latschar, former superintendent at Gettysburg, pointed out that Gettysburg was best known "as being the site of the Confederate major general George Pickett's charge" (rather than the Union major general Winfield S. Hancock's defense) and as the "High Water Mark of the Confederacy" rather than "the Battle that Saved the Union." That Lost Cause mentality began to crumble in the North as well as among certain population brackets of the South as a result of the civil rights movement, forcing yet again a split memory of the Civil War. As more and more politicians and policy makers began to speak out about racial issues, white Southerners turned back to the old divisiveness of the immediate post–Civil War era. As often as Allen Nevins declared that "so far as we can we shall allow the just pride of no national group to be belittled or besmirched" or as New York governor Nelson Rockefeller described the "knowledge that Lincoln's vision of a nation truly fulfilling its spiritual heritage is not yet achieved," Southerners such as Mississippi's Ross Barnett or Alabama's George Wallace stated that former

Confederate states "stand for constitutional government and thousands of people throughout the nation look to the South to restore constitutional rights and the rights of states and individuals." The opposing sides were no longer reunited; rather, they were again divided along the same racial and societal lines that had divided them a hundred years earlier. The same divisiveness that America had witnessed during and in the immediate decades after the war had returned.[74]

And once again, African Americans' place in American society was the chief question to be answered, with Americans' memory of the war revolving primarily around that central question. Yet the battlefield preservation movement in particular and the centennial commemorations in general, including visitation at the battlefields and programs, had hardly reached that level of analysis. African Americans were no more likely to commemorate the Civil War as white Americans were to commemorate African Americans' roles in the war. Likewise, little of the preservation activity in the era was centered around African American history or even the battlefields where they had fought. If there was any inclusion of areas that were connected to the black story, such as Port Hudson or Harpers Ferry, that part of the narrative was left unexplored and the old military history or recreational/natural offerings remained. The only major Civil War–related NPS establishment that included African American history was the 1962 inclusion of Frederick Douglass's home in Washington, D.C. Although there was some movement toward treating race relations and slavery in regard to the Civil War during this time, it tended to be in academic circles or behind the scenes; it would only flower in public memory decades later. Accordingly, although the reconciliationist view of memory was splitting apart in the 1960s, it was not yet being replaced with an emphasis, at least in the public mind, on the emancipationist vision.[75]

The memory of the Civil War that had helped define battlefield preservation and the battlefield preservation that had helped define Americans' memory of the war was consequently changing during this era. But it was changing back to a form that had already appeared rather than forging ahead into new realms. Americans seemed to be going in circles in their views of the Civil War. The same cannot be said of the preservation movement, however. As American popular memory and the nation itself moved beyond the war period, the United States threw off the desire and ability to preserve its historic battlefields associated with the Civil War, leaving it to smaller entities to perform the task. That pattern would only grow in the decades to come as divisiveness over the causes of the Civil War and the present divisiveness over race relations combined to nearly halt Civil War battlefield preservation in America.[76]

6

The Dark Ages,
1965–1990

The fall of the Roman Empire in the fifth century is commonly referred to as the beginning of the Dark Ages in world history, especially in Europe. It was a period between two major cultural and historical epochs of civilization, when academic, economic, and cultural downturns affected the world. Essentially, it was a period of stagnation, marred by little forethought and even less human progress.[1]

As a term, "dark ages" has often been used to define or illustrate other, smaller periods of history, and in one sense it is a fitting description of the late 1960s through the early 1980s in the United States. The nation suffered some of its lowest days during these decades, with crisis after crisis occurring in economics, politics, society, and world affairs. In economics, rampant inflation and gas shortages marred the economy, and political crises rocked the nation, from assassinations such as the brothers Kennedy to demonstrations and riots at political party conventions. The most notable political crisis was the Watergate affair and the resignation of President Richard M. Nixon. In society, the assassination of civil rights leaders, most notably Martin Luther King Jr., ushered in a more violent phase of the civil rights movement, and vast cultural clashes over a plethora of social issues, from civil rights to the death penalty to abortion, caused the nation to wonder about its future. In world affairs, the United States removed its troops from Vietnam, but the plain truth was that it had lost its first war and the "ghost of Vietnam" hung over the nation, particularly the military, for a long time. Rampant drug abuse and counterculture activities only added to the vast transformation. Although there were some bright spots, such as the lunar landings from 1969 to 1972, the late 1960s and 1970s were certainly not America's best years.[2]

Although in a much smaller context and with many fewer lives at stake in comparison to the actual Dark Ages or even the decades of decline in the United States, the term "dark ages" is also a fitting description of the post-centennial American battlefield preservation movement. A growing listlessness among federal officials regarding battlefield establishment had already begun to emerge during the centennial period. During the dark ages, a grand total of one major federal Civil War site was established, and it was not even a battlefield. In fact, focus was being turned away from battlefields toward more recreational endeavors such as seashores and river routes. Kennedy and Johnson liberalism sought to get urban and minority Americans out of the cities for American-based amusement and recreation in natural settings. Consequently, large military battlefields and historic sites, especially in the anti-Vietnam social and fiscal climate of the late 1960s and 1970s, were visited by white men but few minorities. As a result, few parks were established and little land was added to battlefields already existing as parks. As Ronald F. Lee, regional director for the NPS, noted, "It has been made clear to the Director by Congress that requests for additional land for Civil War areas will be looked upon with disfavor."[3]

Government concern over spending too much money on battlefields and preservation reached its high point in the 1980s. President Ronald Reagan infused a new pride in the nation, as evidenced by his famous "Its Morning Again in America" reelection campaign ad in 1984 which resonated with Americans and helped provide a landslide reelection, but he also had definite views regarding domestic government spending and the size of government. His declaration in his first inaugural address in 1981 that "in the present crisis, government is not the solution to our problems; government is the problem" should have forewarned the NPS and other government preservationists that battlefield preservation and a host of other domestic issues were not top priorities. Indeed, in 1981 Secretary of the Interior James Watt proposed a moratorium, which Congress did not accept, on acquiring additional land for parks.[4]

The result was that the federal government almost totally stepped away from the Civil War battlefield preservation movement during this period. The NPS, in fact, switched from emphasizing battlefields and the gore of war in earlier conflicts to more serene modes of commemoration, such as the Vietnam Memorial, which itself had to be erected by a private group. In the federal government's place stood various state governments, which tried valiantly to preserve and protect. But with fewer resources in terms of money and legal advice, and with many suffering their own economic problems, the states simply could not do what the federal government would not do. The result was a downturn in overall battlefield preservation, a low period that in essence had begun decades earlier, despite a small spike in activity around the centennial. These decades formed the darkest days of the Civil War battlefield preservation movement.[5]

I

Having spent years in the U.S. House and Senate, President Lyndon B. Johnson knew how to get bills through Congress. The list of his major legislation that wound its way through Congress and was signed by him was massive, including the famous Civil Rights Act of 1964, the Voting Rights Act of 1965, and the Freedom of Information Act of 1966. One of the lesser known acts signed by Johnson, however, had a distinct impact on historic preservation in America and, by extension, Civil War battlefield preservation.[6]

Although the federal government began to restrict its outright preservation activity after the acquisition of three parks during the centennial years, it did not totally remove itself from the work. In fact, as had been occurring for some decades, the federal government was shifting from outright specific battlefield preservation to larger, more contextual guidance and legislation concerning historic preservation in general. Beginning with the Antiquities Act of 1906, the establishment of the NPS in 1916, the Historic Sites Act in 1935, and the National Trust for Historic Preservation in 1949, a movement to legislate a preservation mentality developed over time, even as less actual historic preservation was taking place on the federal level. Such was the case with the 1964 establishment of the Land and Water Conservation Fund, primarily aimed at recreational opportunities. The capstone of much of this work and evolution in preservation thought emerged in 1966 with the passage of the National Historic Preservation Act, which unfortunately did not serve as a national battlefield preservation policy at all but was at least another building block, and a major one at that. Although there was some desire and talk of a comprehensive battlefield study to foster such a policy in the 1960s, the NPS, which Congress tasked to make the study, never completed it, and the federal government returned to preservation on a reactionary and case-by-case basis. And there was pitifully little of that.[7]

A product of the loss of many historic buildings and sites as a result of earlier legislation, such as urban renewal and interstate highway construction, the National Historic Preservation Act came at a time when Americans could literally see their historic places being destroyed. In an effort to slow this process, the law sought to put a review process in place to delay haphazard or unknowing destruction and set restrictions on the use of federal monies in efforts that would damage historic properties. It also set up a mechanism that could identify, track, and hopefully protect historic sites, including battlefields, in the United States and even abroad.[8]

Working primarily through the NPS as the nation's foremost historic and natural conservation agency, the law set up a tiered system of preservation. The highest tier was reserved for locales placed in the NPS system as national parks, national military parks, national historic sites, national monuments (allowed to be designated by the president in the 1906 Antiquities Act), and various other units of the NPS. These parks, mainly created by Congress, carried park fines and imprisonment for any destruction. There was, however, also a growing list of NPS protective directives and laws that covered the system as a whole.[9]

National Historic Landmarks also achieved a greater level of scrutiny and administration under the National Historic Preservation Act. Although some National Historic Landmarks dated to 1960 as an outgrowth of the Historic Sites Survey of the Historic Sites Act of 1935, the system was renamed and organized under the National Historic Preservation Act in 1966, providing additional incentives to keep designated areas pristine and undamaged. Although no penalty was specified for damaging a National Historic Landmark, there were certain incentives, mostly economic, for staying within the spirit of the law. To reach National Historic Landmark status, a thorough application process was carried out, and a final decision was made by NPS staff. In the decade following the retooling of the program in 1966, several battlefields became National Historic Landmark properties. Still, that designation provided little real preservation.[10]

At a lower degree of national importance and acclaim stood the National Register of Historic Places, a new tier of certification created under the National Historic Preservation Act. This much larger listing likewise carried with it few penalties for tampering, but it nevertheless organized a list of significant areas within the United States that fit certain criteria. Inclusion on the register was through an application process, and it included some economic incentives to keep these areas free from damage. Many battlefields were also listed as National Register sites in the ensuing decades.[11]

Although violation of the 1966 National Historic Preservation Act carried few penalties, the act was instrumental in organizing the effort to identify and determine historic sites. Former NPS director George B. Hartzog went so far as to state that the act allowed the NPS "to elevate history to the equal status of natural history." And the act did have a little punch. Its most potent preservation weapon was the detailed Section 106 review process. This section stipulated that when any federal monies were used in any type of alteration of any historic sites, a review process had to be initiated and conducted to determine what, if any, resources would be damaged and to settle on an understanding of how it would be mitigated. The legislation also created state-level historic preservation officers, and the Section 106 process worked through those officers and their staffs to determine if any damage would be done, how to mitigate the damage, and whether the work should continue. There was also an effort to allow for public involvement. The Section 106 process could not stop work on privately held land, but it nevertheless slowed the work so that clearer heads could prevail and historic sites could be preserved. The effort to involve the state governments in the process also allowed for local attention to sites as well as larger professional historic staffs that included historians, archeologists, and technicians.[12]

Over time, additional amendments and laws that carried stiffer penalties and expanding coverage built on the National Historic Preservation Act. One of the major new pieces of legislation was the 1969 National Environmental Protection Act, which added another layer of investigation, mainly environmental in nature, requiring permits for work on federal land. Perhaps most important to battlefield preservation, the Archeological Resources Protection Act of 1979 added teeth to preservation activities, at least on federal land. The act set up the ability to charge felony penalties for disturbing preserved archeological sites, whether historic or prehistoric; many relic hunters today are charged under this legislation. Other federal laws of this period likewise proved beneficial to slow battlefield destruction, including legislation such as the Department of Transportation Act of 1966 and the Clean Water Act of 1972.[13]

The result of these laws was a much more widespread preservation mentality in America. The National Historic Preservation Act was the first major effort on the part of the United States to identify, categorize, and preserve all of its historic sites. Federal Civil War battlefields then in existence, and those to come, certainly benefited from the passage of this act. Although many of the larger and more famous battlefields were already national parks, others over the ensuing decades became National Historic Landmarks, and increasing numbers were placed on the National Register of Historic Places. Likewise, more than a few parks have taken Archeological Resources Protection Act cases to court for vandals damaging battlefield park resources. Although not tangible or forward-moving efforts to actually preserve more battlefields, the National Historic Preservation Act and the Archeological Resources Protection Act were nonetheless important pieces of legislation that protected many sites and put an umbrella of coverage over many more.

II

Despite a newer focus on preservation theory, the continual theoretical change in federal battlefield preservation resulted in little outright federal conservation of Civil War sites during this dark ages era. No battlefields themselves were established as parks, although there was a continual trickle of additional land acquisition at many of the previously preserved national parks. The only major Civil War sites preserved by the NPS at this time were in fact tangential to the major parks in which they were administratively housed, resulting in major natural parks containing historic sites only by geographical proximity. A prime example was the Chattahoochee River National Recreation Area, established in 1978. Primarily intended for recreation, the park also preserved a small portion of Civil War earthworks and sites dealing with Joseph E. Johnston's river defense line during the Atlanta campaign in 1864. Interestingly, preservation occurred outside the nation's primary historic preservation agency as well; in 1981, the Bureau of Land Management preserved the Fort Craig site in New Mexico, which was a part of the Valverde battlefield. The shifting river took much of the actual battlefield, but New Mexico's recreational Elephant Butte Lake State Park preserved what was left.[14]

An example of the NPS placing minor historic Civil War sites in larger natural parks also included several Gulf Coast fortifications that had remained in army hands until after World War II, including Fort Massachusetts on Ship Island, Mississippi, and Fort Barrancas and Fort Pickens at Pensacola, Florida. Most were let go by the army in 1947, although Barrancas had been somewhat preserved by the Pensacola Naval Air Station since the 1910s. Fort Pickens actually became a Florida state park after World War II, but all were placed under the NPS in 1971 with the establishment of the Gulf Islands National Seashore. The recreational politics behind the move were apparent in NPS director George B. Hartzog's account of a meeting with Mississippi congressman William Colmer, who handled Hartzog easily; after the meeting, Hartzog recalled, "I knew then I had been had by a real pro." Colmer wanted Fort Massachusetts on Ship Island as a part of the NPS, but Hartzog had larger ideas: "Why don't we really do something great down here while we are at it. Why don't we include all of these magnificent islands in one outstanding seashore." Hartzog later told Colmer, "Mr. Chairman, you're in the fort business and I'm in the park business; now why don't we merge our businesses and have a great seashore down there?" Colmer replied, "Well, that's not a bad idea and I'll look into it." The result was Gulf Islands National Seashore. In a similar manner, the NPS also took over the Chesapeake and Ohio Canal in 1971, obtaining areas where armies had crossed the Potomac River and the canal as well as locations near smaller battlefields such as Shepherdstown, West Virginia.[15]

The result was a muted effort to preserve battlefields for the commemoration of battles. And even that was problematic. At Monocacy, for example, there was a new effort to save that battlefield from growing traffic and population concerns as a new highway threatened the integrity of the area. The original 1934 bill was thus amended in 1976 and the park was again promoted, with a hefty appropriation for land acquisition as well as site setup. Still, little was done at the battlefield for a couple more decades, and during this time the park was actually placed under the administration of the superintendent of nearby Antietam National Battlefield.[16]

By far the most significant, and really the only, federal park to emerge in this period was at Andersonville prison in Georgia. Site of the notorious Confederate prison camp, Andersonville was not a battlefield, but it did hold significance in the history of the war. As a result, Andersonville had seen its share of earlier monumentation and commemoration, but Congress finally became involved in 1971 and created the Andersonville National Historic Site.[17]

The earliest effort toward permanent commemoration at Andersonville had been its national cemetery, established in July 1865. Containing the remains of large numbers of prisoners who died while in custody, the cemetery grew to large proportions. It was near enough to the prison for easy access but far enough away to offer some separation. Over the decades, the states of Connecticut, Illinois, Indiana, Iowa, Maine, Minnesota, New Jersey, New York, and Pennsylvania had placed monuments on the site, mostly either in the cemetery itself or on the northern edge of the old prison stockade.[18]

Although the prison site went into private ownership and then bounced around to the Georgia Grand Army of the Republic in 1891 and the Women's Relief Corps in 1896, it returned to federal care in August 1910, when the owners donated the site to the War Department. In 1936, the military set up a small park, naming it Andersonville Prison Park. Although not well known, the small military park did mark the corners of the prison, the gates, and the outline of the stockade walls. It is ironic that this park was not included in the transfer of sites from the War Department to the NPS three years earlier. Writing of 1933, Horace Albright recalled this omission: "To my everlasting regret, I overlooked asking for the Andersonville, Georgia, concentration camp of the Civil War and the nearby cemetery near the site containing the bodies of over 10,000 Union soldiers, for the military cemeteries around Richmond, and for the National Zoological Park in Rock Creek Park, Washington, D.C., which was then and still is under the Smithsonian Institution."[19]

By the mid-1960s, the small park and cemetery at Andersonville were overseen by the Department of the Army, which petitioned the NPS to take custody of it and make it a national park. Various studies occurred thereafter, and almost all saw the need to make Andersonville an NPS site. Whereas the Department of the Interior did not want Pea Ridge and Wilson's Creek, the Advisory Board on National Parks, Historic Sites, Buildings, and Monuments, as well as the secretary of the interior, both pushed for Andersonville's inclusion in the NPS and both the House and Senate insular and interior affairs committees recommended passage of a bill allowing the NPS to take control. Much of the impetus for this action came from the frequent talk of the plight of American prisoners of war in Vietnam, the return of which became a major American strategic goal. Both the congressional committee reports as well as the secretary of the interior's report dwelled on "this grim story of the Civil War prison camps and the general story of military camps through the ages." The committee also noted that "the story of captivity is often as grim as the story of war itself," and the secretary argued that the narrative "should not be forgotten," adding somewhat incorrectly that "Andersonville is the only remaining period prisoner-of-war site and offers the best opportunity to tell that story."[20]

Congressman Jack Brinkley of Georgia provided the bill, H.R. 140, which allowed the secretary of the interior to designate Andersonville a national historic site and the Department of the Army, acting for the Department of Defense, to transfer 201 acres of both cemetery and prison grounds to the NPS. It also allowed the NPS to acquire the intervening privately owned land between the two in order to make a solid park, primarily by swapping other federally owned land in Georgia for land within the authorized boundary. Congress set the acreage limit at five hundred acres and appropriated funds for the purchase and startup.[21]

The NPS began its work in 1971. Among its initial duties were boundary location, land acquisition, staffing, budgeting, and archeological work. Eventually, a visitor center and the National Prisoner of War Museum emerged, all created under the new directives and requirements of the National Historic Preservation Act. Significantly, however, little appropriation was made for the initial land acquisition, continuing the lack of federal monies spent on actually preserving Civil War sites.[22]

Although not technically battlefields, other Civil War prison camps were preserved as state parks and even tangential federal areas. Rock Island, for example, was preserved on the arsenal grounds in Illinois. More traditional state parks preserved other prison sites, one of the earliest being Fort Lawton, which Georgia preserved as a state park in 1939 in the form of the Magnolia Springs State Park. Additional state areas preserved prison sites at Fort Delaware in that state, Point Lookout in Maryland, and Fort Warren in Massachusetts. Local efforts also preserved portions of other prisons sites, such as Johnson's Island in Ohio and Belle Isle in Virginia. Additional sites for prison camps were also marked with earlier national or Confederate cemeteries on or near the grounds.[23]

The massive number of states preserving prison sites in contrast to the lone federal effort at Andersonville was an illustration of the dearth of federal activity throughout the dark ages. The federal government had been slowing its tangible preservation efforts since the massive work of the 1920s and 1930s, but it reached its nadir in the 1970s and 1980s. Civil War battlefield preservation, it seemed, was on life support on the federal level—if not already dead.

III

While the federal government turned almost completely from actual preservation to producing theoretical preservation policies, the individual states were left to carry the load of battlefield preservation. Coming off the enthusiasm of the centennial, or what was left of it, many states continued their work through the next two decades and even started new preservation efforts. Armed with new tools such as the National Historic Preservation Act and its National Historic Landmark and National Register programs as well as vast history staffs to carry on the Section 106 reviews and other policy mandates, the states managed to save an abundance of battlefield land, but it was always a struggle. In comparison to federal efforts, which moved rather quickly in appropriating money and having the NPS almost immediately start work, on the state level preservation and the accompanying education, interpretation, and visitor facilities always seemed to lag behind and in some cases take decades to emerge. The state park mentality of recreation also played into the slow process, as golf courses, swimming pools, and campgrounds often took attention and resources from actual historical preservation, education, and interpretation. Yet the federal parks were also facing increasing recreational development as well, such as the emphasis on environmental aspects in the late 1970s; Gettysburg even created an environmental trail on Big Round Top.[24]

Still, the states did the best they could, and several made significant progress on their battlefields, forming multiple state parks during these years. Missouri, for example, produced three battlefield state parks between 1966 and 1990. In the immediate post-centennial years, the state took control of Pilot Knob and Fort Davidson, which had been a critical engagement in the early stages of Sterling Price's Missouri Raid. Fought in September 1864, Pilot Knob cost Price dearly, despite the Federals withdrawing back toward St. Louis. Early efforts to preserve the battlefield had gone on through descendents of battle participants, chiefly Cyrus Peterson and Thomas Ewing Jr., son of the Union commanding general at the battle. In 1904, the men formed the Pilot Knob Memorial Association and bought the battlefield from a coal company that had depleted all the coal in the area and was liquidating. Eventually, Ewing bought out Peterson and other owners, but he found he could not care for the site alone. He tried to donate the battlefield to the state and local governments, but he had no takers. Eventually, in 1934, he convinced the United States Forest Service to accept donation of the land as part of the Clark National Forest. Despite being government land, little or no marking took place until 1953, when Missouri placed a small highway historical sign at the site. The centennial fortunately revived interest in Fort Davidson, with unexpectedly large crowds at the anniversary programs, and the state began to warm to the idea of a park. Missouri park officials worked out a deal with the Forest Service to oversee the site in 1969, and in 1987 the state fully acquired the battlefield from the federal government, making it a full-fledged state park.[25]

A similar process occurred at Athens. In August 1861, a small force of Missouri state guard failed to capture the town, which was defended by a much smaller force. The battlefield was largely forgotten and the town of Athens was almost deserted by the time of the Civil War centennial, but interest in the battle revived preservation efforts and local residents formed the Athens Park Development Association in 1962. The group raised money and eventually acquired the battlefield, which they donated to the state in 1975, when it became a state park. In the years since, and having been designated the Battle of Athens State Historic Site, archeological and architectural studies have been carried out and recreational facilities added. Similarly, another Missouri state park came to fruition at Carthage, where in July 1861 a Confederate counterattack against Union forces moving into southwest Missouri caused a small skirmish and Confederate victory. The battlefield was unpreserved until 1990, when landowners donated it to the Missouri Department of Natural Resources.[26]

Tennessee was another state that made significant progress in preserving its battlefields. It opened yet another state park along the Tennessee River in 1969 to complement the Nathan Bedford Forrest State Park, which had emerged in the 1920s. The new park sat on the east side of the river, opposite the Forrest park, and was the scene of the fall 1864 action along the river in which Forrest defeated several Union gunboats and shelled the supply depot at Johnsonville from across the river. Unfortunately, much of the original Johnsonville area was then under water as a result of the Tennessee Valley Authority flooding the valley, but there were numerous sites still left above water; the state acquired some three hundred acres from the Tennessee Valley Authority itself in 1969 and created the Johnsonville State Historic Area, opening it to the public in 1971.[27]

One of Tennessee's most famous battlefields preserved as a state park was Fort Pillow, site of the April 1864 attack and massacre by cavalry under Nathan Bedford Forrest. Although heavily debated through time, most modern historians have concluded that a massacre did in fact take place as Confederates killed surrendered black troops after the fighting ended. Backers had long tried to create a large national park along the Mississippi River, which would include Fort Pillow, but these plans never materialized and it was only in 1969 that local promoters of a park plan concentrated their efforts on Fort Pillow itself. The state was open to the idea and began major feasibility studies. Ultimately, Tennessee acquired the historic land, over sixteen hundred acres, although recreation was an important part of the site plan as well. One report stated that "the natural resources and historical features of this area provide a prime recreational prospect for the State of Tennessee." The Tennessee Historical Commission was tasked with performing historical studies and developing an interpretive plan, and the site was listed on the National Register in 1973 and became a National Historic Landmark in 1975. The state also conducted vast archeological surveys in the ensuing years and in 1979 began to reconstruct the fort according to the archeological findings. Unfortunately, extant portions of the original fort were unknowingly destroyed in the process.[28]

The original controversy over the massacre at Fort Pillow created an additional controversy over the founding and interpretation of the park. Illustrating the clear divisiveness that had reemerged between the sections, Tennesseans took exception to a speech made at the dedication of Fort Pillow as a National Historic Landmark in 1975 by NPS regional office official Paul Swartz. He described Fort Pillow as "the place where more than 250 unarmed black Union soldiers were murdered and other atrocities committed," and added that "what happened here will forever shame us as a nation." Swartz hoped that "the 'lesson' of Fort Pillow today might be to keep us utterly realistic about the enigmatic nature of man—ourselves— and what we are capable of if we let the beast be uncaged." Tennessee legislator Edward F. Williams III, who represented Fort Pillow in Nashville, immediately responded, writing Buck R. Allison, head of the Tennessee Department of Conservation. Williams sat on the House committee that oversaw Allison's department. Calling Swartz's statement "Civil War propaganda," Williams told Allison that it was "neither the duty nor the responsibility of the Tenn. Department of Conservation to aid the National Park Service in perpetuating erroneous propaganda which was manufactured more than 111 years ago." Despite not raising objections at the event itself, which he attended, Allison wrote back that he agreed, labeling Swartz's speech "unjustified, stilted, and pedantic." He also noted that "there was an Allison fighting alongside General Forrest at Fort Pillow." Allison called on the NPS to issue an apology, but it was evidently never offered. Others also took exception to a balanced interpretive film and had it changed. Obviously, the reconciliation of the past was no longer a staple of Civil War battlefield preservation.[29]

With much less controversy, eight other states also preserved Civil War battlefields as state parks in the ensuing decades. Texas preserved one of its battlefields in 1971 at Sabine Pass, where in September 1862 Federal vessels caused the departure of Confederate defenders. Little preservation had occurred on the site aside from the placement in 1936 of a statue honoring Confederate commander Richard Dowling and, later, a monument to the Union dead. During World War II the army placed a coastal fortification in the area, but the state of Texas acquired the fifty-eight-acre site in 1971 and made it into a Texas Historical Commission state historic site. An interpretive pavilion was built, and various recreation-related amenities, such as picnic areas and fishing and boating facilities, were also added.[30]

A somewhat more unique process occurred in Georgia at Pickett's Mill, site of one of the many bloody engagements between portions of William T. Sherman's and Joseph E. Johnston's armies during the 1864 Atlanta campaign. Apparently, few even knew where the site of the battlefield was, although secretive local metal detector enthusiasts had hit on a major search area. Consequently, interest in preserving the site, which was owned by a paper company, was low. After Georgia governor Jimmy Carter formed a commission to study statewide historic sites, however, several local residents could not let the battlefield decay and a movement began to purchase part of the field. Led by Phil Secrist and others, several local citizens bought four hundred acres in 1973. Secrist and company then began to lobby the state legislature to make a state park out of their battlefield, and they achieved success in 1974 when the state purchased the site from the citizens and created the Pickett's Mill Battlefield State Historic Site. Planners began to conduct archeological studies through Georgia State University, and additional acreage was added by 1982. Facilities including a pavilion and a visitor center were built in the late 1980s and 1990, and the park, now up to nearly eight hundred acres and including several original earthworks, officially opened to the public in 1992.[31]

Another somewhat unique preservation effort occurred in Kansas. Sterling Price's famous 1864 Missouri Raid had ended in defeat at Westport, but the retreat was tedious and several small actions occurred during that time. One was at Mine Creek, where Federal cavalry caught and defeated the Confederate rear guard in October 1864. Little preservation occurred until 1974, when the Kansas legislature acquired 120 acres of the battlefield, augmented four years later with another 160 acres. It would be decades before the site achieved a visitor center and was opened to the public, but the area nevertheless became the Mine Creek Battlefield State Historic Site, operated by the Kansas Historical Society.[32]

Alabama also created a state park at Fort Blakely, site of one of the last battles of the Civil War. The fort sat on the eastern side of Mobile Bay, where the Federals attacked in April 1865. The battlefield quickly became a "ghost town," but local backers, led by Mary Grice, managed to get the area listed on the National Register of Historic Places. Thereafter, full efforts emerged to preserve the site, and Grice and others established the Historic Blakely Foundation in 1976 to "preserve and re-develop a unique, public, living park." The state took notice, and in 1981 the legislature added Historic Blakely State Park to its list of statewide areas. It also created the Historic Blakely Authority to develop the new park and operate it, with Grice as the new director. Through the years, additional acreage was donated to the park, including a thousand acres in 1990 from International Paper. Although the site offered ample camping and boating facilities, a section of the park was dedicated to the Civil War battlefield and contained earthworks and other war-related signage and exhibits.[33]

In addition to these new parks, there was additional work at several previously semipreserved sites, and full-fledged state parks soon emerged. At Prairie Grove, for instance, where veterans had long cared for and preserved the site of their battle in Arkansas, additional work over the ensuing decades eventually led to the state taking charge. Over the years, the park changed hands, with it going from the local United Daughters of the Confederacy to the state in 1930. Little additional preservation took place, but local citizens did form the Prairie Grove Battlefield Memorial Foundation, and the state even fostered the Prairie Grove Battlefield Park Commission and appropriated fifty thousand dollars to them in the 1950s, with which nearly a hundred additional acres were purchased. The commission also began talking with the state park system about Prairie Grove becoming a full state park, and state officials proved willing. The transfer was made in 1971, and administrators quickly began to raise the local park to the level of a full state park.[34]

A similar process took place in Oklahoma at Honey Springs. A Union victory that secured the Indian Territory for the Union, the July 1863 battle saw several races involved: whites, blacks, and Native Americans. Because of the earlier efforts of local Civil War roundtables and the Oklahoma Historical Society, a site commission had been formed but little progress had occurred through the succeeding decades. In 1981, the tide turned and the state legislature provided funding and designated Honey Springs as a state park. The legislature allowed for as much as nearly three thousand acres, but by 1982 the park contained only 160, although its total acreage would eventually near a thousand. Despite Honey Spring's status as a state park, development moved extremely slowly, and it would be decades before various archeological and historic studies would be performed.[35]

Perhaps one the most important state parks to be finished was at Port Hudson in Louisiana. Although the state had bought much of the battlefield in 1965, it still needed development and state park status, but that unfortunately took quite a while. Aid came from the NPS in making the battlefield a National Historic Landmark in 1975, and the state began to construct various trails, shelters, observation towers, parking lots, and restrooms on the site in the late 1970s. This first phase of planning was completed by March 1982, when the battlefield officially opened as a state park. Later phases included an entrance station, a museum, and infrastructural maintenance support structures, all of which were completed in 1989. Later additions included an interpretive film, and additional acres were eventually added to the park.[36]

In probably the oddest but best-funded state effort, the New Market battlefield in Virginia became a well-known and well-visited state park, sitting as it did aside one of the major highways in the nation, Interstate 81. The origins of the battlefield, where the famous Virginia Military Institute (VMI) cadets had fought in the May 1864 Confederate victory in the Shenandoah Valley, were unique and dated back to the 1940s. Virginia Military Institute graduate George R. Collins became a successful businessman and bought 160 acres of the battlefield in the 1940s. When he died in 1964, he left the battlefield to VMI to be made into a park. To aid in this effort, he also left the institute the majority of his fortune, some three million dollars. Obviously, since VMI was a state school, the battlefield would become a state-owned site, and the institute and Virginia were quick to accept the land and the money. Collins's will left little direction as to how the work should be done, stating only that the land and money had to be used "as a memorial" and "for educational purposes." Gen. George R. E. Shell, superintendent at VMI, and the park's director, James J. Geary, soon dove into the project and opened the New Market Battlefield Park in 1967. A historic house, the Bushong House, served as the visitor center until newer accommodations, paid for with the three million dollars, could be built. Over time, the visitor center was constructed, although not without a controversy that saw the original architect's plan dismissed by the State Art Commission as being "too dominating for the battlefield." The architect resigned. The eventual visitor center and museum, known as the Hall of Valor, was a testament to the VMI cadets as Collins had desired. Restoration of the house, landscaping, an entrance road, three cannon, interpretive exhibits, and a twelve-minute interpretive film were all added over the years. Another one hundred acres was also purchased in 1984.[37]

It is obvious that many states picked up the slack when the federal preservation mentality turned from preservation to theoretic overviews of preservation processes. Fortunately, the states stepped up and provided the money and manpower needed to preserve significant sites. Unfortunately, the preservation of these areas by the states was by and large a lengthy and limited process. States had little money to spend on parks, with the exception of New Market and its bountiful inheritance, so when battlefields were conserved, the preservation was normally partial in nature and achieved only limited success. And in most cases it took decades to get from the initial land acquisition to any kind of formal park that was open to the public and educated and interpreted the site for visitors. Most state parks were also well endowed with money-making recreational attributes, taking the emphasis off their historic importance. Still, the states did the best they could under significant limitations.

IV

Even as the federal government and state officials swapped the preservation baton, many other battlefields fell through the cracks. Most would sadly remain isolated and nearly forgotten for a couple more decades, but a few were preserved by local backers. In several cases where the federal government and state authorities would not do the work, local organizers either on the private or county or city level decided to preserve their own battlefields. There, a continued pattern of limited preservation emerged, with private groups or local governments unable to match the funding levels of the federal or even the state governments. The result was a series of very small and limited local parks.

For example, although a small portion of Buffington Island in Ohio had been in state hands since 1929, another small engagement site of Morgan's famous raid was preserved in 1975. Morgan had crossed into Indiana and met a small force of home guards at Corydon in early July 1863. He captured most of the men and continued on. The site remained in private hands until the Hays family donated five acres to the Harrison County Parks Department in 1975.[38]

More local and private preservation also took place at Franklin in the 1970s. The city itself acquired twenty acres at Fort Granger, and in 1977 another of Franklin's prominent sites was preserved, Carnton Mansion, where several dead Confederate generals had been laid out on the porch. The plantation was also the site of the McGavok Confederate Cemetery. Led by Joseph L. Willoughby, the Carnton Association and Heritage Foundation of Williamson County acquired the house and ten acres in 1977 through donation from physician W. D. Sugg and his wife, Ruth, with the only stipulation being that they restore the mansion. Sugg, then living in Florida, desired "perpetual cherishing and care" and concluded, "We feel that almost no where in America have people shown themselves so worthy of such a trust as you wonderful folks of Williamson County." The Carnton Association opened the house and grounds in 1979, and Ruth Sugg, a widow by 1985, sold more property to the association in that year. Over the next few years the association added a museum and bookstore, and the city added land on Winstead Hill and a historic zoning ordinance.[39]

A similar effort, also foreshadowing the private efforts that would mushroom decades later, was the establishment in 1976 of the Society of Port Republic Preservationists in the Shenandoah Valley. The area had long been a staple in Civil War history, linked as it was to Stonewall Jackson and Phil Sheridan, but little preservation had taken place prior to the modern era. In 1976 the society began an effort that numerous groups would emulate in the ensuing decades.[40]

The 1980s also saw a growth in private and local preservation efforts. One such effort was at the Westport battlefield in Kansas. Touted somewhat presumptuously as the "Gettysburg of the West," Westport was nevertheless the breaking point for Sterling Price's fall 1864 Missouri Raid, where he was defeated and forced to retreat southward. Earlier, Kansas City officials had attempted to focus attention on Westport and there was even an unsuccessful effort to make it into a national military park, but little actual preservation had occurred. In 1975, local Civil War enthusiasts in the Kansas City Civil War Roundtable formed a nonprofit corporation, the Monnett Battle of Westport Fund, named for Howard Monnett, who had researched and written on the battle. The group raised money and placed interpretive signs along a tour route on the expansive battlefield. The corporation began to acquire land in 1983, when a local bank donated about fifty foreclosed acres to the group. Later additions increased the size of what is today Big Blue Battlefield Park, run by the Kansas City Parks Department.[41]

Local preservation also occurred at Davis Bridge in Tennessee, site of the narrow escape of Earl Van Dorn's army after its disastrous attack on Corinth in October 1862. The Davis Bridge Memorial Foundation appeared in the mid-1980s, and under the leadership of Herbert Wood and Rex Brotherton the group managed to purchase in 1987, with the help of the local Sons of Confederate Veterans camp, five acres of land at the river's edge and the old bridge site. The foundation also placed interpretive signs and a monument on the battlefield in 1990. Hundreds of acres have since been added to the site, making Davis Bridge one of the most completely preserved battlefields in the nation.[42]

Ball's Bluff, one of the initial engagements of the war, also saw preservation in 1986. Site of the famous Potomac River Confederate victory in October 1861, which resulted in the death of a United States senator, Edward D. Baker, as well as the establishment of the Joint Committee on the Conduct of the War, Ball's Bluff received a small national cemetery in 1865, containing but fifty-four graves. Thereafter, a few monuments went up on the battlefield, including one to Senator Baker in the 1890s. In 1986, the Beus Corporation, private owner of a 470-acre tract that included the battlefield, decided to create a subdivision out of much of the land. It offered the Northern Virginia Regional Park Authority a sector of 168 acres, with the stipulation that the battlefield be left intact and additional land be made into ball fields and recreational areas. The park authority also acquired additional lands in the ensuing years, making the 223-acre Ball's Bluff Regional Battlefield Park a preserved haven in one of the most densely populated areas of northern Virginia.[43]

There was also a minor attempt at preservation on another northern Virginia battlefield, which by the 1980s was in the middle of expansion and urbanization. In early September 1862, Stonewall Jackson fought at Ox Hill, or Chantilly, in an effort to disrupt the Federal retreat from Second Manassas. The owners of the battlefield had deeded a mere 0.115 acres of land to a trust in 1915 for the purpose of monumentation, and Union veterans had erected monuments there to Brig. Gen. Isaac I. Stevens and Maj. Gen. Philip Kearny, both Union generals killed at the battle. The original trustees died, and the positions went vacant for years before they were filled by court order. By the 1980s, there was some talk of moving the monuments from the very valuable land, but a public outcry developed, as did the Chantilly Battlefield Association, resulting in the eventual donation of some 4.8 acres of additional land. The small area was made into a community park, now known as the Ox Hill Battlefield Park and managed by the Fairfax County Park Authority. Attempts to interest the NPS in the site went unheeded, and only a small portion of the battlefield was saved. Yet in loss came major gains, as Ox Hill became an important rallying cry for future preservation.[44]

Although not as well preserved as other federal- and state-level battlefields, these small parks provided an important source of local Civil War education. Neighborhood organizers did what no one else would try, and in large part they succeeded. And these preservationists were pioneers in a process that would in only a few years become the backbone of battlefield preservation. As the federal government backed away from preservation and the various states and local governments did likewise, it soon fell to local private organizers to carry the torch. These initial efforts illustrated the success that would ensue if only the movement could gather steam.

V

By the late 1980s, a divided battlefield preservation program had been mired in the dark ages for two and a half decades. The federal government had handed tangible preservation activity to the states, which were themselves slowing in the work of preserving their sites. In a time of economic retrenchment, it was little surprise that preservation was not the focus of any government.[45]

Still, there were bright spots. The federal government took a pro-preservation stance with the passage of such legislation as the National Historic Preservation Act, the National Environmental Protection Act, and the Archeological Resources Protection Act, and it would soon take steps to oversee the once-more-blossoming process in the last decade of the twentieth century. Even more important, a vast labor force of local volunteers and benefactors was growing, illustrating what could be done outside the halls of Congress or within state legislatures. With very early examples such as at Franklin, several private associations began to emerge in the late 1980s, and their formula for success became a deluge in the 1990s. All this combined to create a new wave that would see the preservation movement soar in the next generation. But there were foundational activities for this new effort present even in the latter stages of the dark ages, primarily in northern Virginia.[46]

There were few signs pointing to any change in the nation's memory of the war, however. Having plunged headlong into a divisive sectional view of the conflict, actually a recasting of the old Reconstruction generation's stances, the dark ages showed little change in popular mentality from the centennial ideology of the 1960s. As an example, the rancor raised at Fort Pillow state park was a continuation of the centennial's divisiveness. America was still fighting many civil rights battles throughout the dark ages, exacerbated by the 1968 assassination of Martin Luther King Jr. and the continual arguments over school integration in the South well into the 1970s. The nation was perhaps too close to the open wounds and continual history-making process even in the 1980s to be able to reflect objectively as to how race relations could affect the nation's collective memory of the war. Only on the academic front was a move toward the emancipationist vision of memory emerging.[47]

Yet there was welling up in America a vast revitalization, and the changes of the 1990s in terms of tactical preservation would also bring about an embryonic transformation in the nation's view of the war. And that change would be played out dramatically on the battlefields themselves.

Howard L. Landers was the main War Department historian working on preserving battlefields. He implemented the 1925 War Department study at various sites and prepared to preserve others, but was preempted by the transfer of the battlefields to the National Park Service in 1933. This view shows a retired Landers during World War II. Courtesy of U.S. Army Heritage and Education Center.

As the first director the National Park Service, Stephen T. Mather put his mark on the agency but was never quite able to bring it above a nature-leaning approach. Bad health caused Mather to turn over control of the NPS in 1929. Courtesy of Library of Congress.

Horace M. Albright took over the National Park Service in 1929 and succeeded in gaining the historical parks from the War Department in 1933. A chance Sunday afternoon ride with President Roosevelt went a long way in causing the transfer. Courtesy of Library of Congress.

President Franklin D. Roosevelt visited Chickamauga and Chattanooga on several occasions. Here, he is seen high above Chattanooga on Lookout Mountain. Courtesy of Chickamauga and Chattanooga National Military Park.

The Civilian Conservation Corps was one of the most famous of New Deal agencies. This image shows the CCC camp at Shiloh National Military Park in the 1930s. Courtesy of Shiloh National Military Park.

The McLean House went through an interesting history on its path toward preservation. Torn down in the 1890s in preparation to be moved, during the New Deal it was reconstructed on its original site as part of Appomattox Court House National Historical Park. This view from April 1865 shows the house as it looked at the time of the surrender. Courtesy of Library of Congress.

Being the spot where the war began, Fort Sumter, South Carolina, was one of the most iconic Civil War sites in America. This view shows the modernization of the fort in later years, when it became a park after World War II. Courtesy of Library of Congress.

The post–World War II national park at Harpers Ferry, West Virginia, included more than just Civil War history. Over the decades, it would come to be one of the centers of interpretation of the African American experience. This view shows one of the restored streets in the town. Courtesy of Library of Congress.

Ulysses S. Grant III, grandson of the general and president, was an active participant in the memorialization of the Civil War. He was an initial leader in the centennial celebrations in the 1960s. Courtesy of Library of Congress.

The March on Washington in 1963 was a turning point in the civil rights movement. It helped spur a change in the memorialization of the Civil War as well, first on the academic and then eventually on the public level. This view shows the crowd gathered in front of the Lincoln Memorial. Courtesy of Library of Congress.

Despite his reinvigoration of the United States, President Ronald Reagan tried to cut domestic spending, including for parks. The conservatism of the 1980s was a major factor in the "dark ages" of battlefield preservation. Courtesy of Library of Congress.

One of the only parks to be established during the "dark ages," the Andersonville National Historic Site memorialized a prison camp rather than a battlefield. This view shows the prison stockade immediately after the war. Courtesy of Library of Congress.

As chief historian of the National Park Service, Edwin C. Bearss (center) was a major factor in battlefield preservation. Here, he is leading a tour at Shiloh National Military Park. Courtesy of Shiloh National Military Park.

The African American Civil War Memorial, dedicated in Washington, D.C., in 1998, illustrated the changing public perception of race and memory regarding the Civil War. Courtesy of Library of Congress.

The emphasis on African American history and slavery as a cause of the Civil War filtered down into the parks in the Renaissance era, including at the new NPS Corinth Civil War Interpretive Center. The unit of Shiloh National Military Park opened in 2004 and included a portion of the contraband camp that existed there between 1862 and 1864. Courtesy of Shiloh National Military Park.

Today, O. James Lighthizer is the undisputed leader of the Civil War battlefield preservation movement. As president of the Civil War Trust, he leads the first comprehensive, national organization fully committed to battlefield preservation. Courtesy of the Civil War Trust.

7

The Renaissance,
1990–2015

Shelby Foote became a national folk hero in the fall of 1990. Appearing in *The Civil War*, Ken Burns's television documentary that swept the nation that September, Foote's emergence was perhaps the most surprising development to come out of the series. He had written numerous histories and novels, but it was his appealing Southern drawl and sheepish grin that opened the hearts of millions of Americans to him and his passion, the Civil War. The year 1990 was certainly a watershed time for Foote, but it also proved to be decisive in other Civil War–related arenas, including battlefield preservation. In large part due to Ken Burns and Shelby Foote, Civil War history reinvigorated America.[1]

Many other significant events occurred around that shifting of the decades from the 1980s to the 1990s, and America itself changed in many ways. Not only did communism and the Soviet Union fall about that time, but the nation also began to enter a new phase of post–Cold War conflicts, such as the first Gulf War and the rise of terrorism. At home, computers, the Internet, and mobile phones began to emerge in everyday life and increasingly became necessities instead of luxuries.[2]

Drastic change also emerged on the Civil War battlefield preservation front. If the 1970s and 1980s were the dark ages of battlefield preservation, what occurred in the 1990s can only be described as a renaissance. Altogether different from what had preceded it, this modern period, extending into the twenty-first century, has been marked by new thinking, heightened participation, and, most important, undeniable success. An all-out, comprehensive, undeniable, national leader of the effort, something sorely lacking from the beginning, also finally emerged during this era.[3]

Many factors went into this era's new way of thinking and acting, including the emergence of environmental concerns and a growing desire for green space, some of it ushered in by a maturing baby-boomer generation. On the other hand, a lot of the change had to do with public awareness and education. And not a little of that occurred on and around America's Civil War battlefields. For instance, the 135th anniversary of the war took place between 1986 and 1990, fostering an interest in the Civil War not seen since the centennial in the 1960s. Many battlefields held observations on the anniversary dates, including most of the major federal parks and many state parks. Numerous battles were reenacted then and later, and participants will always remember the debacle that was the 125th anniversary of Shiloh, complete with rains that matched only the original event in 1862. In an effort to laugh to keep from crying, many began to refer to the event as "Mudloh."[4]

The American public also took a larger interest in the Civil War due to several media productions in addition to Ken Burns's documentary. Although an academic, James M. McPherson published his highly acclaimed, Pulitzer Prize–winning *Battle Cry of Freedom* in 1988, and it quickly became a national best seller. McPherson presented the war in a spellbinding narrative, offering the reading public an entertaining one-volume history of the war, something much different from the three-volume sets of Catton or Foote dating from the centennial.[5]

The public also began to enjoy better-quality motion pictures utilizing massive numbers of reenactors (by this time reenacting had become a major hobby). Differing from such oddities as the miniseries *North and South* and the similar *Blue and Gray*, the movie *Glory* depicted the travails of the African American Fifty-Fourth Massachusetts in an accurate and compelling format in 1989. Similarly, the 1993 movie *Gettysburg* provided an intimate view into those three days in July 1863. Drawing the public interest by force of their name recognition were the movies' A-list actors, including Morgan Freeman, Martin Sheen, and Jeff Daniels.[6]

Still, no media production spurred interest in the war like Burns's *Civil War*. This eleven-hour documentary, complete with spellbinding narration by David McCullough and commentary by Shelby Foote, showed in American homes each night in the fall of 1990 and took the nation by storm, acquiring some thirty-nine million viewers. Book sales and visitation at Civil War parks surged. Although historians have debated the merits and accuracy of the documentary, Burns unquestionably caused an outcry of interest in the Civil War.[7]

At the same time, amid so much hype about the Civil War, no process did more to galvanize the idea of battlefield preservation than a contemporary series of preservation controversies on the battlefields themselves. One disagreement occurred over the famous National Gettysburg Battlefield Tower, which had opened on private land in 1974 and was regarded as an eyesore ever since. Preservationists fought hard in the 1990s to have the tower removed, which was eventually done in 2000. More significantly, in the 1990s a much more lengthy and complicated set of controversies developed at Manassas over the integrity and view shed of the Manassas National Battlefield. The controversies became national news and accordingly added to the interest and perceived need to preserve historic sites.[8]

The first major modern preservation battle over Manassas occurred in the 1970s as the Marriott Corporation began the process of building an Americana theme park on an unprotected portion of the Second Manassas battlefield. On 513 acres of land adjoining the national park, Marriott announced a plan in 1973 to build a "Great America" theme park that would showcase American history. The tract itself contained the sites of several historic headquarters, including Robert E. Lee's on Stuart's Hill, and it was the jumping-off point for James Longstreet's famous flank attack. The NPS took a neutral position on the development, but several recent federal laws eventually ended the project, most notably environmental procedures set up by the National Environmental Protection Act in 1969. With hopes that the history theme park would be open by 1976, the nation's bicentennial, Marriott instead found the project delayed until 1978, and then, with environmental studies still needing to be performed, it soon gave up the plan altogether.[9]

The withdrawal of Marriott's plan set up another, more forceful encounter. The same plot soon fell into Til Hazel's hands, and the Hazel/Peterson Companies planned to build a mixed-use area of offices and shopping centers named the Williams Center on the site. To some preservationists' dismay, the NPS again took a neutral stance, opting to compromise with the landowners to mitigate the impact on the national park. Then Hazel changed his mind and decided to place a large shopping mall directly on the top of Stuart's Hill, the site of Lee's headquarters. The destruction of such a historic area as well as concern over the attendant population and traffic issues in the vicinity caused the emergence of the Save the Battlefield Coalition, led by Annie Snyder. Forming a broad coalition of supporters, Snyder eventually managed to get political support. Congress stepped in, led initially by Representative Mike Andrews of Texas, Representative Bob Mrazek of New York, and Senator Dale Bumpers of Arkansas. Virginia senator John Warner then came on board. Congress decided the matter by forcing the sale of the property to the government—a government "taking" that added the land (now 558 acres) to the NPS's Manassas park. Such a course was practically un-heard of, because the court granted an extremely high price for the land over the objections of Interior Secretary Donald P. Hodel. Many soon realized that this would probably never happen again, and indeed should not have to happen: it was the result of piecemeal attention to individual preservation threats. Many soon called for a comprehensive national policy on battlefield preservation.[10]

Although the fight over the Hazel/Peterson plan caused an uproar and re-sulted in solid action in the early 1990s, the fight over Manassas was not yet over. One final controversy, perhaps even larger, emerged a few years later. In the early 1990s, the Disney Corporation began to lay groundwork for another theme park; like Marriott's earlier plan, it was to be a tribute to American history. Close to tourist spots in the capital region but far enough away not to compete with its existing parks in Florida and California, the Manassas Disney park was several miles away from the battlefield and not on historic land. Yet preservationists led by Richard Moe of the National Trust for Historic Preservation, as well as other entities such as the Piedmont Environmental Council and Protect Historic America, opposed the plan and eventually had it stopped due to concerns over increased traffic, population, and crowds. Eventually, Disney gave up the idea, but the debate again engulfed the nation as it became headline news in national papers and on nightly news broadcasts. The results not only solidified the obvi-ous need for a national preservation policy but also galvanized preservationists throughout the country to support conservation far and wide, including in their own local areas.[11]

The battlefield preservation movement would never be the same.

I

Annie Snyder's Save the Battlefield Coalition fight had larger implications than just keeping the Hazel/Peterson companies from building their mall on Stuart's Hill. In fact, the controversy sparked a flood of efforts to preserve battlefields, and these fights even rose to the highest levels of government. George H. W. Bush's administration, certainly not as conservative as was Reagan's, sought to show support for the effort amid the increase in popular opinion brought about by Ken Burns and others. All across the board, on the federal, state, local, and private lev-els, battlefield preservationists mobilized, creating what would be a renaissance in preservation, especially compared to the dark ages of the previous decades. And in a major twist of events, even the federal government, almost mute for the past twenty-five years, suddenly became active again.[12]

Although Washington, D.C., reentered the battlefield preservation business in the 1990s, it did so in a different fashion. There would be new parks and new units to emerge in this modern era, but the primary area of federal activity once more became oversight. Preservationists had been calling for nearly a hundred years for a comprehensive national policy on battlefield preservation, yet the federal government had never seen fit to provide one. Calls had first emerged in the massive number of park bills in the late 1890s and early 1900s, but Congress refused to respond. The same call emerged in the 1920s, but Congress again failed to fully address the issue and let the War Department take the lead, which became irrelevant when care of the parks went to the NPS shortly thereafter. Even the centennial years failed to develop a national policy, and at the same time Congress began to shrink from active preservation and turn to larger policy advisement. Although such legislation as the Historic Sites Act and the National Historic Preservation Act emerged, none of it included full-fledged battlefield preservation policy. Amid the renewed interest in the Civil War and a specific call for a national strategy from attorney Tersh Boasberg in the *Washington Post*, the early 1990s was a perfect time for the federal government to begin taking steps toward finally offering that comprehensive policy.[13]

Two major actions resulted, one by Congress and the other by the federal agency tasked with overseeing historic sites in America. At the insistence of Arkansas senator Dale Bumpers, Congress passed in the fall of 1990 the Civil War Sites Study Act. The legislation called for two efforts, including the Shenandoah Valley Civil War Sites Study, which was to "identify the sites, determine the relative significance of such sites, assess short- and long-term threats to their integrity, and provide alternatives for the preservation and interpretation of such sites by Federal, state, and local governments, or other public or private entities, as may be appropriate."[14]

Although the Shenandoah portion of the bill offered help for a critical area of Civil War battlefields, by far the most important portion of the act was the call for a committee of fifteen members and their staff, housed in the NPS, to study the entirety of the nation's Civil War battlefields (Congress would follow later on in 1996 with a similar Revolutionary War and War of 1812 Historic Preservation Study). The Civil War Sites Advisory Commission, composed of legislators, academics, and government bureaucrats, was appointed in 1991, with such notables as filmmaker Ken Burns, historians William J. Cooper and James M. McPherson, and legislator Robert J. Mrazek serving. Edwin C. Bearss was an ex officio member of the commission. Chaired by Holly A. Robinson, the commission began work and over the next year and a half compiled priceless data on the state of the nation's Civil War sites. Tasked with identifying significant battlefields, organizing them in importance, determining their condition and threats to them, and proposing efforts to preserve them, the commission held sixteen public meetings and four workshops in eleven states and in total visited fifty-three battlefields. Commission staff or portions of the commission visited 368 battlefields in total.[15]

A major task was to identify and rate the battlefields so that a plan of preservation could be fostered. The commission identified 384 battlefields as "principal" Civil War sites in twenty-six states. The members organized the battles into four classes, reminiscent of the old 1925 War Department study. Class A fields had "a decisive influence on a campaign and a direct impact on the course of the war," Class B had "a direct and decisive influence on their campaign," Class C had "observable influence on the outcome of a campaign," and Class D had "a limited influence on the outcome of their campaign or operation but achiev[ed] or affec[ed] important local objectives." The 384 battlefields studied were only a small percentage (3.7 percent) of the overall number of battlefields, which by some estimates reached above ten thousand. Still, these were the most important actions and as such constituted the most dire need for preservation.[16]

In terms of the state of preservation, the commission detailed its findings in a lengthy report augmented by a second volume of battle studies for the 384 engagements. Basically, the members found that 43 percent of the battlefields were completely in private hands, with only 4 percent actually being well preserved by a government entity. The rest were protected by a mixture of private, local, or government entities. Furthermore, the commission found that 19 percent of the battlefields were already lost beyond recovery and fully half of the preservable sites faced imminent threat from urbanization. Only a third of the 384 fields faced little or no threat when the report was issued in 1993.[17]

The commission also detailed how little had been done in the previous 125 years. Only thirty-seven battlefields had been preserved by state efforts and fifty-eight as part of the national park system. Even more troubling, only eighty-four fields had been granted National Register status, and only an astounding sixteen sites had been given National Historic Landmark status. Even if the goal was not complete preservation of every Civil War site, in 1993 much work still had to be done, and such a dismal overview resulted from the lack of an overall policy over the previous 130 years.[18]

Significantly, the commission offered its own recommendations to set up a major battlefield policy. It called on the federal government to once more take the lead in preservation, particularly with the Class A and B sites, leaving C and D sites to state, local, or private groups but aiding in their efforts as well. To present an overall policy, the commission called on the federal and state governments to work together to "define directions for battlefield protection. In particular, the national goal should be to provide a national assemblage of key battlefield locations consisting of as many of the 384 sites in the Commission's inventory as can be protected. Such an assemblage of sites is a vital national resource for conveying basic American themes and values that keep us from fragmenting into competing cultures." The commission also called on Congress to establish several other entities, including an "Emergency Civil War Battlefield Land Acquisition Program" and a "Civil War Battlefield Stewardship Pilot Program."[19]

The Civil War Sites Advisory Commission went out of existence after turning in its report, but the federal government did not take its ideas to heart and passed few of its recommendations. Part of the reason was that by the mid-1990s, the renewal brought about by the Burns film as well as the controversies over Manassas had ebbed. Also, a political change in Congress in 1994 ushered in a fiscal conservatism attendant to Newt Gingrich's "Contract with America." Little momentum remained on the federal level, especially concerning the advisory commission's recommendations.[20]

Such limited federal activity was also illustrated by the emergence of the other major federal preservation effort of the early 1990s, the initially small American Battlefield Protection Program (ABPP). After the Manassas debacle, Secretary of the Interior Manuel Lujan Jr. declared the ABPP office open and housed in the NPS in 1991, but the program's initial purpose was merely advisory; it had little power to alter the preservation path. Fortunately, in 1996 Congress passed the American Battlefield Protection Act, which officially created the ABPP, although it was still primarily an advisory program intended "to assist citizens, public and private institutions, and governments at all levels in planning, interpreting, and protecting sites where historic battles were fought on American soil during the armed conflicts that shaped the growth and development of the United States, in order that present and future generations may learn and gain inspiration from the ground where Americans made their ultimate sacrifice." The legislation also declared that the ABPP "shall encourage, support, assist, recognize, and work in partnership with citizens, Federal, State, local, and tribal governments, other public entities, educational institutions, and private nonprofit organizations in identifying, researching, evaluating, interpreting, and protecting historic battlefields and associated sites on a National, State, and local level." The program received a three-million-dollar appropriation annually for ten years, bumped up to ten million annually in an amended format in 2002, which was primarily distributed through grants to battlefield preservation groups. Congress stipulated, however, that the program would run only ten years (to 2008), at which time it would, if successful, need reauthorization. Congress reauthorized the program for another ten years in 2009, at the same level of funding.[21]

The work of the American Battlefield Protection Program has been stellar, supporting the work of various state, local, and private preservation efforts. In its outreach, the ABPP mainly focused on two areas of need. The first was actual money for the acquisition of battlefield land. Since 1998, the program's land-acquisition grant program has helped save parts of seventy-five battlefields in sixteen different states. The second need was money for the study of how best to preserve sites. Here the ABPP has helped numerous local and even larger en-tities in planning for preservation; in fact, since 1992, the ABPP has given out more than five hundred planning grants to over a hundred battlefield preservation groups in forty-two states and territories. The ABPP's Civil War Battlefield Pres-ervation Program is its main effort focusing on the Civil War.[22]

The American Battlefield Protection Program has also recently worked to update the original 1993 advisory commission report. Although a new commis-sion has not been appointed, Congress gave the program the authority through amendments and reauthorizations to resurvey the original sites to see what has changed over the past twenty years. The ABPP staff conducted its update sur-veys beginning in 2008 and continued through 2010, issuing twenty-four detailed reports for states and the District of Columbia, including one grouping of three "Far Western Battlefields" in Colorado, Idaho, and New Mexico. These detailed documents delineated the changes since 1993, sometimes updating, correcting, or changing classifications in the original report and certainly providing more information on each site. These individual reports also listed the grants issued to preservationists in each state to that date.[23]

Despite the stellar work done by the advisory commission and the American Battlefield Protection Program, the federal government still did not take the full reins of leadership by issuing a comprehensive battlefield preservation policy. Al-though this era would indeed prove to be a renaissance in terms of new method-ology and action, it was not going to be led by the federal government.

II

The federal government provided some preservation effort, but it failed once again to construct an overall policy. And the federal government was not that effective in individual preservation during this period either, leaving the process mainly to its American Battlefield Protection Program to provide preservation guidance for other groups. That said, the federal government, primarily through the NPS, did add a few distinct sites to its park system after 1990, which demonstrated some movement away from the lethargy of the dark ages. But there was somewhat of a caveat even in these newer parks. The new sites were not necessarily preserved for their military significance, as had been the case for the previous 130 years, but were results of a major shift in American perception and memory of the war, pri-marily on racial grounds. The renaissance in thinking that emerged in the 1990s, when the emancipationist vision of memory finally emerged as an accepted public view outside the halls of academia, shifted Americans' views on the Civil War, and the federal government likewise shifted its focus on battlefield preservation.[24]

Much of the impetus for the federal government's change of thinking, as well as the larger American public's transition, came from the same sources that inspired the nation in the late 1980s and early 1990s, such as Ken Burn's documentary and the 125th anniversary events. Although historians argued that Burns did not go far enough on the slavery issue, there was no doubt that Burns considered slavery the key cause of the Civil War and many of his talking heads illustrated that fact. Ed Bearss declared that John Brown's slave raid on Harpers Ferry was the single most important spark for the war, and Barbara Fields eloquently posited that the war was about battles and weapons only to the extent that they joined a larger argument over freedom and liberty. An illustration of the change in thinking emerged at Gettysburg as two very different commemorative efforts went forward in July 1988. One was the old martial reenactment, but the other, which gained much less attention yet foreshadowed the future, focused on the rededication of the Eternal Light Peace Memorial, originally dedicated at the battle's seventy-fifth anniversary. As Edward Linenthal suggests, the rededication "sought to deepen and universalize the ideology of reconciliation," and speaker Carl Sagan tied the desire for eternal peace to the Cold War's potential nuclear destruction. While the nation was still in the throes of the Cold War in 1988, it was but a small step to include racial matters.[25]

The effect was huge in the federal government, especially when Illinois congressman Jesse Jackson Jr. added language to a 2000 appropriations bill that required NPS Civil War units to interpret not just their individual site histories but also slavery as the chief cause of the war as a whole: "To encourage Civil War battle sites to recognize and include in all of their public displays and . . . educational presentations the unique role that the institution of slavery played in causing the Civil War." Such a suggestion had been made earlier in 1990, but this time a firestorm developed, especially from heritage groups in the South. Nevertheless, the agency began to implement Jackson's wishes under the guidance of the NPS's chief historian, Dwight Pitcaithley. Perhaps no greater result was the NPS symposium Rally on the High Ground, held at Ford's Theatre in Washington, D.C., in May 2000. There, participants heard from such historians as Eric Foner and David Blight as well as from Jackson himself. The symposium brought issues to light that illustrated the changing nature of racial interpretation at Civil War battlefields, often using technology such as the "virtual" Underground Railroad Park. Historian David Blight summed up the major question at issue: "Did they remember the meanings of the war, or merely the drama of the fight"?[26]

The effects of this new emphasis were soon seen in several national parks added to the system in the 1990s and 2000s, including those outside the Civil War arena that touched on such subjects as the civil rights movement. Sites dealing with the *Brown v. Board of Education* case, the Selma, Alabama, demonstrations, and Little Rock's Central High School all came to fruition during this period. In terms of a strictly Civil War focus, the NPS added a unit to the Shiloh National

Military Park at Corinth, Mississippi, where a significant siege as well as a later brutal battle took place in 1862. Yet much of the impetus for preserving the area and adding the unit came with the emphasis on the famous contraband camp that existed at Corinth from 1862 to 1864. A portion of the contraband camp's site itself was included in the unit, as well as major interpretation at the new interpretive center that opened in 2004 at the Battery Robinett site. The interpretive center, different from a museum in that it interpreted history more than it showcased artifacts, went far beyond just interpreting the contraband camp. It was one of the first NPS sites to wholeheartedly educate the public on slavery's role in the causes of the Civil War. Giving Mississippi's proslavery secession convention declaration of causes a prominent hearing, the center sought to discuss the causes of the war as much as it did to interpret the military actions around the town.[27]

Another illustration of the rise of racial issues as prominent factors in establishing federal battlefield parks was the Sand Creek Massacre National Historic Site in Colorado. The location of the exact site of the November 1864 Indian massacre had been debated for decades, but archeological studies done under 1998 federal legislation resulted in a collaborative agreement between the federal government, the state of Colorado, and the various Native American tribes that the actual site had finally been determined. A Special Resource Study and Site Location Study allowed Congress to authorize the park in 2000, and the national park opened in 2007. Unlike much earlier interpretations of Native American sites, the NPS took a more objective view of the events and included the native side of the story as well. Although not related to the history of African Americans or slavery, the work at Sand Creek nevertheless illustrated the changing federal government policy and ideals concerning minorities and their actions on Civil War battlefields.[28]

In 2002, the NPS also began operating the Cedar Creek and Belle Grove National Historic Park in Virginia. Originally supported by the National Trust for Historic Preservation, a local preservation group, the Cedar Creek Battlefield Foundation, began to work in the late 1980s. The area had been designated a National Historic Landmark in 1969, but for decades little preservation had gone forward. Then several private enterprises began to acquire land around the various battlefields in the area, and although the NPS owned only eight acres when the park came into existence, local battlefield preservationists owned a total of nearly twelve hundred acres. The Cedar Creek battle was a major part of the desire for the park, but the NPS was also careful to interpret a much broader history, including slavery at the Belle Grove plantation as well as the earlier Native American history of the area. Cedar Creek and Belle Grove National Historic Park illustrated the broader effort to move beyond narrow battle history in NPS interpretation.[29]

While major changes were occurring on the federal level in terms of racial awareness, the NPS was also developing other battlefields along more traditional ideals. The small fight at Glorieta Pass, New Mexico, in March 1862 had allowed the Federals to blunt Confederate offensive movements in the far West. Little in terms of preservation had occurred thereafter, although the nearby area of Pecos had been declared a national monument under the Antiquities Act in the 1960s. Pecos National Historical Park itself had been created in 1990 by an act of Congress, raising the site from the status of a national monument. In that same year, perhaps in reaction to the discovery of thirty Confederate soldiers' remains in 1987, the Glorieta unit of the Pecos park, with subunits at Pigeon's Ranch and Canoncito, was added in order to preserve and interpret the Civil War battle. Land was acquired slowly, with the superintendent's reports describing the effort as a "hot button" issue in which the federal government did not appropriate money for acquisition and outside buyers were not forthcoming either, leading trapped landowners to complain of "reverse condemnation." It was only during the sesquicentennial, through the efforts of the Glorieta Coalition, that the area was actually opened to visitors, with an interpretive trail allowing access and viewing of the Pigeon's Ranch unit.[30]

The Glorieta unit also illustrated the changing attitudes toward Civil War battlefield preservation, interpretation, and ideology. Immediately after its establishment, the Glorieta unit became a target for monumentation. One organization, the Glorieta Battlefield Memorial Planning Group, desired to erect a monument to Colorado volunteers at the battle, but it met opposition from NPS officials. Park leaders met with the group and voiced "concerns with monuments/ memorials within National Park Units," but as the park did not yet own the land, they could not stop the proposed effort and the monument was dedicated in 1993. NPS officials did, however, ask to be involved in creating the text for the monument. In another change of ideology, the NPS decided to rebury the thirty Confederate soldiers found on the battlefield in 1987 in the Santa Fe National Cemetery. Finally, it seemed, the animosity of sides was again beginning to lessen.[31]

One other battlefield began to see increased attention in this more modern age as well. Although established by Congress in 1934, the Monocacy battlefield had never received the promised donated land and had sat idle for decades. Only in 1976 did Congress rectify the situation and provide funds for land acquisition (up to sixteen hundred acres). Unfortunately, the sponsor of the legislation and major supporter of the park, local congressman Goodloe Byron, died of a heart attack just two days before Congress passed his bill, so he never saw the results of his work. Nevertheless, he had worked with the Monocacy Battlefield Advisory Commission and developed plans for boundaries and preservation of prime land set to be urbanized. As one congressional staffer noted after Byron's death, "Without this change, half of the battlefield would be under industrial development within the next five years." Once again, Ed Bearss drew a large boundary, this time of some twenty-five hundred acres, but progress was slow. Some success came in the 1980s, but it was not until 1991 that a small portion of the park was opened to the public. Throughout the remainder of the 1990s and into the 2000s, the park focused on opening more land, stabilizing historic structures, and obtaining a new visitor center outside the flood-prone areas of the Monocacy River basin. Making the park complete was the 2003 administrative act that separated Monocacy from Antietam's administration.[32]

Although the federal government restarted its Civil War battlefield preservation efforts in the years after 1990, with new comprehensive studies and the battlefield protection program as well as additional sites, the sad fact was that government officials did not heed the warning in the 1993 advisory commission report that the federal government needed to take the lead in the process. Despite calls for an overall comprehensive battlefield preservation policy, Congress did not see fit to institute it. No doubt the later War on Terror and its attendant ground wars in Iraq and Afghanistan raised more concern over spending. Consequently, what federal work that was done was still site specific, and often the NPS found itself in a compromising situation in which it had to bargain and compromise, losing precious land to save what it deemed was more significant. With the failure of the federal government to take the lead, it fell to other entities to seize the standard of battlefield preservation and carry it forward on a nationwide basis.[33]

III

It would seem logical that if the federal government would not step in and take control of the battlefield preservation process, the individual states would take the lead. But that did not happen. Despite some success at the state level, the states did not take a leadership role. The reasons for this included states opting for local preservation efforts and the desire for recreational parks rather than history parks, which did not make money. Still, the result was an almost leaderless government preservation effort.[34]

Nevertheless, some states did preserve battlefield land in this more modern era, including a portion of the Secessionville battlefield near Charleston, South Carolina. Fort Lamar was part of the Confederate defenses of the area, and it was there that Federal attacks were turned away in June 1862. The state's Department of Natural Resources, working through one of its agencies—the Heritage Trust—purchased thirteen and a half acres in 1996 and created the Fort Lamar Heritage Preserve.[35]

Louisiana also preserved a portion of its historic Civil War fields, including two forts near Alexandria on the Red River. Fort Randolph and Fort Buhlow helped defend the river, and the United Daughters of the Confederacy erected monuments there in 1928. The two forts, which saw no action, were nevertheless eventually preserved, one by the city of Pineville and the other by the state on the grounds of the Louisiana Hospital for the Insane. In 2007, after a long delay, the state provided funds to create the Forts Randolph and Buhlow State Historic Site, complete with a staff, visitor center, hiking trails, and exhibits. Work was completed by 2010, when the park opened to the public. Of perhaps more historic interest, the state park on each side of the river was also the site of the famous Bailey's Dam, which was constructed to allow the trapped Union fleet under David Dixon Porter high enough water to escape the falling river during the Red River campaign.[36]

Georgia was the most active of all the states in this modern era, preserving in some form at least three battlefields. It added seventeen acres of the Griswoldville battlefield to its state park system in 1997. The site of the Confederate militia's unsuccessful attempt to delay Sherman's March to the Sea in November 1864, the Griswoldville battlefield was placed under the nearby Jarrell Plantation State Historic Site and contained only a monument and small parking area.[37]

The opening of other battlefields took much longer and were more complex affairs. Indeed, the state's acquisition of the Allatoona battlefield was a decades-long process. Part of the post–Atlanta campaign, when John Bell Hood marched northward, the October 1864 battle was fierce and bloody but yielded no long-term effects, except the religious hymn "Hold the Fort." The Army Corps of Engineers had purchased the land around the battlefield in the 1940s, but it had accomplished little historic interpretation over the decades. In fact, the site soon became a party area for local youth. In the early 1990s, however, the Etowah Valley Historical Society began to work at the site, providing signage and trails. Still, it was not until 2007 that the federal government leased the land to the Georgia state park system. The state park was then attached to Red Top Mountain State Park, which occupied other areas around Lake Allatoona.[38]

Of similarly lengthy duration, and still incomplete as of the sesquicentennial, was the work at Resaca. In a joint effort begun in 2002, state and local county officials banded together to create a park that would be run by the county. The battle was one of the earliest and most significant conflicts of the Atlanta campaign in May 1864, and the project to preserve it turned out to be a multilevel operation. The state worked with the Friends of Resaca Battlefield to establish the Resaca Battlefield State Historic Site and was still constructing the park during the sesquicentennial but leaving its management to Gordon County. The county also acquired and operated the Fort Wayne Civil War Historic Site on the Resaca battlefield.[39]

In addition to the work in Gordon County, other local governments toiled in Georgia, including Atlanta and the counties of Fulton, Henry, and Whitfield, saving land around Lovejoy Station, Peachtree Creek, and Utoy. Local governments in other states also worked to preserve historic battlefields. Hanover County, Virginia, attained 172 acres of the North Anna battlefield, opening the North Anna Battlefield Park in 1996. In addition, numerous other county and city governments in Virginia preserved hundreds of acres of battlefield land, mostly around Newport News and Saltville and in Henrico County. The same occurred in Tennessee, mostly around the Nashville area but also in Chattanooga and Collierville. In North Carolina, Wayne County preserved 31 acres of the Goldsborough Bridge battlefield, Brunswick County acquired approximately 625 acres of the Wilmington battlefield, Lenoir County preserved 125 acres at Kinston and Wise Fork, and the city of Washington acquired an easement of over 192 acres of the Washington battlefield. In Kentucky, Madison County preserved 597 acres of the Richmond battlefield, and in Arkansas the cities of Jacksonville (Bayou Meto) and Helena preserved land at those sites. In South Carolina, Charleston and Charleston County acquired much of their local battlefields, and Adams County in Pennsylvania preserved many of the Gettysburg area historic sites outside that park.[40]

Local and county governments also began to establish zoning ordinances to restrict disturbances to battlefields. Easements, wherein landowners promised not to develop the land, were often found to be an easier and cheaper means to this end, and many local governments opted for local historic districts to provide preservation cover instead of the outright preservation of historic sites. But in an effort to steer clear of government involvement, many conservative rural officials opted not to pass zoning ordinances. Boge and Boge highlighted this phenomenon, noting that "residents of rural communities commonly deplore the idea of land-use controls even when such protection would guarantee the maintenance of rural values."[41]

As a result, state and local governments, using limited and piecemeal efforts, were not able to foster any type of concerted preservation initiative. But they can hardly be blamed for failure in that regard, as states and local governments by definition cannot foster a national process. Still, in the wake of a lackluster federal effort, states and local governments were not much more successful at preserving battlefields than the national government.

IV

Despite several new national parks and a few scattered state and local parks, even the renaissance age did not see the massive outpouring of government effort that previous generations had enjoyed. In what became a pattern over the decades, the chief leadership in the effort once again changed. Where once the federal government was the leader in the effort to preserve Civil War battlefields, it gave that role over to the states by the 1960s, and then the states handing the effort over to local officials, who could do little. Government in its entirety stepped away from the leadership of battlefield preservation, and the process was once again handed off to new organizers.[42]

As governments at all levels turned over battlefield preservation to private entities, with the majority of governmental work increasingly coming in support, advisory, or financial grant roles, local private groups took the standard. The recent success of the Civil War battlefield preservation effort certainly resulted in part from the grass roots—mostly local people who fought, scratched, clawed, and almost begged for every acre of ground they could get. But local participation has been a hallmark of battlefield preservation from the beginning, especially with private associations supporting every site that became a federal park. Secretary of the Interior Manuel Lujan Jr. summed up the process in the early 1990s when he noted, "Preservation is best achieved when the people closest to the place in question are closely involved—when preservation is happening not for them or to them, but with them." And the sheer number of these small, localized groups that emerged after 1990 illustrated the widespread nature and power of the combined effort in this era.[43]

Numerous states saw private enterprises begin work in the 1990s. In Oklahoma, for example, the Friends of Honey Springs Battlefield (established in 1991) and Friends of Cabin Creek Battlefield (1994) appeared at those sites. Similarly, in South Carolina, the South Carolina Battleground Preservation Trust (1993) and the Fort Sumter–Fort Moultrie Historical Trust (2001) preserved land in that state, and in West Virginia the Rich Mountain Battlefield Foundation (1991), the Falling Waters Battlefield Association (2004), and the Shepherdstown Battlefield Preservation Association (2004) preserved land at those battlefields and were assisted in their work by the U.S. Forestry Service. In Arkansas, the Reed's Bridge Battlefield Preservation Society (1997) at Bayou Meto and the Friends of Devil's Backbone Ridge Battlefield (2010) performed needed work; larger statewide efforts included work carried out by the Friends of Arkansas's Battlefields (2010). In Kentucky, the Mill Springs Battlefield Association (1992), the Middle Creek National Battlefield Foundation (1992), the Camp Wildcat Preservation Foundation (1994), the Battle for the Bridge Historic Preserve Project of the Hart County Historical Society (1996), and the Battle of Richmond Association (2001) all worked to preserve Kentucky's battlefields. In Louisiana, the Friends of Fort DeRussy (1994) and the Plaquemines Historic Association (1996), as well as the Friends of the Mansfield Battlefield (2003), worked to preserve that state's historic ground. In Maryland, an early effort to recast the namesake of the Antietam Plan began with the establishment of the Save Historic Antietam Foundation

(1986), and more recently the Friends of South Mountain State Battlefield (2002) emerged. The Friends of Monterey Pass Battlefield (2010) sought to preserve that battlefield in Pennsylvania.[44]

Other states that saw larger numbers of battles contained even more grass-roots efforts. Mississippi, for example, developed one of the most active private commission networks. The Siege and Battle of Corinth Commission, Friends of the Siege and Battle of Corinth (1993), and Brices Cross Roads National Battle-field Commission (1993) performed wonders in preserving their respective sites. The Friends of Raymond (1998) likewise preserved much of that battlefield, and later additions such as the Friends of the Battle of Okolona (2001), Okolona De-velopment Foundation Charities, and Iuka Battlefield Commission (2002) worked hard in northern Mississippi and the Sid J. Champion Heritage Foundation (2005) and Friends of Vicksburg National Military Park and Campaign (2008) added much preserved land connected to the Vicksburg campaign. In addition, other entities, such as the Mississippi Department of Archives and History and various state and federal forest services and even the city of Jackson, acquired additional land ranging from small plots to larger tracts. Retired NPS historian Terry Winschel has remarked that "the preservation efforts across Mississippi present an enviable record of perseverance, commitment, and dedication that has thus far achieved remarkable results and promises even greater success."[45]

Missouri also saw a vast assortment of private enterprises develop, includ-ing early efforts such as the Friends of Fort D/Cape Girardeau Parks Develop-ment Foundation (1993), Newtonia Battlefields Protection Association (1994), and Civil War Roundtable of Western Missouri (1994), which worked at several battlefields, including Independence, Liberty, and Little Blue River. More recent work came under the Foundation for Historic Preservation (1998), working at Fredericktown, and the Lone Jack Historical Society (1999). Other entities, such as the U.S. Fish and Wildlife Service and the Agriculture Department's Forestry Service, preserved land as well, with the state and local county and city govern-ments also preserving land at various battlefields.[46]

Several groups also emerged in North Carolina, including the Averasboro Battlefield Commission (1994), the Historical Preservation Group (2002) at Kin-ston and Wyse Fork, the Goldsborough Bridge Battlefield Association (2006), and the Friends of Brunswick Town/Fort Anderson (2008) at Wilmington. A remarkable effort to preserve and interpret the New Bern battlefield took place under the New Bern Historical Society, which acquired more than twenty-five acres of that historic site. State, county, and city efforts, such as the North Car-olina Coastal Land Trust and the Conservation Trust for North Carolina, also acquired battlefield land.[47]

Georgia likewise had a number of advocacy groups helping to preserve battlefield land. These included the Friends of Civil War Paulding County (1993) at New Hope Church, Dallas, and Pickett's Mill, the Etowah Valley Historical Society (1995) at Allatoona, Friends of Resaca Battlefield (1996), the Kolb Farm Coalition (2001) at Kennesaw Mountain, and the Friends of Nash Farm (2006) at Lovejoy's Station. Statewide efforts also emerged, such as the Trust for Public Land, the Nature Conservancy of Georgia, and the Georgia Battlefield Association, as well as numerous other local private interests such as the Atlanta History Center's work at Marietta and New Hope Church.[48]

In Tennessee, many active battlefield preservation groups developed, including the large Tennessee Civil War Preservation Association and Tennessee Wars Commission. In addition, more local efforts included the Davis Bridge Memorial Foundation (1991), Parker's Crossroads Battlefield Association (1993), Battle of Nashville Preservation Society (1998), Lakeway Civil War Preservation Association (2006) at Bean's Station and Bull's Gap, and Battle of Hartsville Preservation Association and Salem Cemetery Battlefield Association. Some of the best work was done at Franklin, where a succession of entities such as the Save the Franklin Battlefield (1989) and Heritage Foundation of Franklin and Williamson County morphed into the Franklin Trust.[49]

Not surprisingly, Virginia had the most active private preservation entities. Some of the earliest efforts, even in the late 1980s, were the Chantilly Battlefield Association (1986), the Cedar Creek Battlefield Foundation (1988), the Brandy Station Foundation (1989), and the Sailor's Creek Reenactment and Preservation Committee (1989). The 1990s saw a mushroom effect in Virginia, with the development of groups including the Historic Staunton River Foundation (1994), Fort Pocahontas Limited (1995) at Wilson's Wharf battlefield, Friends of Wilderness Battlefield (1995), Kernstown Battlefield Association (1996), Trevilian Station Battlefield Foundation (1996), Friends of Fredericksburg Area Battlefields (1997), and Totopotomoy Battlefield at Rural Plains Foundation (1999). The first decade of the twenty-first century only saw this activity increase, with the Citizen's Committee for the Civil War Cavalry Battles of Aldie, Middleburg, and Upperville (2000), the Historic Sandusky Foundation (2000) at Lynchburg, the Richmond Battlefields Association (2001), the Buckland Preservation Society (2003), and the Friends of Cedar Mountain (2004). Moreover, a remarkable joint effort emerged in 2000 in the form of the Shenandoah Valley Battlefields Foundation, preserving land at battlefields such as Cedar Creek, Cross Keys, Fisher's Hill, Kernstown, McDowell, New Market, Opequon, Port Republic, and Tom's Brook. Although the federal government had established the Shenandoah National Park in 1935, many of the area's battlefields had not been included in the park proper. Based on the 1990 Civil War Sites Act report, Congress established the Shenandoah Valley Battlefield National Historic District in 1996, and a foundation emerged in 2000 in order to manage it. In ten years, the foundation saved three thousand acres, with that many more also preserved by partner organizations. Under the leadership of Executive Director W. Denman Zirkle, the foundation planned to double that number in the future.[50]

One of the most innovative private preservation efforts in Virginia came at Pamplin Park near Petersburg. Businessman Robert B. Pamplin took advantage of the opportunity to acquire his ancestral land and purchased over four hundred acres of Petersburg battlefield and earthworks, including the area where the federal breakthrough occurred in April 1865. Pamplin's foundation funded a state-of-the-art museum and interpretive center as well as renovation of historic houses and lands. The National Museum of the Civil War Soldier opened in 1999, and the park added additional interpretive and educational exhibits and buildings over the years.[51]

Given their numbers and successes, these local groups have done more than all levels of government combined in this most recent generation. Part of their success was due to the local-level work involved, as they did not have to battle state- or federal-level politicians worried about losing votes. Were it not for these local efforts, many acres of battlefields would have been lost, and the entire process would probably have stalled through government channels, just like it did in the 1970s and 1980s and after the temporary governmental excitement in the early 1990s. These groups consequently picked up where the government on all levels failed the American people in terms of Civil War battlefield preservation.[52]

V

Local efforts by definition could do little on the larger canvas of national battlefield preservation without some sort of national entity to coordinate and focus that local attention. The federal government was not willing to take on the leadership role, so the process continued to be local and limited. And only a few called for such leadership in the midst of the dark ages, including the self-appointed head of the Civil War Roundtable Associates, Arkansas lobbyist Jerry Russell. He often called for greater preservation efforts, and as Ed Bearss stated, long before anyone else was interested in preservation, "Jerry Russell was." Others called him "the lone voice in the wilderness."[53]

Several larger corporate and charitable entities eventually emerged to offer a semblance of a national campaign to preserve battlefields, although they did not constitute the major guiding hand that was required. Many nonprofit sponsors of battlefield preservation nevertheless did amazing work in this new era—groups such as the Nature Conservancy, the Trust for Public Land, the Melon Founda-tion, and the Union Camp Corporation. They not only preserved land but also fostered awareness among the public. Certainly the best-known group among these was the Conservation Fund, whose president, Patrick Noonan, organized the Civil War Battlefield Campaign. He described the time as a crossroads that demanded action: "I believe future generations will praise our foresight or curse our blindness." Working with other preservation groups, the Conservation Fund eventually saved many acres of battlefield land, including the famous cornfield at Antietam, the East Cavalry battlefield at Gettysburg, and land at Five Forks and Reams Station at Petersburg. The Conservation Fund also brought height-ened attention to battlefield preservation through its popular *Civil War Battlefield Guide*, edited by Francis H. Kennedy. The melding of battlefield preservation with the environmental concerns of conservation and green space, as desired by many of these groups, offered a broad formula for success. Still, on the Civil War battlefield preservation policy front, the Conservation Fund did nothing compre-hensive in and of itself.[54]

By 2000, however, the comprehensive entity that had been missing for the entire 140 years of Civil War battlefield preservation emerged in the form of the modern Civil War Trust. Although its history was rocky in the beginning, the CWT is nevertheless today the unmistakable national leader in Civil War bat-tlefield preservation. That duty should have gone to the federal government many decades before, but the federal government did not take the helm and state and local governments by definition could not take on a national leadership role. It consequently fell to the private sector to take that leap, and the CWT did so remarkably well.[55]

The beginnings of what would evolve into the Civil War Trust of today had its birth in the massive urbanization of northern Virginia in the late 1980s. Watching battlefield land be swamped and destroyed almost around the clock, local Civil War buffs and historians Ed Wenzel, Bud Hall, and Brian Pohanka watched in agony as northern Virginia battlefields such as Ox Hill were swamped with urbanization and no one did anything about it. It quickly became clear that assuming battlefields were sacred, especially in comparison to making money by development, was not a reality. Wenzel noted, "I just assumed the county (of Fairfax) would be doing something with the site as far as making it a park. . . . Whatever the county was doing, I just sort of assumed they had it under control. But they didn't." Wenzel, Hall, and Pohanka began to act. "You talk about three angry guys," Wenzel said. They managed to get some coverage from the *Wash-ington Post* as well as preserve a tiny portion of the battlefield around the original monuments. Others watched in horror as well, including several NPS historians such as Robert K. Krick at Fredericksburg and Donald Pfanz at Petersburg. Pfanz contacted Krick, who pointed him toward Pohanka. The historians agreed that a meeting to organize a national preservation group was mandatory.[56]

That meeting (preceded by an organizational caucus at historian A. Wilson Greene's home) took place in July 1987 at Arbuckle's Restaurant in downtown Fredericksburg, Virginia, and resulted in the Association for the Preservation of Civil War Sites (APCWS), a name Pfanz presented (among many other names). Pfanz noted that "the group voted to adopt it, not because it was a good name but because everyone by then was tired and wanted to get home." The small group with the big name nevertheless began with a bang, garnering support from academic historians such as Gary Gallagher, who quickly became president of the board, and James McPherson. It also hired its first executive director, A. Wilson Greene, then an NPS historian at Fredericksburg. Obviously slanted toward the eastern theater with all the Virginia historians, the APCWS soon achieved tax-exempt status and also began publishing a preservation newsletter, *Hallowed Ground*, which was printed by Morningside publisher Bob Younger as a donation. The members also wrote letters, attended Civil War reenactments, and sold T-shirts to raise money. With headquarters in Fredericksburg, the APCWS also began to seek funding from members and outside charitable history organizations.[57]

Of profound early influence was philanthropist Richard Gilder, who attended one of the board meetings in 1988. After listening to the debate, he interrupted, saying, "You all are thinking like a bunch of school teachers. You're thinking much too small." He pointed them toward larger monetary sums, offering his own funds if the group could match them. They did, and more, prompting Gilder to increase his giving, which allowed the APCWS to add staff to work on the preservation efforts. The member-based APCWS saved its first land in December 1988 at Port Republic, although it was donated, and later acquired land around Petersburg. It eventually saved land at eight battlefields in Virginia and North Carolina in the first three years and was negotiating with a dozen or more. In those years, the group raised over six hundred thousand dollars for land acquisition and dealt with site zoning. The overall idea was not to keep the land but to donate it to respectable national, state, and local historic preservation entities such as the NPS or state parks. But the key was to acquire the land; one of the founding members of the APCWS and its first executive director, A. Wilson Greene, stated that "the Association is built around the premise that only by acquiring deeded interest in historically significant property can that property's integrity be guaranteed."[58]

As stated in the modern Civil War Trust's *Hallowed Ground*, "Their act changed the very nature of battlefield preservation, taking it from solely the realm and mission of government bodies and providing individual Americans with the opportunity to contribute and make a tangible difference in decisions regarding the future of this hallowed ground. Groups focusing on the protection of a particular battlefield had existed previously, but for the first time a single entity would pursue a holistic approach to preservation, spreading its attentions across the map. It is from these efforts that the modern battlefield preservation movement . . . traces their beginnings."[59]

Unfortunately, the rush of preservation instigated by the APCWS, which totaled over six thousand acres in twelve states by 1999, sowed seeds of controversy as well. The success of saving hundreds of acres at Malvern Hill and Glendale as well as over a thousand acres at Brandy Station led to deep debt, as most of the group's purchasing power had been acquired through loans. A change in leadership was also a problem. Greene left the APCWS to become head of Pamplin Park in late 1994. Pamplin did amazing work in saving a major area of the Petersburg battlefield, but he had been a major donor to the APCWS; he now put most of his money into his own park rather than into the APCWS. In Greene's place came Harpers Ferry historian Dennis Frye as executive director, and that produced complaints about change, leadership, and, primarily, the huge debt that now faced the organization.[60]

At the same time, a similar organization was also at work under the name Civil War Battlefield Foundation, later changed to the Civil War Trust. Organized in 1991, the original CWT was actually a hybrid government organization established by the federal government to oversee the American Battlefield Protection Program. Secretary of the Interior Lujan desired a better remedy than the recent legislative "taking" of Manassas battlefield land and thought the CWT would allow that flexibility. The primary funding for the CWT was revenue from the sale of Civil War commemorative coins struck by the U.S. Mint. Some wondered why another organization was needed, but contemporary APCWS executive director Greene noted, "The APCWS had just not quite been around long enough or established a strong enough foundation for the government to have turned to us to administer that commemorative coin program." Accordingly, the original CWT became financially solid with millions of dollars, which they placed in the bank, using the interest to preserve battlefields. The CWT, with its government mandate and better financial footing, continued to work independently from the APCWS throughout the 1990s.[61]

Although the two groups were polar opposites and had two separate sources of funding, the APCWS grass-roots movement and the CWT large corporate donations, animosity developed between them, significantly stunting the preservation effort. The divide even reached into the individual groups themselves, particularly in the APCWS, when the early 1990s Disney fight, led primarily by the National Trust, split the group. The academic historians in the association, such as McPherson and Gallagher, were very much against Disney, whereas association leaders and public (NPS) historians Will Greene and Dennis Frye sided with Disney. With such controversy within and without, the two organizations rarely worked together, and in fact they did not get along that well, especially when the CWT began to solicit private memberships along the lines of the grass-roots APCWS, thus leading to direct competition. Conversely, the APCWS tried to get access to some of the CWT's money through political maneuvering. The "higher class" CWT, according to historian Bob Zeller, "looked down on the grassroots APCWS. It envisioned the APCWS as a division of the Trust, 'best used as the (Trust's) land acquisition, management and evaluation division.'" Alternatively, the APCWS viewed the CWT as "an arrogant new recruit with a big gun, a fancy uniform and no battle experience." Animosity also reigned between the staff of the two organizations, each having little love lost for the other. Meanwhile, the process of battlefield preservation suffered.[62]

Despite such animosity, a common bond was actually forged on the board level. APCWS board member John D. Haynes Sr. of Mississippi, who was instrumental in the Brices Cross Roads preservation effort, worked with his friend Mississippi senator Trent Lott to push for federal aid for battlefield preservation. Senators and representatives seemed reluctant to take sides in the conflict between the two national organizations and desired common action before they invested money. A major alliance was therefore formed out of necessity when O. James Lighthizer of the CWT board joined Haynes of the APCWS in lobbying for a preservation funding bill in 1998. The combined effort produced the major federal legislation advances in the late 1990s. "It was crucial that we went up to the Hill as one entity," Haynes noted.[63]

This commonality continued to exist among the board members, which led to talk of joining the two groups into one efficient organization. The staff of both were against such a move, as was the APCWS executive director. However, the board members prevailed under the subtle leadership of John Haynes, with each group appointing three members to a merger committee. This small group met at Annapolis, Maryland, in June 1999, declaring "it was the unanimous conclusion of each and every member of both committees that a merger of the two organizations would galvanize the Civil War community as never before and give us the opportunity to move this precious cause forward on a scale never accomplished in the past." In November, the two groups accordingly merged into the Civil War Preservation Trust, both with symbolic unanimous votes. Carrington Williams of the APCWS board became chairman of the combined board, but Williams demanded that Lighthizer of the CWT board be named the first president of the organization.[64]

It was a momentous decision. Longtime board member Henry E. Simpson described Lighthizer as "really the right guy at the right place at the right time."

Indeed, Lighthizer proved to be exactly what the CWPT needed, both to stream-line the merged organization and heal bruised egos. Lighthizer, in fact, described himself as a "manager and salesman." He had a history of public service and po-litical acumen, having served in the Maryland legislature as well as a county ex-ecutive of Anne Arundel County for eight years. Most recently, he had served as Maryland's transportation secretary, bringing Southwest Airlines to Baltimore's airport, making it a major hub. In all this time as county executive and transpor-tation czar, Lighthizer always kept an eye out for preservation, helping utilize easements at Antietam and creating a multi-hundred-acre park in his county. He even had thoughts of running for governor, but several life changes brought him to a change in priorities and ideals, with battlefield preservation quickly be-coming his major passion and focus. He soon became the face of the national Civil War battlefield preservation movement, taking his rightful place alongside the greats in the pantheon of movement leaders: Henry V. Boynton, George B. Davis, Howard L. Landers, and Edwin C. Bearss. And his staff loved him; retired Civil War Trust chief operating officer Ron Cogswell recently noted, "So Jim. . . . If we didn't have him, we'd have to invent him, given his background in local gov-ernment, state government, his passion for the Civil War and land preservation and his ability to deliver a great speech when called upon, either to our members or government officials."[65]

Lighthizer first had to cajole and heal before he could lead, however, espe-cially among the board members, some of whom were not totally in favor of the merger but showed a united front in a symbolic unanimous vote. As one APCWS board member stated, "I went along [and] stayed on the board because I wanted to be part of the movement, and it looked like that was where the movement was heading." The first combined board meeting was tense. Mary Abroe remem-bered watching as Lighthizer began the meeting, thinking, "I'm glad I'm not in his shoes. He's got to deal with all of these people and all of this." Ultimately, Lighthizer and Carrington Williams won most members over, original CWT board chairman Ruff Fant comparing the merger to denominations: "The Episco-palians and the hard-shell Baptists, what developed instead from the merger was the organization with the energy of the hard-shell Baptists, but with the financial responsibility of the Episcopalians. And that's a great organization. And I think the success speaks for itself. And it could have been just an internal war. But I think instead, it worked out, thanks to Jim Lighthizer's leadership, fantastically well, because the best of both organizations were brought to bear at the time."[66]

Yet it was not easy, especially at first. The nagging APCWS debt was a ma-jor issue to be dealt with. Likewise, the merger went better on the board level than it did on the staff level. Lighthizer traveled to the APCWS offices and took stock of his new employees. He met stiff resistance and realized he had to purge.

Twenty-four employees dwindled down to thirteen after only two months, and then to four in six months—the result of employees either leaving or being fired. Next Lighthizer had to figure out exactly what the new organization owned. The group's former director of real estate, Noah Mehrkam, recalled: "I remember Jim Lighthizer one day . . . had a list and said, 'This is the stuff we own.' He threw it down on my desk, and said, 'Go figure out where it is. Figure out what we own, what's going on there, what it looks like, is it developed for access at all, does it have trails on it, does it have earthworks; what do we have? Inventory it.' And so I spent a couple of months in the fall of 2000, in addition to trying to get this money shaken loose to pay off the big debt, to figure out in inventory what we owned."[67]

Lighthizer quickly retired the debt of the APCWS, which current CWT board member Bill Vodra commented was the "wedding . . . dowry." He then moved forward, obtaining major funding and acquiring major battlefield land. Despite a name change in 2011 to the old Civil War Trust, the group has to date saved a total of nearly forty-three thousand acres at over a hundred different battlefields in twenty-one states. The CWT now has fifty thousand members, dwarfing what the separated APCWS or original CWT could do and outpacing what anyone could have expected. Historian Gary Gallagher admitted, "No one envisioned that many thousands and thousands of acres would be saved and millions of dollars (spent) on the scale that has come about. That was absolutely beyond what anyone would have imagined." Perhaps Ed Bearss said it best, comparing the merger to a shotgun wedding: "But whether it's a shotgun wedding, it's the most important shotgun wedding I've ever seen take place."[68]

Lighthizer and the CWT performed their work in a number of ways. The organization quickly mastered the art of raising funds under the careful leadership of David Duncan. "We never ask for outright grants," Lighthizer advised. "I was in government. I know that when people come in with their hand out, you want them to have some skin in the game." As a result, all the CWT's actions revolved around matching grants. "'You give me a million, and I will make it two,'" Lighthizer added. "'And, by the way, I will give the land back to you, if you want it.' It's a good argument." Lighthizer also proved willing to get into the trenches and get dirty in political fights. The *Washington Post* characterized the CWT as "part conservation fund, part lobbying shop, part political pit bull." And it was a learning experience even for the veteran politician Lighthizer. "When I took the job . . . did I say we were going to start a political organization? No," Lighthizer recalled. "But as the facts presented themselves, I recognized . . . if we don't get political, we are not going to be in business." He got political by lobbying on the national level as well as the state and even local level. The consummate politician certainly knew how to operate among local political activities. "The land-use process at the local level is often very political," he noted, adding, "I knew how to stop rezoning." One such local effort that carried national implications came in one of the first major efforts of the combined organization. Lighthizer tried to negotiate with developers around the Chancellorsville battlefield in 2002, but they ignored him. He then pushed hard to save the land, and in the next election he turned the local county board of supervisors into a preservation oriented entity. It certainly gained the attention of local politicians elsewhere. "If we can compromise, we will do it—and have done it," Lighthizer noted. But the real philosophy was this: "If we engage [developers] in battle, we want to make the battle so nasty and so brutal that even if we lose, they won't ever want to cross our path again."[69]

Despite all the land acquisition, the CWT went to extremes to not be a land-owning organization. Its basic intent was to preserve the land by moving it on to capable partners who could administer it. "With every piece of property that we buy," Lighthizer said, "we have an exit strategy for every one. And ultimately we want to get rid of it all. We're in the land preservation business, not in the land ownership business. . . . And we look to hand off every single place we buy, ultimately to the National Park Service or to a state park or county park. We always try to get rid of it. We like perpetual groups, which is to say governments. We have handed them off to counties, individual groups, states and the federal government. But if we hand it off to local groups, we have reverted clauses; that if they don't comply with the agreement, it comes back to us." At other times, the CWT found it difficult to pass the land along to a nearby partner. In those cases, the group also developed a plan: "We have a written policy that if we're going to keep it longer than two years, and we don't believe we can get rid of it in two years, then we develop a plan to interpret it, for the public. And if we think we're going to keep it less than two years, then we don't invest in it other than maintenance."[70]

As the years passed, Lighthizer and his board and staff fashioned a first-rate organization that became the long-awaited national leader in Civil War battle-field preservation. Although the major focus remained saving battlefield land forever through purchases and easements, the difficult economic times of the late 2000s and early 2010s caused a rethinking in how to raise money. Yet during that time the CWT significantly increased its acreage of saved land, mostly by carefully finding grant opportunities to match donations so that every dollar donated effectively turned into multiple dollars. Running major campaigns on proposed battlefield acquisitions and keeping the membership and public focused on battlefields through efforts such as Park Day, its annual list of most endangered battlefields, and its award-winning magazine *Hallowed Ground* (which moved from newsletter to magazine format at the time of the merger), the CWT survived the economic downturn and actually prospered during it. Later using the sesquicentennial of the war as a focal point, the CWT in June 2011 launched its "Campaign 150: Our Time, Our Legacy" project, intending to raise forty million dollars. It reached its goal by April 2014 and set a new goal of fifty million for 2015, which was met and more. And it was all done with the highest level of integrity, which mirrored the patriotic effort itself; in fact, the CWT continuously received the highest marks from agencies that ranked charitable groups.[71]

More recently, the CWT also branched out from its strict land acquisition efforts into other areas, including razing nonhistoric buildings, stabilizing historic structures, and retimbering various tracts. Perhaps the biggest effort came in education. Historically, it has generally fallen to the preserver to do the interpretation and education at each site, and the CWT has made great strides in accepting that responsibility in recent years, particularly for land they had to keep. Although much of the land acquired by the CWT was passed on to other entities such as the NPS, the CWT saw high stakes in education and interpretation of the battlefields, believing that those who are knowledgeable and care about sites are more apt to help save them. Consequently, the CWT developed a wide-ranging effort to educate its members and the public, even creating the position of director of history and education, currently held by historian Garry Adelman. In addition to its annual conference, which provides lectures and tours of the battlefields by renowned historians, the CWT routinely offers national and regional teacher institutes. It has also moved into the digital age by running a first-rate website, giving tours of battlefields (known as "battle apps") on smart phones, and providing animated maps of major Civil War battles. Lighthizer and the other leadership quickly realized the key to continuing the success was reaching a younger generation, and the CWT determined to move forward successfully into the digital age.[72]

By 2015, the list of CWT victories was impressive, with a total of over forty-three thousand acres preserved. The organization had saved over a thousand acres at eight different battlefields, including Brices Cross Roads, Brandy Station, Trevilian Station, Bentonville, Kelly's Ford, Shiloh, Resaca, and Cool Spring. Major national victories came in opposing a new Walmart at the Wilderness battlefield and casinos at Gettysburg, as well as saving a monumental piece of the Fredericksburg battlefield at the Slaughter Pen for twelve and a half million dollars. Perhaps preservationist John L. Nau summed it up best: "I would suggest that as an impact on Civil War battlefield preservation and the ability to expose more people to the war, to the period of American history and preservation, the merger of those two groups probably did more for the future—meaning from the merger time forward to today and beyond—than any other action since the war ended and the formation of the national battlefield parks. It was a huge effort."[73]

What had eluded veterans, government officials, and preservationists alike for nearly 150 years was finally a reality. It had been desired as early as the 1902 hearings in Congress, but it had never materialized. The foundations were placed in the 1925 War Department studies, but the next step had never been taken. The NPS had missed a major chance to take the lead in the New Deal and centennial eras. Even the major revitalization of the 1990s never resulted in a solid governmental leadership role, and the two private "national" organizations wasted a lot of time and effort in fighting each other almost as much as they fought the loss of battlefields. Yet what finally emerged in late 1999, at long last, was a national leader in Civil War battlefield preservation.[74]

VI

For all its success in preserving battlefields and interpreting them, the Civil War Trust, perhaps most remarkably, did so amid a time of momentous change in terms of the memory of the Civil War. Having been a source of contention in the immediate decades after the conflict, the war became a source of reconciliation for white Americans beginning in the 1880s, rising to a flood in the 1890s and early twentieth century. Americans, and veterans in particular, sought to reconcile on equal terms and emphasized the bravery, heroism, and military ability of both sides. Joint reunions, monuments, and celebrations fostered white supremacist and reconciliationist visions of memory to force out any acceptance of the emancipationist vision of the war. Nowhere was this ethos of reconciliation more apparent than at the military parks this generation created. Yet the feelings of mutual respect did not last but were slowly eroded by later generations, who began to reform the competing visions of the Civil War to fit their agendas. Beginning in the 1920s and 1930s, and rising to a national level in the 1960s, Northerners and Southerners again split apart over issues revolving around the war, namely race relations and the status of African Americans as free and equal citizens. Such divisiveness continued as the civil rights generation remained in power.[75]

It has only been in the last few decades that a newer generation has emerged, holding to very new ideas regarding race relations and by extension the memory of the Civil War. The effects of the war still resonate today; although large issues such as secession and slavery were settled in 1865, their parent issues, states' rights and racism, were not, and each is still a factor in today's world, albeit not to the extent that caused war in the 1860s. Still, the current generation of American leaders, and certainly the most current generation of children they are raising, live in a very different world of race relations than did their parents and grandparents.[76]

Fueling the change in race relations have been larger questions of equality, participation, and access. A remarkable thrust of the change also revolved around the growing acceptance of African American history as an acceptable form of study, first in academia and then in the larger context in popular culture.

Growing from the New Left revisionism of the 1960s, African American history became a popular area of study among academics, but the infusion came much more slowly in popular culture. Yet it came. Entertainment blockbusters such as Alex Haley's *Roots* and the major motion picture *Glory* presented African American history to the public in much different terms than did the historians and filmmakers of the previous decades. At times this change met fierce resistance, such as with the 1995 effort to place a statue in Richmond, Virginia, to Arthur Ashe on Monument Avenue as well as the neo-Confederate response to Jesse Jackson Jr.'s insistence on a broader interpretation at national parks. Still, most whites in the South are coming to accept African American history as a part of America's history, particularly in dealing with the Civil War, but it is a slow process. Indeed, only recently has Blight's "emancipationist vision" of Civil War memory actually become viable in the public mind.[77]

The emergence of white American acceptance of African American participation and influence on the Civil War can be seen in many areas in the most recent era, particularly on the battlefields. The year 1998 saw the creation of the African American Civil War Memorial in Washington, D.C., as well as celebrations around the centennial of the Fifty-Fourth Massachusetts Monument in Boston. Moreover, the National Park Service also took the lead in commemorating black history in the war and at the parks, largely due to Jesse Jackson Jr.'s mandate to include in its interpretations the role of slavery in causing the war. The resulting Rally on the High Ground symposium, as well as an agreement among NPS Civil War sites superintendents at the Nashville Holding the High Ground conference, infused the mandate into NPS leadership, and the effect slowly but surely filtered down into the parks themselves.[78]

As a result, many sites began to implement the interpretive changes regarding the newer emphasis on the African American role in the war. The 2003 NPS interpretive center in Richmond at Tredegar Iron Works illustrated such a change. The interpretive exhibits showcased a broader understanding of the war as a whole, and the inclusion of the statue of Abraham Lincoln and son Tad, in the heart of the Confederate capital no less, clearly illustrated the changing ideals of Civil War memory. The depiction of Father Abraham in Richmond also carried with it a racial connotation regarding freeing the slaves.[79]

Other sites added a new interpretation and emphasis on the black role during the war as well. The 2004 Corinth Civil War Interpretive Center provided significant space to the interpretation of African Americans during the war, the role of slavery in causing the war, and life at and the effects of the local contraband camp at Corinth. The unit of Shiloh National Military Park also preserved a portion of the original contraband camp and provided interpretation and bronze statue memorials on the site. Similarly, recent activity at Vicksburg National Military

Park emphasized the African American contribution to Union victory; an African American monument went up in that park in 2004. Likewise, fresh exhibits at Fort Sumter were expanded at the new Liberty Square visitor center in Charleston (the debarking point for the fort itself), which opened in 2001. Other sites such as Stones River and Chickamauga also added new and broader exhibits, which one NPS official pointedly added was "one of addition rather than replacement." In other words, the battlefields still interpreted and educated the public about the battles themselves, the tactics and the generals, but they also added the causes to the exhibits.[80]

A special emphasis on reaching "beyond the battlefield" was incorporated into the planning for the Civil War's sesquicentennial. The NPS's Southeast Region, for example, created a strategic plan to guide events during the four years, and it highly advocated inclusion of racial issues as well as other nonmilitary aspects such as the home front. Part of the document read, "In particular, the NPS will address the Institution of slavery as the principal cause of the Civil War, as well as the transition from slavery to freedom—after the war—for the 4 million previously enslaved African Americans. The service must introduce the people of the battlefront and home front, who they were, and how they lived." It also stated as a main goal that "the Southeast Region has a special responsibility to interpret serious messages, including slavery, due to the purpose, significance, and primary themes of so many of its parks."[81]

Although major battles in which African American troops fought were relatively few, additional monumentation and interpretation also developed at those sites. No organized black units fought in the Vicksburg siege itself, causing some to wonder if a monument to black troops was out of place in the park, but United States Colored Troops fought in the campaign, particularly at Milliken's Bend. That sight was not preserved, nor were other sites such as Battery Wagner (due to no longer being extant) or Nashville (due to urbanization). Moreover, Fort Pillow and Port Hudson, where U.S. Colored Troops fought, were preserved as state parks but were done so by Southern states that did little to commemorate African American action on Civil War battlefields. Still, in addition to numerous monuments in cemeteries and at historic sites across the North, monuments to African American soldiers emerged at such isolated and unpreserved battlefields as Fort Butler, Louisiana, Honey Springs (monuments to the famous African American First Kansas Cavalry) and Cabin Creek, Oklahoma, and Island Mound, Missouri.[82]

Perhaps the best opportunity for a federally managed park to interpret and commemorate African American participation in battle action was at the Petersburg National Battlefield. Thinking began to change at Petersburg as early as 1974, when a marker went up at Battery 9 interpreting events during which the U.S. Colored Troops captured the fort. The battlefield was also included in the National Historic Landmark program about the same time, with some of its justification being the role the battle played in racial terms. Still, as at many other NPS sites with mainly white visitation, there was little impetus to change. Change nevertheless slowly occurred, with a monument going up in 1993 to U.S. Colored Troops at Battery 9. Petersburg park officials also expanded their interpretation in the 1990s to embrace race, including new waysides at the Crater that told of U.S. Colored Troops and Confederate reactions regarding the famous massacre of black troops.[83]

Another major area where the NPS shifted its emphasis to African American history was at Harpers Ferry. There, a major museum rose in the 1990s that placed John Brown's raid into a larger context, and the African American History Museum took visitors through the history of slavery in America, obviously concentrating on John Brown but also taking the story into the present. Similarly, NPS officials at Gettysburg National Military Park recently altered exhibits and provided new interpretation with the opening of the new visitor center in 2008. Major exhibits sought to reflect the racial implications of Abraham Lincoln's Gettysburg Address rather than the purely military aspects of the High Water Mark thesis so long in vogue. Interpretation stressed not only the race-related causes of the war but also the "new birth of freedom" that was made available to African Americans as a result of the war.[84]

Other battlefields also saw an increase in monumentation and interpretive texts. Monocacy, for example, recently celebrated its sesquicentennial with numerous programs on the African American experience, including "Fighting for Freedom: United States Colored Troops," "The Revolution is Complete: Emancipation in Maryland," "Archeological Stories of a Slave Village," "Recruiting Maryland Colored Troops," "U.S. Colored Troops—Wreath Laying Ceremony," and "Beneath a Blanket of Stars: Soldier & Slave Perspectives on the Night Sky."[85]

This change in racial awareness regarding Civil War battlefields was not related to African American history alone, however. With expanding minority recognition from Black History Month, numerous parks also routinely provided interpretive programs and site bulletins dealing with such events as Women's History Month, National American Indian Heritage Month, and National Hispanic Heritage Month. The increased emphasis on Native American participation and victimization in the war was also illustrative of the widespread sensitivity to minorities and their history and has most notably brought about broader changes at Little Big Horn, although it is not a Civil War battlefield. The recent establishment of the Sand Creek Massacre National Historic Site was one Civil War example, but subtle changes took place elsewhere as well. At Killdeer Mountain Battlefield State Historic Site in North Dakota, a recent monument text change illustrated the evolving nature of dealing with minority history. The original monument placed in the 1950s was extremely one sided, listing the Federal actions and casualties and educating the public on what the Federal campaign was about. The new text, placed in 2001, was much more evenhanded, even listing the Native American leaders and admitting to Federal soldier depredations such as killing unarmed men, women, and children as well as destroying the Indians' winter housing and supplies. The new text also admitted that the battle further strained relations and brought on even more bloodshed in the next decade.[86]

A renaissance has thus occurred not only in the manner in which battlefield preservation is done and in the scope of that preservation, but it has also transpired in the way Americans view the Civil War as a whole. Now that major entities are embracing broader contexts and interpreting the wider cause-and-effect nature of these battles, the American public has begun to shift its ideals and its memory of the war as well. Significantly, although some opposition emerged to the sweeping changes, it mostly came from fringe groups that were not able to cause stoppages or even delays. Accordingly, even while the memory of the war was changing, it still surged forward, in large part on the Civil War battlefields themselves.

Epilogue

The Future

Excitement filled the air in April 2012. Tennessee's "signature event" for that year, a program commemorating the Civil War sesquicentennial by focusing on western Tennessee and the climactic battle at Shiloh 150 years earlier, had begun. Numerous Shiloh and western theater historians such as John F. Marszalek, James L. McDonough, Wiley Sword, and Larry J. Daniel offered talks and roundtable discussions, but perhaps the highlight of the event was the governor's presence and the announcement by Civil War Trust president Jim Lighthizer of a major land acquisition at Shiloh National Military Park—some 925 acres either transferred or in the process of being preserved. Lighthizer spoke about his group's effort: "As a permanent and meaningful legacy of the sesquicentennial, we give our children and grandchildren the opportunity to walk these same fields unblemished and undisturbed." His announcement was a festive addition to a heartfelt commemoration. Although some states participated more than others during the four-year-long Civil War sesquicentennial, the entire process, certainly not by design but by necessity, highlighted the role of the acknowledged leader in battlefield preservation, the Civil War Trust.[1]

Debate raged over how successful or relative the Civil War sesquicentennial was, with one major historian, Gary Gallagher, even calling the process and its response "anemic." Many disagreed, but what is fully clear is that the sesquicentennial was a resounding success in terms of battlefield preservation, and most of the credit went to the Civil War Trust. From 2000 to 2010, the CWT averaged saving some twenty-one hundred acres per year; as an indicator of the economic problems the CWT had faced more recently, between 2006 and 2010, the average fell to a little over fifteen hundred acres per year. Yet in the five sesquicenten-nial years (2011–15), the average was over twenty-four hundred acres per year. Obviously, local grass-roots supporters as well as big donors gave more, even in the midst of economic stagnation, but the CWT also made sure that money was spent wisely and located every matching dollar it could to make donations go that much further.[2]

Perhaps the ending of the sesquicentennial in 2015 is a logical place to stop and examine where the movement has been, determine patterns, and look to the future. Obviously, the events of 150 years enable a major sampling from which we can learn, and definite patterns and results have emerged over the course of those decades. One pattern that developed was the continual pendulum swings back and forth between the Boynton Chickamauga Plan of total preservation and the Boynton/Davis Antietam Plan of limited preservation. Although Boynton's idea dominated in the 1890s, the more limited Antietam style emerged as the winner as much of the preservation work done from then until the 1990s, with a couple of exceptions at Pea Ridge and Wilson's Creek, was done in the most cost-effective manner on the federal level. And that does not even consider the state and local parks, which almost all followed the more limited plan. Yet Boynton's plan has reemerged as the Civil War Trust is vying to save as much battlefield land as possible, obviously within the constraints of limited funding, which ne-cessitates choices as to what is most critical. Still, the day of *choosing* to preserve a battlefield in limited fashion is long gone, and no other battlefield exemplifies this fact better than Antietam itself, where the Antietam Plan now lies on the scrap heap of history. Congress expanded the park's boundaries in 1960 and again in 1988, and the park has added many acres and had zoning ordinances established. Today, it consists of about three thousand acres of historic ground.[3]

A similar pattern has been the evolution of the leadership and activity of the four major entities that have historically preserved battlefield land. The process started out as nongovernment efforts by soldiers or veterans in private organiza-tions, but soon the federal government entered the picture and led the effort for some five or six decades, all the while slowly backing away from preservation it-self, certainly along the Boynton theory. As the federal government slowly backed away and then became almost absent in the dark ages, choosing rather to take a theoretical and oversight orientation, the states began to take over the process, particularly during the centennial era and in the dark ages. The states could by definition do little on the national front, however, and near the end of the dark ages they turned the process over to local county and even city governments. All the while, private efforts began to bloom, leading to an explosion of private work in the modern renaissance era. Led by the Civil War Trust, private preservation efforts are still leading the way today. Yet it has taken a combined effort of all the groups to reach the success that is so evident at the end of the sesquicentennial.

Other, smaller patterns include personal attributions of the work, not just merely the work itself. Each generation has had its major leaders, whether it be Boynton and Davis in the golden age, Howard Landers and Ed Bearss in the mid-twentieth century, or Jim Lighthizer in the modern era. Likewise, the recognition of local lobbying for preservation is essential, as almost every preserved battlefield today has had at some point a local association backing its preservation.

A list of the patterns that developed over the past 150 years could go on and on, but it is much more instructive to use those patterns to determine the course of future preservation. There is obviously plenty of work still ahead. Civil War Trust president Jim Lighthizer recently described the effort in context: "A conservative estimate of the universe of significant battlefields that ought to be saved is about 200,000 acres that's in private ownership and will ultimately be developed. So it's like drinking out of a fire hose. There's a huge threat. It's a gargantuan area to try and save. If we save a fraction of it, we'll be happy. And remarkably successful. A billion dollars could put a dent in it. It wouldn't solve it, wouldn't completely save the minimal amount that needs to be saved, but it would help a lot. But you're probably looking at two billion dollars to do it right."[4]

Still, there are discernable lessons from the past that need to be implemented in order to ensure the future success of Civil War battlefield preservation. The first, and probably the key, lesson is the dependence on continued grass-roots, local involvement and work. As noted earlier, each of the preserved battlefields today came about first and foremost because they had local preservationists lobbying Congress, state legislatures, or local governments. And the local impact obviously extends to the private sector as well; the Civil War Trust, for example, is heavily dependent on its tens of thousands of individual members paying dues each year and responding even more to calls for special projects. The CWT's Color Bearers society is especially critical in much of the group's work.[5]

Just because much of battlefield preservation hinges on local grass-roots work, however, does not mean that larger governmental agencies no longer have a place of critical importance. Although the federal government has been a major player in preservation throughout the decades, it nevertheless still has a duty, and indeed a responsibility, to lead the effort. Major calls and opportunities for a concerted battlefield preservation policy and plan came in the 1890s, the early 1900s, the 1920s, the 1960s, and again in the 1990s, but each time Congress failed to take the ultimate step and lead the way, dooming the process to a piecemeal effort that has until 2000 been almost leaderless and as a result less comprehensive. The Civil War Trust has emerged as that leader, but it took nearly 140 years for such an organization to arrive, and in that time priceless battlefield land was lost. It also goes without saying that the Civil War Trust, as good as it is, is not clothed with the necessary statutory ability to completely govern and lead the battlefield preservation process. Although the government has become reengaged over recent decades from its low point in the dark ages, there is still no reason why the federal government should not take the critical leadership responsibility it has always shunned. And the pathway to the future is even more clear now, as the Civil War Trust has emerged as the undisputed leader and has proven its integrity, discernment, and success. Congress should immediately pass a national battlefield preservation policy that provides statutory oversight and leadership ability for the Civil War Trust.

Such a dual government/private cooperation could be powerful. Working on all levels, the government-backed Civil War Trust could deal with such issues as zoning ordinances, easements, and other processes that historians Boge and Boge described so well in 1993. Although their plan of action did not, and rightfully could not, envision the remarkable success of the Civil War Trust in the coming decades, it is not mutually exclusive to what has occurred and still needs careful consideration. In fact, Boge and Boge were almost prophetic when they described how the "task at hand is not one of choosing between preservation and development but rather one of formulating a policy of *planned* development." The Civil War Trust continues that theme today, recently declaring in *Hallowed Ground* that "preservation is not inherently anti-development; it is merely pro-smart development."[6]

All these factors reflect one larger contextual need, that of combining various groups that seek a common goal in the fight for preservation. "Lone wolf" Jerry Russell preached combining efforts for years, and it really is key to success. Civil War preservationists who do so for the commemoration of historic events should have no problem combining resources with other groups that want certain lands preserved but for very different reasons. Why should ideology get in the way of Civil War enthusiasts joining with local tourism and business owners who would benefit economically from a preserved park? Why should they battle environmentalists who seek green space, when battlefields could satisfy both? Why, as Boge and Boge pointed out, battle farmers over land protection when a preserved easement could aid everyone through economic agriculture? Basically, the more leverage Civil War battlefield preservation can gain from combining competing groups, the more it can benefit all.[7]

Other future aspects are also clear, such as the need to continually educate the public on history. Boge and Boge discussed this need decades ago, writing that education "holds the greatest potential to influence the course of battlefield preservation." Yet perhaps the greatest need that is critical today, and no doubt will be in the future, is something that has plagued the battlefield preservation effort for its entire history, and that is continuity in leadership. The War Department commissioners working in the 1890s were primarily, except for a couple at Gettysburg, unknown in the battlefield preservation process prior to their work. Accordingly, there was little continuity between Reconstruction and the golden age. Likewise, Boynton and Davis were long gone by the time Landers and the War Department restarted their work in the 1920s. Perhaps most significantly, the break between the War Department stewards and the National Park Service was nearly complete, allowing for almost no continuity at all. The same lack of continuity can be seen between the New Deal leaders and centennial-era preservationists; Ed Bearss was not involved in New Deal–era or World War II–era preservation, yet he became a stalwart in the centennial era and dark ages, almost a lone wolf himself as NPS chief historian. Certainly, the lack of almost anyone leading except Bearss caused the renaissance generation to start over almost from scratch. Thus, almost each generation has had to restart its preservation efforts, seemingly having to reinvent the wheel each time because the federal government never provided a comprehensive national battlefield preservation policy. Consequently, the effort died with each generation, only to be restarted again by the next.[8]

This need for leadership is as critical today as it has ever been, and perhaps even more so. Today, the Civil War Trust is doing things never before dreamed of; it is no stretch to say that more has been accomplished in the renaissance era than ever before, although unfortunately that work cannot quite compare in quality to that of the golden age, when the veterans themselves were able to mark whole parks; we will never see that opportunity again. Yet much of the current success is due to one man, Jim Lighthizer, president of the Civil War Trust. But it is possible for that success to evaporate if his leadership is not carried forward. Obviously, Lighthizer will not be able to lead the CWT indefinitely, and when his retirement comes the organization, and indeed the entire battlefield preservation movement, will be at a crossroads. If Lighthizer is not followed by a competent leader of his caliber, future historians will write the next chapters in the history of battlefield preservation and lament the Civil War Trust as yet another of the capable but temporary organizations on the larger preservation scene. Its demise will result from a failure to provide continuity in leadership, which marked the exact same rise and fall of every other generation prior to the renaissance era. On the other hand, if another charismatic, capable leader follows Lighthizer, it will for the first time carry over that leadership, and success, into a new generation, and there will be no limit to what can be accomplished. Fortunately, the organization's management has begun the process of formulating continuity in leadership even now, so the Civil War Trust will no doubt be the first group to transcend generations and as a result propel the preservation movement to a higher level.

Yet if the federal government would finally accept its responsibility to create an overall policy with the Civil War Trust as its centerpiece, even more could be done in the bright future. And bright it is. In fact, there is also emerging one other new theory of Civil War battlefield preservation, and it has the potential to completely revolutionize previous theories. Almost all work in the past has been the preservation of existing pristine battlefield land, but a new construct, taken somewhat from another genre of preservation, that of historic houses, is gaining acceptance. When a historic structure has been changed or damaged, it is often not preserved in its current state but is changed back to its original state, or the state it was in when it saw its most famous events. The same, as has been recently demonstrated, can be done on battlefields: rehabilitation and reclamation.

There have been a few instances of such rehabilitation on battlefields, such as at Fort Pulaski and the McLean House at Appomattox. At Gettysburg, preservationists have filled in the electric railroad bed and removed car dealerships, towers, and hotels from the site. Probably the most popular effort in this arena is the ongoing work to remove trees and provide an accurate view shed of what soldiers during the Civil War saw. This was done to some complaint in major ways at Gettysburg and Vicksburg, and to lesser degrees at Chickamauga, Antietam, and Shiloh.[9]

Doing so at national parks was one thing, and tree-clearing efforts rarely affected the actual lay of the ground but only the view sheds, important as that is. Reclamation of completely altered private land is quite another issue. Actually leading the way in this pioneering effort once again on the private level is Franklin, where the Carter House and Carnton Plantation private efforts long ago foreshadowed future modern preservation concepts. The preservationists at Franklin have taken the communal approach that is so necessary in their work; various preservation associations around Franklin have joined together to create Franklin's Charge, combining their resources and efforts. One participant has gone so far as describing the new group as "the unprecedented formation of a unique public/private partnership." Success came as a famous pizza restaurant went down, but the biggest effort occurred on the eastern side of the battlefield where the Confederate attack moved through the Carnton Plantation toward the Union lines. This area was for many years a 110-acre golf course, but it has now been returned to its original state as the Eastern Flank Battle Park. One local preservationist described the effort as the "largest battlefield reclamation project in North American history." Future plans include turning the cotton gin area back into a park and rebuilding the gin itself.[10]

This new approach, so successfully demonstrated at Franklin, has awakened national preservationists to that battlefield and, more important, to the use of reclamation in preservation. So impressive has been the work of Franklin's Charge and other groups that the Civil War Trust, not a major actor at Franklin before, is now actively engaged there. Likewise, Congress recently authorized a resource study carried out by the National Park Service. Federal and state grants have also begun to flood the coffers of Franklin's Charge.[11]

Obviously, it would have been better if rehabilitation or reclamation was not needed at Franklin; if only Congressman Cox's Franklin National Military Park bill had been passed when he offered it in 1900, when the veterans could have marked the battlefield when it was still primarily pristine. That unfortunately did not happen, but the modern preservationists at Franklin have continued the fight, emerging as successful in their own way over time by employing a myriad of efforts and policies.

And it is that evolution of policies and places, and the continual dedication of the people behind them, that make the story of Civil War battlefield preservation so instructive as the nation moves forward and newer generations preserve and honor the ground we cherish so deeply as Americans.

Abbreviations

ABPP	American Battlefield Protection Program, Washington, D.C.
APPO	Appomattox Court House National Historical Park, Appomattox, Virginia
ARPO	Arkansas Post National Memorial, Gillett, Arkansas
BBBP	Big Blue Battlefield Park, Kansas City, Missouri
BBRBP	Ball's Bluff Regional Battlefield Park, Leesburg, Virginia
BBSHS	Bentonville Battlefield State Historic Site, Four Oaks, North Carolina
BLSHS	Battle of Lexington State Historic Site, Lexington, Missouri
CARN	Carnton Plantation, Franklin, Tennessee
CH	Carter House, Franklin, Tennessee
CHCH	Chickamauga and Chattanooga National Military Park, Fort Oglethorpe, Georgia
CHS	Chicago Historical Society
CWT	Civil War Trust, Washington, D.C.
CBSP	Columbus-Belmont State Park, Columbus, Kentucky
COLO	Colonial National Historical Park, Yorktown, Virginia
CR	*Congressional Record*
FB	Fort Bragg, Fort Bragg, North Carolina
FCPA	Fairfax County Park Authority, Fairfax, Virginia
FFSHS	Fort Fisher State Historic Site, Kure Beach, North Carolina
FMSP	Fort McAllister State Park, Savannah, Georgia
FN	Fort Negley Visitor Center and Park, Nashville, Tennessee
FODO	Fort Donelson National Battlefield, Dover, Tennessee
FOLA	Fort Lamar Heritage Preserve, Charleston, South Carolina
FOPU	Fort Pulaski National Monument, Savannah, Georgia

FOSU	Fort Sumter National Monument, Charleston, South Carolina
FPSHP	Fort Pillow State Historic Park, Henning, Tennessee
FRCH	Franklin's Charge, Franklin, Tennessee
FRSP	Fredericksburg and Spotsylvania National Military Park, Fredericksburg, Virginia
GDNR	Georgia Department of Natural Resources, Parks and Historic Sites Division, Atlanta, Georgia
GGMP	Grand Gulf Military Park, Port Gibson, Mississippi
GNMP	Gettysburg National Military Park, Gettysburg, Pennsylvania
HAFE	Harpers Ferry National Historical Park, Harpers Ferry, West Virginia
HBSP	Historic Blakely State Park, Spanish Fort, Alabama
HFC	Harpers Ferry Center, Charleston, West Virginia
KEMO	Kennesaw Mountain National Battlefield Park, Kennesaw, Georgia
LC	Library of Congress, Washington, D.C.
LLC	Law Library of Congress, Washington, D.C.
MANA	Manassas National Battlefield Park, Manassas, Virginia
MDAH	Mississippi Department of Archives and History, Jackson
MDNR	Missouri Department of Natural Resources, Jefferson City
MHS	Massachusetts Historical Society, Boston
MONO	Monocacy National Battlefield, Frederick, Maryland
MSHS	Mansfield State Historic Site, Mansfield, Louisiana
MTSU	Middle Tennessee State University, Murfreesboro, Tennessee
NARA	National Archives and Records Administration, Washington, D.C.
NARAAT	National Archives at Atlanta
NARAPH	National Archives at Philadelphia
NARE	National Register of Historic Places, Washington, D.C.
NBHS	New Bern Historical Society, New Bern, North Carolina
NCA	National Cemetery Administration, Washington, D.C.
NCDAH	North Carolina Division of Archives and History, Raleigh
NMBSHP	New Market Battlefield State Historical Park, New Market, Virginia
NPS	National Park Service, Washington, D.C.
NYPL	New York Public Library, New York, New York
OBHSP	Olustee Battlefield Historic State Park, Olustee, Florida
PBSHS	Perryville Battlefield State Historic Site, Perryville, Kentucky
PECO	Pecos National Historical Park, Pecos, New Mexico
PERI	Pea Ridge National Military Park, Garfield, Arkansas
PETE	Petersburg National Battlefield, Petersburg, Virginia

Abbreviations

PGBSP	Prairie Grove Battlefield State Park, Prairie Grove, Arkansas
POHU	Port Hudson State Historic Site, Jackson, Louisiana
RBSHS	Rivers Bridge State Historic Site, Ehrhardt, South Carolina
RICH	Richmond National Battlefield Park, Richmond, Virginia
SCBSP	Sailor's Creek Battlefield State Park, Rice, Virginia
SI	Smithsonian Institution, Washington, D.C.
SNMP	Shiloh National Military Park, Shiloh, Tennessee
STRI	Stones River National Battlefield, Murfreesboro, Tennessee
SVBF	Shenandoah Valley Battlefields Foundation, New Market, Virginia
TSLA	Tennessee State Library and Archives, Nashville
UARK	University of Arkansas, Fayetteville
UI	University of Iowa, Iowa City
USMA	United States Military Academy, West Point, New York
UTA	University of Texas at Austin
VNMP	Vicksburg National Military Park, Vicksburg, Mississippi
WHS	Wisconsin Historical Society, Madison
WICR	Wilson's Creek National Battlefield, Republic, Missouri

Notes

Preface

1. Ken Burns, prod., *The Civil War*, documentary series, PBS, 1990.
2. Georgie Boge and Margie Holder Boge, *Paving Over the Past: A History and Guide to Civil War Battlefield Preservation* (Washington, D.C.: Island Press, 1993), 9.
3. The history of battlefield preservation is a growing topic among historians, especially in recent years. Early efforts include Ronald F. Lee, *The Origin and Evolution of the National Military Park Idea* (Washington, D.C.: National Park Service, 1973); and Michael W. Panhorst, "Lest We Forget: Monuments and Memorial Sculpture in National Military Parks on Civil War Battlefields, 1861–1917" (Ph.D. diss., Univ. of Delaware, 1988). The 1990s saw more work, including Edward T. Linenthal, *Sacred Ground: Americans and Their Battlefields* (Urbana: Univ. of Illinois Press, 1991); Mary Munsell Abroe, "'All the Profound Scenes': Federal Preservation of Civil War Battlefields, 1861–1990" (Ph.D. diss., Loyola Univ., 1996); and Boge and Boge, *Paving Over the Past*. The twenty-first century has seen an explosion of work, including overall works such as Richard W. Sellars's *Pilgrim Places: Civil War Battlefields, Historic Preservation, and America's First National Military Parks, 1863–1900* (Fort Washington, Pa.: Eastern National, 2005); and Timothy B. Smith's *The Golden Age of Battlefield Preservation: The Decade of the 1890s and the Establishment of America's First Five Military Parks* (Knoxville: Univ. of Tennessee Press, 2008). The individual battlefields have also received greater treatment, especially Gettysburg. For that battle, see Amy J. Kinsel, "'From These Honored Dead': Gettysburg in American Culture, 1863–1938" (Ph.D. diss., Cornell Univ., 1992); Jennifer M. Murray, *On a Great Battlefield: The Making, Management, and Memory of Gettysburg National Military Park, 1933–2012* (Knoxville: Univ. of Tennessee Press, 2014); Jennifer M. Murray, "'Far Above Our Poor Power to Add or Detract': National Park Service Administration of the Gettysburg Battlefield, 1933–1938," *Civil War History* 55, no. 1 (Mar. 2009): 56–81; Jim Weeks, *Gettysburg: Memory, Market, and an American Shrine* (Princeton: Princeton Univ. Press, 2003); and Thomas A. Desjardin, *These Honored Dead: How*

the *Story of Gettysburg Shaped American Memory* (Cambridge, Mass.: Da Capo, 2003). For Shiloh, see Timothy B. Smith, *This Great Battlefield of Shiloh: History, Memory, and the Establishment of a Civil War National Military Park* (Knoxville: Univ. of Tennessee Press, 2004); Timothy B. Smith, *The Untold Story of Shiloh: The Battle and the Battlefield* (Knoxville: Univ. of Tennessee Press, 2006); and Timothy B. Smith, *Rethinking Shiloh: Myth and Memory* (Knoxville: Univ. of Tennessee Press, 2013). For Vicksburg, see Christopher Waldrep, *Vicksburg's Long Shadow: The Civil War Legacy of Race and Remembrance* (New York: Rowman and Littlefield, 2005); and Terrence J. Winschel, "Stephen D. Lee and the Making of an American Shrine," *Journal of Mississippi History* 63, no. 1 (2001): 17–32. For Chickamauga, see Timothy B. Smith, *A Chickamauga Memorial: The Establishment of America's First Civil War National Military Park* (Knoxville: Univ. of Tennessee Press, 2009). For Antietam, see Susan T. Trail, "Remembering Antietam: Commemoration and Preservation of a Civil War Battlefield" (Ph.D. diss., Univ. of Maryland, 2005). For Manassas, see Joan M. Zenzen, *Battling for Manassas: The Fifty-Year Preservation Struggle at Manassas National Battlefield Park* (Univ. Park: Pennsylvania State Univ. Press, 1998). In addition, almost each federal site has numerous administrative histories, special studies, and reports and archives on the history of the park in question, although these are generally more technical and less academic in nature.

4. Lee, *Origin and Evolution*, 7; "Study of National Military Parks—Proposed Battlefields, Monuments, etc. 1870's Compilations, Legislation, Reports to Congress, Survey," Box 13, Ronald F. Lee Papers, HFC; G. Kurt Piehler, *Remembering War the American Way* (Washington, D.C.: Smithsonian Institution Press, 1995), 3, 184; Richard West Sellars, "Vigil of Silence: The Civil War Memorials," *History News* 41, no. 4 (July–Aug. 1986): 20–21; Boge and Boge, *Paving Over the Past*, 81; Charles B. Hosmer Jr., *Presence of the Past: A History of the Preservation Movement in the United States before Williamsburg* (New York: G. P. Putnam's Sons, 1965). See also Thomas A. Chambers, *Memories of War: Visiting Battlegrounds and Bonefields in the Early American Republic* (Ithaca, N.Y.: Cornell Univ. Press, 2012).

5. William H. Stauffer, "There's No General Rule about Position of Feet on Equestrian Statues," *Civil War Times* 2 (July 1960): 6; Harry A. Butowsky, "Nomenclature Used in the National Parks," *CRM Bulletin* 2, no. 4 (Dec. 1979): 3, 7–8.

6. The literature on America's larger historic preservation policy is also extensive. See Norman Tyler, Ted J. Ligabel, and Ilene R. Tyler, *Historic Preservation: An Introduction to Its History, Principles, and Practice*, 2nd ed. (New York: Norton, 2009); William J. Murtagh, *Keeping Time: The History and Theory of Preservation in America* (New York: Wiley, 2005); Robert E. Stipe, ed., *A Richer Heritage: Historic Preservation in the Twenty-first Century* (Chapel Hill: Univ. of North Carolina Press, 2003). For an older perspective, see Hosmer, *Presence of the Past*; and Charles B. Hosmer Jr., *Preservation Comes of Age: From Williamsburg to the National Trust, 1926–1949*, 2 vols. (Charlottesville: Univ. Press of Virginia, 1981).

7. Richard West Sellars, "The Granite Orchards of Gettysburg," *History News* 41, no. 4 (July—Aug. 1986): 23; Sellars, "Vigil of Silence," 21; Lawrence A. Kreiser Jr. and Randal Allred, *The Civil War in Popular Culture: Memory and Meaning* (Lexington:

Univ. Press of Kentucky, 2014); Abroe, "All the Profound Scenes," 1:6, 14; Linenthal, *Sacred Ground*, 1. The literature on historical memory is growing. For general reference, see Maurice Halbwachs, *The Collective Memory* (New York: Harper and Row, 1980). For distinctly American historical memory, see John Bodnar, *Remaking America: Public Memory, Commemoration, and Patriotism in the Twentieth Century* (Princeton, N.J.: Princeton Univ. Press, 1992); Michael Kammen, *Mystic Chords of Memory: The Transformation of Tradition in American Culture* (New York: Knopf, 1991); and Linenthal, *Sacred Ground*. Memory literature dealing specifically with the Civil War is a growing body. See first and foremost David W. Blight, *Race and Reunion: The Civil War in American Memory* (Cambridge, Mass.: Belknap Press, 2001); David W. Blight, *Beyond the Battlefield: Race, Memory, and the American Civil War* (Amherst: Univ. of Massachusetts Press, 2002); Alice Fahs and Joan Waugh, *The Memory of the Civil War in American Culture* (Chapel Hill: Univ. of North Carolina Press, 2004); William Blair, *Cities of the Dead: Contesting the Memory of the Civil War in the South, 1865–1914* (Chapel Hill, Univ. of North Carolina Press, 2003); and Caroline E. Janney, *Remembering the Civil War: Reunion and the Limits of Reconciliation* (Chapel Hill: Univ. of North Carolina Press, 2013). The literature on memory and actual Civil War battlefields is much smaller, but several good works have recently appeared. See Abroe, "All the Profound Scenes"; Bradley S. Keefer, *Conflicting Memories on the River of Death: The Chickamauga Battlefield and the Spanish American War, 1863–1933* (Kent, Ohio: Kent State Univ. Press, 2013); and Kevin M. Levin, *Remembering the Battle of the Crater: War as Murder* (Lexington: Univ. Press of Kentucky, 2012).
8. John A. Farrell, "McMansionizing History: Can Anyone Save Some of the Civil War's Most Important Battlefields?" *Washington Post Magazine*, Nov. 16, 2008, 25.

Prologue

1. Lucius W. Barber, *Army Memoirs of Lucius W. Barber, Company "D," 15th Illinois Volunteer Infantry. May 24, 1861, to Sept. 30, 1865* (Chicago: J. M. W. Jones Stationary and Printing, 1894), 60.
2. Fred True to sister, Apr. 10, 1862, 41st Illinois File, SNMPRF; Smith, *This Great Battlefield of Shiloh*, 10–11.
3. George Carrington Diary, Apr. 8, 1862, CHS.
4. For the site of the White Post Burial Place, see Shiloh National Military Park marker BG3.
5. "History," undated, Administrative History #1 Folder, WICR. For tourism, see Reiko Hillyer, *Designing Dixie: Tourism, Memory, and Urban Space in the New South* (Charlottesville: Univ. of Virginia Press, 2014).
6. Benson J. Lossing, *Pictorial History of the Civil War in the United States of America*, 3 vols. (Hartford, Conn.: Thomas Belknap, 1877), 3:76–77.
7. Rock L. Comstock Jr., "Short History: Fort Sumter," 1956, FOSU, 7.
8. "The Grand Army," *National Tribune*, Nov. 13, 1884; "Western Battle-Fields," *National Tribune*, Sept. 9, 1882.
9. Charles H. Lothrop, *A History of the First Regiment Iowa Cavalry Veteran Volunteers, from Its Organization in 1861 to Its Muster Out of the United States Service in 1866*

(Lyons, Iowa: Beers and Eaton, 1890), 206; Alfred Seelye Roe, *History of the First Regiment of Heavy Artillery Massachusetts Volunteers, Formerly the Fourteenth Regiment of Infantry, 1861–1865* (Boston: Commonwealth Press, 1917), 171.

10. F. M. Smith Letter [to uncle], Nov. 8, 1861, Post Battle Visits, WICR; W. O. Gulick Letter, undated, Post Battle Visits, WICR; Griffin Frost, *Camp and Prison Journal* (Iowa City, Iowa: Camp Pope Bookshop, 1994), 4, copy in Post Battle Visits, WICR; Albert D. Richardson, *The Secret Service, the Field, the Dungeon, and the Escape* (Hartford, Conn.: American Publishing, 1865), 203–204.

11. W. A. Love, "Forward and Back," *Confederate Veteran* 33, no. 1 (Jan. 1925): 9–10; Harold Adams Small, ed., *The Road to Richmond: The Civil War Letters of Major Abner R. Small of the 16th Maine Volunteers* (Bronx, N.Y.: Fordham Univ. Press, 2000), 180–81.

12. Arnold Gates, ed., *The Rough Side of War: The Civil War Journal of Chesley A. Mosman, 1st Lieutenant, Company D, 59th Illinois Volunteer Infantry Regiment* (Garden City, N.Y.: Basin, 1987), 135–37; B. F. McGee, *History of the 72d Indiana Volunteer Infantry of the Mounted Lightening Brigade* (Lafayette, Ind.: S. Vater, 1882), 237–38; "A Relic of Chickamauga," *New York Times*, Apr. 10, 1881; "A National Military Park," *Washington Post*, Feb. 24, 1890.

13. Love, "Forward and Back," 9–10; J. W. Reid, *History of the Fourth Regiment S. C. Volunteers, from the Commencement of the War until Lee's Surrender* (Greeneville, S.C.: Shannon, 1892), 62–63; Stewart Bennett and Barbara Tillery, eds., *The Struggle for the Life of the Republic: A Civil War Narrative by Brevet Major Charles Dana Miller, 76th Ohio Volunteer Infantry* (Kent, Ohio: Kent State Univ. Press, 2004), 214.

14. "The Wilson Creek Battle Ground," *St. Louis Democrat*, Nov. 12, 1861, copy in WICR.

15. Frank Moore, ed., *The Rebellion Record: A Diary of American Events, with Documents, Narratives Illustrative Incidents, Poetry, etc.*, 11 vols. (New York: D. Vann Nostrand, 1861–68), 6:43; Frost, *Camp and Prison Journal*, 4.

16. E. B. Long, *The Civil War Day by Day: An Almanac 1861–1865* (New York: Doubleday, 1971), 219; R. G. Horton, *A Youth's History of the Great Civil War in the United States, from 1861 to 1865* (New York: Van Evrie, Horton, 1866), 241; Smith, *Chickamauga Memorial*, 7.

17. Timothy B. Smith, *Champion Hill: Decisive Battle for Vicksburg* (New York: Savas Beatie, 2004), 390.

18. For more on death and the Civil War, and all its attributes and connotations, see Drew Gilpin Faust, *This Republic of Suffering: Death and the American Civil War* (New York: Alfred A. Knopf, 2008).

19. Lossing, *Pictorial History of the Civil War* 3:78.

20. Dean W. Holt, *American Military Cemeteries: A Comprehensive Illustrated Guide to the Hallowed Grounds of the United States, Including Cemeteries Overseas* (Jefferson, N.C.: McFarland, 1992), 2–3.

21. U.S. Quartermaster Department, *Roll of Honor: Names of Soldiers Who Died in Defense of the American Union Interred in the National Cemeteries*, 27 vols. (Wash-

ington, D.C.: Government Printing Office, 1869), 15:2, 16:76; Charles W. Snell and Sharon A. Brown, *Antietam National Battlefield and National Cemetery* (Washington, D.C.: National Park Service, 1986), 26; Holt, *American Military Cemeteries*, 2–3, 429; "National Cemeteries Dates Established and First Burials," 201, NCA; Gary Wills, *Lincoln at Gettysburg: The Words that Remade America* (New York: Simon and Shuster, 1992); Abroe, "All the Profound Scenes," 43.

22. Quartermaster Department, *Roll of Honor* 11:11–13; Piehler, *Remembering War the American Way*, 50; Holt, *American Military Cemeteries*, 65, 67.

23. David Charles Sloane, *The Last Great Necessity: Cemeteries in American History* (Baltimore: Johns Hopkins Univ. Press, 1991); James J. Farrell, *Inventing the American Way of Death, 1830–1920* (Philadelphia: Temple Univ. Press, 1980); Piehler, *Remembering War the American Way*, 6, 50. See also the various descriptions of the physical makeup of the cemeteries contained in Quartermaster Department, *Roll of Honor.*

24. Piehler, *Remembering War the American Way*, 51.

25. Michael W. Panhorst, "'The First of Our Hundred Battle Monuments': Civil War Battlefield Monuments Built by Active-Duty Soldiers During the Civil War," *Southern Cultures* 20, no. 4 (Winter 2014): 22–43.

26. "Army Correspondence," *Macon Journal and Messenger*, Sept. 6, 1861; "Letters from the Army," Sept. 5, 1861, Bartow Monument File, MANA; Robert E. L. Krick, "The Civil War's First Monument: Bartow's Marker at Manassas," *Blue and Gray* 8, no. 4 (Apr. 1991): 33; Zenzen, *Battling for Manassas*, 2.

27. Panhorst, "First of Our Hundred Battle Monuments," 31.

28. James H. Laubach to Vicksburg superintendent, Oct. 12, 1934, Park Administrative History—Vicksburg, Box 93, RG 79, NARAPH; Abroe, "All the Profound Scenes," 91–92.

29. Daniel A. Brown, *Marked for Future Generations: The Hazen Brigade Monument, 1863–1929* (Murfreesboro, Tenn.: Stones River National Battlefield, 1985), 5–8.

30. Long, *Civil War Day by Day*, 687; S. P. Heintzelman Journal, June 10, 1865, LC, copy at MANA; *House Document 481*, 63rd Cong., 2nd sess., 43–46; "The Bull Run Battlefield," *New York Times*, June 12, 1865; Samuel R. Fisher Letter [to Montgomery Miegs], June 16, 1866, 1865 Monuments File, MANA; Zenzen, *Battling for Manassas*, 2; "Is the United States Too Poor to Own Its Own Monuments," 1917, 1865 Monuments File, MANA; Abroe, "All the Profound Scenes," 92–93.

31. For analysis of the postwar divisiveness over death, see Faust, *This Republic of Suffering*; and John R. Neff, *Honoring the Civil War Dead: Commemoration and the Problem of Reconciliation* (Lawrence: Univ. Press of Kansas, 2005).

32. See the still-extant Manassas monuments for the text.

Chapter 1

1. Blight, *Race and Reunion*, 37–38.
2. Ibid., 44.
3. Kenneth M. Stampp, *The Imperiled Union: Essays on the Background of the Civil War* (New York: Oxford Univ. Press, 1980), 4–5; Robert J. Cook, William L. Barney, and

Elizabeth R. Varon, *Secession Winter: When the Union Fell Apart* (Baltimore: Johns Hopkins Univ. Press, 2013), 90.

4. Blight, *Race and Reunion*, 44–46.

5. For Reconstruction, see Eric Foner, *Reconstruction: America's Unfinished Revolution, 1863–1877* (New York: Harper Collins, 1989); and Heather Cox Richardson, *West from Appomattox: The Reconstruction of America After the Civil War* (New Haven, Conn.: Yale Univ. Press, 2008).

6. Ibid., 98–139; Linenthal, *Sacred Ground*, 90; Thomas Adams Upchurch, *Legislating Racism: The Billion Dollar Congress and the Birth of Jim Crow* (Lexington: Univ. Press of Kentucky, 2004).

7. "Honoring the Dead," June 2, 1871, *Fredericksburg Star*.

8. Abroe, "All the Profound Scenes," 19; Blight, *Race and Reunion*, 80. For the lost cause and bloody shirt, see Gaines M. Foster, *Ghosts of the Confederacy: Defeat, the Lost Cause, and the Emergence of the New South* (New York: Oxford Univ. Press, 1987); and Neff, *Honoring the Civil War Dead*.

9. Gloria Peterson, *Administrative History: Fort Donelson National Military Park, Dover, Tennessee* (Washington, D.C.: National Park Service, 1968), 12.

10. Holt, *American Military Cemeteries*, 2; "National Cemeteries Dates Established and First Burials," NCA.

11. Abroe, "All the Profound Scenes," 33, 63; Quartermaster Department, *Roll of Honor* 24:7; Holt, *American Military Cemeteries*, 445; "Dear Amy," undated, Asa Fitch Papers, Cornell University, Ithaca, New York.

12. Ephraim P. Abbott to Mother, July 11, 1867, Shiloh National Cemetery, Vertical Files, SNMP; Timothy B. Smith, "'The Handsomest Cemetery in the South': Shiloh National Cemetery," *West Tennessee Historical Society Papers* 56 (2002): 1–16; Quartermaster Department, *Roll of Honor* 20:119.

13. Peterson, *Administrative History*, 12–14.

14. Ann Wilson Willett, "A History of Stones River National Military Park" (master's thesis, Middle Tennessee State College, 1958), 50–59; Abroe, "All the Profound Scenes," 59–60.

15. John M. Vanderslice, *Gettysburg Then and Now: The Field of American Valor—Where and How Troops Fought and the Troops They Encountered, an Account of the Battle Giving Movements, Positions, and Losses of the Commands Engaged* (Philadelphia: Gettysburg Battlefield Memorial Association, 1899), 355–56; Harlan D. Unrau, *Administrative History: Gettysburg National Military Park and National Cemetery* (Denver: National Park Service, 1991), 22, 25; Abroe, "All the Profound Scenes," 93–94; Snell and Brown, *Antietam National Battlefield*, 23–24.

16. For the text of An Act to Establish and Protect National Cemeteries, see Richard Myers, *The Vicksburg National Cemetery: An Administrative History* (Washington, D.C.: National Park Service, 1968), 200–201.

17. Smith, *Golden Age of Battlefield Preservation*, 21; Blight, *Race and Reunion*, 22, 27–28, 30, 64. For more on postwar divisiveness concerning burials, see Blair, *Cities of the Dead*; and Neff, *Honoring the Civil War Dead*.

18. E. B. Whitman Letter [to Quartermaster], Mar. 8, 1866, Series 1, Box 1, Folder 3, National Cemetery Files, FODO; untitled article, *Keowee Courier*, May 19, 1866; untitled article, *Columbia Daily Phoenix*, May 12, 1866; "The Battle of Franklin," *Western Kansas World*, May 29, 1886; "Western Battle-Fields," *National Tribune*, Sept. 9, 1882; "Grand Army," *National Tribune*, Nov. 13, 1884; James L. McDonough, *Nashville: The Western Confederacy's Final Gamble* (Knoxville: Univ. of Tennessee Press, 2004), 137–38; Franklin Battlefield National Register of Historic Places Inventory—Nomination Form, Nov. 5, 1982, NARE; Virginia McDaniel Bowman, *Historic Williamson County: Old Homes and Sites* (Nashville: Blue and Grey Press, 1971), 60–61.

19. Ralph Happel, "A History of the Fredericksburg and Spotsylvania County Battlefields Memorial National Military Park," 1955, FRSP, 25; Kenneth W. Noe, *Perryville: This Grand Havoc of Battle* (Lexington: Univ. Press of Kentucky, 2001), 359; Patrick A. Schroeder, *The Confederate Cemetery at Appomattox* (Lynchburg, Va.: Schroeder Publications, 1999), 6–9; Abroe, "All the Profound Scenes," 36. For more on the Ladies' Memorial Associations, see Caroline E. Janney, *Burying the Dead but Not the Past: Ladies' Memorial Associations and the Lost Cause* (Chapel Hill: Univ. of North Carolina Press, 2012).

20. "The Memorial Association," *Bamberg Herald*, Apr. 19, 1900, copy in RBSHS; J. Tracy Power and Daniel J. Bell, "Rivers Bridge State Park Visitor's Guide," 1992, 13, RBSHS.

21. Comstock, "Short History," 6; Lossing, *Pictorial History of the Civil War* 3:402; Blight, *Race and Reunion*, 154–55.

22. E. B. Whitman Letter, Mar. 8, 1866, FODO.

23. "Make a National Park at Franklin," *Confederate Veteran* 17, no. 1 (Jan. 1909): 15; "Grand Army," *National Tribune*, Nov. 13, 1884.

24. William H. Tunnard, *A Southern Record: The History of the Third Regiment Louisiana Infantry* (Baton Rouge, La.: Published by the Author, 1866), 208.

25. Peterson, *Administrative History*, 12; "Through the South," *New York Times*, July 4, 1867; "The Chickamauga Park," *New York Times*, Apr. 28, 1891; *Society of the Army of the Cumberland: Nineteenth Reunion, Chicago, Illinois, 1888* (Cincinnati: Robert Clarke, 1889), 19:53–55; "Western Battle-Fields," *National Tribune*, Sept. 9, 1882. For environmental change, see Lisa M. Brady, *War upon the Land: Military Strategy and the Transformation of Southern Landscapes during the American Civil War* (Athens: Univ. of Georgia Press, 2012).

26. George B. Davis to Secretary of War, Mar. 18, 1895, Folder 267, Box 19, Series 1, SNMP; B. G. Brazelton, *A History of Hardin County* (Nashville: Cumberland Presbyterian Publishing House, 1885), 35, 82; George W. McBride, "Shiloh, After Thirty-Two Years," in *Under Both Flags: A Panorama of the Great Civil War as Represented in Story, Anecdote, Adventure, and the Romance of Reality*, ed. C. R. Graham (Philadelphia: People's Publishing, 1896), 221; "A Writer," *Southern Bivouac* 3, no. 2 (Oct. 1884): 87; "Shocking Conditions of the Confederate Dead at Shiloh," Jan. 2, 1878, *Talladega (Ala.) Reporter and Watchtower*.

27. "Virginia Battlefields," *Philadelphia Weekly Times*, Aug. 6 and 13, 1881; Levin, *Remembering the Battle of the Crater*, 36–37.

28. Andrew Carroll, ed., *War Letters: Extraordinary Correspondence from American Wars* (New York: Scribner, 2001), 121.

29. Hosmer, *Presence of the Past*, 81; "Editorial Article No. 5," *New York Times*, Sept. 12, 1874, 6; Blight, *Race and Reunion*, 84, 199–200; Piehler, *Remembering War the American Way*, 75–76; "The Atlanta Celebration," *Washington Post*, Oct. 19, 1880, 1; "Blended Blue and Gray," *Washington Post*, Aug. 12, 1883, 4; "The Blue and the Gray," *New York Times*, July 2, 1888, 4; "First Reunion at Pea Ridge, September 1st, 1887," *Benton County Pioneer* 7, no. 3 (Mar. 1962): 5–6. For reunions at Wilson's Creek, see *Springfield Express*, July 29, 1887, and Aug. 17, 1883; and *Springfield Daily Herald*, July 18, 1883.

30. *House Reports*, 59th Cong., 1st sess., H.R. Rep. 4431, 10; James B. Shaw, *History of the Tenth Indiana Volunteer Infantry* (Lafayette, Ind.: Burt-Hayward, 1912), 274–75; Glenn Tucker, *Chickamauga: Bloody Battle in the West* (Indianapolis: Bobbs-Merrill, 1961), 420.

31. Smith, "Handsomest Cemetery in the South," 1–16; E. B. Whitman to J. L. Donelson, Apr. 29, 1866, E 576, Box 53, RG 92, NARA; "A Visit to the Battle-Field of Shiloh—Appalling Picture," *Oxford Falcon*, May 24, 1866; "Shocking Condition of the Confederate Dead at Shiloh," *Talladega Reporter and Watchtower*, Jan. 2, 1878; W. B. Ellis, "Who Lost Shiloh to the Confederacy," *Confederate Veteran* 22, no. 7 (July 1914): 313; F. A. Shoup, "How We Went to Shiloh," *Confederate Veteran* 2, no. 5 (May 1894): 138. For the national cemetery, see Series 4, SNMPAF.

32. Margaret E. Wagner, Gary W. Gallagher, and Paul Finkelman, eds., *Library of Congress Civil War Desk Reference* (New York: Simon and Shuster, 2002), 816; Blight, *Race and Reunion*, 164; Lossing, *Pictorial History of the Civil War*; Robert Underwood Johnson and Clarence Clough Buel, eds., *Battles and Leaders of the Civil War: Being for the Most Part Contributions by Union and Confederate Officers: Based upon "The Century" War Series*, 4 vols. (New York: Century, 1884–87).

33. Thure de Thulstrup, *Battle of Shiloh Lithograph* (L. Prang, 1888); Wagner, Gallagher, and Finkelman, *Library of Congress Civil War Desk Reference*, 830.

34. *Manual of the Panorama of the Battle of Shiloh* (Chicago: A. T. Andreas, 1885), 5, 14; "Battle of Shiloh," *Chicago Daily Tribune*, Aug. 15, 1885; Rachel Stephens, "The Battle of Shiloh Cyclorama: A Biased Commemoration," *Montage* 2 (2008): 105. For more on Prentiss, see Timothy B. Smith, "Shiloh's False Hero," *Civil War Times* 47, no. 6 (Dec. 2008): 28–35.

35. Wagner, Gallagher, and Finkelman, *Library of Congress Civil War Desk Reference*, 827; Harold Holzer, "Vanished Heritage," *American Heritage* 56, no. 4 (Sept. 2005): 41.

36. David G. Martin, *The Campaign of Shiloh, March–April, 1862* (New York: Fairfax Press, 1987), 105; David Nevin, *The Road to Shiloh: Early Battles in the West* (Alexandria, Va.: Time-Life Books, 1983), 130–35; *Manual of the Panorama of the Battle of Shiloh*, 5, 14; Don Carlos Buell, "Shiloh Reviewed," in Johnson and Buel, *Battles and Leaders of the Civil War* 1:504–505, 510–11; "Battle of Shiloh—Apr. 6th 1862,"

McCormick Harvesting Machine Co., 1885; Stephens, "Battle of Shiloh Cyclorama," 103–16.

37. Holzer, "Vanished Heritage," 41; Frank Harrell, "The Case of the Missing Manassas Cyclorama," http://nps-vip.net/history/museum/cycloram/painting.htm. For photos of the Shiloh panorama, see the H. H. Bennett Collection, WHS.

38. Holzer, "Vanished Heritage," 41; David S. Heidler and Jeanne T. Heidler, eds., *Encyclopedia of the American Civil War: A Political, Social, and Military History*, 5 vols. (Santa Barbara, Calif.: ABC-CLIO, 2000), 1:542.

39. Holzer, "Vanished Heritage," 41; Gettysburg Foundation, "The Film & Cyclorama," http://www.gettysburgfoundation.org/13; Stephens, "Battle of Shiloh Cyclorama," 105.

40. See Civil War Trust, "The Cycloramic Connection," http://www.civilwar.org /education/history/cycloramas/index.html; *Manual of the Panorama of the Battle of Shiloh*, 5, 14; Stephens, "Battle of Shiloh Cyclorama," 103–104.

41. Vanderslice, *Gettysburg Then and Now*, 360–63; Unrau, *Administrative History*, 41–43, Minute Book Gettysburg Battlefield Memorial Association, 1872–1895, 49, 51, GNMP; Abroe, "All the Profound Scenes," 79. Quite a large literature has emerged on Gettysburg; see Weeks, *Gettysburg*; Desjardin, *These Honored Dead*; and Carol Reardon, *Pickett's Charge in History and Memory* (Chapel Hill: Univ. of North Carolina Press, 1997).

42. Vanderslice, *Gettysburg Then and Now*, 364.

43. Ibid., 363–64, 367; Unrau, *Administrative History*, 47.

44. Vanderslice, *Gettysburg Then and Now*, 367–68.

45. Ibid., 368–71; Unrau, *Administrative History*, 50–51.

46. Vanderslice, *Gettysburg Then and Now*, 371–88; Abroe, "All the Profound Scenes," 84; Unrau, *Administrative History*, 58.

47. "An Act Donating Condemned Cannon and Cannon-balls to the Posts of the Grand Army of the Republic of Philadelphia and Other Associations, for Monumental Purposes," June 3, 1874, Box 11, Ronald F. Lee Papers, HFC; Lee, *Origin and Evolution*, 7–11; U.S. War Department, *Annual Report of the Secretary of War—1895* (Washington, D.C.: U.S. War Department, 1895), 31; Unrau, *Administrative History*, 47–48.

48. Unrau, *Administrative History*, 57–59, 63.

49. Vanderslice, *Gettysburg Then and Now*, 368, 372–79; Abroe, "All the Profound Scenes," 81, 118, 125–28; Minute Book Gettysburg Battlefield Memorial Association, 135, 151–52, GNMP.

50. Minute Book Gettysburg Battlefield Memorial Association, 146, GNMP; John P. Nicholson, William M. Robbins, and C. A. Richardson to Secretary of War, Feb. 15, 1898, E 711, Box 2, RG 92, NARA; Unrau, *Administrative History*, 61–62; Abroe, "All the Profound Scenes," 146, 151.

51. Smith, "Handsomest Cemetery in the South," 1–16; E. B. Whitman to J. L. Donelson, Apr. 29, 1866, NARA; Ellis, "Who Lost Shiloh to the Confederacy," 313; Shoup, "How We Went to Shiloh," 138; "Western Battle-Fields," *National Tribune*, Sept. 9, 1882; "Make a National Park at Franklin," 15; James L. McDonough and Thomas L. Connelly, *Five Tragic Hours: The Battle of Franklin* (Knoxville: Univ. of Tennessee

Press, 1983), 183–84; National Park Service, *Battle of Franklin Sites, Williamson County, Tennessee: Special Resource Study* (Washington, D.C.: National Park Service, n.d.), 71; Dan M. Robison, "The Carter House, Focus of the Battle of Nashville," *Tennessee Historical Quarterly* 22, no. 1 (Mar. 1963): 17; *Keedysville Antietam Wavelet*, Oct. 15, 1887; "Antietam Memorial Association," *Keedysville Antietam Wavelet*, May 24, 1890; David W. Reed, "National Cemeteries and National Military Parks," in *War Sketches and Incidents as Related by the Companions of the Iowa Commandery Military Order of the Loyal Legion of the United States*, 70 vols. (Des Moines, Iowa: n.p., 1898), 2:371; James R. McConaghie and Daniel J. Keeffe, "A History of Vicksburg National Military Park," 1954, 12, Folder 49, Box 2, Edwin C. Bearss Series, VNMP.

52. Sean M. Styles, "Stones River National Battlefield Historic Resource Study," 2004, 63, 65, STRI; Donald C. Pfanz, "History Through Eyes of Stone: A Survey of Civil War Monuments near Fredericksburg, Virginia," rev. ed., 2006, 57–61, 124–36, 211–16, FRSP; Christopher J. Huggard, "Pea Ridge National Military Park: An Administrative History," 1998, 23–26, PERI.

53. "Antietam Memorial Association," *Keedysville Antietam Wavelet*, May 24, 1890; *Keedysville Antietam Wavelet*, Oct. 15, 1887; Reed, "National Cemeteries and National Military Parks," 371.

54. *House Reports*, 59th Cong., 1st sess., H.R. Rep. 4431, 10; *Society of the Army of the Cumberland: Twenty-Second Reunion, Columbus, Ohio, 1891* (Cincinnati: Robert Clarke, 1892), 22:18; *Society of the Army of the Cumberland: Twenty-Third Reunion, Chickamauga, Georgia, 1892* (Cincinnati: Robert Clarke, 1892), 23:53; Henry V. Boynton, *Dedication of the Chickamauga and Chattanooga National Military Park, September 18–20, 1895: Report of the Joint Committee to Represent the Congress at the Dedication of the Chickamauga and Chattanooga National Military Park* (Washington, D.C.: Government Printing Office, 1896), 318; Henry V. Boynton, *The National Military Park: Chickamauga-Chattanooga: An Historical Guide, with Maps and Illustrations* (Cincinnati: Robert Clarke, 1895), 219, 224; *Chickamauga Memorial Association Proceedings at Chattanooga, Tenn., and Crawfish Springs, Ga., September 19 and 20, 1889* (n.p.: Chattanooga Army of the Cumberland Reunion Entertainment Committee, n.d.), 8; "A Park of Battlefields," *New York Times*, Mar. 24, 1887.

55. "Chickamauga Battle-Field," *Washington Post*, Sept. 26, 1888; "The Chickamauga Battlefield," *New York Times*, Oct. 6, 1879; "Death of Jeff C. Davis," *Washington Post*, Dec. 1, 1879; editorial, *New York Times*, Nov. 12, 1888; Stones River Mission 66 Plan, Box 27, RG 79, NARAPH; Hazen Monument Report, undated, E 5, Box 60, RG 79, NARA.

56. "The Field of Chickamauga," *New York Times*, Nov. 11, 1888; "Battle of Chickamauga," *Washington Post*, May 5, 1889; "The Chattanooga Battlefield," *Washington Post*, Nov. 12, 1888; "The Chickamauga Maps," *Washington Post*, Jan. 31, 1890.

57. Abroe, "All the Profound Scenes," 103.

58. William L. Shea and Earl J. Hess, *Pea Ridge: Civil War Campaign in the West* (Chapel Hill: Univ. of North Carolina Press, 1992), 328; Blight, *Race and Reunion*, 112; Abroe, "All the Profound Scenes," 62, 141; "Camping on Chickamauga," *Washington Post*, Sept. 16, 1892.

Chapter 2

1. "The Chickamauga Bill Signed," *Washington Post*, Aug. 20, 1890; CR, 51st Cong., 1st sess., vol. 21, 7335, 8473, 8693, 8695, 8903; Boynton, *National Military Park*, 260; James W. Livingood, "Chickamauga and Chattanooga National Military Park," *Tennessee Historical Quarterly* 23, no. 1 (Mar. 1964): 15.
2. "Camping on Chickamauga," *Washington Post*, Sept. 16, 1892, 4.
3. For the Spanish-American War and imperialism, see Ivan Musicant, *Empire by Default: The Spanish-American War and the Dawn of the American Century* (New York: Henry Holt, 1998).
4. C. Vann Woodward, *The Strange Career of Jim Crow*, 3rd ed. (New York: Oxford Univ. Press, 1989); Blight, *Race and Reunion*, 2, 264, 256. For more on this subject, especially the religious aspects, see Edward J. Blum, *Reforging the White Republic: Race, Religion, and American Nationalism, 1865–1898* (Baton Rouge: Louisiana State Univ. Press, 2005). For winning war and losing peace, see A. J. Langguth, *After Lincoln: How the North Won the Civil War and Lost the Peace* (New York: Simon and Shuster, 2014).
5. Blight, *Race and Reunion*, 2; Linenthal, *Sacred Ground*, 91.
6. Abroe, "All the Profound Scenes," 108; Blight, *Race and Reunion*, 2.
7. CR, 51st Cong., 2nd sess., vol. 21, 1:559; *House Reports*, 51st Cong., 2nd sess., H.R. Rep. 3024, 1–6; Abroe, "All the Profound Scenes," 115; Lee, *Origin and Evolution*, 6.
8. CR, 53rd Cong., 2nd sess., vol. 26, 7:6722; *House Reports*, 53rd Cong., 2nd sess., H.R. Rep. 1139, 1–5; Abroe, "All the Profound Scenes," 145.
9. Unpublished quantitative study by the author.
10. Smith, *Golden Age of Battlefield Preservation*, 6–7.
11. For a nice overview of the 1890s battlefield establishment, see Richard W. Sellars, "Pilgrim Places: Civil War Battlefields, Historic Preservation, and America's First National Military Parks, 1863–1900," 22–52. This article was also published in booklet form; see Sellars, *Pilgrim Places*.
12. Boynton, *National Military Park*, 224. For Boynton, see Timothy B. Smith, "Henry Van Ness Boynton and Chickamauga: The Pillars of the Modern Military Park Movement," in *The Chickamauga Campaign*, ed. Steven E. Woodworth (Carbondale: Southern Illinois Univ. Press, 2010), 165–87.
13. Boynton, *Dedication of the Chickamauga and Chattanooga National Military Park*, 317; Henry V. Boynton, "The Chickamauga Memorial Association," *Southern Historical Society Papers* 16 (1888): 339, 344; Boynton, *National Military Park*, 219, 222, 225, 245; *Chickamauga Memorial Association Proceedings*, 7, 29; CR, 51st Cong., 1st sess., vol. 21, 8:7335; CR, 51st Cong., 1st sess., vol. 21, 9:8473, 8693, 8695, 8903.
14. Smith, *Chickamauga Memorial*, 26–27; Timothy B. Smith, "A Chattanooga Plan: The Gateway City's Critical Role in Civil War Battlefield Preservation," in *The Chattanooga Campaign*, ed. Steven E. Woodworth and Charles D. Grear (Carbondale: Southern Illinois Univ. Press, 2012), 204–206.
15. Boynton, *National Military Park*, 273.
16. Smith, *Chickamauga Memorial*, 155.
17. Edward C. Walthall to Henry V. Boynton, Mar. 17, 1896, Folder 3, Box 4, Ezra A. Carman Papers, NYPL; Park Commission Annual Report—1892, Folder 1, Box 1,

Series 1, CHCH; Boynton, *National Military Park*, 272; "The Chickamauga Park," *Washington Post*, May 10, 28, and 30, 1891; John C. Paige and Jerome A. Greene, *Administrative History of Chickamauga and Chattanooga National Military Park* (Denver: National Park Service, 1983), 21; Lee, *Origin and Evolution*, 36; "Tablets at Chickamauga," *Washington Post*, Apr. 21, 1894.

18. "Prince Henry Surveys Civil War Battleground," *New York Times*, Mar. 3, 1902; "President's Riding Pace Too Fast for Troopers," *New York Times*, Sept. 8, 1902; "On Battle-Fields," *Washington Post*, Sept. 8, 1902; Smith, "Chattanooga Plan," 203–15.

19. Boynton, *Dedication of the Chickamauga and Chattanooga National Military Park*, 7, 9–10, 12, 14; Livingood, "Chickamauga and Chattanooga National Military Park," 17.

20. "The Father of the Chickamauga National Park Enterprise," undated newspaper clipping, Henry Van Ness Boynton Papers, MHS; Smith, "Henry Van Ness Boynton and Chickamauga," 183.

21. "Antietam Memorial Association," *Keedysville Antietam Wavelet*, May 24, 1890; J. C. Stearns and H. Heth to R. N. Bachelder, June 10, 1892; J. C. Stearns to R. N. Bachelder, Aug. 27, 1892; and Antietam Board to R. N. Bachelder, Jan. 13, 1894, all in E 707, Box 1, RG 92, NARA; Daniel S. Lamont to Quartermaster General, July 14, 1894, and R. N. Bachelder to J. C. Stearns, July 19, 1894, both in E 707, Box 1, RG 92, NARA. For an overview of Antietam's preservation, see Trail, "Remembering Antietam."

22. *House Reports*, 59th Cong., 1st sess., H.R. Rep. 4431, 9.

23. Smith, *Chickamauga Memorial*, 23, 27; Smith, "Chattanooga Plan," 205–206.

24. George B. Davis to Secretary of War, Mar. 18, 1895, SNMP; George B. Davis to Cornelius Cadle, Mar. 28, 1895, Folder 618, Box 37, Series 1, SNMP; *House Reports*, 59th Cong., 1st sess., H.R. Rep. 4431, 10; Smith, *This Great Battlefield of Shiloh*, 29.

25. For Henderson, see Timothy B. Smith, "The Politics of Battlefield Preservation: David B. Henderson and the National Military Parks," *Annals of Iowa* 66, nos. 3 and 4 (Summer/Fall 2007): 293–320; *Report of the Proceedings of the Society of the Army of the Tennessee at the Twenty-Sixth Meeting Held at Council Bluffs, Iowa, October 3rd and 4th, 1894* (Cincinnati: F. W. Freeman, 1895), 26:127–28.

26. Daniel S. Lamont to Cornelius Cadle, Mar. 12, 1895, E 713, RG 92, NARA; E. C. Dawes to George B. Davis, Jan. 24, 1895, E 712, Box 1, RG 92, NARA; George B. Davis to Secretary of War, Mar. 12, 1895, E 713, RG 92, NARA; Smith, "Politics of Battlefield Preservation," 306.

27. D. B. Henderson to D. W. Reed, Jan. 13, 1895, Folder 90, Box 1, Series 3, SNMP; D. W. Reed appointment, Mar. 26, 1895, E 713, RG 92, NARA; Alexander P. Stewart to Chickamauga and Chattanooga National Military Park Commission, Feb. 14, 1895, Folder 618, Box 37, Series 1, SNMP; H. V. Boynton to Secretary of War, Mar. 25, 1905, Folder 92, Box 12, Series 1, SNMP.

28. Jacob Dickinson to Cornelius Cadle, Jan. 15, 1910, E 82, Vol. 44, RG 107, NARA; David W. Reed, *The Battle of Shiloh and the Organizations Engaged* (Washington, D.C.: Government Printing Office, 1902), 7–23, 48–49; "First Reunion of Iowa Hornet's Nest Brigade," Oct. 12–13, 1887, Folder 216, Box 4, Series 3, SNMP.

29. Daniel S. Lamont to Cornelius Cadle, Apr. 20, 1895, and Daniel S. Lamont to George B. Davis, Mar. 19, 1895, both in E 713, RG 92, NARA; George B. Davis to Cornelius Cadle, Mar. 23, 1895, Folder 570, Box 35, Series 1, SNMP; unknown to Editor, *Commercial-Gazette*, Dec. 24, 1895, Folder 153, Box 13, Series 1, SNMP; George B. Davis to Cornelius Cadle, Apr. 17 and June 25, 1895, "Letter Book of the Shiloh National Military Park Commission," E 713, RG 92, NARA.

30. Gettysburg National Military Park Commission, *Annual Reports to the Secretary of War, 1893–1901* (Washington, D.C.: Government Printing Office, 1902), 9, 11–12; U.S. War Department, *Annual Report of the Secretary of War, 1893* (Washington, D.C.: U.S. War Department, 1893), 32–33. See also Weeks, *Gettysburg*; Desjardin, *These Honored Dead*; and Reardon, *Pickett's Charge*.

31. Minute Book Gettysburg Battlefield Memorial Association, 251, GNMP; Gettysburg National Military Park Commission, *Annual Reports to the Secretary of War*, 5; J. P. Nicholson Journals, 1:1, GNMP.

32. U.S. War Department, *Annual Report of the Secretary of War—1894* (Washington, D.C.: U.S. War Department, 1894), 29; CR, 53rd Cong., 3rd sess., vol. 27, 1:105, 402; Desjardin, *These Honored Dead*, 80.

33. John P. Nicholson, William M. Robbins, and C. A. Richardson to Secretary of War, Feb. 15, 1898, NARA; Gettysburg National Military Park Commission, *Annual Reports to the Secretary of War*, 5, 8, 11; George B. Davis to Secretary of War, May 25, 1893, J. P. Nicholson Journals, 1:13, GNMP; Secretary of War to Justice Department, J. P. Nicholson Journals, 1:19, GNMP; Daniel S. Lamont to Attorney General, May 1, 1895, E 709, RG 92, NARA; John P. Nicholson to G. W. Davis, Feb. 5, 1895, E 710, NARA; Abroe, "All the Profound Scenes," 205; Lee, *Origin and Evolution*, 15.

34. CR, 51st Cong., 1st sess., vol. 21, 6:5393; Boynton, *National Military Park*, 259; CR, 53rd Cong., 3rd sess., vol. 27, 1:430.

35. William T. Rigby Report, Dec. 7, 1899, Administrative Series, Box 7, Folder 158, VNMP; W. T. Rigby, "History and Views of the Vicksburg National Military Park," *Vicksburg Monday Morning Democrat*, Sept. 6, 1909, Folder 128, Box 6, Administrative Series, VNMP; "Father of Park Delighted with Progress," *Vicksburg Evening Post*, Nov. 30, 1908; D. B. Henderson to J. F. Merry, Nov. 6, 1896; D. B. Henderson to W. T. Rigby, Dec. 14, 1896; and D. B. Henderson to W. T. Rigby, Dec. 28, 1896, all in Box 2, Wilfliam T. Rigby Papers, UI; "Charter of Incorporation of the Vicksburg National Military Park Association," Folder 158, Box 7, Administrative Series, VNMP; *Report of the Proceedings of the Society of the Army of the Tennessee at the Thirty-First Meeting Held at Chicago, Ill., October 10–11, 1899* (Cincinnati: F. W. Freeman, 1900), 31:41; CR, 55th Cong., 3rd sess., vol. 32, 2:1518, 1529, 1640, 1678, 1760.

36. D. B. Henderson to W. O. Mitchell, Feb. 14, 1899, Box 3, William T. Rigby Papers, UI; William T. Rigby Appointment, Mar. 1, 1899, Folder 7, Box 1, William T. Rigby Series, VNMP; *Report of the Proceedings of the Society of the Army of the Tennessee at the Thirty-First Meeting* 31:41; Rigby, "History and Views of the Vicksburg National Military Park"; "Facts Concerning Early Park Personalities," Folder 145, Box 6, Administrative Series, VNMP; U.S. War Department, *Annual Report of the Secretary of*

War—1899 (Washington, D.C.: U.S. War Department, 1899), 341–42; Josiah Patterson to Stephen D. Lee, Aug. 18, 1900, Box 1, Letters Received—Vicksburg National Military Park Commission, RG 79, NARAAT.

37. H. V. Boynton to William T. Rigby, May 9, 1901, Folder 1, Box 2, Letters Received—Vicksburg National Military Park Commission, RG 79, NARAAT; S. D. Lee to William T. Rigby, July 29, 1901, S. D. Lee to William T. Rigby, July 31, 1901, and S. D. Lee to William T. Rigby, Oct. 31, 1901, all in Folder 33, Box 1, William T. Rigby Series, VNMP; S. D. Lee to William T. Rigby, July 29, 1901, Folder 33, Box 1, William T. Rigby Series, VNMP; U.S. War Department, *Annual Report of the Secretary of War—1901* (Washington, D.C.: U.S. War Department, 1901), 391; Secretary of War to H. V. Boynton, May 20, 1902, and E. E. Betts to Secretary of War, Apr. 12, 1902, both in E 715, Box 1, RG 92, NARA.

38. Robert Shaw Oliver to William T. Rigby, Mar. 21, 1905, Folder 4, Box 1, Administrative Series, VNMP; War Department, *Annual Report of the Secretary of War—1899*, 341–43; Hosmer, *Presence of the Past*, 75. For monumentation at Vicksburg, see Michael W. Panhorst, *The Memorial Art and Architecture of Vicksburg National Military Park* (Kent, Ohio: Kent State Univ. Press, 2015).

39. "Protection of Military Parks," *United States Statutes at Large*, vol. 29, 599–600.

40. Lee, *Origin and Evolution*, 37; Boge and Boge, *Paving Over the Past*, 23; Boynton, *National Military Park*, 11; Boynton, *Dedication of the Chickamauga and Chattanooga National Military Park*, 11, 274, 341. For more on state monument commemorations, see William C. Lowe, "'A Grand and Patriotic Pilgrimage': The Iowa Civil War Monuments Dedication Tour of 1906," *Annals of Iowa* 69, no. 1 (Winter 2010): 1–50; and James H. Madison, "Civil War Memories and 'Pardnership Forgittin',' 1865–1913," *Indiana Magazine of History* 99, no. 3 (Sept. 2003): 198–230. For more on monuments as commemoration, see Thomas J. Brown, *The Public Art of Civil War Commemoration: A Brief History with Documents* (Boston: Bedford/St. Martin's, 2004).

41. For the Spanish-American War, see Musicant, *Empire by Default*.

42. *House Reports*, 54th Cong., 1st sess., H.R. Rep. 374, 1–3; *Senate Reports*, 54th Cong., 1st sess., S. Rep. 526, 1–3; *CR*, 54th Cong., 1st sess., vol. 28, 3:2443–44, 2491–92; *CR*, 54th Cong., 1st sess., vol. 28, 6:5042, 5380; "Practical Use for Chickamauga Park," *Washington Post*, Feb. 10, 1898; Lee, *Origin and Evolution*, 35–36; "A National Parade Ground," *New York Times*, Dec. 7, 1895; "To Use for Military Purposes," *New York Times*, Feb. 26, 1896.

43. Atwell Thompson to Cornelius Cadle, Apr. 29 and May 16, 1898, and Atwell Thompson to D. W. Reed, July 9, 1898, all in Folder 625, Box 38, Series 1, SNMP; H. V. Boynton to A. P. Stewart, Sept. 14, 1897, Folder 159, Box 6, Series 1, CHCH; U.S. War Department, *Annual Report of the Secretary of War—1897* (Washington, D.C.: U.S. War Department, 1897), 57; U.S. War Department, *Annual Report of the Secretary of War—1898* (Washington, D.C.: U.S. War Department, 1898), 400–401, 532, 582; Paige and Greene, *Administrative History of Chickamauga and Chattanooga National Military Park*, 44, 76, 138–39, 171–74, 178, 184–85, 187–92; War Department, *Annual Report of the Secretary of War—1899*, 321. For a fascinating comparison study of memory, see Keefer, *Conflicting Memories on the River of Death*.

44. Smith, *Golden Age of Battlefield Preservation*, 6–8.
45. "Our National Military Park," undated newspaper clipping in "Reminiscences of Chickamauga," Henry Van Ness Boynton Papers, MHS; Boynton, *National Military Park*, 251; Smith, "Henry Van Ness Boynton and Chickamauga," 165–87.
46. Smith, "Chattanooga Plan," 206; Smith, *Golden Age of Battlefield Preservation*, 39–40.
47. *House Reports*, 59th Cong., 1st sess., H.R. Rep. 4431, 11–12.
48. *House Reports*, 59th Cong., 1st sess., H.R. Rep. 4431, 12–14; *Grant and Lee: The Appomattox Land and Improvement Company, Niagara Falls, N.Y.* (Niagara Falls, N.Y.: Niagara Falls Printing House, 1891); "Appomattox—Then and Now," *Newark Daily Advertiser*, Nov. 25, 1893; Master Plan draft, 1962, 2, APPO; *Senate Reports*, 57th Cong., 1st sess., S. Rep. 1344, 1–3; Henry C. Jewett to Chief of Engineers, Apr. 19, 1928, E 5, Box 7, RG 79, NARA. See also William Marvel, *A Place Called Appomattox* (Chapel Hill: Univ. of North Carolina Press, 2000), 308–19.
49. War Department, *Annual Report of the Secretary of War—1895*, 31–32; *House Reports*, 59th Cong., 1st sess., H.R. Rep. 4431, 11.
50. *House Reports*, 59th Cong., 1st sess., H.R. Rep. 4431, 8.
51. Ibid., 9, 12.
52. George B. Davis to John P. Nicholson, May 13, 1902, E 12B, Box 1, RG 153, George B. Davis Papers, NARA; George B. Davis Testimony, undated, E 12B, Box 1, RG 153, George B. Davis Papers, NARA; *House Reports*, 59th Cong., 1st sess., H.R. Rep. 4431, 10. See William G. Robertson, *The Staff Ride* (Washington, D.C.: Center of Military History, 1987).
53. Smith, "Politics of Battlefield Preservation," 310–14.
54. H.R. 1996, 54th Cong., 1st sess., LLC; H.R. 1647, 55th Cong., 1st sess., LLC; Willett, "History of Stones River National Military Park," 60.
55. Smith, "Politics of Battlefield Preservation," 310–11.
56. "National Battlefields Park," *Fredericksburg Star*, May 31, 1904; "Battlefield Park," *National Tribune*, Jan. 20, 1898; "To Preserve Virginia Battlefields," *New York Times*, Feb. 8, 1898; "Chancellorsville Battle Field," *New York Times*, Dec. 10, 1894; Chancellorsville Battlefield Association Prospectus, undated, FRSP; *Senate Reports*, 57th Cong., 1st sess., S. Rep. 165, 1, 10; S. 1287, 58th Cong., 1st sess., LLC; *Senate Reports*, 56th Cong., 1st sess., S. Rep. 335, 1–3. For members of the park association, see *House Reports*, 56th Cong., 1st sess., H.R. Rep. 717, 3–4.
57. H.R. 113, 58th Cong., 1st sess., LLC.
58. H.R. 7345, 56th Cong., 1st sess., LLC.
59. H.R. 946, 56th Cong., 1st sess., LLC; *House Report*, 56th Cong., 1st sess., H. Rep. 688, 1; Atlanta Business Men's League, *The Proposed Atlanta National Military Park: A Brief Outline of the Project* (Atlanta: Atlanta Business Men's League, 1899), 9–10.
60. H.R. 9567, 56th Cong., 1st sess., LLC; McDonough and Connelly, *Five Tragic Hours*, 179; National Park Service, *Battle of Franklin Sites*, 74.
61. H.R. 7837, 56th Cong., 1st sess., LLC; *House Reports*, 59th Cong., 1st sess., H.R. Rep. 4431, 12. See notes on proposed battlefields in Box 11, Ronald F. Lee Papers, HFC.
62. Richard Waldbauer and Sherry Hutt, "The Antiquities Act of 1906 at Its Centennial," *CRM: The Journal of Heritage Stewardship* 3, no. 1 (Winter 2006):

36–48; Abroe, "All the Profound Scenes," 236. See also David Harmon, Francis P. McManamon, and Dwight T. Pitcaithley, *The Antiquities Act: A Century of American Archaeology, Historic Preservation, and Nature Conservation* (Tucson: Univ. of Arizona Press, 2006).

63. CR, 53rd Cong., 3rd sess., vol. 27, 1:430; Nell Irvin Painter, *Standing at Armageddon: The United States, 1877–1919* (New York: W. W. Norton, 1987); Vincent P. DeSantis, *The Shaping of Modern America, 1877–1920* (Wheeling, WVa.: Forum Press, 1973); William Gardner Bell, *Secretaries of War and Secretaries of the Army: Portraits and Biographical Sketches* (Washington, D.C.: Center of Military History, 1982), 100.

64. Lee, *Origin and Evolution*, 46–52.

65. For Henderson's life, see Smith, "Politics of Battlefield Preservation," 293–320.

66. CR, 56th Cong., 1st sess., vol. 33, 1:55, 221, 579, 594, 637; CR, 56th Cong., 1st sess., vol. 33, 2:1218, 1372, 1425, 1663, 1760; CR, 56th Cong., 1st sess., vol. 33, 3:2866–67, 2913, 2956; CR, 56th Cong., 1st sess., vol. 33, 4:3108; CR, 56th Cong., 1st sess., vol. 33, 6:4961–62, 5104; CR, 56th Cong., 2nd sess., vol. 34, 4:3265; CR, 57th Cong., 1st sess., vol. 35, 1:52, 54–56, 95–96, 130, 183, 186, 230, 686; CR, 57th Cong., 1st sess., vol. 35, 2:1109–10, 1198, 1203, 1318; CR, 57th Cong., 1st sess., vol. 35, 3:2470, 2714; CR, 57th Cong., 1st sess., vol. 35, 5:4854; CR, 57th Cong., 2nd sess., vol. 36, 1:984; CR, 57th Cong., 2nd sess., vol. 36, 3:2300.

67. *House Reports*, 57th Cong., 1st sess., H.R. Rep. 771, 8–10; *Senate Reports*, 57th Cong., 1st sess., S. Rep. 1344, 1–3.

68. CR, 56th Cong., 1st sess., vol. 33, 1:55, 221, 579, 594, 637; CR, 56th Cong., 1st sess., vol. 33, 2:1218, 1372, 1425, 1663, 1760; CR, 56th Cong., 1st sess., vol. 33, 3:2866–67, 2913, 2956; CR, 56th Cong., 1st sess., vol. 33, 4:3108; CR, 56th Cong., 1st sess., vol. 33, 6:4961–62, 5104; CR, 56th Cong., 2nd sess., vol. 34, 4:3265; CR, 57th Cong., 1st sess., vol. 35, 1:52, 54–56, 95–96, 130, 183, 186, 230, 686; CR, 57th Cong., 1st sess., vol. 35, 2:1109–10, 1198, 1203, 1318; CR, 57th Cong., 1st sess., vol. 35, 5:4854; CR, 57th Cong., 2nd sess., vol. 36, 1:984; CR, 57th Cong., 2nd sess., vol. 36, 3:2300; "Battlefield Park," *Fredericksburg News*, May 30, 1900.

69. "Father of Park Delighted with Progress"; Smith, *This Great Battlefield of Shiloh*, 23, 26–27; H. W. Brands, *T. R.: The Last Romantic* (New York: Basic Books, 1997), 13–19, 82, 119, 316, 334; CR, 53rd Cong., 3rd sess., vol. 27, 1:19.

70. L. White Busbey, *Uncle Joe Cannon: The Story of a Pioneer American* (New York: Holt, 1927); Blair Bolles, *Tyrant from Illinois: Uncle Joe Cannon's Experiment with Personal Power* (New York: W. W. Norton, 1951); William Rea Gwinn, *Uncle Joe Cannon, Archfoe of Insurgency: A History of the Rise and Fall of Cannonism* (New York: Bookman Associates, 1957).

71. *House Reports*, 57th Cong., 1st sess., H.R. Rep. 2043, 2; Lee, *Origin and Evolution*, 39, 42–43.

72. H. V. Boynton to John P. Nicholson, Apr. 22, 1902, and Cornelius Cadle to D. W. Reed, Mar. 2, 1904, both in Folder 628, Box 38, Series 1, SNMP.

73. *House Reports*, 59th Cong., 1st sess., H.R. Rep. 4431, 13.

74. Ibid., 8, 10, 12–14, 18–19, 22–25.

75. Ibid., 13, 17.

76. *House Reports*, 57th Cong., 1st sess., H.R. Rep. 2043, 3–4.

77. *House Reports*, 57th Cong., 1st sess., H.R. Rep. 771, 9; Lee, *Origin and Evolution*, 44; *House Reports*, 59th Cong., 1st sess., H.R. Rep. 4431, 16; Cornelius Cadle to Josiah Patterson, Mar. 24, 1902, and Cornelius Cadle to D. W. Reed, Mar. 24, 1902, both in Folder 628, Box 38, Series 1, SNMP; Andrew Hickenlooper to D. B. Henderson, May 10, 1902, Folder 1, Box 1, Administrative Series, VNMP; John S. Kountz to William T. Rigby, Mar. 13, 1902, Folder 34, Box 2, William T. Rigby Series, VNMP; D. B. Henderson to Elihu Root, May 20, 1902, and John P. Nicholson to Secretary of War, May 15, 1902, both in E 715, Box 1, RG 92, NARA; D. B. Henderson to George D. Meiklejohn, Mar. 10, 1898, Folder 173, Box 14, Series 1, SNMP.

78. *House Reports*, 59th Cong., 1st sess., H.R. Rep. 4431, 16; U.S. War Department, *Annual Report of the Secretary of War—1904* (Washington, D.C.: U.S. War Department, 1904), 39; Bell, *Secretaries of War and Secretaries of the Army*, 100, 102; Lee, *Origin and Evolution*, 44; *House Reports*, 58th Cong., 2nd sess., H.R. Rep. 2325, 1–5; H.R. 14748, 58th Cong., 2nd sess., LLC.

79. *House Reports*, 59th Cong., 1st sess., H.R. Rep. 4431, 1–5; S. Rep. 5794, 59th Cong., 1st sess., LLC; U.S. War Department, *Annual Report of the Secretary of War—1905* (Washington, D.C.: U.S. War Department, 1905), 39; Lee, *Origin and Evolution*, 44–45. See also the extensive notes on the consolidation of the commissions in Box 11, Ronald F. Lee Papers, HFC.

80. *United States Statutes at Large*, vol. 37, pt. 1, 417–18.

81. Styles, "Stones River National Battlefield Historic Resource Study," 65; Noe, *Perryville*, 362; Pfanz, "History Through Eyes of Stone," 297; Lee A. Wallace Jr. and Martin R. Conway, *A History of Petersburg Battlefield* (Washington, D.C.: National Park Service, 1983), 36–39; Patrick A. Schroeder, ed., *Tarheels: Five Points in the Record of North Carolina in the Great War of 1861–65* (Lynchburg, Va.: Schroeder, 2000), 80; Master Plan draft, 3, APPO; "Report on Certain New York Monuments Adjacent to Manassas National Battlefield Park," Box 39, New York Monuments, RG 79, NARAPH; "7th Georgia Regiment Position Markers at Manassas National Battlefield Park," undated, Georgia Monuments File, MANA; "Tribute to Col. Webster," *Manassas Journal*, Oct. 23, 1914, and Joseph Mills Hanson to Emily C. Round, Feb. 6, 1940, both in Webster Monument File, MANA; "Bentonville Battlefield: A History of Preservation," undated, BBSHS.

82. For the state park phenomenon, see Ney C. Landrum, *The State Park Movement in America: A Critical Review* (Columbia: Univ. of Missouri Press, 2013).

83. *Whitestone Hill: Class I and Class III Cultural Resource Inventories, Dickey County, North Dakota* (Bismarck: State Historical Society of North Dakota, 2010); National Park Service, *Update to the Civil War Sites Advisory Commission Report on the Nation's Civil War Battlefields: State of North Dakota* (Washington, D.C.: National Park Service, 2010); Aaron L. Barth, "Imagining a Battlefield at a Civil War Mistake: The Public History of Whitestone Hill, 1863 to 2013," *Public Historian* 35, no. 3 (Aug. 2013): 81–84.

84. William Watts Folwell, *A History of Minnesota*, 4 vols. (St. Paul: Minnesota Historical Society, 1924), 2:386–91; Roy W. Meyer, *Everyone's Country Estate: A History*

of Minnesota's State Parks (St. Paul: Minnesota Historical Society Press, 1991), 1, 3, 15–17, 23–28.

85. "Olustee Battlefield Historic State Park Unit Management Plan," 2008, OBHSP, 1, 31, A1–1; David J. Nelson, "Florida Crackers and Yankee Tourists: The Civilian Conservation Corps, the Florida Park Service and the Emergence of Modern Florida Tourism" (Ph.D. diss., Florida State Univ., 2008), 96.

86. Lacy personal communication.

87. Don Montgomery and Holly Houser, "History of Prairie Grove Battlefield State Park: 1862–2008," 1, 10–15, PGBSP; "Prairie Grove Battlefield State Park Time-line—1862–2008," 1–2, PGBSP; "History of the Prairie Grove Chapter," 1, PGBSP.

88. Michael A. Capps, "Kennesaw Mountain National Battlefield Park: An Administrative History," 5, National Park Service, 1994, KEMO; Earl J. Hess, *Kennesaw Mountain: Sherman, Johnston and the Atlanta Campaign* (Chapel Hill: Univ. of North Carolina Press, 2013), 235–38.

89. Smith, *Golden Age of Battlefield Preservation*, 6–8.

90. Ibid.

91. Abroe, "All the Profound Scenes," 160, 183–84. See also Upchurch, *Legislating Racism*, for the effort to restart Reconstruction in the Billion Dollar Congress. For examples of reconciliation in the various speeches, see Smith, *Untold Story of Shiloh*, 97–138.

92. Paige and Greene, *Administrative History of Chickamauga and Chattanooga National Military Park*, 21; Abroe, "All the Profound Scenes," 253; George C. Osborn, ed., "Letters of Senator Edward Cary Walthall to Robert W. Banks," *Journal of Mississippi History* 9 (July 1949): 191. Several historians have made the point that even in reconciliation, there were still ill feelings among many veterans. See Neff, *Honoring the Civil War Dead*; Janney, *Remembering the Civil War*, 189–96; Caroline E. Janney, "No 'Sickly Sentimental Gush': Chickamauga and Chattanooga National Military Park and the Limits of Reconciliation," in *Gateway to the Confederacy: New Perspectives on the Chickamauga and Chattanooga Campaigns, 1862–1863*, ed. Wiley Sword and Evan C. Jones (Baton Rouge: Louisiana State Univ. Press, 2014), 285–310; and Caroline E. Janney, "War over a Shrine of Peace: The Appomattox Peace Monument and Retreat from Reconciliation," *Journal of Southern History* 77, no. 1 (Feb. 2011): 91–120. See also M. Keith Harris, *Across the Bloody Chasm: The Culture of Commemoration among Civil War Veterans* (Baton Rouge: Louisiana State Univ. Press, 2014); Barbara A. Gannon, *The Won Cause: Black and White Comradeship in the Grand Army of the Republic* (Chapel Hill: Univ. of North Carolina Press, 2011); Megan Kate Nelson, *Ruin Nation: Destruction and the American Civil War* (Athens: Univ. of Georgia Press, 2012); and Robert E. Hunt, *The Good Men Who Won the War: Army of the Cumberland Veterans and the Emancipation Memory* (Tuscaloosa: Univ. of Alabama Press, 2010).

93. *Pennsylvania at Chickamauga and Chattanooga: Ceremonies at the Dedication of the Monuments Erected by the Commonwealth of Pennsylvania to Mark the Positions of the Pennsylvania Commands Engaged in the Battles* (n.p.: Wm. Stanley Ray, 1897), 46; George Mason, *Illinois at Shiloh* (Chicago: M. A. Donohue, n.d.), 177; John Latschar, "Coming to Terms with the Civil War at Gettysburg National Military Park," *CRM:*

The Journal of Heritage Stewardship 4, no. 2 (Summer 2007): 12; Abroe, "All the Profound Scenes," 258–59; Zenzen, *Battling for Manassas*, 6.

94. E. A. Carman, Alex. P. Stewart, and Frank G. Smith to Secretary of War, July 1, 1907, and Robert Shaw Oliver Endorsement, July 11, 1907, both in Folder 195, Box 11, Series 2, CHCH; U.S. War Department, *Annual Report of the Secretary of War—1906* (Washington, D.C.: U.S. War Department, 1906), 304; S. F. Stewart to Henry Breckinridge, Dec. 8, 1914, E 588, Folder 2, Box 1, RG 92, NARA; Paige and Greene, *Administrative History of Chickamauga and Chattanooga National Military Park*, 153; Archibald Gracie, *The Truth about Chickamauga* (Dayton, Ohio: Morningside, 1997), xl–xliiii, 5, 30, 33, 226; Jim Ogden, personal communication with author, Oct. 20, 2003; Reed, *Battle of Shiloh*, 7–23, 48–49; "First Reunion of Iowa Hornet's Nest Brigade," SNMP; David W. Reed, *Campaigns and Battles of the Twelfth Regiment Iowa Veteran Volunteer Infantry: From Organization, September, 1861, to Muster-Out, January 20, 1866* (n.p.: n.p., n.d.), 1.

95. Desjardin, *These Honored Dead*, 94; Garry E. Adelman, *The Myth of Little Round Top: Gettysburg, PA* (Gettysburg, Pa.: Thomas Publications, 2003), 37–84; Linenthal, *Sacred Ground*, 107. See also Reardon, *Pickett's Charge*; and Kent Masterson Brown, *Retreat from Gettysburg: Lee, Logistics, and the Pennsylvania Campaign* (Chapel Hill: Univ. of North Carolina Press, 2005).

Chapter 3

1. "Ruth Hit Starts Yanks to Victory," *New York Times*, Apr. 11, 1930.
2. Abroe, "All the Profound Scenes," 291, 300. For an overview of the period, see George D. Moss, *The Rise of Modern America* (Upper Saddle River, N.J.: Prentice Hall, 1995).
3. Hosmer, *Presence of the Past*, 22; Montgomery and Houser, "History of Prairie Grove Battlefield State Park," 16; Abroe, "All the Profound Scenes," 291; Lee, *Origin and Evolution*, 47.
4. Smith, *Golden Age of Battlefield Preservation*, 211–12.
5. Ibid., 211–13.
6. For the NPS, see Dayton Duncan and Ken Burns, *The National Parks: America's Best Idea* (New York: Knopf, 2009).
7. Abroe, "All the Profound Scenes," 225, 239, 304.
8. Smith, *Golden Age of Battlefield Preservation*, 211–13.
9. *Establishment of National Military Parks—Battle Fields* (Washington, D.C.: Government Printing Office, 1930), 17, 32, 34.
10. "South Greets GAR," *Washington Post*, Sept. 17, 1913; Blight, *Race and Reunion*, 383; "Confederate Reunion to Be Held for First Time on a Battlefield," *New York Times*, May 25, 1913; U.S. War Department, *Annual Report of the Secretary of War—1913* (Washington, D.C.: U.S. War Department, 1913), 178; "Chickamauga Men Are to Meet Again," *Christian Science Monitor*, July 14, 1913; Gettysburg Battle-Field Commission, *Pennsylvania at Gettysburg: Ceremonies at the Dedication of the Monuments Erected by the Commonwealth of Pennsylvania to Major-General George G. Meade, Major General Winfield S. Hancock, Major General John F. Reynolds, and to Mark the*

Positions of the Pennsylvania Commands Engaged in the Battle, 3 vols. (Harrisburg, Pa.: Wm. Stanley Ray, 1914), 3:174.

11. Smith, *Golden Age of Battlefield Preservation*, 211–13.

12. Ibid.

13. Commission Meeting Minutes, Dec. 11, 1918, Folder 58, Box 2, Series 1, CHCH; U.S. War Department, *Annual Report of the Secretary of War—1915* (Washington, D.C.: U.S. War Department, 1915), 859; U.S. War Department, *Annual Report of the Secretary of War—1918* (Washington, D.C.: U.S. War Department, 1918), 1459; Charles Grosvenor obituary, *Columbus Evening Dispatch*, Oct. 30, 1917; Mary Wilder to R. B. Randolph, Oct. 20, 1917, Folder 140, Box 5, Series 1, CHCH; John T. Wilder obituary, *Chattanooga Times*, Oct. 21, 1917; 1922 Annual Report, Folder 31, Box 1, Series 1, CHCH.

14. Richard Randolph obituary, *Chattanooga Times*, Oct. 8, 1937; U.S. War Department, *Annual Report of the Secretary of War—1912* (Washington, D.C.: U.S. War Department, 1912), 171; E. E. Betts to Richard Randolph, Jan. 8, 1915, E 588, Folder 6, Box 1, RG 92, NARA; Superintendent's 1922 Report, July 11, 1922, Folder 31, Box 1, Series 1, CHCH.

15. U.S. War Department, *Annual Report of the Secretary of War—1914* (Washington, D.C.: U.S. War Department, 1914), 659; D. W. Reed to DeLong Rice, May 20, 1913, Folder 558, Box 35, Series 1, SNMP; War Department, *Annual Report of the Secretary of War—1912*, 196; War Department, *Annual Report of the Secretary of War—1913*, 200. For Rice, see Timothy B. Smith, "DeLong Rice: Shiloh's Poet Preservationist," *Tennessee Historical Quarterly* 63, no. 2 (2004): 128–43.

16. DeLong Rice to A. J. Earl, Apr. 20, 1916, Folder 533, Box 35, Series 1, SNMP; "Invoices" Ledger Book, RG 79, NARAAT; Shiloh National Military Park Daily Events, Feb., Apr., and Aug. 1912, 18, 20, 24, SNMP; R. A. Livingston Appointment, Sept. 13, 1916, Folder 533, Box 35, Series 1, SNMP; DeLong Rice, *The Story of Shiloh* (Jackson, TN: McCowat-Mercer, 1924).

17. J. P. Nicholson Journals, 13:34, GNMP; W. C. Storrick, *Gettysburg: The Place, the Battles, the Outcome* (Harrisburg, Pa.: J. Horace McFarland, 1932), 131, 144; U.S. War Department, *Annual Report of the Secretary of War—1907* (Washington, D.C.: U.S. War Department, 1907), 327; War Department, *Annual Report of the Secretary of War—1915*, 871; U.S. War Department, *Annual Report of the Secretary of War—1919* (Washington, D.C.: U.S. War Department, 1919), 5245; Unrau, *Administrative History*, 91; Murray, *On a Great Battlefield*, 20.

18. William T. Rigby to Quartermaster General of the Army, Apr. 23, 1924, Folder 29, Box 2, Administrative Series, VNMP; U.S. War Department, *Annual Report of the Secretary of War—1909* (Washington, D.C.: U.S. War Department, 1909), 44; "Facts Concerning Early Park Personalities," Folder 145, Box 6, Administrative Series, VNMP; "Annual Report of the Vicksburg National Military Park Commission," July 30, 1929, Administrative Series, Box 6, Folder 126, VNMP; Smith, *Golden Age of Battlefield Preservation*, 208.

19. M. J. Ludington to Depot Quartermaster, Mar. 30, 1898, and Assistant Quartermaster to Depot Quartermaster, Apr. 7, 1898, both in E 89, File 109863, RG 92, NARA;

Elihu Root to Charles W. Adams, June 14, 1900, E 89, File 152827, RG 92, NARA;
J. M. Dalzell to General, Oct. 19, 1903, and A. W. Butt to Quartermaster General,
Nov. 14, 1903, both in E 89, File 109863, RG 92, NARA; J. L. Pettus to Quartermaster General, June 7, 1912, and John L. Cook to Depot Quartermaster, June 6, 1912,
both in E 89, File 370969, RG 92, NARA; George W. Graham Oath, Aug. 5, 1912,
E 89, File 371906, RG 92, NARA; Henry Breckinridge Memo, Aug. 1, 1913, E 89,
File 457776, RG 92, NARA; Snell and Brown, *Antietam National Battlefield*, 129, 561.

20. "Famous Charge at Battle of Chickamauga Re-Enacted; Cry of 'Steam Roller' Resented
   by Commander Entenz," *Chattanooga Times*, Sept. 19, 1923; Richard Randolph obituary, *Chattanooga Times*, Oct. 9, 1937; Paige and Greene, *Administrative History of
   Chickamauga and Chattanooga National Military Park*, 56, 155–56, 201; DeLong Rice
   to Assistant Secretary of War, Jan. 24, 1919, and Benedict Crowell to DeLong Rice,
   Jan. 28, 1919, both in E 588, Box 5, RG 92, NARA; War Department, *Annual Report
   of the Secretary of War—1919*, 5255.

21. U.S. Congress, *Hearing before the Committee on Military Affairs, House of Representatives, Seventieth Congress, First Session, on H.R. 10291* (Washington, D.C.: Government Printing Office, 1928).

22. *House Reports*, 69th Cong., 1st sess., H.R. Rep. 1071, 1; *House Reports*, H.R. Rep.
   1525, 71st Cong., 2nd sess., 2; *Establishment of National Military Parks*, 17.

23. *House Reports*, 69th Cong., 1st sess., H.R. Rep. 1071, 1–4, 8; *House Reports*, 71st
   Cong., 2nd sess., H.R. Rep. 1525 2; *Establishment of National Military Parks*, 17–18;
   Abroe, "All the Profound Scenes," 296. For more on the army's history efforts, see
   Stetson Conn, *Historical Work in the United States Army, 1862–1954* (Washington,
   D.C.: Center of Military History, 1980).

24. *House Reports*, 69th Cong., 1st sess., H.R. Rep. 1071, 3–7.

25. Ibid., 4–8.

26. Ibid.

27. H.R. 9765, 69th Cong., 1st sess., LLC, copy in Box 11, Ronald F. Lee Papers, HFC;
   House Reports, 69th Cong., 1st sess., H.R. Rep. 1071, 1, 9–10; *House Reports*, 71st
   Cong., 2nd sess., H.R. Rep. 1525, 2.

28. *House Reports*, 69th Cong., 2nd sess., H.R. Rep. 574, 1–3; *Senate Reports*, 70th Cong.,
   2nd sess., S. Rep. 187, 1–3, 10; *House Reports*, 71st Cong., 2nd sess., H.R. Rep. 1525. 2.

29. *Senate Reports*, 72nd Cong., 1st sess., S. Rep. 27, Dec. 19, 1931, 2. For more on Landers, see the Howard L. Landers Papers, UTA.

30. *Senate Reports*, 70th Cong., 2nd sess., S. Rep. 187, 1–10; *Senate Reports*, 71st Cong.,
   2nd sess., S. Rep. 46, 1–10; *House Reports*, 71st Cong., 2nd sess., H.R. Rep. 1525, 2;
   Establishment of National Military Parks, 18, 21.

31. Ruth Graham to Olinus Smith, Mar. 6, 1937, Park History—Vertical Files, KEMO;
   John T. Willett, "A History of Richmond National Battlefield Park," undated,
   40–41, RICH; Howard L. Landers to Colonel Gibson, Oct. 12, 1928, H2215, Folder
   226, STRI; H. J. Connor to Archibald Runner, Oct. 20, 1931, H14, Folder 82, STRI;
   H. L. Landers to Colonel Gibson, Oct. 12, 1928, Box 1, Series 1, Resource Management Collection, FODO; Howard L. Landers Diaries, 1929–1933, Box 3G428,
   Howard L. Landers Papers, UTA; Sean M. Styles, *Stones River National Battlefield*

Historic Resource Study (Atlanta: National Park Service Southeast Region, 2004), 66; Wallace and Conway, *History of Petersburg National Battlefield*, 66.

32. CR, 69th Cong., 1st sess., vol. 69, 1,566; CR, 70th Cong., 2nd sess., vol. 70, 3135, 4156; Agnew Deed, June 28, 1930, E 5, Box 8, RG 79, NARA; Conrad L. Worth to Superintendent, Natchez Trace Parkway, Jan. 30, 1956, Brice's Crossroads File, Box 25, RG 79, NARAPH; Brices Cross Roads Monument Completion Report, Mar. 14, 1931, E 5, Box 8, RG 79, NARA; Malcolm Gardner to Regional Director, Nov. 18, 1947, Brice's Crossroads File, Box 34, RG 79, NARAPH.

33. "Report of Inspection," Nov. 3, 1926, E 5, Box 7, RG 79, NARA; Master Plan draft, 3–4, APPO; *House Reports*, 74th Cong., 1st sess., H. Rep. 851, 1–2; Lee, *Origin and Evolution*, 52. See also Janney, "War over a Shrine of Peace," 91–120.

34. Mission 66 File, Colonial National Historical Park, Box 25, RG 79, NARAPH, 43; Brehon Sommerville to Chief of Engineers, Dec. 6, 1929, E 5, Box 81, RG 79, NARA; "Outline of Development, Colonial National Monument, Yorktown, Virginia," 1933, 16, COLO.

35. *House Reports*, 71st Cong., 2nd sess., H.R. Rep. 1525, 1–28; *Establishment of National Military Parks*, 1, 20, 24, 26, 30–32, 37.

36. *House Reports*, 71st Cong., 2nd sess., H.R. Rep. 1525, 1–28; *Establishment of National Military Parks*, 1, 20.

37. *House Reports*, 71st Cong., 2nd sess., H.R. Rep. 1525, 28; Boge and Boge, *Paving Over the Past*, 28; *Senate Reports*, 72nd Cong., 1st sess., S. Rep. 27, Dec. 19, 1931, 5–6.

38. "General G. B. Davis Dies Suddenly," undated newspaper clipping, George B. Davis File, USMA; General Orders No. 61, Dec. 17, 1914, George B. Davis File, USMA; *Forty-sixth Annual Reunion of the Association Graduates of the United States Military Academy at West Point, New York, June 11th, 1915* (Saginaw, Mich.: Seeman and Peters, 1915), 133, 137.

39. Master Plan, 1970, FOPU, 4, 49; C. P. Summerall to Charles C. Edwards, undated, E 5, Box 25, RG 79, NARA; Fort Pulaski Mission 66 File, 27, Box 26, RG 79, NARAPH; J. Faith Meader, *Fort Pulaski National Monument Administrative History* (Atlanta: National Park Service Southeast Region, 2003), 18–21; Lee, *Origin and Evolution*, 51.

40. Meghan Hagerty, "Park Service Works to Connect Washington's Fort Circle Parks," *Hallowed Ground* 9, no. 3 (Fall 2008): 45–46; Benjamin F. Cooling III, *The Day Lincoln Was Almost Shot: The Fort Stevens Story* (Lanham, Md.: Scarecrow Press, 2013), 248–49.

41. Lee, *Origin and Evolution*, 51; P. H. Drewry to E. J. Nixon, Feb. 28, 1924, and unknown to I. B. Brown, June 11, 1909, Davis L. Davis et. al. Memorandum, undated, and City resolution, undated, all in Folder 8, Box 2, War Department Files, PETE; Minutes of the Meeting of the Petersburg Commission, Apr. 18, 1925, and Petersburg Commission to Secretary of War, Nov. 19, 1925, all in Folder 5, Box 2, War Department Files, PETE; Petersburg Mission 66 Plan, 24, Box 27, RG 79, NARAPH.

42. *House Reports*, 69th Cong., 1st sess., H.R. Rep. 887, 1–3; Minutes of the Meeting of the Petersburg Commission, May 2, 1925, Minutes of the Meeting of the Petersburg

Commission, May 14, 1925, and Petersburg Commission to Secretary of War, Nov. 19, 1925, all in Folder 5, Box 2, War Department Files, PETE.

43. *CR*, 69th Cong., 1st sess., vol. 67, 9536–37, 10836–37, 12632, 13094; *House Reports*, 69th Cong., 1st sess., H.R. Rep. 887, 1–3; *Senate Reports*, 69th Cong., 1st sess., S. Rep. 1179, 1.

44. Petersburg Commission to Secretary of War, July 2, 1928, Folder 5, Box 2, War Department Files, PETE; "Crater Battlefield is Now A Gold Course," 1930, Folder 3, Box 15, NPS Files, PETE; Petersburg Mission 66 Plan, 24, NARAPH; Wallace and Conway, *History of Petersburg National Battlefield*, 61.

45. Petersburg Commission to Secretary of War, Apr. 5, 1929, Arthur E. Wilbourn to Charles Hall Davis, Nov. 12, 1930, "Report on Development of Petersburg Battlefield Park," Nov. 24, 1933, and James Blyth to Quartermaster General, Dec. 10, 1929, all in Folder 5, Box 2, War Department Files, PETE; "Dedication of Petersburg National Military Park Monday June 20, 1932," Box 2, Folder 4, War Department Files, PETE; "Military Park Is Memorial to Warriors of '65," *Petersburg Progress Index*, June 20, 1932; "National Battlefield Park Here Rapidly Taking Shape," Petersburg Mission 66 Plan, 24, NARAPH; Will Be Beautiful Section," *Petersburg Progress Index*, July 21, 1929; "Fort Mahone Given to Park by Local Man," *Petersburg Progress Index*, Jan. 19, 1930; Wallace and Conway, *History of Petersburg National Battlefield*, 70.

46. "Report on Inspection of Battlefields in and Around Fredericksburg and Spotsylvania Court House, Virginia," Dec. 1, 1925, FRSP; Fredericksburg Park Mission 66 Plan, undated, Box 26, RG 79, NARAPH; *CR*, 69th Cong., 1st sess., vol. 68, 3579, 9529, 10836; *CR*, 69th Cong., 2nd sess., vol. 68, 1013, 1797–98, 3153, 4938; *House Reports*, 69th Cong., 1st sess., H.R. Rep. 814, 1–2; *Senate Reports*, 69th Cong., 2nd sess., S. Rep. 1400, 1–2; "President Signs Local Park Bill," Feb. 15, 1927, *Fredericksburg Free Lance Star*. For a listing of monuments and dates, see Donald C. Phanz, "History Through the Eyes of Stone," Sept. 2006, FRSP.

47. George F. Hobson Appointment, Jan. 9, 1928, Hobson Folder, Drawer 1, Cabinet 6, FRSP; Tenney Ross Appointment, May 18, 1929, Ross Folder, Drawer 1, Cabinet 6, FRSP; Arthur Wilbourn Appointment, May 29, 1930, Wilbourn Folder, Drawer 1, Cabinet 6, FRSP; Arthur E. Wilbourn to Quartermaster General, Nov. 12, 1930, and Testimonial of Appreciation, Dec. 13, 1929, both in Fleming Folder, Drawer 1, Cabinet 6, FRSP; R. D. Valliant to Commission, Mar. 28, 1930, Fencing Folder, Drawer 1, Cabinet 6, FRSP; A. J. McGehee to Oswald E. Camp, Jan. 29, 1929, Bronze Castings Folder, Drawer 1, Cabinet 6, FRSP; Fredericksburg Park Mission 66 Plan, NARAPH; Branch Spaulding to Frank McHichester, Jan. 31, 1940, E 10B, Box 2465, RG 79, NARA; Happel, "History of the Fredericksburg and Spotsylvania County Battlefields," 49, 56.

48. *CR*, 69th Cong., 2nd sess., vol. 68, 3189–90, 5197, 5964; *House Reports*, 69th Cong., 1st sess., H.R. Rep. 788, 1–7; *Senate Reports*, 69th Cong., 2nd sess., S. Rep. 1517, 1–7. For a detailed look at Stones River, see John Riley George, "Stones River: Creating a Battlefield Park, 1862–1932" (Ph.D. diss.: Middle Tennessee State Univ., 2013).

49. "Report on Inspection of Battlefield of Stones River, Tennessee," July 17, 1928, H17, Folder 216, STRI.

50. John F. Conklin to Quartermaster General, Oct. 9, 1928, E 5, Box 65, RG 79, NARA; John F. Conklin to H. L. Landers, June 15, 1928, and "Address by Capt. Connor," July 15, 1932, both in H2215, Folder 226, STRI.
51. H. J. Connor to Quartermaster General, July 18, 1932, "Progress Report, Stones River National Military Park," Apr. 1, 1931, and "Address by Capt. Connor," July 15, 1932, all in H2215, Folder 226, STRI; J. Crawford Biggs to Harold L. Ickes, May 4, 1934, and "Press Release Re: Stones River National Military Park," May 17, 1935, both in H14, Folder 82, STRI; C. A. Bach to Inspector General, Nov. 2, 1931, E 5, Box 63, RG 79, NARA; *Historic Listing of National Park Service Officials* (Washington, D.C.: National Park Service, 1991), 179.
52. *CR*, 70th Cong., 1st sess., vol. 69, 1533, 4961, 5914; *House Reports*, 70th Cong., 1st sess., H.R. Rep. 64, 1; *Senate Reports*, 70th Cong., 1st sess., S. Rep. 563, 1; "Report on Fort Donelson National Military Park," Nov. 28, 1928, Folder 1, Series 1, War Department Files, FODO; Peterson, *Administrative* History, 27–28.
53. "Report on Fort Donelson National Military Park," Nov. 28, 1928, Folder 1, Series 1, War Department Files, FODO.
54. John F. Conklin to H. L. Landers, Aug. 16, 1928, Box 1, Series 1, Resource Management Collection, FODO; "Termination of the Commission," May 13, 1932, Box 4, Series 1, War Department Records, FODO; "Report on the Construction of Fort Donelson National Military Park, Dover, Tennessee," June 14, 1932, Folder 2, Series 1, War Department Files, FODO; "Program," July 14, 1932, Folder 3, Series 1, War Department Files, FODO; "Progress Report, Fort Donelson National Military Park," Jan. 1, 1931, Box 2, Series 3, Resource Management Collection, FODO; "Confederate Monument," undated, Folder 4, Series 1, War Department Files, FODO; Peterson, *Administrative* History, 40, 47, 56; Van L. Riggins, *A History of Fort Donelson National Military Park Tennessee* (Washington, D.C.: National Park Service, 1958), 38.
55. Hosmer, *Preservation Comes of Age* 1:471, 473; Abroe, "All the Profound Scenes," 287.
56. Horace M. Albright, *Origins of National Park Service Administration of Historic Sites* (Philadelphia: Eastern National Park & Monument Association, 1971), 1–24; U.S. War Department, *Annual Report of the Secretary of War—1923* (Washington, D.C.: U.S. War Department, 1923), 161; U.S. War Department, *Annual Report of the Secretary of War—1931* (Washington, D.C.: U.S. War Department, 1931), 21; Richard B. Randolph to Joseph B. Cumming, Aug. 23, 1921, Folder 63, Box 2, Series 1, CHCH; U.S. Congress, *Hearings before the Committee on Military Affairs House of Representatives Seventieth Congress Second Session on S. 4173 to Transfer Jurisdiction over Certain National Military Parks and National Monuments from the War Department to the Department of the Interior, and for Other Purposes* (Washington, D.C.: Government Printing Office, 1929), 6, 8–9, 11–12, 15, 19.
57. H.R. 8502, 72nd Cong., 1st sess., LLC; *Senate Reports*, 70th Cong., 1st sess., S. Rep. 1026, 1–2; *Senate Reports*, 70th Cong., 1st sess., S. Rep. 4173, LLC; U.S. Congress, *Hearings before the Committee on Military Affairs House of Representatives Seventieth Congress Second Session on S. 4173*, 1–3; Terry Winschel, personal communication with author, Aug. 18, 2004. For more on the transfer and Landers's opposition, see

Harlan D. Unrau and George F. Williss, *Administrative History: Expansion of the National Park Service in the 1930s* (Washington, D.C.: National Park Service, 1983).

58. Hosmer, *Preservation Comes of Age* 1:477; U.S. Congress, *Hearings before the Committee on Military Affairs House of Representatives Seventieth Congress Second Session on S. 4173*, 9, 13–14; Albright, *Origins of National Park Service Administration of Historic Sites*, 1–24.

59. U.S. Congress, *Hearings before the Committee on Military Affairs House of Representatives Seventieth Congress Second Session on S. 4173*, 7, 16–18; Albright, *Origins of National Park Service Administration of Historic Sites*, 1–24.

60. U.S. Congress, *Hearings before the Committee on Military Affairs House of Representatives Seventieth Congress Second Session on S. 4173*, 19, 20–21.

61. Ibid., 6, 8, 10, 13, 16.

62. Ibid., 5, 22.

63. Albright, *Origins of National Park Service Administration of Historic Sites*, 1–24; U.S. Congress, *Hearing before the Committee on Military Affairs, House of Representatives, Seventieth Congress, First Session, on H.R. 10291*, 5–7; U.S. Congress, *Hearings before the Committee on Military Affairs House of Representatives Seventieth Congress Second Session on S. 4173*, 10.

64. *Establishment of National Military Parks*, 21–23.

65. Hosmer, *Preservation Comes of Age* 1:477; *Opinions of the Attorneys General*, vol. 36, 1929–32, 75–79, copy in Box 11, Ronald F. Lee Papers, HFC; Albright, *Origins of National Park Service Administration of Historic Sites*, 1–24.

66. Hosmer, *Preservation Comes of Age* 1:532; Albright, *Origins of National Park Service Administration of Historic Sites*, 1–24; Lee, *Origin and Evolution*, 51–52; Abroe, "All the Profound Scenes," 309–310, 315.

67. "Division of State Parks: Acquisition Date of the State Parks," undated, FPSHP.

68. See Georgia Department of Natural Resources, State Parks and Historic Sites, http://gastateparks.org/item/67911#JeffDavis.

69. Richard Schriver Barry, "Fort Macon: Its History," *North Carolina Historical Review* 27, no. 2 (Apr. 1950): 176; Fort Morgan National Register of Historic Places Inventory—Nomination Form, Oct. 4, 1975, NARE; Fort Pike State Historic Site History, undated, courtesy of Raymond Berthelot, Louisiana Office of State Parks.

70. Gregory L. Wade, "Nashville's Fort Negley Opens to the Public," *Civil War News*, Jan. 2005; "1,150 Men to Rebuild Fort Negley Breastworks," *Nashville Tennessean*, June 14, 1935; Dixie Johnson, "Silent-Gunned Fort," May 5, 1946, FN.

71. Blight, *Race and Reunion*, 2; Tennessee GenWeb, "The Beginnings Of Nathan Bedford Forrest State Park," pt. 4, http://tngenweb.org/benton/bentonhistory26.html; "Division of State Parks: Acquisition Date of the State Parks," FPSHP.

72. "Erects Shaft to Comrades Lost Near Old Shelton House," *Richmond Times-Dispatch*, Sept. 16, 1924; Edmund B. Rogers, "History of Legislation Relating to the National Park System Through the 82d Congress," n.d., RICH; Willett, "History of Richmond National Battlefield Park," 27–28, 30, 32, 38, 44; J. Ambler Johnston, *Echoes of 1861–1961* (n.p.: n.p., 1971); "The Dedication by the Richmond

Battlefield Parks Corporation of the Battlefield Area Around Richmond," June 22, 1932, Early Park History File, RICH.

73. Kermit McKeever, *Where People and Nature Meet: A History of the West Virginia State Parks* (Charleston, WVa.: Pictorial Histories, 1988), 89–94.

74. McKeever, *Where People and Nature Meet*, 66, 70.

75. "Columbus-Belmont Battlefield State Park," *Hickman County Gazette*, 1953.

76. "Story of Arkansas Post," undated, Mission 66 Proposal, Box 82, RG 79, NARAPH; "Superintendent's Annual Report—1972," Arkansas Post File, HFC.

77. Fort Bragg Historical Tour brochure, undated, FB; Eric J. Wittenberg, *The Battle of Monroe's Crossroads and the Civil War's Final Campaign* (El Dorado Hills, Calif.: Savas Beatie, 2006), 226; "Report on Development of Petersburg Battlefield Park," Nov. 24, 1933, Folder 5, Box 2, War Department Files, PETE.

78. "Park History, Colonel Dan McCook Brigade Association," undated, Monument Research Files, KEMO; Capps, "Kennesaw Mountain National Battlefield Park," 5–7.

79. "Cheatham Hill Description," undated, Monument Research Files, KEMO; Memo for Assistant Secretary of War, Dec. 20, 1924, E 5, Box 43, RG 79, NARA; Richard Randolph to A. E. Demaray, Aug. 18, 1933, E 10, Box 2435B, RG 79, NARA; Capps, "Kennesaw Mountain National Battlefield Park," 5–7.

80. Lorrie K. Owen, ed., *Dictionary of Ohio Historic Places*, 2 vols. (Minneapolis: Somerset, 1999), 2:985–86; Michael J. Matts and Stephen J. Roberts, "Battle of Buffington Island Battlefield Preservation Plan," 2006, ABPP, 32–33; "Fort Gaines Named One of America's Most Endangered," *Preservation: Alabama Historical Commission Report* 37, no. 6 (Sept.–Oct. 2011): 1.

81. "Timeline of Mansfield State Historic Site's History and Development," undated, MSHS; Mansfield Battle Park Association Charter, July 2, 1907, MSHS; UDC Scrapbook, MSHS.

82. Zenzen, *Battling for Manassas*, 15; E. R. W. Ewing to Rufus W. Pearson, Feb. 1, 1928, unknown to R. Walton Moore, Feb. 28, 1927, and Walter L. Hopkins to Sir, June 1927, all in Park Development—Various Letters 1927–28 Re. Manassas Battlefield Confederate Park, MANA.

83. U.S. War Department, *Official Army Register—January 1, 1922* (Washington, D.C.: War Department, 1922), 518.

84. Ed Bearss interview, Aug. 11, 2004, SNMP.

85. *Establishment of National Military Parks*, 21; Abroe, "All the Profound Scenes," 270–72, 298, 321.

86. *House Reports*, 69th Cong., 1st sess., H.R. Rep. 887, 1–3; *Senate Reports*, 69th Cong., 2nd sess., S. Rep. 1400, 1–2.

87. "Stones River Park Is Dedicated with Fitting Ceremonies," *Murfreesboro News Journal*, July 16, 1932; *House Reports*, 69th Cong., 1st sess., H.R. Rep. 887, 1–3.

88. "Historic Park Will Attract Tourists Here," Sept. 19, 1926, Folder 9, Box 2, War Department Files, PETE; Levin, *Remembering the Battle of the Crater*, 105; Abroe, "All the Profound Scenes," 302.

Chapter 4

1. Linenthal, *Sacred Ground*, 97.
2. Smith, *Chickamauga Memorial*, 135–36.
3. For Roosevelt, see Jean Edward Smith, *FDR* (New York: Random House, 2007).
4. Ed Bearss interview, Aug. 11, 2004, SHIL; Murray, *On a Great Battlefield*, 30, 43.
5. "Report on Development of Petersburg Battlefield Park," Nov. 24, 1933, Folder 5, Box 3, War Department Files, PETE; Murray, *On a Great Battlefield*, 39; Ed Bearss interview, Aug. 11, 2004, SHIL.
6. Murray, *On a Great Battlefield*, 20, 26, 31; Abroe, "All the Profound Scenes," 322, 398.
7. Abroe, "All the Profound Scenes," 322, 398; "Press Release Re: Stones River National Military Park," May 17, 1935, H14, Folder 82, STRI.
8. *Historic Listing of National Park Service Officials*, 58, 107, 158, 185.
9. *Historic Listing of National Park Service Officials*, 80, 99, 111, 174, 179; "Livingston Resigns as Supt. Park," *Savannah Courier*, Apr. 17, 1936; Zeb McKinney, personal communication with author, Jan. 25, 2006; Smith, *This Great Battlefield of Shiloh*, 136; Randolph obituary, *Chattanooga Times*, Oct. 8, 1937. It must be noted, however, that McConaghie went directly to Vicksburg as superintendent.
10. Kammen, *Mystic Chords of Memory*, 470–71.
11. Hosmer, *Preservation Comes of Age* 1:548–76; Bodnar, *Remaking America*, 178–79; Kammen, *Mystic Chords of Memory*, 468; Abroe, "All the Profound Scenes," 351; Lee, *Origin and Evolution*, 55; Boge and Boge, *Paving Over the Past*, 28.
12. Hosmer, *Preservation Comes of Age* 1:548–576; Bodnar, *Remaking America*, 178–79; Kammen, *Mystic Chords of Memory*, 468; Abroe, "All the Profound Scenes," 351; Lee, *Origin and Evolution*, 5; Boge and Boge, *Paving Over the Past*, 28.
13. Bodnar, *Remaking America*, 178–79; Abroe, "All the Profound Scenes," 365.
14. Abroe, "All the Profound Scenes," 378–79, 381; Cape Hatteras Mission 66 Plan, undated, Box 25, RG 79, NARAPH; Cumberland Gap Mission 66 Plan, undated, Box 25, RG 79, NARAPH; Barry Mackintosh, *C&O Canal: The Making of a Park* (Washington, D.C.: National Park Service, 1991), 19–20; National Park Service, *Update to the Civil War Sites Advisory Commission Report on the Nation's Civil War Battlefields: State of Maryland* (Washington, D.C.: National Park Service, 2010), 15; National Park Service, *Update to the Civil War Sites Advisory Commission Report on the Nation's Civil War Battlefields: Commonwealth of Virginia* (Washington, D.C.: National Park Service, 2009), 27.
15. Constructing Division to Quartermaster, Aug. 28, 1931, and John A. Gilman to quartermaster, Dec. 10, 1930, both in E 5, Box 48, RG 79, NARA; Paula Stoner Reed, "Cultural Resources Study: Monocacy National Battlefield," 1999, 54–55, MONO; *House Reports*, Apr. 3, 1934, 73rd Cong., 2nd sess., H.R. Rep. 1134, 5.
16. *Senate Reports*, June 6, 1934, 73rd Cong., 2nd sess., S. Rep. 1403; *House Reports*, Apr. 3, 1934, 73rd Cong., 2nd sess., H.R. Rep. 1134; *CR*, 73rd Cong., 2nd sess., vol. 78, 8791, 11167, 12453; Reed, "Cultural Resources Study," 54–55; Abroe, "All the Profound Scenes," 568.

17. *CR*, 74th Cong., 1st sess., vol. 79, 2902, 4782, 8308, 10291; "Park History," undated, Park History, Vertical Files, KEMO.

18. Kennesaw Mountain Mission 66 Plan, undated, Box 26, RG 79, NARAPH; Capps, "Kennesaw Mountain National Battlefield Park," 8–15; *Historic Listing of National Park Service Officials*, 132; Hess, *Kennesaw Mountain*, 238–39.

19. *CR*, 74th Cong., 1st sess., vol. 79, 8734, 11977, 13992; Master Plan draft, 4, APPO; Hosmer, *Preservation Comes of Age* 1:620–626; Hosmer, *Preservation Comes of Age* 2:733–36, 948–50; Janney, "War over a Shrine of Peace," 91–120.

20. Master Plan draft, 5–6, APPO; Mission 66 Plan, Box 25, RG 79, NARAPH; Charles W. Porter, "Supplementary Report on Appomattox Court House, Va.," 1937, APPO; Appomattox Court House National Register of Historic Places Continuation Sheet, Section 8, 79–80, APPO. See also "Appomattox Court House NHP: Cultural Landscape Report," APPO.

21. *CR*, 74th Cong., 2nd sess., vol. 80, 714, 2435, 3140; Willett, "History of Richmond National Battlefield Park," 39, 42, 45; *Historic Listing of National Park Service Officials*, 163; "Saving Richmond's Battlefields—Gaines' Mill," *Hallowed Ground* 13, no. 2 (Summer 2012): 10–11.

22. Manassas Mission 66 Plan, undated, Box 27, RG 79, NARAPH; Zenzen, *Battling for Manassas*, 19, 21. See also Bull Run Recreational Area Folder, MANA.

23. Zenzen, *Battling for Manassas*, 24, 26–32; Abroe, "All the Profound Scenes," 374; Manassas Mission 66 Plan, NARAPH; "Administration and Museum Building Final Report," Aug. 27, 1942, Manassas National Battlefield Park Visitor Center or Museum File, MANA; "Jackson Monument to Be Done by Pollia," *New York Times*, Mar. 5, 1939; "Statue Plans Irk Virginia," *New York Times*, Apr. 9, 1939; "Assail Jackson Memorial," *New York Times*, Mar. 24, 1939; "'Stonewall' Jackson Rides Again," *Hartford Courant*, Apr. 23, 1939; Raleigh C. Taylor Memo, Aug. 28, 1940, and Joseph Mills Hanson Memo, Nov. 12, 1943, both in Stonewall Jackson File, MANA.

24. *CR*, 74th Cong., 1st sess., vol. 79, 2902, 4782, 8308, 10291; H. C. Bryant to Verne Chatelain, June 13, 1935, E 10B, Box 2596A, RG 79, NARA.

25. For the state park effort, see Landrum, *State Park Movement in America*.

26. Arno B. Cammerer to Senator Byrd, Oct. 10, 1934, and Oliver Taylor to director, Feb. 5, 1944, both in E 7, Box 3047, RG 79, NARA; "The History of Sailor's Creek (a.k.a. Sayler's Creek) Battlefield Historical State Park, 1937–2010," 2010, SCBSP.

27. H.R. 113, 58th Cong., 1st sess., LLC; Perryville Deed, Jan. 12, 1931, PBSHS; Robert S. Cameron, *Staff Ride Handbook for the Battle of Perryville, 8 October 1862* (Fort Leavenworth, Kans.: Combat Studies Institute Press, 2005), 243; Noe, *Perryville*, 362.

28. "Speakers at Rivers Bridge Memorial Services, 1876–Present," undated, RBSHS; Power and Bell, "Rivers Bridge State Park," 14; Daniel J. Bell, "The Strongest Position I Ever Saw in My Life: Mapping and Site Study of the Rivers Bridge Battlefield," 2005, 70–78, ABPP.

29. R. Jervis Cooke, "Sand and Grit: The Story of Fort McAllister, a Confederate Earthwork on the Great Ogeechee River, Genesis Point, Georgia," 1938, 70–71, FMSP; Christopher A. Whitfield, "Restoration: The Recapturing of Fort McAllister During the Henry Ford Years," 2005, FMSP.

30. Murray, *On a Great Battlefield*, 31.
31. For the New Deal, see David M. Kennedy, *Freedom from Fear: The American People in Depression and War, 1929–1945* (New York: Oxford Univ. Press, 1999).
32. W. A. Ronan, "History of CCC Veterans Company 1364, Petersburg, Va.," 1934, Box 2, War Department Files, PETE.
33. Unrau, *Administrative History*, 155; "Report on Development of Petersburg Battlefield Park," Nov. 24, 1933, Folder 5, Box 2, War Department Files, PETE.
34. William E. Leuchtenburg, *Franklin D. Roosevelt and the New Deal, 1932–1940* (New York: Harper and Row, 1963), 164–65; "Some Blame Dam for High Erosion Rate," *Nashville Tennessean*, 1998, copy in Shiloh National Military Park Scrapbook, SNMP; Charles E. Shedd, *A History of Shiloh National Military Park, Tennessee* (Washington, D.C.: Government Printing Office, 1954), 52; "The Preservation of Fort Henry and Associated Sites," 2011, 16–17, ABPP.
35. "Civil Works Program—Statistical Summary" and "Final Report of Civil Work Program," undated, both in Box 4, Series 1, FODO; Unrau, *Administrative History*, 155; Snell and Brown, *Antietam National Battlefield*, 151; Capps, "Kennesaw Mountain National Battlefield Park," 16; Abroe, "All the Profound Scenes," 339.
36. Leuchtenburg, *Franklin D. Roosevelt and the New Deal*, 120–23; Lewis M. Anderson to "All C.W.A. Foremen," Jan. 30, 1934, and Lewis M. Anderson to "All Foremen Working on Civil Works Program," Jan. 29, 1934, both in Box 8, RG 79, NARAAT; Paul D. Welch, *Archeology at Shiloh Indian Mounds, 1899–1999* (Tuscaloosa: Univ. of Alabama Press, 2006), 2; Frank H. H. Roberts Field Notebook, National Anthropological Archives, National Museum of Natural History, SI; Moreau B. Chambers Field Notebook, National Anthropological Archives, National Museum of Natural History, SI; Frank H. H. Roberts Jr., *Indian Mounds on Shiloh Battlefield*, photograph in *Explorations and Fieldwork of the Smithsonian Institution in 1934* (Washington, D.C.: Smithsonian Institution, 1935), 65–68; W. W. Luckett to Verne E. Chatelain, Nov. 18, 1935, "Research Studies, Shiloh National Military Park," undated, Charles S. Dunn to Branch Spalding, Nov. 22, 1937, and "Research Studies Made During the CWA Period, Shiloh National Military Park," undated, all in Historical Reports, Vertical Files, SNMP.
37. Carolyn S. Childress, "A Grassroots Study of the Civilian Conservation Corps: An In Depth Look at the Three Camps under the Direction of the Fredericksburg and Spotsylvania National Military Park, Virginia," 1982, FRSP; Leuchtenburg, *Franklin D. Roosevelt and the New Deal*, 174; John C. Paige, *The Civilian Conservation Corps and the National Park Service, 1933–1942: An Administrative History* (Washington, D.C.: National Park Service, 1985), 97; "Petersburg National Battlefield Resource Management Records, 1873, 1922–2004," 15; Ronan, "History of CCC Veterans Company 1364." Much of the discussion of the CCC at Shiloh is based on Timothy B. Smith, "Black Soldiers and the CCC at Shiloh National Military Park," *CRM: The Journal of Heritage Stewardship* 3, no. 2 (Summer 2006): 73–84.
38. "Short History of National Monuments and Historical Areas," undated, Box 91, RG 79, NARAPH; Fort Pulaski Restoration Data, Oct. 15, 1934, FOPU; "A Summary

of Work Accomplishments of the Civilian Conservation Corps at Fort Pulaski National Monument, Savannah, Georgia, May 10, 1934–June 5, 1940," 1940, FOPU; Waldrep, *Vicksburg's Long Shadow*, 277, 290; Fort Donelson Mission 66 Plan, Box 26, RG 79, NARAPH; Paige and Greene, *Administrative History of Chickamauga and Chattanooga National Military Park*, 100–101; Capps, "Kennesaw Mountain National Battlefield Park," 17–20; Peterson, *Administrative History*, 67; Happel, "History of the Fredericksburg and Spotsylvania County Battlefields," 56–57.

39. "Camp Report, Nov. 1, 1934, CCC Folder, RICH; Rogers, "History of Legislation Relating to the National Park System"; Mission 66 Plan, Box 25, RG 79, NARAPH; Murray, *On a Great Battlefield*, 23; Unrau, *Administrative History*, 155; John A. Salmond, *The Civilian Conservation Corps, 1933–1942: A New Deal Case Study* (Durham, N.C.: Duke Univ. Press, 1967).

40. "ECW Monthly Progress and Cost Report," Feb. 1937, E 75, Box 7, RG 79, NARA; "Dedication of THC Marker for CCC Co. 2425, MP-3, Shiloh National Military Park, July 14, 1990," Dedication Remarks for Placement of CCC Marker—July 14, 1990, Vertical Files, SNMP; "Camp Inspection Report," Oct. 3, 1938, E 115, Box 199, RG 35, NARA; "2425th Company, MP-3, Pittsburg Landing, Tennessee," *Official Annual Civilian Conservation Corps "C" District, Fourth Corps Area—1937*, Patsy Weiler Collection, MTSU; "Tennessee Camp MP-7," May 25, 1937; Narrative Report of Tennessee Camp MP-7, Mar. 31, 1935, E 42, Box 28, RG 79, NARA; Erosion Control Memo, Mar. 11, 1935, Folder 168, Box 9, Series 2, SNMP; Alex Bradford to R. A. Livingston, Mar. 31, 1935, E 42, Box 27, RG 79, NARA; O. E. Van Cleve to Governor Hill McAlister, July 19, 1935, and Secretary of War to Senator Kenneth McKellar, July 15, 1935, both in Hill McAlister Papers, Folder 8, Box 77, TSLA.

41. Leuchtenburg, *Franklin D. Roosevelt and the New Deal*, 133–34; Robert A. Livingston to Verne A. Chatelain, Dec. 12, 1933, Folder 328, Box 20, Series 2, SNMP; Shedd, *History of Shiloh National Military Park*, 46; Blueprints, "Entrance Stations," Folder 91, Map Drawer 11, Series 8, SNMP; Fort Donelson Mission 66 Plan, NARAPH; Paige and Greene, *Administrative History of Chickamauga and Chattanooga National Military Park*, 99; Willett, "History of Richmond National Battlefield Park," 90; Unrau, *Administrative History*, 156, 159; Snell and Brown, *Antietam National Battlefield*, 158–59.

42. "Press Release Re: Stones River National Military Park," May 17, 1935, H14, Folder 82, STRI; Snell and Brown, *Antietam National Battlefield*, 156–57; Unrau, *Administrative History*, 159, 163, 165; "Restoration of Fort Negley Finally Complete," Dec. 13, 1936, unattributed newspaper column, FN; Floyd B. Taylor to Branch Spaulding, Apr. 16, 1936, Box 1, RG 79, NARAPH; "Monumentation-Topo Maps," Folder 93, Map Drawer 5, Series 7, SNMP; Blueprints, "Proposed Eastern Corinth, Hamburg-Crump and Peabody Monument Roads," Folder 43, Map Drawer 8, Series 8, SNMP; "Maintenance and Post Construction for Shiloh National Military Park," Folder 343, Box 21, Series 2, SNMP; "Final Construction Report—Project 4A1," Miscellaneous Files, SNMP. For the Bureau of Public Roads, see RG 30 in the National Archives; for the United States Geological Survey, see RG 57.

43. "Columbus-Belmont Battlefield State Park," *Hickman County Gazette*, 1953; "Come Share Our Heritage.... The History of Kentucky State Parks," 1999, CBSP, 4; Barry, "Fort Macon," 176; Fort Morgan National Register of Historic Places Inventory—Nomination Form, Oct. 4, 1975, NARE; "Arkansas Post National Memorial Administrative History," undated, ARPO.

44. Conrad L. Wirth, *Parks, Politics, and the People* (Norman: Univ. of Oklahoma Press, 1980), 185.

45. T. Sutton Jett memorandum, Apr. 9, 1936, Box 2, RG 79, NARAPH.

46. *Federal Register*, Title 36, 9 FR 12868–69, 1944; Unrau, *Administrative History*, 217.

47. Wallace and Conrad, *Petersburg*, 126–29.

48. Unrau, *Administrative History*, 219–20.

49. Paige and Greene, *Administrative History of Chickamauga and Chattanooga National Military Park*, 195, 205–206.

50. Fort Pulaski Mission 66 File, 27, Box 26, RG 79, NARAPH; Barry, "Fort Macon," 176–77; Fort Morgan National Register of Historic Places Inventory—Nomination Form, Oct. 4, 1975, NPS.

51. Mission 66 Plan, Box 25, RG 79, NARAPH; Floyd B. Taylor, "Narrative Report," Aug. 1944, Miscellaneous History Files, RICH; Zenzen, *Battling for Manassas*, 35; Waldrep, *Vicksburg's Long Shadow*, 283.

52. Noe, *Perryville*, 363; Abroe, "All the Profound Scenes," 341; Paige and Greene, *Administrative History of Chickamauga and Chattanooga National Military Park*, 102; Murray, *On a Great Battlefield*, 54–56.

53. George F. Emery to Regional Director, Apr. 9, 1947, Box 3, RG 79, NARAPH.

54. For social change during this period, see Kennedy, *Freedom from Fear*.

55. Abroe, "All the Profound Scenes," 316–431.

56. Ibid., 391.

57. Ibid., 411; Waldrep, *Vicksburg's Long Shadow*, 267.

58. Abroe, "All the Profound Scenes," 322, 324, 415–16.

59. "Press Release Re: Stones River National Military Park," May 17, 1935, H14, Folder 82, STRI; CR, 74th Cong., 1st sess., vol. 79, 2902, 4782, 8308, 10291; "Park History," KEMO; "The Development of Fort Harrison Battlefield Park," undated, Miscellaneous History, RICH.

60. Abroe, "All the Profound Scenes," 382, 387, 394–95, 407.

61. Ibid., 397.

62. Ibid., 403, 410–11.

Chapter 5

1. For the *Enola Gay* in memory, see Edward T. Linenthal and Tom Engelhardt, *History Wars: The Enola Gay and Other Battles for the American Past* (New York: Henry Holt, 1996).

2. Duncan and Burns, *National Parks*, 333–34.

3. Allan R. Millett, Peter Maslowski, and William B. Feis, *For the Common Defense: A Military History of the United States from 1607–2012* (New York: Free Press, 2012), 440.

4. For the mobilization and demobilization of America's armed forces, see Russell F. Weigley, *The American Way of War: A History of United States Military Strategy and Policy* (New York: Macmillan, 1973).

5. For the end of the Civil War veterans, see Richard A. Serrano, *Last of the Blue and Gray: Old Men, Stolen Glory, and the Mystery that Outlived the Civil War* (Washington, D.C.: Smithsonian, 2013).

6. For a general overview of the period, including the civil rights movement, see James T. Patterson, *Grand Expectations: The United States 1945–1974* (New York: Oxford Univ. Press, 1996).

7. James Hamilton, personal communication with author, June 4, 2014; "Short History of the Park," Fort Caroline National Monument, undated, Box 91, RG 79, NARAPH.

8. Millett, Maslowski, and Feis, *For the Common Defense*, 440; Comstock, "Short History," 8–19; Mission 66 Approved Prospectus for Fort Sumter National Monument, undated, Box 26, RG 79, NARAPH. See also Thomas J. Brown, *Civil War Canon: Sites of Confederate Memory in South Carolina* (Chapel Hill: Univ. of North Carolina Press, 2015).

9. CR, 80th Cong., 2nd sess., vol. 94, 4632, 4691, 4745, 5075; Comstock, "Short History," 20–21.

10. Comstock, "Short History," 21–22.

11. A. C. Manuey Memo, Apr. 29, 1948, Fort Sumter 1948–52 Folder, FOSU; Comstock, "Short History," 8–17, 22; Roy E. Appleman to Regional Director, Dec. 8, 1950, Fort Sumter 1948–52 Folder, FOSU.

12. William W. Luckett to Regional Director, Apr. 20, 1950, Fort Sumter 1948–52 Folder, FOSU; Maurie Fring to E. J. Pratt, Aug. 29, 1861, Box 91, RG 79, NARAPH; Abroe, "All the Profound Scenes," 518.

13. *House Report*, 78th Cong., 2nd sess., H.R. Rep. 1315, Mar. 30, 1944, 2; Hosmer, *Preservation Comes of Age* 1:664–68; "State Not Sure of Contribution to Harpers Ferry National Park," Mar. 8, 1951, Folder 2, Henry Temple McDonald Papers, HAFE. For more on Harper's Ferry, see Teresa S. Moyer and Paul A. Shackel, *The Making of Harpers Ferry National Historical Park: A Devil, Two Rivers, and a Dream* (Lanham, Md.: Altamira Press, 2008).

14. Ronald F. Lee to Henry T. McDonald, Mar. 30, 1937, Folder 1, Henry Temple McDonald Papers, HAFE; "Harpers Ferry Will Become National Park," Feb. 25, 1938, *Martinsburg News*, copy in Folder 2, Henry Temple McDonald Papers, HAFE; Dennis Frye, "Harpers Ferry Park—Yesterday and Today," Harpers Ferry National Historical Park 50th Anniversary, 1944–1994, commemorative program, 1994, 4–5, HAFE.

15. CR, 78th Cong., 2nd sess., vol. 90, 3499, 6483, 6712; *House Report*, 78th Cong., 2nd sess., H.R. Rep. 1315, Mar. 30, 1944, 3; *Senate Reports*, 78th Cong., 2nd sess., S. Rep. 1001, June 21, 1944, 3; Frye, "Harpers Ferry Park—Yesterday and Today," 4–5, 10; Harpers Ferry Mission 66 Prospectus, undated, Box 9, RG 79, NARAPH; Conrad L. Wirth to Henry T. McDonald, Oct. 10, 1944, Folder 2, Henry Temple McDonald Papers, HAFE; Maryland Senate Bill 148, Feb. 7, 1951, and West Virginia House

Bill 432, Feb. 22, 1951, both in Folder 3, Box 8, Henry Temple McDonald Papers, HAFE; A. E. Demaray to Jennings Randolph, Mar. 15, 1945, Folder 1, Box 1, Henry Temple McDonald Papers, HAFE; Okey L. Patteson to Conrad L. Wirth, Apr. 17, 1950, Folder 6, Box 1, Henry Temple McDonald Papers, HAFE.

16. Frye, "Harpers Ferry Park—Yesterday and Today," 5–6.
17. Kammen, *Mystic Chords of Memory*, 611. For Mission 66, see National Park Service, *Our Heritage: A Plan for Its Protection and Use: "Mission 66"* (Washington, D.C.: National Park Service, n.d.) and National Park Service, *Mission 66 for the National Park System* (Washington, D.C.: National Park Service, 1956).
18. See the various Mission 66 proposal plans for the different parks in Boxes 25–28, RG 79, NARAPH.
19. Ibid.
20. Ibid.
21. Abroe, "All the Profound Scenes," 456, 458–59; Timothy B. Smith, "Shiloh: Portrait of a Battle: Fifty Years Later," *Tennessee Historical Quarterly* 65, no. 2 (Summer 2006): 147–61.
22. Murray, *On a Great Battlefield*, 82, 153. See the various Mission 66 proposal plans for the different parks in Boxes 25–28, RG 79, NARAPH.
23. Bodnar, *Remaking America*, 197; Abroe, "All the Profound Scenes," 459–60, 463.
24. Wirth, *Parks, Politics, and the People*, 294.
25. Public Law 801, Chapter 971; CR, 81st Cong., 2nd sess., vol. 96, 14676, 15628; *Senate Reports*, 81st Cong., 2nd sess., S. Rep. 2550; Abroe, "All the Profound Scenes," 425; Ed Bearss interview, Aug. 11, 2004, SHIL; Vicksburg National Military Park Roads and Bridges, HAER No. MS-14, undated, 41–46, VICK; Vicksburg National Military Park Land Protection Plan, 2010, 5, VICK; Ed Bearss interview, Feb. 16, 2012, CWT. For the Cairo, see Edwin C. Bearss, *Hardluck Ironclad: The Sinking and Salvage of the Cairo*, rev. ed. (Baton Rouge: Louisiana State Univ. Press, 1980).
26. "History of Georgia State Parks and Historic Sites System," 2008, GDNR; Billy Townsend, "Georgia Historic Marker List," 2001, GDNR; Crampton's Gap National Register of Historic Places Registration Form, July 8, 2010, NARE; Turner's and Fox's Gap National Register of Historic Places Registration Form, July 8, 2010, NPS; South Mountain Battlefields National Register of Historic Places Multiple Property Documentation Form, Mar. 14, 2008, NPS; Boge and Boge, *Paving Over the Past*, 45–46; "Fire on the Mountain: The Battle of South Mountain, Sept. 14, 1862: Battlefield Guide," 1998, ABPP.
27. Historic Staunton River Foundation and Staunton River Battlefield State Park, "History of the Park," http://www.stauntonriverbattlefield.org/parkhist.html.
28. Diane Rogness, personal communication with author, May 22 and 30, 2014.
29. "Timeline of Mansfield State Historic Site's History and Development," undated, MSHS; untitled newspaper clipping, *Mansfield Enterprise*, June 2, 1955; "Unprecedented Mansfield Preservation," *Hallowed Ground* 15, no. 2 (Summer 2014): 8.
30. Bentonville Battlefield Historic Association Application, 1996, 9, ABPP; "Bentonville Battlefield: A History of Preservation," BBSHS; Bentonville Battleground Preservation Plan, 1998, 1, ABPP.

31. William C. Wright, *Confederate Magazine at Fort Wade, Grand Gulf, Mississippi, Excavations 1980–1981*, Archeological Report No. 8 (Jackson: Mississippi Department of Archives and History, 1982), 21; William C. Wright, *The Confederate Upper Battery Site, Grand Gulf, Mississippi, Excavations 1982*, Archeological Report No. 13 (Jackson: Mississippi Department of Archives and History, 1984), 32–33; "Dedication," May 6, 1962, "Dedication of Grand Gulf Military Monument," May 6, 1962, "Dedication Museum and Visitor Center," Apr. 7, 1968, and "Parade and Barbeque Part of Dedication," Mar. 24, 1968, all in Grand Gulf Military Park Subject File, MDAH.

32. "The Built Environment" and "Cultural Landscapes," both undated and in BLSHS.

33. Lacy, personal communication with author, July 1, 2014.

34. Hosmer, *Preservation Comes of Age* 2:809–65; Abroe, "All the Profound Scenes," 428; "Address of William Lobdell Clark, Jr., on May 10th, 1930. At the Unveiling of the Confederate Monument on the Port Hudson Battlefield," 1930, POHU; Raymond Berthelot, personal communication with author, Jan. 13, 2011.

35. National Park Service, *Battle of Franklin Sites*, 16–17, 76; Robison, "Carter House," 17–18; Bowman, *Historic Williamson County*, 144–46.

36. "Charter of Incorporation," Apr. 10, 1952, CH; Robison, "Carter House," 17–20; National Park Service, *Battle of Franklin Sites*, 14.

37. For the centennial, see Robert J. Cook, *Troubled Commemoration: The American Civil War Centennial, 1961–1965* (Baton Rouge: Louisiana State Univ. Press, 2011); and Jon Wiener, "Civil War, Cold War, Civil Rights: The Civil War Centennial in Context, 1960–1965," in Fahs and Waugh, *Memory of the Civil War in American Culture*, 237–57.

38. Cook, *Troubled Commemoration*, 2, 9–10, 13; Levin, *Remembering the Battle of the Crater*, 114; Bodnar, *Remaking America*, 206–209, 211–12, 218–20; Kammen, *Mystic Chords of Memory*, 594, 598–99. For a view of a state level commission, see James J. Geary, "When Dedication Was Fierce and from the Heart: Planning Virginia's Civil War Centennial, 1958–1965," NMBSHP.

39. Cook, *Troubled Commemoration*, 2, 9–10, 13; Murray, *On a Great Battlefield*, 104; Bodnar, *Remaking America*, 206–209, 211–12, 218–20; Kammen, *Mystic Chords of Memory*, 594, 598–99; Levin, *Remembering the Battle of the Crater*, 120–22.

40. Cook, *Troubled Commemoration*, 264; Bodnar, *Remaking America*, 212; Stanley F. Horn to Bernard C. Campbell, Dec. 13, 1961, Box 24, RG 79, NARAPH.

41. Linenthal, *Sacred Ground*, 97–98; Smith, "Shiloh," 147–61; Abroe, "All the Profound Scenes," 474, 494; Superintendent to Regional Director, July 26, 1961, Box 24, RG 79, NARAPH.

42. Kammen, *Mystic Chords of Memory*, 601; Lawrence W. Quist to Regional Director, June 13, 1961, Box 24, RG 79, NARAPH; "Summary of Civil War Centennial Activities—1961–1965," undated, Civil War Centennial File, HFC; Power and Bell, "Rivers Bridge State Park," 14.

43. Bodnar, *Remaking America*, 213–15; Abroe, "All the Profound Scenes," 498, 503.

44. Bernard C. Campbell to Regional Director, June 23, 1961, and Bernard C. Campbell to Allan Nevins, Dec. 12, 1961, both in Box 24, RG 79, NARAPH; Arthur C.

Menius, "The Bennett Place," 1979, NCDAH, 17–20; Kammen, *Mystic Chords of Memory*, 599, 602; Bodnar, *Remaking America*, 211.

45. Bodnar, *Remaking America*, 226.

46. Boge and Boge, *Paving Over the Past*, 29–30.

47. Edmund B. Rogers, *History of Legislation Relating to the National Park System Through the 82d Congress* (Washington, D.C.: National Park Service, 1958), 2; Shea and Hess, *Pea Ridge*, 329; Huggard, "Pea Ridge National Military Park," 32; Alaric Parrish, "Pea Ridge National Military Park Administrative History," 1974, 7–10, PERI; Secretary of War to John M. Morin, undated, PERI.

48. "Report of Inspection of Pea Ridge Battlefield, Benton County, Arkansas, Apr. 8, 1941," Administrative History Folder, PERI; Huggard, "Pea Ridge National Military Park," 28, 39; Parrish, "Pea Ridge National Military Park Administrative History," 7–10; unknown to Clyde T. Ellis, Apr. 12, 1940, and Clyde T. Ellis to Floyd Sharp, Jan. 21, 1941, both in Clyde T. Ellis Papers, UARK, copies in PERI.

49. CR, 84th Cong., 2nd sess., vol. 102, 10516, 12810, 15154; *House Reports*, 84th Cong., 2nd sess., H.R. Rep. 2346, June 13, 1956, 1, 8, 9–10; *Senate Reports*, 84th Cong., 2nd sess., S. Rep. 2514, July 11, 1956, 9–10; Huggard, "Pea Ridge National Military Park," 46; Parrish, "Pea Ridge National Military Park Administrative History," 11–16; Ed Bearss interview, Feb. 16, 2012, CWT.

50. CR, 84th Cong., 2nd sess., vol. 102, 10516, 12810, 15154; *House Reports*, 84th Cong., 2nd sess., H.R. Rep. 2346, June 13, 1956, 1, 8, 9–10; *Senate Reports*, 84th Cong., 2nd sess., S. Rep. 2514, July 11, 1956, 9–10; Huggard, "Pea Ridge National Military Park," 46; Parrish, "Pea Ridge National Military Park Administrative History," 11–16; Ed Bearss interview, Feb. 16, 2012, CWT.

51. Ed Bearss interview, Feb. 16, 2012, CWT; Parrish, "Pea Ridge National Military Park Administrative History," 17–18; "Brief Facts Concerning Pea Ridge National Military Park," 1960, Box 92, RG 79, NARAPH, 1.

52. Ed Bearss interview, Feb. 16, 2012, CWT.

53. Ibid.; Parrish, "Pea Ridge National Military Park Administrative History," 17–18; "Brief Facts Concerning Pea Ridge National Military Park," NARAPH.

54. "Brief Facts Concerning Pea Ridge National Military Park," 1; Director to Robert Dickson III, Nov. 26, 1962, Mission 66 Proposal, Box 27, RG 79, NARAPH; Ed Bearss interview, Aug. 11, 2004, SHIL; Linenthal, *Sacred Ground*, 109; Huggard, "Pea Ridge National Military Park," 40, 48, 85, 113–14, 119, 131; Pea Ridge National Military Park Master Plan, 1964, PERI, 3; Shea and Hess, *Pea Ridge*, 327, 329; John T. Willett to Regional Director, July 13, 1961, John T. Willett to Dennis C. Kurjack, Nov. 21, 1960, and John T. Willett to Gilbert Twiss, Sept. 29, 1960, in "Brief Facts Concerning Park," Box 92, RG 79, NARAPH.

55. "Tablet Placed on Spot Where Gen. Lyon Fell," *Springfield Leader*, May 27, 1928, copy in Administrative History #1 Folder, WICR; Robert R. Pollock, "The Battle of Wilson's Creek in History and Memory" (master's thesis, Missouri State Univ., 2008), 34–35; G. R. Young to Lon Scott, Mar. 30, 1928, WICR; H. L. Robb to Chief Engineers, Apr. 21, 1928, WICR; "Souvenir Program of Battle of Wilson Creek," 1938, Administrative History #2 Folder, WICR; "Wilson's Creek Foundation

History," undated, Administrative History #1 Folder, WICR; "History," Administrative History #1 Folder, WICR; John K. Hulston, *An Ozark Lawyer's Story, 1946–1976* (Republic, Mo.: Western Printing, 1976), 349–50.

56. *House Reports*, 86th Cong., 1st sess., H.R. Rep. 1071, copy in WICR; "Wilson's Creek Foundation History," undated, Administrative History #1 Folder, WICR; *Senate Reports*, 86th Cong., 2nd sess., S. Rep. 1213, 5; Hulston, *Ozark Lawyer's Story*, 352, 354–55; "History," Administrative History #1 Folder, WICR; "Unpublished Hearings Held by the Committee on Interior and Insular Affairs over H. R. 725 Legislation to Establish Wilson's Creek Battlefield National Park," 1959, WICR.

57. *CR*, 86th Cong., 2nd sess., vol. 106, 2517, 7872, 9078; *Senate Reports*, 86th Cong., 2nd sess., S. Rep. 1213, and *House Reports*, 86th Cong., 1st sess., H.R. Rep. 1071, copies of both in WICR; "Wilson's Creek Foundation History," Administrative History #1 Folder, WICR; Hulston, *Ozark Lawyer's Story*, 352, 354–55; "History," Administrative History #1 Folder, WICR; "Wilson's Creek National Battlefield Park," Apr. 22, 1960, Administrative History #2 Folder, WICR.

58. "History," Administrative History #1 Folder, WICR; "Wilson's Creek Foundation History," Administrative History #1 Folder, WICR.

59. Ed Bearss interview, Feb. 16, 2012, CWT; *Wilson's Creek National Battlefield, Republic, Missouri, Cultural Landscape Report*, vol. 1 (Omaha: National Park Service Midwest Region, 2004), 2–105; Hulston, *Ozark Lawyer's Story*, 375, 381.

60. Conrad L. Wirth to D. D. Terry, Aug. 18, 1948, and J. C. Harrington to Director, Nov. 29, 1956, both in Box 82, RG 79, NARAPH; "Superintendent's Annual Report—1972," Arkansas Post File, HFC.

61. *CR*, 86th Cong., 2nd sess., vol. 106, 14750, 15844; *Senate Reports*, 86th Cong., 2nd sess., S. Rep. 1743, June 27, 1960, 2; "Superintendent's Annual Report—1972," Arkansas Post File, HFC; William L. Bowen to Regional Director, July 2, 1962, Box 26, RG 79, NARAPH; W. E. O'Neil Jr. to Hot Springs Superintendent, Sept. 8, 1964, Box 64, RG 79, NARAPH; NPS Press Release, June 22, 1962, Arkansas Post File, HFC; "Arkansas Post National Memorial Administrative History," ARPO.

62. Roger S. Durham, *Fort McAllister* (Mount Pleasant, S.C.: Arcadia, 2004), 8.

63. Joseph E. Brent and Maria Campbell Brent, "Jenkins Ferry Battlefield Preservation Plan," 2013, 77–78, ABPP.

64. "History of Fort Fisher," undated, FFSHS.

65. Menius, "Bennett Place," 4–9.

66. Ibid., 9–16.

67. Charles R. Eatherly, ed., *Arizona State Parks: The Beginning* (Phoenix: Arizona State Parks, 2007), 195; see also Arizona State Parks, Picacho Peak State Park, "History of Picacho Peak State Park," http://azstateparks.com/Parks/PIPE/history.html.

68. Karen Hanna, "Honey Springs Battlefield Park Master Plan Report," 1997, 5–6, ABPP.

69. Fort Jackson National Register of Historic Places Inventory Nomination Form, 1977, NARE; Alvin Phillips, personal communication with author, July 28, 2010.

70. Bodnar, *Remaking America*, 222.

71. See the long held desire to create a national park at Westport, Missouri, as one example.

72. Robert Dallek, *An Unfinished Life: John F. Kennedy, 1917–1963* (Boston: Little, Brown, 2003), 640–43.

73. Abroe, "All the Profound Scenes," 476.

74. Linenthal, *Sacred Ground*, 99; Latschar, "Coming to Terms with the Civil War," 12; Abroe, "All the Profound Scenes," 482–85, 506; Blight, *Race and Reunion*, 44.

75. Abroe, "All the Profound Scenes," 518, 523; Murray, *On a Great Battlefield*, 114; Blight, *Race and Reunion*, 2.

76. Blight: *Race and Reunion*, 2.

Chapter 6

1. For the Dark Ages, see Chris Wickham, *The Inheritance of Rome: Illuminating the Dark Ages, 400–1000* (New York: Viking, 2009).

2. For a synopsis of the era, see Patterson, *Grand Expectations*; and James T. Patterson, *Restless Giant: The United States from Watergate to Bush v. Gore* (New York: Oxford Univ. Press, 2007).

3. Ed Bearss interview, Aug. 11, 2004, SHIL; Kammen, *Mystic Chords of Memory*, 610; Abroe, "All the Profound Scenes," 514–17; Boge and Boge, *Paving Over the Past*, 40; George B. Hartzog Jr., *Battling for the National Parks* (Mt. Kisco, N.Y.: Moyer Bell, 1988), 152, 275.

4. Boge and Boge, *Paving Over the Past*, 40; Ronald Reagan, *Ronald Reagan: An American Life* (New York: Simon and Schuster, 1990), 226–27, 326; Hartzog, *Battling for the National Parks*, 152, 275; Ed Bearss interview, Aug. 11, 2004, SHIL.

5. Piehler, *Remembering War the American Way*, 177, 186.

6. For Johnson, see Robert Dallek, *Lyndon B. Johnson: Portrait of a President* (New York: Oxford Univ. Press, 2004).

7. Hartzog, *Battling for the National Parks*, 266–67; Kammen, *Mystic Chords of Memory*, 613; Boge and Boge, *Paving Over the Past*, 30–31, 145.

8. Kammen, *Mystic Chords of Memory*, 610.

9. For the NPS role in the NHPA, see Barry Macintosh, *The National Historic Preservation Act and the National Park Service: A History* (Washington, D.C.: National Park Service, 1986).

10. Abroe, "All the Profound Scenes," 453.

11. Leslie H. Blythe, *National Park System Properties in the National Register of Historic Places* (Washington, D.C.: National Park Service, 1994).

12. William C. Everhart, Janet A. McDonnell, and George B. Hartzog, *Oral History Interview with George B. Hartzog, Jr., Director, National Park Service, 1964* (Washington, D.C.: National Park Service, 2007), 53; Boge and Boge, *Paving Over the Past*, 43.

13. Kammen, *Mystic Chords of Memory*, 611, 614; Boge and Boge, *Paving Over the Past*, 43, 97.

14. Lenard E. Brown, *Historic Resource Study: Chattahoochee River National Recreation Area and the Chattahoochee River Corridor* (Atlanta: National Park Service, 1980), ii;

National Park Service, *Update to the Civil War Sites Advisory Commission Report on the Nation's Civil War Battlefields—Far Western Battlefields: States of Colorado, Idaho, and New Mexico* (Washington, D.C.: National Park Service, 2010), 27; Peggy A. Gerow, *Guardian of the Trail: Archeological and Historical Investigations at Fort Craig* (Santa Fe, N.M.: Bureau of Land Management, 2004), 10.

15. Hartzog, *Battling for the National Parks*, 129–32.
16. Abroe, "All the Profound Scenes," 568.
17. For Andersonville, see William Marvel, *Andersonville: The Last Depot* (Chapel Hill: Univ. of North Carolina Press, 1994).
18. Secretary of the Interior to Henry M. Jackson, undated, E 11, Box 2746, RG 79, NARA; *Senate Reports*, 91st Cong., 2nd sess., S. Rep. 91-1258; Edwin C. Bearss, *Andersonville National Historic Site Historic Resource Study and Historical Base Map* (Washington, D.C.: National Park Service, 1970), 143–50. As an example of dedication services, see Pennsylvania Andersonville Memorial Commission, *Pennsylvania at Andersonville, Georgia: Ceremonies at the Dedication of the memorial Erected by the Commonwealth of Pennsylvania in the National Cemetery at Andersonville, Georgia* (n.p.: C. E. Aughinbaugh, 1905).
19. Bearss, *Andersonville National Historic Site*, 172; *Senate Reports*, 91st Cong., 2nd sess., S. Rep. 91-1258; Secretary of the Interior to Henry M. Jackson, undated, E 11, Box 2746, RG 79, NARA; Albright, *Origins of National Park Service Administration of Historic Sites*, 1–24.
20. Secretary of the Interior to Henry M. Jackson, undated, E 11, Box 2746, RG 79, NARA; *Senate Reports*, 91st Cong., 2nd sess., S. Rep. 91-1258.
21. *CR*, 91st Cong., 2nd sess., vol. 116, 31454, 35403, 37348; *House Reports*, 91st Cong., 2nd sess., H.R. Rep. 91-1394; *Senate Reports*, 91st Cong., 2nd sess., S. Rep. 91–1258; Secretary of the Interior to Henry M. Jackson, undated, E 11, Box 2746, RG 79, NARA.
22. Joe Holt to Jack Brinley, Dec. 8, 1970, Lawrence C. Hadley to Regional Director, Dec. 3, 1971, and Joe Holt to Regional Director, Nov. 13, 1970, all in E 11, Box 2717, RG 79, NARA.
23. "History of Georgia State Parks and Historic Sites System," 2008, GDNR. For an examination of many of these prison camps, see Maria Campbell Brent and Joseph E. Brent, *Confederate Historic Resource Study* (Washington, D.C.: National Cemetery Administration, 2014).
24. *Balancing Historic Preservation Needs with the Operation of Highly Technical or Scientific Facilities* (Washington, D.C.: Advisory Council on Historic Preservation, 1991); Murray, *On a Great Battlefield*, 116.
25. Walter E. Busch, *Fort Davidson and the Battle of Pilot Knob* (Charleston, S.C.: History Press, 2010), 47, 51–52, 55, 57.
26. Missouri State Parks, "At Battle of Athens State Historic Site," http://mostateparks.com/page/54082/general-information; "Missouri Department of Natural Resources 1974–2014 Timeline," MDNR, 43.
27. Johnsonville National Register of Historic Places Registration Form, 2000, NARE.

28. Tennessee State Parks, *Fort Pillow State Historic Park General Management Plan* (Nashville: Tennessee Department of Conservation, 1989), 9–10, FPSHP; "Division of State Parks: Acquisition Date of the State Parks," FPSHP; Colin A. Strickland and Timothy S. Huebner, "From Civil War Fort to State Park: A History of Fort Pillow," 40–41, FOPI.

29. Benjamin Hayes, "Without Controversy: The Development of Fort Pillow State Historic Park," in *Rethinking Protected Areas in a Changing World: Proceedings of the 2011 George Wright Society Biennial Conference on Parks, Protected Areas, and Cultural Sites*, ed. Samantha Weber (Hancock, Mich.: George Wright Society, 2012), 137–41.

30. Steven D. Hoyt and Jim Bruseth, "Defining the Battles of Sabine Pass: A Survey of Blockaders, Blockade-Runners, and Coastal Fortifications," 2010, ABPP; Edward T. Cotham Jr., *Sabine Pass: The Confederacy's Thermopylae* (Austin: Univ. of Texas Press, 2004), 195.

31. Brad Butkovich, *The Battle of Pickett's Mill: Along the Dead Line* (Charleston, S.C.: History Press, 2013), 161–63.

32. Kansas Historical Society, http://kshs.org/p/mine-creek-battlefield-about/15868# friends.

33. "Historic Blakely State Park," undated, HBSP.

34. Montgomery and Houser, "History of Prairie Grove Battlefield State Park," 20, 27–29, 31, 35; "Prairie Grove Battlefield State Park Timeline—1862–2008," 3, 5, PGBSP.

35. Hanna, "Honey Springs Battlefield Park Master Plan Report," 5–6.

36. Raymond Berthelot, personal communication with author, Jan. 13, 2011; Michael Fraering, personal communication with author, July 27, 2010.

37. James Geary, "History of the Battlefield," undated, 1, 4, 6, 8–10, NMBSHP.

38. Harrison County Parks, "Battle of Corydon Park's History," http://www.harrison countyparks.com/about/history-heritage/battle-of-corydon-memorial-park.

39. Franklin Battlefield National Register of Historic Places Inventory—Nomination Form, NARE; Robison, "Carter House," 20; Joseph L. Willouby to unknown, Sept. 25, 1978, CARN; "Department of State Certificate," Nov. 21, 1977, CARN; W. D. Sugg to Joe Willoughby, Sept. 17, 1977, CARN; Carnton Deed, Aug. 21, 1985, CARN; Warranty Deed, Aug. 21, 1985, CARN; W. D. Sugg and wife to unknown, undated, CARN; National Park Service, *Battle of Franklin Sites*, 15–16, 19, 77, 79; Bowman, *Historic Williamson County*, 61–63, 111.

40. *Update to the Civil War Sites Advisory Commission Report on the Nation's Civil War Battlefields: State of Virginia*, 2009, ABPP, 35.

41. Daniel L. Smith, "Interpretive and Development Plan for Byram's Ford Big Blue Battlefield," 2005, 16–21, BBBP.

42. "Davis Bridge Battlefield Preservation Plan," 2002, 3, 32, 36, ABPP.

43. "Ball's Bluff National Register of Historic Places Inventory Nomination Form," 1984, NARE; "General Management Plan for Ball's Bluff Regional Battlefield Park Fairfax County, Virginia," 2004, BBRBP, no pages listed; Ball's Bluff Battle Awareness Project Application, 1996, 3, 9, ABPP.

44. "Ox Hill Battlefield Park General Management Plan and Conceptual Development Plan," Fairfax, Va., 2005, 11–12, 15–16, FCPA; Boge and Boge, *Paving Over the Past,* 65, 68.

45. Hartzog, *Battling for the National Parks,* 275.

46. Abroe, "All the Profound Scenes," 525–70.

47. Blight, *Race and Reunion,* 2. For the King assassination, see Gerald Posner, *Killing the Dream: James Earl Ray and the Assassination of Martin Luther King, Jr.* (New York: Random House, 1998).

Chapter 7

1. Geoffrey C. Ward, Ric Burns, and Ken Burns, *The Civil War: An Illustrated History* (New York: Knopf, 1990), 264–73.

2. For an overview of the times, see Patterson, *Restless Giant.*

3. For the Renaissance, see Gordon Campbell, *The Oxford Dictionary of the Renaissance* (New York: Oxford Univ. Press, 2003).

4. Abroe, "All the Profound Scenes," 542.

5. James M. McPherson, *Battle Cry of Freedom: The Civil War Era* (New York: Oxford Univ. Press, 1988); Abroe, "All the Profound Scenes," 525.

6. Abroe, "All the Profound Scenes," 544.

7. Burns, *Civil War;* Boge and Boge, *Paving Over the Past,* 6; Robert Brent Toplin, ed., *Ken Burns's* The Civil War: *Historians Respond* (New York: Oxford Univ. Press, 1996).

8. Abroe, "All the Profound Scenes," 529–30; Boge and Boge, *Paving Over the Past,* 4.

9. Zenzen, *Battling for Manassas,* 85–86, 98.

10. Catharine M. Gilliam, "Taking Law: Fact and Fiction," *CRM: Cultural Resources Management* 20, no. 5 (1997): 15–18; Abroe, "All the Profound Scenes," 535–39; Zenzen, *Battling for Manassas,* 128, 133, 137, 146, 151, 153, 155; Boge and Boge, *Paving Over the Past,* 97.

11. Zenzen, *Battling for Manassas,* 160, 166, 168, 174, 177–78, 181; Boge and Boge, *Paving Over the Past,* 4.

12. For Bush, see Timothy Naftali, *George H. W. Bush* (New York: Times Books, 2007).

13. Boge and Boge, *Paving Over the Past,* 135.

14. Public Law 101-628; Boge and Boge, *Paving Over the Past,* 135.

15. Ed Bearss interview, Feb. 16, 2012, CWT; Public Law 101-628; Public Law 104-333 Sec 603 (16 USC 1a-5 note); "Protecting Battlefields," *CRM Bulletin* 13, no. 5 (1990): 2; Jan Townsend, "Catalyst for Battlefield Preservation: The Civil War Sites Advisory Commission Study," *CRM: Cultural Resources Management* 20, no. 5 (1997): 7–10.

16. Staff of the Civil War Sites Advisory Commission, *Civil War Sites Advisory Commission Report on the Nation's Civil War Battlefields* (Washington, D.C.: National Park Service, 1993), 1–10.

17. Ibid., 1–10.

18. Ibid.

19. Ibid.

20. For the Contract with America, see John B. Bader, *Taking the Initiative: Leadership Agendas in Congress and the "Contract with America"* (Washington, D.C.: Georgetown Univ. Press, 1996).

21. Bryan Mitchell interview, Feb. 18, 2013, CWT; Ed Bearss interview, Feb. 16, 2012, CWT; Public Law 104-333, 16 U.S.C. 469k as amended; 16 U.S.C 469k-1; Boge and Boge, *Paving Over the Past*, 136; "Protecting Battlefields," 1–2; "Report to Congress Pursuant to the Civil War Battlefield Preservation Act of 2002," undated, ABPP.

22. Stephen A. Morris, "American Battlefield Protection Program: Evolving Relationships," *CRM: Cultural Resource Management* 14, no. 4 (1991): 10–11; National Park Service, http://www.nps.gov/history/hps/abpp/aboutus.htm; National Park Service, http://www.nps.gov/history/hps/abpp/grants/planninggrants.htm; National Park Service, http://www.nps.gov/history/hps/abpp/grants/CWBLAGgrants.htm.

23. See the state updates in ABPP.

24. Blight, *Race and Reunion*, 2.

25. Linenthal, *Sacred Ground*, 102–103. See Burns, *Civil War*, for narration by Bearss and Fields.

26. Dwight T. Pitcaithley, "The American Civil War and the Preservation of Memory," *CRM: Cultural Resources Management* 25, no. 4 (2002): 5–9; Joe Baker, "Haunted History: Slavery and the Landscape of Myth at America's Civil War Sites," *Common Ground* 10, no. 3 (Fall 2005): 16; Latschar, "Coming to Terms with the Civil War," 13–14; Robert K. Sutton, ed., *Rally on the High Ground: The National Park Service Symposium on the Civil War* (Fort Washington, Pa.: Eastern National, 2001); Blight, *Race and Reunion*, 340.

27. Murray, *On a Great Battlefield*, 156; National Park Service, *Corinth Civil War Boundary Adjustment Study: Corinth Unit of the Shiloh National Military Park: Environmental Assessment* (Washington, D.C.: National Park Service, 2004), 1–3; Corinth National Historic Register Nomination, 1976, Corinth Battlefield 0–1999 Subject File, MDAH; Corinth National Historic Landmark Nomination, 1971, Corinth Civil War 1 Subject File, MDAH; Chester L. Sumners to Theodore G. Bilbo, Mar. 30, 1940, Corinth Civil War 2 Subject File, MDAH; National Park Service, *Special Resource Study: Corinth, Mississippi* (Washington, D.C.: National Park Service, 2003); Timothy B. Smith, *Corinth 1862: Siege, Battle, Occupation* (Lawrence: Univ. of Kansas Press, 2012), 307. For the Mississippi Secession Convention and its emphasis on slavery, see Timothy B. Smith, *The Mississippi Secession Convention: Delegates and Deliberations in Politics and War, 1861–1865* (Jackson: Univ. Press of Mississippi, 2014). See also James O. Horton and Lois E. Horton, eds., *Slavery and Public History: The Tough Stuff of American Memory* (Chapel Hill: Univ. of North Carolina Press, 2008).

28. National Park Service, *Sand Creek Massacre National Historic Site Natural Resource Condition Assessment* (Fort Collins, Colo.: National Park Service, 2013), xv. See also Ari Kelman, *A Misplaced Massacre: Struggling over the Memory of Sand Creek* (Cambridge: Harvard Univ. Press, 2013).

29. Boge and Boge, *Paving Over the Past*, 75; Michale Commisso, *Land Use History for Cedar Creek and Belle Grove National Historical Park* (Boston: National Park Service, 2007), 11, 13.

30. "1990 Annual Narrative Report," 1990, Pecos National Historic Park File, HFC; "1992 Annual Narrative Report," 1992, Pecos National Historic Park File, HFC; Public Law 101-536; "Construct Interpretive Foot Trail from the Old Denver Highway to Arrowhead Ridge and Windmill Hill: Environmental Assessment," 2007, ii, PECO; Superintendent's Memorandum, Jan. 25, 1996, Pecos National Historic Park File, HFC; Superintendent's Memorandum, Feb. 23, 2005, Pecos National Historic Park File, HFC; Superintendent's Memorandum, Aug. 24, 2006, Pecos National Historic Park File, HFC; "Pecos National Historical Park—Glorieta Battlefield Trail Progress," *Hallowed Ground* 8, no. 4 (Winter 2007): 38; "Glorieta National Battlefield: Its Economic Benefits for San Miguel and Santa Fe Counties," 2001, 2, ABPP.

31. "1992 Annual Narrative Report," 1992, Pecos National Historic Park File, HFC; "1993 Annual Narrative Report," 1993, Pecos National Historic Park File, HFC.

32. "Planning for the Future," Monocacy National Battlefield Newsletter, Dec. 2002, Monocacy National Battlefield File, HFC; "Congress Passes Byron-Sponsored Bill Approving Monocacy Battlefield Park Funds," *Frederick News-Post*, Oct. 14, 1978, copy in Monocacy National Battlefield File, HFC; Ed Bearss interview, Feb. 16, 2012, CWT; "Monocacy Battlefield Park Plans, Land Acquisition Can Begin Oct. 1," *Frederick News*, Nov. 22, 1976, copy in Monocacy National Battlefield File, HFC; "Monocacy Battlefield Park Expansion Efforts Under Way," undated clipping, Monocacy National Battlefield File, HFC; Superintendent's 1997 Annual Narrative Report, 1998, Monocacy National Battlefield File, HFC; Superintendent's 2003 Annual Narrative Report, Feb. 24, 2004, Monocacy National Battlefield File, HFC.

33. Boge and Boge, *Paving Over the Past*, 54.

34. Ibid., 46.

35. Fort Lamar brochure, undated, FOLA.

36. "Forts Randolph and Buhlow State Historic Site," undated, in Raymond Berthelot, personal communication with author, Jan. 14, 2011.

37. "History of Georgia State Parks and Historic Sites System," 2008, GDNR.

38. James Hamilton, personal communication with author, June 4, 2014.

39. Resaca Battlefield Historical Site Park, "Sneak Preview!," http://www.resacabattlefield.org/SneakPreview.htm.

40. National Park Service, *Update to the Civil War Sites Advisory Commission Report on the Nation's Civil War Battlefields: State of North Carolina* (Washington, D.C.: National Park Service, 2010), 18; National Park Service, *Update to the Civil War Sites Advisory Commission Report on the Nation's Civil War Battlefields: State of Kentucky* (Washington, D.C.: National Park Service, 2008), 15; National Park Service, *Update to the Civil War Sites Advisory Commission Report on the Nation's Civil War Battlefields: State of Georgia* (Washington, D.C.: National Park Service, 2010), 18; National Park Service, *Update to the Civil War Sites Advisory Commission Report on the Nation's Civil War Battlefields: State of South Carolina* (Washington, D.C.: National Park Service, 2010), 21; National Park Service, *Update to the Civil War Sites Advisory Commission Report on the Nation's Civil War Battlefields: State of Arkansas* (Washington, D.C.: National Park Service, 2010), 20; National Park Service, *Update to the Civil*

War Sites Advisory Commission Report on the Nation's Civil War Battlefields: State of Tennessee (Washington, D.C.: National Park Service, 2009), 24; *Update to the Civil War Sites Advisory Commission Report on the Nation's Civil War Battlefields: State of Virginia*, 2009, 28, ABPP; National Park Service, *Update to the Civil War Sites Advisory Commission Report on the Nation's Civil War Battlefields: Commonwealth of Pennsylvania* (Washington, D.C.: National Park Service, 2010), 14.

41. Boge and Boge, *Paving Over the Past*, 36, 44, 47–48. See also Francis H. Kennedy, *The Dollar and Sense of Battlefield Preservation: The Economic Benefits of Protecting Civil War Battlefields: A Handbook for Community Leaders* (Washington, D.C.: Preservation Press, 1994).

42. Ed Bearss interview, Feb. 16, 2012, CWT.

43. Joseph E. Brent, "Community Consensus Planning for Battlefield Preservation," *CRM: Cultural Resource Management* 23, no. 7 (2000): 7–11; "The Siege and Battle of Corinth: A Strategy for Preservation, Protection and Interpretation," 1991, 1, ABPP. For more on the importance of community in battlefield preservation, see Katherine Curran, "An Enduring Legacy: Community Engagement in American Battlefield Preservation" (master's thesis, Marist College, 2016).

44. National Park Service, *Update to the Civil War Sites Advisory Commission Report on the Nation's Civil War Battlefields: State of Oklahoma* (Washington, D.C.: National Park Service, 2010), 18; National Park Service, *Update to the Civil War Sites Advisory Commission Report on the Nation's Civil War Battlefields: State of South Carolina*, 25; National Park Service, *Update to the Civil War Sites Advisory Commission Report on the Nation's Civil War Battlefields: State of West Virginia* (Washington, D.C.: National Park Service, 2010), 16–17, 19; National Park Service, *Update to the Civil War Sites Advisory Commission Report on the Nation's Civil War Battlefields: State of Arkansas*, 18–22, 24; National Park Service, *Update to the Civil War Sites Advisory Commission Report on the Nation's Civil War Battlefields: State of Kentucky*, 17; Maria C. Brent and Joseph E. Brent, "Interpretive Plan for the Mill Springs Battlefield, Pulaski and Wayne Counties, Kentucky," 2 vols., 2011, ABPP; Maria C. Brent and Joseph E. Brent, "Battle of Richmond Interpretive Plan," 2005, 5, ABPP; "Preserving Kentucky Battlefields," *Hallowed Ground* 11, no. 1 (Spring 2010): 26–35; National Park Service, *Update to the Civil War Sites Advisory Commission Report on the Nation's Civil War Battlefields: State of Louisiana* (Washington, D.C.: National Park Service, 2010), 21; National Park Service, *Update to the Civil War Sites Advisory Commission Report on the Nation's Civil War Battlefields: State of Maryland*, 18; Brent, "Community Consensus Planning for Battlefield Preservation," 9–11; William McWhorter, James E. Bruseth, Toni S. Turner, and Rolando Garza, "The Last Battle: Telling the Story of Palmito Ranch Battlefield," 2010, ABPP.

45. National Park Service, *Update to the Civil War Sites Advisory Commission Report on the Nation's Civil War Battlefields: State of Mississippi* (Washington, D.C.: National Park Service, 2010), 20–22, 25. For detail on Brices Cross Roads, see "An Entire Battlefield Saved," *Hallowed Ground* 15, no. 2 (Summer 2014): 10–11; Terry Winschel, personal communication with author, Sept. 19, 2014.

46. National Park Service, *Update to the Civil War Sites Advisory Commission Report on the Nation's Civil War Battlefields: State of Missouri* (Washington, D.C.: National Park Service, 2011), 22–24, 27–28.

47. National Park Service, *Update to the Civil War Sites Advisory Commission Report on the Nation's Civil War Battlefields: State of North Carolina*, 17–18, 21; "The Battle of New Bern," undated, NBHS.

48. National Park Service, *Update to the Civil War Sites Advisory Commission Report on the Nation's Civil War Battlefields: State of Georgia*, 18–19, 24.

49. National Park Service, *Update to the Civil War Sites Advisory Commission Report on the Nation's Civil War Battlefields: State of Tennessee*, 20–24, 27–28; Robert Hicks to attendees, "Why Franklin Matters: Exploring the Preservation and Interpretation of Franklin's Civil War Story," undated, and "Why Franklin Matters," in handbooks given out at the June 21–24, 2007, conference, Franklin, Tenn., FRCH.

50. *Update to the Civil War Sites Advisory Commission Report on the Nation's Civil War Battlefields: State of Virginia*, 2009, 27–29, 33–36, ABPP; "Shenandoah Valley Battlefields Foundation: A Case for Support," undated, SVBF; "Shenandoah Valley Battlefields Foundation 2011 Annual Report," 2011, SVBF; "Shenandoah Valley Battlefields National Historic District, Virginia: Executive Summary Final Management Plan," 2000, iii, SVBF.

51. A. Wilson Greene, "The Origins of the National Museum of the Civil War Soldier at Pamplin Historical Park," *Hallowed Ground* 14, no. 4 (Winter 2013): 32–34.

52. Boge and Boge, *Paving Over the Past*, 149.

53. Ed Bearss interview, Feb. 16, 2012, CWT; Tersh Boasberg interview, June 14, 2012, CWT.

54. Abroe, "All the Profound Scenes," 555, 557–59; Boge and Boge, *Paving Over the Past*, 10, 40, 132; Francis H. Kennedy, ed., *The Civil War Battlefield Guide* (Boston: Houghton Mifflin, 1990), xi.

55. For the history of the trust, see the voluminous oral interviews in CWT.

56. Bob Zeller, "The Birth of the Modern Battlefield Preservation Movement," *Hallowed Ground* 13, no. 2 (Summer 2012): 6–7; Bob Zeller, "The Birth of the Civil War Trust and the Modern Battlefield Preservation Movement," undated, 4–5, CWT.

57. APCWS Meeting Minutes, July 18, 1987, and Jan. 16 and Mar. 15, 1988, CWT; A. Wilson Greene, "The Association for the Preservation of Civil War Sites," *CRM Bulletin* 13, no. 53 (1990): 3; Zeller, "Birth of the Modern Battlefield Preservation Movement," 6–7; Zeller, "Birth of the Civil War Trust," 7.

58. Greene, "Association for the Preservation of Civil War Sites," 3; Zeller, "Birth of the Modern Battlefield Preservation Movement," 6–7; Zeller, "Birth of the Civil War Trust," 7–9.

59. "History Under Siege: Dispatches from 150 Years of Civil War Battlefield Preservation," *Hallowed Ground* 12, no. 3 (Fall 2011): vii.

60. APCWS Meeting Minutes, Dec. 10, 1994, CWT; Paul Bryant interview, Nov. 22, 2012, CWT; Zeller, "Birth of the Civil War Trust," 11–12.

61. "Certificate," CWT Board Minutes, Oct. 8, 1992, CWT; A. Wilson Greene interview, June 21, 2011, CWT; Zeller, "Birth of the Civil War Trust," 10.

62. James M. McPherson interview, Jan. 30, 2011, CWT; Ruff Fant interview, Aug. 30, 2012, CWT; Childs F. Burden interview, May 15, 2012, CWT; Zeller, "Birth of the Civil War Trust," 10–11; Dennis Frye interview, Feb. 15, 2012, CWT.

63. Zeller, "Birth of the Civil War Trust," 12–13.

64. "Merger Memorandum," July 12, 1999, APCWS Board Minutes, CWT; O. James Lighthizer interview, July 14, 2011, CWT; Mary Abroe interview, Apr. 27, 2012, CWT; "Carrington Williams Was a Leading Preservationist," *Civil War News*, Sept. 2002; Zeller, "Birth of the Civil War Trust," 13; O. James Lighthizer interview, July 14, 2011, CWT.

65. CWPT Board Minutes, Nov. 12, 1999, CWT; Henry E. Simpson interview, May 16, 2012, CWT; Farrell, "McMansionizing History," 26; Ron Cogswell interview, Mar. 8, 2012, CWT.

66. Mary Abroe interview, Apr. 27, 2012, CWT; Farrell, "McMansionizing History," 27; Zeller, "Birth of the Civil War Trust," 15; Ruff Fant interview, Aug. 30, 2012, CWT.

67. CWPT Board Minutes, Jan. 22, 2000, CWT; O. James Lighthizer interview, July 14, 2011, CWT; Mary Abroe interview, Apr. 27, 2012, CWT; Farrell, "McMansionizing History," 27; Zeller, "Birth of the Civil War Trust," 15; Noah Mehrkam interview, May 1, 2012, CWT.

68. Bill Vodra interview, July 24, 2012, CWT; Mary Abroe interview, Apr. 27, 2012, CWT; Farrell, "McMansionizing History," 27; Zeller, "Birth of the Civil War Trust," 15; Ed Bearss interview, Feb. 16, 2012, CWT.

69. Farrell, "McMansionizing History," 16–17, 26–28.

70. O. James Lighthizer interview, July 14, 2011, CWT.

71. Civil War Trust Annual Report, 2011, CWT, 11, 20, 27; Civil War Trust Annual Report, 2012, 3, 24, CWT; Civil War Trust Annual Report, 2013, 24–25, CWT; "Campaign 150 Success!" *Hallowed Ground* 15, no. 1 (Spring 2014): 6.

72. Civil War Trust Annual Report, 2012, 15, CWT; Civil War Trust Annual Report, 2013, 3–4, 15–19, CWT; Garry Adelman interview, Nov. 9, 2012, CWT.

73. Civil War Trust Annual Report, 2013, 4, CWT; "Did You Know," *Hallowed Ground* 15, no. 2 (Summer 2014): 11; "Walmart Controversy Fully Resolved," *Hallowed Ground* 15, no. 1 (Spring 2014): 14–15; "Gettysburg Casino Controversy Nears Conclusion," *Hallowed Ground* 11, no. 42 (Winter 2010): 6–7; James Lighthizer, "Gambling with History," *New York Times*, Sept. 27, 2005; Farrell, "McMansionizing History," 28; John Nau interview, May 2, 2012, CWT.

74. For the modern Civil War Trust, view its website at http://www.civilwar.org.

75. Blight, *Race and Reunion*, 2.

76. For the continual change in race relations even to the present, see John Hope Franklin and Evelyn Higginbotham, *From Slavery to Freedom: A History of African Americans*, 9th ed. (New York: McGraw Hill, 2010).

77. Baker, "Haunted History," 20, 24; Latschar, "Coming to Terms with the Civil War," 9; Blight, *Race and Reunion*, 2.

78. John Hennessy, "Interpreting the Civil War: Moving Beyond Battlefields," *CRM: Cultural Resources Management* 25, no. 4 (2002): 10; Baker, "Haunted History," 18; Levin, *Remembering the Battle of the Crater*, 130; Richard E. Miller, "The National

Park Service and the Afro-American Experience, 1990: An Independent Assessment from the Black Perspective," 1991, NPS. For a newer account of the USCT, see William A. Dobak, *Freedom by the Sword: The U.S. Colored Troops, 1862–1867* (Washington, D.C.: Center of Military History, 2011).

79. Baker, "Haunted History," 24.

80. Carlin Timmons and Sandy Pusey, "Fort Sumter National Monument's New Facility at Liberty Square," *CRM: Cultural Resources Management* 25, no. 4 (2002): 40–41; Baker, "Haunted History," 18–20, 23; Richard D. Stone and Mary M. Graham, "Selective Civil War Battlefield Preservation as a Method of Marketing the Southern 'Lost Cause,'" *Charm*, 2007, 223.

81. "A Strategic Plan for Commemorating the Civil War's Important Places and Compelling Stories within the National Park Service's Southeast Region," 2010, NPS.

82. For USCT participation in the war, see Dudley Taylor Cornish, *The Sable Arm: Negro Troops in the Union Army, 1861–1865* (New York: W. W. Norton, 1966); and Joseph T. Glatthaar, *Forged in Battle: The Civil War Alliance of Black Soldiers and White Officers* (New York: Free Press, 1989).

83. Levin, *Remembering the Battle of the Crater*, 125, 128–29, 131; Latschar, "Coming to Terms with the Civil War," 11.

84. J. Christian Spielvogel, *Interpreting Sacred Ground: The Rhetoric of National Civil War Parks and Battlefields* (Tuscaloosa: Univ. of Alabama Press, 2013), 50–54, 68–82; Latschar, "Coming to Terms with the Civil War," 13; Murray, *On a Great Battlefield*, 165.

85. National Park Service, http://www.nps.gov/mono/planyourvisit/150-events-12–13 .htm.

86. Danyelle A. Nelson, "No Place for Women: Interpreting Civil War Battlefields," *CRM: Cultural Resource Management* 20, no. 3 (1997): 59; "National American Indian Heritage Month," *CRM Bulletin* 13, no. 5 (1990): 16; Richard West Sellars, "The National Park System and the Historic American Past: A Brief Overview and Reflection," *George Wright Forum* 24, no. 1 (2007): 18–19; "Diamond C Ranch Marks Anniversary Near Battlefield," *Dunn County Herald*, Nov. 16, 1983; Diane Rogness, personal communication with author, May 22 and 30, 2014. See the new monument text for the modern approach.

Epilogue

1. "For Shiloh Sesquicentennial, Major Preservation Victories," *Hallowed Ground* 13, no. 2 (Summer 2012): 4–5.

2. Civil War Trust, "Understanding Our Past," http://www.civilwar.org/education /history/civil-war-history-and-scholarship/gary-gallagher-interview.html; see the Civil War Trust annual reports in CWT for figures.

3. Boge and Boge, *Paving Over the Past*, 157–58.

4. O. James Lighthizer interview, July 14, 2011, CWT.

5. Curran, "Enduring Legacy."

6. Boge and Boge, *Paving Over the Past*, 13, 87–88; "History Under Siege," ix.

7. Boge and Boge, *Paving Over the Past*, 103–17, 126.
8. Ibid., 133.
9. Murray, *On a Great Battlefield*, 52, 159, 167, 183–84.
10. "History Under Siege," xiii; Civil War Trust Annual Report, 2012, 23, CWT; Civil War Trust Annual Report, 2013, 4, CWT; Hicks, "Why Franklin Matters: Exploring the Preservation and Interpretation" and "Why Franklin Matters," FRCH; "Franklin, Tenn. Celebrates Demise of the Pizza Hut," *Civil War News*, Jan. 2006; Adam Goodheart, "Civil War Battlefields: Saving the Landscape of America's Deadliest War," *National Geographic* (Apr. 2005): 74–75; National Park Service, *Battle of Franklin Sites*, 16, 19, 79.
11. National Park Service, *Battle of Franklin Sites*, 80–82.

Bibliography

Manuscripts and Reports

American Battlefield Protection Program, Washington, D.C.
    Ball's Bluff Battle Awareness Project Application.
    Bell, Daniel J. "The Strongest Position I Ever Saw in My Life: Mapping and Site Study of the Rivers Bridge Battlefield."
    Bentonville Battlefield Historic Association Application.
    Bentonville Battleground Preservation Plan.
    Brent, Joseph E., and Maria Campbell Brent. "Jenkins Ferry Battlefield Preservation Plan."
    Brent, Maria C., and Joseph E. Brent. "Battle of Richmond Interpretive Plan."
    ———. "Interpretive Plan for the Mill Springs Battlefield, Pulaski and Wayne Counties, Kentucky."
    Davis Bridge Battlefield Preservation Plan.
    "Fire on the Mountain: The Battle of South Mountain, Sept. 14, 1862: Battlefield Guide."
    "Glorieta National Battlefield: Its Economic Benefits for San Miguel and Santa Fe Counties."
    Hanna, Karen. "Honey Springs Battlefield Park Master Plan Report.
    Hoyt, Steven D., and Jim Bruseth. "Defining the Battles of Sabine Pass: A Survey of Blockaders, Blockade-Runners, and Coastal Fortifications."
    Matts, Michael J., and Stephen J. Roberts. "Battle of Buffington Island Battlefield Preservation Plan."
    McWhorter, William, James E. Bruseth, Toni S. Turner, and Rolando Garza. "The Last Battle: Telling the Story of Palmito Ranch Battlefield."
    "The Preservation of Fort Henry and Associated Sites."
    "Report to Congress Pursuant to the Civil War Battlefield Preservation Act of 2002."
    "The Siege and Battle of Corinth: A Strategy for Preservation, Protection and Interpretation."

Appomattox Court House National Historical Park, Appomattox, Virginia
  Appomattox Court House National Register of Historic Places Continuation Sheet,
    Section 8.
  "Appomattox Court House NHP: Cultural Landscape Report."
  Master Plan draft, 1962.
  Porter, Charles W. "Supplementary Report on Appomattox Court House, Va."

Arkansas Post National Memorial, Gillett, Arkansas
  "Arkansas Post National Memorial Administrative History."

Ball's Bluff Regional Battlefield Park, Leesburg, Virginia
  "General Management Plan for Ball's Bluff Regional Battlefield Park Fairfax County,
    Virginia."

Battle of Lexington State Historic Site, Lexington, Missouri
  "The Built Environment."
  "Cultural Landscapes."

Bentonville Battlefield State Historic Site, Four Oaks, North Carolina
  "Bentonville Battlefield: A History of Preservation."

Big Blue Battlefield Park, Kansas City, Missouri
  Smith, Daniel L. "Interpretive and Development Plan for Byram's Ford Big Blue
    Battlefield."

Carnton Plantation, Franklin, Tennessee
  Carnton Deed.
  Sugg, W. D. Letters.
  Warranty Deed.
  Willouby, Joseph L. Letters.

Carter House, Franklin Tennessee
  "Charter of Incorporation."

Chicago Historical Society
  Carrington, George. Diary.

Chickamauga and Chattanooga National Military Park, Fort Oglethorpe, Georgia
  Series 1—General Administration.
  Series 2—Monuments, Tablets, Markers, and Historical Tablets.

Civil War Trust, Washington, D.C.
  Abroe, Mary. Interview.
  Adelman, Garry. Interview.
  Association for the Preservation of Civil War Sites, Board Meeting Minutes,
    1987–99.
  Bearss, Ed. Interview.
  Boasberg, Tersh. Interview.
  Bryant, Paul. Interview.
  Burden, Childs F. Interview.

Civil War Preservation Trust Board Minutes, 2000–2011.
Civil War Preservation Trust / Civil War Trust Annual Reports, 2000–2014.
Civil War Trust Board Minutes, 1991–99.
Cogswell, Ron. Interview.
Fant, Ruff. Interview.
Frye, Dennis. Interview.
Greene, A. Wilson. Interview.
Lighthizer, O. James. Interview.
McPherson, James M. Interview.
Mehrkam, Noah. Interview.
Mitchell, Bryan. Interview.
Nau, John. Interview.
Simpson, Henry E. Interview.
Vodra, Bill. Interview.
Zeller, Bob. "The Birth of the Civil War Trust and the Modern Battlefield Preservation Movement."

Colonial National Historical Park, Yorktown, Virginia
"Outline of Development, Colonial National Monument, Yorktown, Virginia."

Columbus-Belmont State Park, Columbus, Kentucky
"Come Share Our Heritage. . . . The History of Kentucky State Parks."

Cornell University, Ithaca, New York
Fitch, Asa. Papers.

Fairfax County Park Authority, Fairfax, Virginia
"Ox Hill Battlefield Park General Management Plan and Conceptual Development Plan."

Fort Bragg, Fort Bragg, North Carolina
Fort Bragg Historical Tour brochure.

Fort Donelson National Battlefield, Dover, Tennessee
National Cemetery Files.
Whitman, E. B. Letter.
Resource Management Collection.
War Department Files.

Fort Fisher State Historic Site, Kure Beach, North Carolina
"History of Fort Fisher."

Fort Lamar Heritage Preserve, Charleston, South Carolina
Fort Lamar brochure.

Fort McAllister State Park, Savannah, Georgia
Cooke, R. Jervis. "Sand and Grit: The Story of Fort McAllister, a Confederate Earthwork on the Great Ogeechee River, Genesis Point, Georgia."
Whitfield, Christopher A. "Restoration: The Recapturing of Fort McAllister During the Henry Ford Years."

Fort Negley Visitor Center and Park, Nashville, Tennessee
> Johnson, Dixie. "Silent-Gunned Fort."
> "Restoration of Fort Negley Finally Complete."

Fort Pillow State Historic Park, Henning, Tennessee
> "Division of State Parks: Acquisition Date of the State Parks."
> Strickland, Colin A., and Timothy S. Huebner. "From Civil War Fort to State Park: A History of Fort Pillow."

Fort Pulaski National Monument, Savannah, Georgia
> "A Summary of Work Accomplishments of the Civilian Conservation Corps at Fort Pulaski National Monument, Savannah, Georgia, May 10, 1934–June 5, 1940"
> Fort Pulaski Restoration Data.
> Master Plan.

Fort Sumter National Monument, Charleston, South Carolina
> Comstock, Rock L., Jr. "Short History: Fort Sumter."
> Fort Sumter 1948–52 Folder.

Franklin's Charge, Franklin, Tennessee
> Hicks, Robert. "Why Franklin Matters."
> ———. "Why Franklin Matters: Exploring the Preservation and Interpretation of Franklin's Civil War Story."

Fredericksburg and Spotsylvania National Military Park, Fredericksburg, Virginia
> Bronze Castings Folder.
> Chancellorsville Battlefield Association Prospectus.
> Childress, Carolyn S. "A Grassroots Study of the Civilian Conservation Corps: An In Depth Look at the Three Camps under the Direction of the Fredericksburg and Spotsylvania National Military Park, Virginia."
> Fencing Folder.
> Fleming Folder.
> Happel, Ralph. "A History of the Fredericksburg and Spotsylvania County Battlefields Memorial National Military Park."
> Hobson Folder.
> Pfanz, Donald C. "History Through Eyes of Stone: A Survey of Civil War Monuments near Fredericksburg, Virginia."
> "Report on Inspection of Battlefields in and Around Fredericksburg and Spotsylvania Court House, Virginia."
> Ross Folder.
> Wilbourn Folder.

Georgia Department of Natural Resources, Parks and Historic Sites Division, Atlanta
> Townsend, Billy. "Georgia Historic Marker List."
> "History of Georgia State Parks and Historic Sites System."

Gettysburg National Military Park, Gettysburg, Pennsylvania
> Minute Book Gettysburg Battlefield Memorial Association, 1872–1895.
> Nicholson, John P. Journals.

Harpers Ferry Center, Charleston, West Virginia
  Arkansas Post File.
  Brice's Cross Roads File.
  Civil War Centennial File.
  Lee, Ronald F. Papers.
  Monocacy National Battlefield File.
  Pecos National Historic Park File.

Harpers Ferry National Historical Park, Harpers Ferry, West Virginia
  Frye, Dennis. "Harpers Ferry Park—Yesterday and Today." Harpers Ferry National
    Historical Park 50th Anniversary, 1944–1994. Commemorative program.
  McDonald, Henry Temple. Papers.

Historic Blakely State Park, Spanish Fort, Alabama
  "Historic Blakely State Park."

Kennesaw Mountain National Battlefield Park, Kennesaw, Georgia
  Capps, Michael A. "Kennesaw Mountain National Battlefield Park: An Administra-
    tive History."
  Monument Research Files.
  "Park History."
  Vertical Files.

Law Library of Congress, Washington, D.C.
  House Bills
      H.R. 1996. 54th Cong., 1st sess.
      H.R. 1647. 55th Cong., 1st sess.
      H.R. 7345. 56th Cong., 1st sess.
      H.R. 946. 56th Cong., 1st sess.
      H.R. 9567. 56th Cong., 1st sess.
      H.R. 7837. 56th Cong., 1st sess.
      H.R. 113. 58th Cong., 1st sess.
      H.R. 113. 58th Cong., 1st sess.
      H.R. 14748. 58th Cong., 2nd sess.
      H.R. 9765. 69th Cong., 1st sess.
      H.R. 8502. 72nd Cong., 1st sess.
  Senate Bills
      S. 1287. 58th Cong., 1st sess.
      S. 5794. 59th Cong., 1st sess.
      S. 4173. 70th Cong., 1st sess.

Library of Congress, Washington, D.C.
  Heintzelman, S. P. Journal.

Manassas National Battlefield Park, Manassas, Virginia
  1865 Monuments File.
      Fisher, Samuel R. Letter.
      "Is the United States Too Poor to Own Its Own Monuments."

Bartow Monument File.
Bull Run Recreational Area Folder.
Georgia Monuments File.
Heintzelman, S. P. Journal.
Manassas National Battlefield Park Visitor Center or Museum File.
Park Development—Various Letters 1927–28 Re. Manassas Battlefield Confederate
    Park.
Stonewall Jackson File.
Webster Monument File.

Mansfield State Historic Site, Mansfield, Louisiana
    Mansfield Battle Park Association Charter.
    "Timeline of Mansfield State Historic Site's History and Development."
    UDC Scrapbook.

Massachusetts Historical Society, Boston
    Boynton, Henry Van Ness. Papers.

Middle Tennessee State University, Murfreesboro, Tennessee
    Weiler, Patsy. Collection.

Mississippi Department of Archives and History, Jackson
    Corinth Subject Files.
    Corinth Battlefield 0–1999.
    Corinth Civil War 1.
    Corinth Civil War 2.
    Grand Gulf Military Park Subject File.
    "Dedication."
    "Dedication of Grand Gulf Military Monument."
    "Dedication Museum and Visitor Center."
    "Parade and Barbeque Part of Dedication."

Missouri Department of Natural Resources, Jefferson City
    "Missouri Department of Natural Resources 1974–2014 Timeline."

Monocacy National Battlefield, Frederick, Maryland
    Reed, Paula Stoner Reed. "Cultural Resources Study: Monocacy National
        Battlefield."

National Archives and Records Administration, Washington, D.C.
    RG 30. Records of the Bureau of Public Roads.
    RG 35. Records of the Civilian Conservation Corps.
        E 115. Division of Investigations: Camp Inspection Reports, 1933–1942.
    RG 79. Records of the National Park Service.
        E 5. War Department Records Relating to Military Parks, Monuments, and
            Cemeteries, 1892–1937.
        E 7. Vicksburg National Cemetery: Copies of Letters Sent by the Superintendent
            to the Office of the Quartermaster General, 1869–1907.
        E 10. Central Classified Files, 1907–1932.

E 10B. Central Classified Files, 1933–1949.

E 11. Index Files.

E 42. "Mission 66" Program: Revised Prospectuses, 1960–1961.

E 75. Branch of Engineering: Final Construction Reports, 1934–1942.

RG 92. Records of the Office of the Quartermaster General.

E 89. General Correspondence, 1890–1914.

E 576. General Correspondence and Reports Relating to National and Post Cemeteries, 1865–1890.

E 588. Correspondence, Maps, and Other Papers of the Mail and Record Division, Office of the Secretary of War, Relating to National Battlefield Parks at Chickamauga-Chattanooga, Vicksburg, and Other Battlefield Parks, 1913–1923.

E 707. Antietam Battlefield Commission—General Correspondence, Mainly Letters Received, 1894–1898.

E 709. Gettysburg National Military Park Commission—Press Copies of Letters Sent, Related to the Gettysburg Battlefield Commission, 1895–1898.

E 710. Gettysburg National Military Park Commission—Register of Letters Received by the Gettysburg Battlefield Commission, 1895–1897.

E 711. Gettysburg National Military Park Commission—General Correspondence, Mainly Letters, 1898–191.

E 712. General Correspondence, Chiefly Letters Received, 1895–1911.

E 713. Press Copies of Letters Sent, Feb. 1895–Apr. 1899.

E 715. Vicksburg National Military Park—General Correspondence and Reports, 1899–1913.

RG 107. Records of the Office of the Secretary of War.

E 82. Press Copies of Letters Sent, Jan. 1896–July 1913.

RG 153. Records of the Office of the Judge Advocate General (Army).

E 12B. Papers of Brigadier General George B. Davis, 1901–1910.

National Archives at Atlanta

RG 79. Records of the National Park Service.

Shiloh National Military Park, Tennessee, 1869–1950.

Vicksburg National Military Park, Mississippi, 1865–1949.

National Archives at Philadelphia

RG 79. Records of the National Park Service.

National Cemetery Administration, Washington, D.C.

"National Cemeteries Dates Established and First Burials."

National Park Service, Washington, D.C.

"A Strategic Plan for Commemorating the Civil War's Important Places and Compelling Stories within the National Park Service's Southeast Region."

Miller, Richard E. "The National Park Service and the Afro-American Experience, 1990: An Independent Assessment from the Black Perspective."

National Register of Historic Places, Washington, D.C.

Ball's Bluff National Register of Historic Places Inventory Nomination Form.

Corinth National Historic Register Nomination Form.

Crampton's Gap National Register of Historic Places Registration Form.

Fort Jackson National Register of Historic Places Inventory Nomination Form.

Fort Morgan National Register of Historic Places Inventory—Nomination Form.

Franklin Battlefield National Register of Historic Places Inventory—Nomination Form.

Johnsonville National Register of Historic Places Registration Form.

South Mountain Battlefields National Register of Historic Places Multiple Property Documentation Form.

Turner's and Fox's Gap National Register of Historic Places Registration Form.

New Bern Historical Society, New Bern, North Carolina
"The Battle of New Bern."

New Market Battlefield State Historical Park, New Market, Virginia
Geary, James J. "When Dedication Was Fierce and from the Heart: Planning Virginia's Civil War Centennial, 1958–1965."

New York Public Library, New York, New York
Carman, Ezra A. Papers.

North Carolina Division of Archives and History, Raleigh
Menius, Arthur C. "The Bennett Place."

Olustee Battlefield Historic State Park, Olustee, Florida
"Olustee Battlefield Historic State Park Unit Management Plan."

Pea Ridge National Military Park, Garfield, Arkansas
Administrative History Folder.
Ellis, Clyde T. Papers.
Huggard, Christopher J. "Pea Ridge National Military Park: An Administrative History."
Parrish, Alaric. "Pea Ridge National Military Park Administrative History."
Pea Ridge National Military Park Master Plan.

Pecos National Historical Park, Pecos, New Mexico
"Construct Interpretive Foot Trail from the Old Denver Highway to Arrowhead Ridge and Windmill Hill: Environmental Assessment."

Perryville Battlefield State Historic Site, Perryville, Kentucky
Perryville Deed.

Petersburg National Battlefield, Petersburg, Virginia
NPS Files.
Resource Management Records, 1873, 1922–2004.
War Department Files.

Port Hudson State Historic Site, Jackson, Louisiana
"Address of William Lobdell Clark, Jr., on May 10th, 1930. At the Unveiling of the Confederate Monument on the Port Hudson Battlefield."

Prairie Grove Battlefield State Park, Prairie Grove, Arkansas
"History of the Prairie Grove Chapter."
Montgomery, Don, and Holly Houser. "History of Prairie Grove Battlefield State Park: 1862–2008."
"Prairie Grove Battlefield State Park Timeline—1862–2008."

Richmond National Battlefield Park, Richmond, Virginia
CCC Folder.
Early Park History File.
Miscellaneous History Files.
Rogers, Edmund B. "History of Legislation Relating to the National Park System Through the 82d Congress."
Willett, John T. "A History of Richmond National Battlefield Park."

Rivers Bridge State Historic Site, Ehrhardt, South Carolina
"The Memorial Association."
Power, J. Tracy, and Daniel J. Bell. "Rivers Bridge State Park Visitor's Guide."
Speakers at Rivers Bridge Memorial Services, 1876–Present.

Sailor's Creek Battlefield State Park, Rice, Virginia
"The History of Sailor's Creek (a.k.a. Sayler's Creek) Battlefield Historical State Park, 1937–2010."

Shenandoah Valley Battlefields Foundation, New Market, Virginia
"Shenandoah Valley Battlefields Foundation 2011 Annual Report."
"Shenandoah Valley Battlefields Foundation: A Case for Support."
"Shenandoah Valley Battlefields National Historic District, Virginia: Executive Summary Final Management Plan."

Shiloh National Military Park, Shiloh, Tennessee
Administrative Files.
Series 1. Administration #1.
Series 2. Administration #2.
Series 3. D. W. Reed Papers.
Series 4. Shiloh National Cemetery.
Series 7. Maps #2.
Series 8. Blueprints/Plans.
Shiloh National Military Park Daily Events.
Bearss, Ed. Interview.
Miscellaneous Files.
Regimental Files.
41st Illinois File.
Shiloh National Military Park Scrapbook.
Vertical Files.
Dedication Remarks for Placement of CCC Marker—July 14, 1990.
Historical Reports.
"Research Studies Made During the CWA Period, Shiloh National Military Park."

"Research Studies, Shiloh National Military Park."
Shiloh National Cemetery.

Smithsonian Institution, Washington, D.C.
Chambers, Moreau B. Notebook.
National Anthropological Archives, National Museum of Natural History.
Roberts, Frank H. H. Field Notebook.

Stones River National Battlefield, Murfreesboro, Tennessee
H14. Area and Service History Files.
H2215. Cultural Resource Studies and Research Files, National Park Service Areas.
Styles, Sean M. "Stones River National Battlefield Historic Resource Study."

Tennessee State Library and Archives, Nashville
McAlister, Hill. Papers.

United States Military Academy, West Point, New York
Davis, George B. File.

University of Arkansas, Fayetteville
Ellis, Clyde T. Papers.

University of Iowa, Iowa City, Iowa
Rigby, William T. Papers.

University of Texas at Austin, Austin, Texas
Landers, Howard L. Papers.

Vicksburg National Military Park, Vicksburg, Mississippi
Administrative Series.
Edwin C. Bearss Series.
Vicksburg National Military Park Land Protection Plan.
Vicksburg National Military Park Roads and Bridges. HAER No. MS-14.
William T. Rigby Series.

Wilson's Creek National Battlefield, Republic, Missouri
Administrative History #1 Folder.
Administrative History #2 Folder.
Frost, Griffin. *Camp and Prison Journal.*
Gulick, W. O. Letter.
Post Battle Visits Folder.
Smith, F. M. Letter.
"Unpublished Hearings Held by the Committee on Interior and Insular Affairs over
H. R. 725 Legislation to Establish Wilson's Creek Battlefield National Park."

Wisconsin Historical Society, Madison
Bennett, H. H. Collection.

Government Documents

Annual Report of the Secretary of War. 1890–1932. Washington, D.C.: U.S. War Department.

Congressional Record. 1889–1971. Washington, D.C.

Federal Register. 1944. Washington, D.C.

House Reports. Washington, D.C.

Opinions of the Attorneys General. Vol. 36. Washington, D.C.

Senate Reports. Washington, D.C.

United States Statutes at Large. Vols. 29 and 37. Washington, D.C.

U.S. Congress. House. *Hearing before the Committee on Military Affairs, House of Representatives, Seventieth Congress, First Session, on H.R. 10291.* Washington, D.C.: Government Printing Office, 1928.

———. *Hearings before the Committee on Military Affairs House of Representatives Seventieth Congress Second Session on S. 4173 to Transfer Jurisdiction over Certain National Military Parks and National Monuments from the War Department to the Department of the Interior, and for Other Purposes.* Washington, D.C.: Government Printing Office, 1929.

Newspapers

Bamberg Herald

Chattanooga Times

Chicago Daily Tribune

Christian Science Monitor

Columbia Daily Phoenix

Columbus Evening Dispatch

Dunn County Herald

Frederick News

Frederick News-Post

Fredericksburg Free Lance Star

Fredericksburg News

Fredericksburg Star

Hartford Courant

Hickman County Gazette

Keedysville Antietam Wavelet

Keowee Courier

Macon Journal and Messenger

Manassas Journal

Mansfield Enterprise

Martinsburg News

Murfreesboro News Journal

Nashville Tennessean

Newark Daily Advertiser

New York Times

Oxford Falcon

Petersburg Progress Index

Philadelphia Weekly Times

Richmond Times-Dispatch

Savannah Courier

Springfield Daily Herald

Springfield Express

Springfield Leader

St. Louis Democrat

Talladega Reporter and Watchtower

Vicksburg Evening Post

Vicksburg Monday Morning Democrat

Washington Post

Western Kansas World

Published Primary Sources

Albright, Horace M. *Origins of National Park Service Administration of Historic Sites.* Philadelphia: Eastern National Park and Monument Association, 1971.

Atlanta Business Men's League. *The Proposed Atlanta National Military Park: A Brief Outline of the Project.* Atlanta: Atlanta Business Men's League, 1899.

Balancing Historic Preservation Needs with the Operation of Highly Technical or Scientific Facilities. Washington, D.C.: Advisory Council on Historic Preservation, 1991.

Barber, Lucius W. *Army Memoirs of Lucius W. Barber, Company "D," 15th Illinois Volunteer Infantry. May 24, 1861, to Sept. 30, 1865.* Chicago: J. M. W. Jones Stationary and Printing, 1894.

"Battlefield Park." *National Tribune,* Jan. 20, 1898.

Bearss, Edwin C. *Andersonville National Historic Site Historic Resource Study and Historical Base Map.* Washington, D.C.: National Park Service, 1970.

Bennett, Stewart, and Barbara Tillery, eds. *The Struggle for the Life of the Republic: A Civil War Narrative by Brevet Major Charles Dana Miller, 76th Ohio Volunteer Infantry.* Kent, Ohio: Kent State Univ. Press, 2004.

Boynton, Henry V. "The Chickamauga Memorial Association." *Southern Historical Society Papers* 16 (1888): 339–349.

———. *Dedication of the Chickamauga and Chattanooga National Military Park, September 18–20, 1895: Report of the Joint Committee to Represent the Congress at the Dedication of the Chickamauga and Chattanooga National Military Park.* Washington, D.C.: Government Printing Office, 1896.

———. *The National Military Park: Chickamauga-Chattanooga: An Historical Guide, with Maps and Illustrations.* Cincinnati: Robert Clarke, 1895.

Brazelton, B. G. *A History of Hardin County.* Nashville: Cumberland Presbyterian Publishing House, 1885.

Brown, Lenard E. *Historic Resource Study: Chattahoochee River National Recreation Area and the Chattahoochee River Corridor.* Atlanta: National Park Service, 1980.

Buell, Don Carlos. "Shiloh Reviewed." In Johnson and Buel, *Battles and Leaders of the Civil War* 1:487–536.

Carroll, Andrew, ed. *War Letters: Extraordinary Correspondence from American Wars.* New York: Scribner, 2001.

Chickamauga Memorial Association Proceedings at Chattanooga, Tenn., and Crawfish Springs, Ga., September 19 and 20, 1889. N.p.: Chattanooga Army of the Cumberland Reunion Entertainment Committee, n.d.

Commisso, Michael. *Land Use History for Cedar Creek and Belle Grove National Historical Park.* Boston: National Park Service, 2007.

Ellis, W. B. "Who Lost Shiloh to the Confederacy?" *Confederate Veteran* 22, no. 7 (July 1914): 313–14.

Everhart, William C., Janet A. McDonnell, and George B. Hartzog. *Oral History Interview with George B. Hartzog, Jr., Director, National Park Service, 1964–1972.* Washington, D.C.: National Park Service, 2007.

"First Reunion at Pea Ridge, September 1st, 1887." *Benton County Pioneer* 7, no. 3 (Mar. 1962): 5–6.

Forty-sixth Annual Reunion of the Association Graduates of the United States Military Academy at West Point, New York, June 11th, 1915. Saginaw, Mich.: Seeman and Peters, 1915.

Frost, Griffin. *Camp and Prison Journal.* Iowa City, Iowa: Camp Pope Bookshop, 1994.

Gates, Arnold, ed. *The Rough Side of War: The Civil War Journal of Chesley A. Mosman, 1st Lieutenant, Company D, 59th Illinois Volunteer Infantry Regiment.* Garden City, N.Y.: Basin, 1987.

Gettysburg Battle-Field Commission. *Pennsylvania at Gettysburg: Ceremonies at the Dedication of the Monuments Erected by the Commonwealth of Pennsylvania to Major-General George G. Meade, Major General Winfield S. Hancock, Major General John F. Reynolds, and to Mark the Positions of the Pennsylvania Commands Engaged in the Battle.* 3 vols. Harrisburg, Pa.: Wm. Stanley Ray, 1914.

Gettysburg National Military Park Commission. *Annual Reports to the Secretary of War, 1893–1901.* Washington, D.C.: Government Printing Office, 1902.

Gracie, Archibald. *The Truth about Chickamauga.* Dayton, Ohio: Morningside, 1997.

"The Grand Army." *National Tribune*, Nov. 13, 1884.

Grant and Lee: The Appomattox Land and Improvement Company, Niagara Falls, N.Y. Niagara Falls, N.Y.: Niagara Falls Printing House, 1891.

Hartzog, George B., Jr. *Battling for the National Parks*. Mt. Kisco, N.Y.: Moyer Bell, 1988.

Horton, R. G. *A Youth's History of the Great Civil War in the United States, from 1861 to 1865*. New York: Van Evrie, Horton, 1866.

Hulston, John K. *An Ozark Lawyer's Story, 1946–1976*. Republic, Mo.: Western Printing, 1976.

Johnson, Robert Underwood, and Clarence Clough Buel, eds. *Battles and Leaders of the Civil War: Being for the Most Part Contributions by Union and Confederate Officers: Based upon "The Century" War Series*, 4 vols. New York: Century, 1884–87.

Johnston, J. Ambler. *Echoes of 1861–1961*. N.p.: n.p., 1971.

Kennedy, Francis H. *The Dollar and Sense of Battlefield Preservation: The Economic Benefits of Protecting Civil War Battlefields: A Handbook for Community Leaders*. Washington, D.C.: Preservation Press, 1994.

Lossing, Benson J. *Pictorial History of the Civil War in the United States of America*. 3 vols. Hartford, Conn.: Thomas Belknap, 1877.

Lothrop, Charles H. *A History of the First Regiment Iowa Cavalry Veteran Volunteers, from Its Organization in 1861 to Its Muster Out of the United States Service in 1866*. Lyons, Iowa: Beers and Eaton, 1890.

Love, W. A. "Forward and Back." *Confederate Veteran* 33, no. 1 (Jan. 1925): 9–10.

"Make a National Park at Franklin." *Confederate Veteran* 17, no. 1 (Jan. 1909): 15.

Manual of the Panorama of the Battle of Shiloh. Chicago: A. T. Andreas, 1885.

Mason, George. *Illinois at Shiloh*. Chicago: M. A. Donohue, n.d.

McBride, George W. "Shiloh, After Thirty-Two Years." In *Under Both Flags: A Panorama of the Great Civil War as Represented in Story, Anecdote, Adventure, and the Romance of Reality*, edited by C. R. Graham. 220–27. Philadelphia: People's Publishing, 1896.

McGee, B. F. *History of the 72d Indiana Volunteer Infantry of the Mounted Lightening Brigade*. Lafayette, Ind.: S. Vater, 1882.

Moore, Frank, ed. *The Rebellion Record: A Diary of American Events, with Documents, Narratives Illustrative Incidents, Poetry, etc.* 11 vols. New York: D. Vann Nostrand, 1861–68.

National Park Service. *Battle of Franklin Sites, Williamson County, Tennessee: Special Resource Study*. Washington, D.C.: National Park Service, n.d.

———. *Corinth Civil War Boundary Adjustment Study: Corinth Unit of the Shiloh National Military Park: Environmental Assessment*. Washington, D.C.: National Park Service, 2004.

———. *Mission 66 for the National Park System*. Washington, D.C.: National Park Service, 1956.

———. *Our Heritage: A Plan for Its Protection and Use: "Mission 66."* Washington, D.C.: National Park Service, n.d.

————. *Sand Creek Massacre National Historic Site Natural Resource Condition Assessment.* Fort Collins, Colo.: National Park Service, 2013.

————. *Special Resource Study: Corinth, Mississippi.* Washington, D.C.: National Park Service, 2003.

————. *Update to the Civil War Sites Advisory Commission Report on the Nation's Civil War Battlefields: Commonwealth of Pennsylvania.* Washington, D.C.: National Park Service, 2010.

————. *Update to the Civil War Sites Advisory Commission Report on the Nation's Civil War Battlefields: Commonwealth of Virginia.* Washington, D.C.: National Park Service, 2009.

————. *Update to the Civil War Sites Advisory Commission Report on the Nation's Civil War Battlefields: State of Arkansas.* Washington, D.C.: National Park Service, 2010.

————. *Update to the Civil War Sites Advisory Commission Report on the Nation's Civil War Battlefields—Far Western Battlefields: Colorado, Idaho, and New Mexico.* Washington, D.C.: National Park Service, 2010.

————. *Update to the Civil War Sites Advisory Commission Report on the Nation's Civil War Battlefields: State of Georgia.* Washington, D.C.: National Park Service, 2010.

————. *Update to the Civil War Sites Advisory Commission Report on the Nation's Civil War Battlefields: State of Kentucky.* Washington, D.C.: National Park Service, 2008.

————. *Update to the Civil War Sites Advisory Commission Report on the Nation's Civil War Battlefields: State of Louisiana.* Washington, D.C.: National Park Service, 2010.

————. *Update to the Civil War Sites Advisory Commission Report on the Nation's Civil War Battlefields: State of Maryland.* Washington, D.C.: National Park Service, 2010.

————. *Update to the Civil War Sites Advisory Commission Report on the Nation's Civil War Battlefields: State of Mississippi.* Washington, D.C.: National Park Service, 2010.

————. *Update to the Civil War Sites Advisory Commission Report on the Nation's Civil War Battlefields: State of Missouri.* Washington, D.C.: National Park Service, 2011.

————. *Update to the Civil War Sites Advisory Commission Report on the Nation's Civil War Battlefields: State of North Carolina.* Washington, D.C.: National Park Service, 2010.

————. *Update to the Civil War Sites Advisory Commission Report on the Nation's Civil War Battlefields: State of North Dakota.* Washington, D.C.: National Park Service, 2010.

————. *Update to the Civil War Sites Advisory Commission Report on the Nation's Civil War Battlefields: State of Oklahoma.* Washington, D.C.: National Park Service, 2010.

————. *Update to the Civil War Sites Advisory Commission Report on the Nation's Civil War Battlefields: State of South Carolina.* Washington, D.C.: National Park Service, 2010.

————. *Update to the Civil War Sites Advisory Commission Report on the Nation's Civil War Battlefields: State of Tennessee.* Washington, D.C.: National Park Service, 2009.

————. *Update to the Civil War Sites Advisory Commission Report on the Nation's Civil War Battlefields: State of West Virginia.* Washington, D.C.: National Park Service, 2010.

Osborn, George C., ed. "Letters of Senator Edward Cary Walthall to Robert W. Banks." *Journal of Mississippi History* 9 (July 1949): 185–203.

Pennsylvania Andersonville Memorial Commission. *Pennsylvania at Andersonville, Georgia: Ceremonies at the Dedication of the memorial Erected by the Commonwealth of Pennsylvania in the National Cemetery at Andersonville, Georgia.* N.p.: C. E. Aughinbaugh, 1905.

Pennsylvania at Chickamauga and Chattanooga: Ceremonies at the Dedication of the Monuments Erected by the Commonwealth of Pennsylvania to Mark the Positions of the Pennsylvania Commands Engaged in the Battles. N.p.: Wm. Stanley Ray, 1897.

Reagan, Ronald. *Ronald Reagan: An American Life.* New York: Simon and Schuster, 1990.

Reed, David W. *The Battle of Shiloh and the Organizations Engaged.* Washington, D.C.: Government Printing Office, 1902.

———. *Campaigns and Battles of the Twelfth Regiment Iowa Veteran Volunteer Infantry: From Organization, September, 1861, to Muster-Out, January 20, 1866.* N.p.: n.p., n.d.

———. "National Cemeteries and National Military Parks." In *War Sketches and Incidents as Related by the Companions of the Iowa Commandery Military Order of the Loyal Legion of the United States,* 2:355–74. 70 vols. Des Moines, Iowa: n.p., 1898).

Reid, J. W. *History of the Fourth Regiment S.C. Volunteers, from the Commencement of the War until Lee's Surrender.* Greeneville, S.C.: Shannon, 1892.

Report of the Proceedings of the Society of the Army of the Tennessee at the Thirty-First Meeting held at Chicago, Ill., October 10–11, 1899. Cincinnati: F. W. Freeman, 1900.

Report of the Proceedings of the Society of the Army of the Tennessee at the Twenty-Sixth Meeting Held at Council Bluffs, Iowa, October 3rd and 4th, 1894. Cincinnati: F. W. Freeman, 1895.

Rice, DeLong. *The Story of Shiloh.* Jackson, TN: McCowat-Mercer, 1924.

Richardson, Albert D. *The Secret Service, the Field, the Dungeon, and the Escape.* Hartford, Conn.: American Publishing, 1865.

Roberts, Frank H. H., Jr. *Indian Mounds on Shiloh Battlefield.* Photograph in *Explorations and Fieldwork of the Smithsonian Institution in 1934,* 65–68. Washington, D.C.: Smithsonian Institution, 1935.

Roe, Alfred Seelye. *History of the First Regiment of Heavy Artillery Massachusetts Volunteers, Formerly the Fourteenth Regiment of Infantry, 1861–1865.* Boston: Commonwealth Press, 1917.

Rogers, Edmund B. *History of Legislation Relating to the National Park System Through the 82d Congress.* Washington, D.C.: National Park Service, 1958.

Shaw, James B. *History of the Tenth Indiana Volunteer Infantry.* Lafayette, Ind.: Burt-Hayward, 1912.

Shoup, F. A. "How We Went to Shiloh." *Confederate Veteran* 2, no. 5 (May 1894): 137–40.

Small, Harold Adams, ed. *The Road to Richmond: The Civil War Letters of Major Abner R. Small of the 16th Maine Volunteers.* Bronx, N.Y.: Fordham Univ. Press, 2000.

Society of the Army of the Cumberland: Nineteenth Reunion, Chicago, Illinois, 1888. Cincinnati: Robert Clarke, 1889.

Society of the Army of the Cumberland: Twenty-Second Reunion, Columbus, Ohio, 1891. Cincinnati: Robert Clarke, 1892.

Society of the Army of the Cumberland: Twenty-Third Reunion, Chickamauga, Georgia, 1892. Cincinnati: Robert Clarke, 1892.

Staff of the Civil War Sites Advisory Commission. *Civil War Sites Advisory Commission Report on the Nation's Civil War Battlefields.* Washington, D.C.: National Park Service, 1993.

Storrick, W. C. *Gettysburg: The Place, the Battles, the Outcome.* Harrisburg, Pa.: J. Horace McFarland, 1932.

Sutton, Robert K., ed. *Rally on the High Ground: The National Park Service Symposium on the Civil War.* Fort Washington, Pa.: Eastern National, 2001.

Tennessee State Parks. *Fort Pillow State Historic Park General Management Plan.* Nashville: Tennessee Department of Conservation, 1989.

Thulstrup, Thure de. *Battle of Shiloh Lithograph.* L. Prang, 1888.

Trail, Susan W. "Remembering Antietam: Commemoration and Preservation of a Civil War Battlefield." Ph.D. diss., Univ. of Maryland, 2005.

Tunnard, William H. *A Southern Record: The History of the Third Regiment Louisiana Infantry.* Baton Rouge, La.: Published by the Author, 1866.

U.S. Congress. House. *Establishment of National Military Parks—Battle Fields: Hearings Before the Committee and Subcommittee No. 8 of the Committee on Military Affairs, House of Representatives, March 21 and February 8, 1930.* 71st Cong., 2nd sess. Washington, D.C.: Government Printing Office, 1930.

U.S. Quartermaster Department. *Roll of Honor: Names of Soldiers Who Died in Defense of the American Union Interred in the National Cemeteries,* 27 vols. Washington, D.C.: Government Printing Office, 1869.

U.S. War Department. *Official Army Register—January 1, 1922.* Washington, D.C.: War Department, 1922.

Vanderslice, John M. *Gettysburg Then and Now: The Field of American Valor—Where and How Troops Fought and the Troops They Encountered, an Account of the Battle Giving Movements, Positions, and Losses of the Commands Engaged.* Philadelphia: Gettysburg Battlefield Memorial Association, 1899.

"Western Battle-Fields." *National Tribune,* Sept. 9, 1882.

Whitestone Hill: Class I and Class III Cultural Resource Inventories, Dickey County, North Dakota. Bismarck: State Historical Society of North Dakota, 2010.

Wilson's Creek National Battlefield, Republic, Missouri, Cultural Landscape Report. Vol. 1. Omaha: National Park Service Midwest Region, 2004.

Wirth, Conrad L. *Parks, Politics, and the People.* Norman: Univ. of Oklahoma Press, 1980.

Wright, William C. *Confederate Magazine at Fort Wade, Grand Gulf, Mississippi, Excavations 1980–1981.* Archaeological Report No. 8. Jackson: Mississippi Department of Archives and History and Grand Gulf State Military Monument, 1982.

———. *The Confederate Upper Battery Site, Grand Gulf, Mississippi, Excavations 1982.* Archaeological Report No. 13. Jackson: Mississippi Department of Archives and History and Grand Gulf State Military Monument, 1984.

"A Writer." *Southern Bivouac* 3, no. 2 (Oct. 1884): 87.

Secondary Sources

Abroe, Mary Munsell. "'All the Profound Scenes': Federal Preservation of Civil War Battlefields, 1861–1990." Ph.D. diss., Loyola Univ. Chicago, 1996.

Adelman, Garry E. *The Myth of Little Round Top: Gettysburg, PA.* Gettysburg, Pa.: Thomas Publications, 2003.

"An Entire Battlefield Saved." *Hallowed Ground* 15, no. 2 (Summer 2014): 10–11.

Bader, John B. *Taking the Initiative: Leadership Agendas in Congress and the "Contract with America."* Washington, D.C.: Georgetown Univ. Press, 1996.

Baker, Joe. "Haunted History: Slavery and the Landscape of Myth at America's Civil War Sites." *Common Ground* 10, no. 3 (Fall 2005): 14–27.

Barry, Richard Schriver. "Fort Macon: Its History." *North Carolina Historical Review* 27, no. 2 (Apr. 1950): 163–77.

Barth, Aaron L. "Imagining a Battlefield at a Civil War Mistake: The Public History of Whitestone Hill, 1863 to 2013." *Public Historian* 35, no. 3 (Aug. 2013): 81–84.

Bearss, Edwin C. *Hardluck Ironclad: The Sinking and Salvage of the Cairo.* Rev. ed. Baton Rouge: Louisiana State Univ. Press, 1980.

Bell, William Gardner. *Secretaries of War and Secretaries of the Army: Portraits and Biographical Sketches.* Washington, D.C.: Center of Military History, 1982.

Blair, William A. *Cities of the Dead: Contesting the Memory of the Civil War in the South, 1865–1914.* Chapel Hill: Univ. of North Carolina Press, 2003.

Blight, David W. *Beyond the Battlefield: Race, Memory, and the American Civil War.* Amherst: Univ. of Massachusetts Press, 2002.

———. *Race and Reunion: The Civil War in Memory and Reunion.* Cambridge: Harvard Univ. Press, 2001.

Blum, Edward J. *Reforging the White Republic: Race, Religion, and American Nationalism, 1865–1898.* Baton Rouge: Louisiana State Univ. Press, 2005.

Blythe, Leslie H. *National Park System Properties in the National Register of Historic Places.* Washington, D.C.: National Park Service, 1994.

Bodnar, John. *Remaking America: Public Memory, Commemoration, and Patriotism in the Twentieth Century.* Princeton, N.J.: Princeton Univ. Press, 1992.

Boge, Georgie, and Margie Holder Boge. *Paving Over the Past: A History and Guide to Civil War Battlefield Preservation.* Washington, D.C.: Island Press, 1993.

Bolles, Blair. *Tyrant from Illinois: Uncle Joe Cannon's Experiment with Personal Power.* New York: Norton, 1951.

Bowman, Virginia McDaniel. *Historic Williamson County: Old Homes and Sites.* Nashville: Blue and Grey Press, 1971.

Brady, Lisa M. *War upon the Land: Military Strategy and the Transformation of Southern Landscapes during the American Civil War.* Athens: Univ. of Georgia Press, 2012.

Brands, H. W. *T. R.: The Last Romantic.* New York: Basic Books, 1997.

Brent, Joseph E. "Community Consensus Planning for Battlefield Preservation." *CRM: Cultural Resource Management* 23, no. 7 (2000): 7–11.

Brent, Maria Campbell, and Joseph E. Brent. *Confederate Historic Resource Study*. Washington, D.C.: National Cemetery Administration, 2014.

Brown, Daniel A. *Marked for Future Generations: The Hazen Brigade Monument, 1863–1929*. Murfreesboro, Tenn.: Stones River National Battlefield, 1985.

Brown, Kent Masterson. *Retreat from Gettysburg: Lee, Logistics, and the Pennsylvania Campaign*. Chapel Hill: Univ. of North Carolina Press, 2005.

Brown, Thomas J. *Civil War Canon: Sites of Confederate Memory in South Carolina*. Chapel Hill: Univ. of North Carolina Press, 2015.

———. *The Public Art of Civil War Commemoration: A Brief History with Documents*. Boston: Bedford/St. Martin's, 2004.

Burns, Ken. prod. *The Civil War*. Documentary series. PBS, 1990.

Busbey, L. White. *Uncle Joe Cannon: The Story of a Pioneer American*. New York: Holt, 1927.

Busch, Walter E. *Fort Davidson and the Battle of Pilot Knob*. Charleston, S.C.: History Press, 2010.

Butkovich, Brad. *The Battle of Pickett's Mill: Along the Dead Line*. Charleston, S.C.: History Press, 2013.

Butowsky, Harry A. "Nomenclature Used in the National Parks." *CRM Bulletin* 2, no. 4 (Dec. 1979): 3, 7–8.

Cameron, Robert S. *Staff Ride Handbook for the Battle of Perryville, 8 October 1862*. Fort Leavenworth, Kans.: Combat Studies Institute Press, 2005.

"Campaign 150 Success!" *Hallowed Ground* 15, no. 1 (Spring 2014): 6.

Campbell, Gordon. *The Oxford Dictionary of the Renaissance*. New York: Oxford Univ. Press, 2003.

"Carrington Williams Was a Leading Preservationist." *Civil War News*, Sept. 2002.

Chambers, Thomas A. *Memories of War: Visiting Battlegrounds and Bonefields in the Early American Republic*. Ithaca, N.Y.: Cornell Univ. Press, 2012.

Conn, Stetson. *Historical Work in the United States Army, 1862–1954*. Washington, D.C.: Center of Military History, 1980.

Cook, Robert J. *Troubled Commemoration: The American Civil War Centennial, 1961–1965*. Baton Rouge: Louisiana State Univ. Press, 2011.

Cook, Robert J., William L. Barney, and Elizabeth R. Varon. *Secession Winter: When the Union Fell Apart*. Baltimore: Johns Hopkins Univ. Press, 2013.

Cooling, Benjamin F., III. *The Day Lincoln Was Almost Shot: The Fort Stevens Story*. Lanham, Md.: Scarecrow Press, 2013.

Cornish, Dudley Taylor. *The Sable Arm: Negro Troops in the Union Army, 1861–1865*. New York: W. W. Norton, 1966.

Cotham, Edward T., Jr. *Sabine Pass: The Confederacy's Thermopylae*. Austin: Univ. of Texas Press, 2004.

Curran, Katherine. "An Enduring Legacy: Community Engagement in American Battlefield Preservation." Master's thesis, Marist College, 2016.

Dallek, Robert. *Lyndon B. Johnson: Portrait of a President*. New York: Oxford Univ. Press, 2004.

———. *An Unfinished Life: John F. Kennedy, 1917–1963*. Boston: Little, Brown, 2003.

DeSantis, Vincent P. *The Shaping of Modern America, 1877–1920*. Wheeling, WVa.: Forum Press, 1973.

Desjardin, Thomas A. *These Honored Dead: How the Story of Gettysburg Shaped American Memory*. Cambridge, Mass.: Da Capo, 2003.

"Did You Know." *Hallowed Ground* 15, no. 2 (Summer 2014): 11.

Dobak, William A. *Freedom by the Sword: The U.S. Colored Troops, 1862–1867*. Washington, D.C.: Center of Military History, 2011.

Duncan, Dayton, and Ken Burns. *The National Parks: America's Best Idea*. New York: Knopf, 2009.

Durham, Roger S. *Fort McAllister*. Mount Pleasant, S.C.: Arcadia, 2004.

Eatherly, Charles R., ed. *Arizona State Parks: The Beginning*. Phoenix: Arizona State Parks, 2007.

Fahs, Alice, and Joan Waugh, eds. *The Memory of the Civil War in American Culture*. Chapel Hill: Univ. of North Carolina Press, 2004.

Farrell, James J. *Inventing the American Way of Death, 1830–1920*. Philadelphia: Temple Univ. Press, 1980.

Farrell, John A. "McMansionizing History: Can Anyone Save Some of the Civil War's Most Important Battlefields?" *Washington Post Magazine*, Nov. 16, 2008, 14–17, 25–29.

Faust, Drew Gilpin. *This Republic of Suffering: Death and the American Civil War*. New York: Alfred A. Knopf, 2008.

Folwell, William Watts. *A History of Minnesota*. 4 vols. St. Paul: Minnesota Historical Society, 1924.

Foner, Eric. *Reconstruction: America's Unfinished Revolution, 1863–1877*. New York: Harper Collins, 1989.

"For Shiloh Sesquicentennial, Major Preservation Victories." *Hallowed Ground* 13, no. 2 (Summer 2012): 4–5.

"Fort Gaines Named One of America's Most Endangered." *Preservation: Alabama Historical Commission Report* 37, no. 6 (Sept.—Oct. 2011): 1.

Foster, Gaines M. *Ghosts of the Confederacy: Defeat, the Lost Cause, and the Emergence of the New South*. New York: Oxford Univ. Press, 1987.

Franklin, John Hope, and Evelyn Higginbotham. *From Slavery to Freedom: A History of African Americans*. 9th ed. New York: McGraw Hill, 2010.

"Franklin, Tenn. Celebrates Demise of the Pizza Hut." *Civil War News*, Jan. 2006.

Gannon, Barbara A. *The Won Cause: Black and White Comradeship in the Grand Army of the Republic*. Chapel Hill: Univ. of North Carolina Press, 2011.

George, John Riley. "Stones River: Creating a Battlefield Park, 1862–1932." Ph.D. diss., Middle Tennessee State Univ., 2013.

Gerow, Peggy A. *Guardian of the Trail: Archeological and Historical Investigations at Fort Craig.* Santa Fe, N.M.: Bureau of Land Management, 2004.

"Gettysburg Casino Controversy Nears Conclusion." *Hallowed Ground* 11, no. 42 (Winter 2010): 6–7.

Gilliam, Catharine M. "Taking Law: Fact and Fiction." *CRM: Cultural Resources Management* 20, no. 5 (1997): 15–18.

Glatthaar, Joseph T. *Forged in Battle: The Civil War Alliance of Black Soldiers and White Officers.* New York: Free Press, 1989.

Goodheart, Adam. "Civil War Battlefields: Saving the Landscape of America's Deadliest War." *National Geographic* (Apr. 2005): 62–85.

Greene, A. Wilson. "The Association for the Preservation of Civil War Sites." *CRM Bulletin* 13, no. 53 (1990): 3.

———. "The Origins of the National Museum of the Civil War Soldier at Pamplin Historical Park." *Hallowed Ground* 14, no. 4 (Winter 2013): 32–34.

Gwinn, William Rea. *Uncle Joe Cannon, Archfoe of Insurgency: A History of the Rise and Fall of Cannonism.* New York: Bookman Associates, 1957.

Hagerty, Meghan. "Park Service Works to Connect Washington's Fort Circle Parks." *Hallowed Ground* 9, no. 3 (Fall 2008): 45–46.

Halbwachs, Maurice. *The Collective Memory.* New York: Harper and Row, 1980.

Harmon, David, Francis P. McManamon, and Dwight T. Pitcaithley. *The Antiquities Act: A Century of American Archaeology, Historic Preservation, and Nature Conservation.* Tucson: Univ. of Arizona Press, 2006.

Harris, M. Keith. *Across the Bloody Chasm: The Culture of Commemoration among Civil War Veterans.* Baton Rouge: Louisiana State Univ. Press, 2014.

Hayes, Benjamin. "Without Controversy: The Development of Fort Pillow State Historic Park." In *Rethinking Protected Areas in a Changing World: Proceedings of the 2011 George Wright Society Biennial Conference on Parks, Protected Areas, and Cultural Sites,* edited by Samantha Weber, 137–41. Hancock, Mich.: George Wright Society, 2012.

Heidler, David S., and Jeanne T. Heidler, eds. *Encyclopedia of the American Civil War: A Political, Social, and Military History.* 5 vols. Santa Barbara, Calif.: ABC-CLIO, 2000.

Hennessy, John. "Interpreting the Civil War: Moving Beyond Battlefields." *CRM: Cultural Resources Management* 25, no. 4 (2002): 10–12.

Hess, Earl J. *Kennesaw Mountain: Sherman, Johnston and the Atlanta Campaign.* Chapel Hill: Univ. of North Carolina Press, 2013.

Hillyer, Reiko. *Designing Dixie: Tourism, Memory, and Urban Space in the New South.* Charlottesville: Univ. of Virginia Press, 2014.

Historic Listing of National Park Service Officials. Washington, D.C.: National Park Service, 1991.

"History Under Siege: Dispatches from 150 Years of Civil War Battlefield Preservation." *Hallowed Ground* 12, no. 3 (Fall 2011): i–xvi.

Holt, Dean W. *American Military Cemeteries: A Comprehensive Illustrated Guide to the Hallowed Grounds of the United States, Including Cemeteries Overseas.* Jefferson, N.C.: McFarland, 1992.

Holzer, Harold. "Vanished Heritage." *American Heritage* 56, no. 4 (Sept. 2005): 41.

Horton, James O., and Lois E. Horton, eds. *Slavery and Public History: The Tough Stuff of American Memory.* Chapel Hill: Univ. of North Carolina Press, 2008.

Hosmer, Charles B., Jr. *Presence of the Past: A History of the Preservation Movement in the United States before Williamsburg.* New York: G. P. Putnam's Sons, 1965.

———. *Preservation Comes of Age: From Williamsburg to the National Trust, 1926–1949.* 2 vols. Charlottesville: Univ. Press of Virginia, 1981.

Hunt, Robert E. *The Good Men Who Won the War: Army of the Cumberland Veterans and the Emancipation Memory.* Tuscaloosa: Univ. of Alabama Press, 2010.

Janney, Caroline E. *Burying the Dead but Not the Past: Ladies' Memorial Associations and the Lost Cause.* Chapel Hill: Univ. of North Carolina Press, 2012.

———. "No 'Sickly Sentimental Gush': Chickamauga and Chattanooga National Military Park and the Limits of Reconciliation." In *Gateway to the Confederacy: New Perspectives on the Chickamauga and Chattanooga Campaigns, 1862–1863,* edited by Wiley Sword and Evan C. Jones, 285–310. Baton Rouge: Louisiana State Univ. Press, 2014.

———. *Remembering the Civil War: Reunion and the Limits of Reconciliation.* Chapel Hill: Univ. of North Carolina Press, 2013.

———. "War over a Shrine of Peace: The Appomattox Peace Monument and Retreat from Reconciliation." *Journal of Southern History* 77, no. 1 (Feb. 2011): 91–120.

Kammen, Michael. *Mystic Chords of Memory: The Transformation of Tradition in American Culture.* New York: Vintage Books, 1991.

Keefer, Bradley S. *Conflicting Memories on the River of Death: The Chickamauga Battlefield and the Spanish American War, 1863–1933.* Kent, Ohio: Kent State Univ. Press, 2013.

Kelman, Ari. *A Misplaced Massacre: Struggling over the Memory of Sand Creek.* Cambridge: Harvard Univ. Press, 2013.

Kennedy, David M. *Freedom from Fear: The American People in Depression and War, 1929–1945.* New York: Oxford Univ. Press, 1999.

Kennedy, Francis H., ed. *The Civil War Battlefield Guide.* Boston: Houghton Mifflin, 1990.

Kinsel, Amy. "'From These Honored Dead': Gettysburg in American Culture, 1863–1938." Ph.D. diss., Cornell Univ., 1992.

Kreiser, Lawrence A., Jr., and Randal Allred. *The Civil War in Popular Culture: Memory and Meaning.* Lexington: Univ. Press of Kentucky, 2014.

Krick, Robert E. L. "The Civil War's First Monument: Bartow's Marker at Manassas." *Blue and Gray* 8, no. 4 (Apr. 1991): 33.

Landrum, Ney C. *The State Park Movement in America: A Critical Review.* Columbia: Univ. of Missouri Press, 2013.

Langguth, A. J. *After Lincoln: How the North Won the Civil War and Lost the Peace.* New York: Simon and Shuster, 2014.

Latschar, John. "Coming to Terms with the Civil War at Gettysburg National Military Park." *CRM: The Journal of Heritage Stewardship* 4, no. 2 (Summer 2007): 6–17.

Lee, Ronald F. *The Origin and Evolution of the National Military Park Idea.* Washington, D.C.: National Park Service, 1973.

Leuchtenburg, William E. *Franklin D. Roosevelt and the New Deal, 1932–1940.* New York: Harper and Row, 1963.

Levin, Kevin M. *Remembering the Battle of the Crater: War as Murder.* Lexington: Univ. Press of Kentucky, 2012.

Linenthal, Edward T. *Sacred Ground: America and Their Battlefields.* Urbana: Univ. of Illinois Press, 1991.

Linenthal, Edward T., and Tom Engelhardt. *History Wars: The Enola Gay and Other Battles for the American Past.* New York: Henry Holt, 1996.

Livingood, James W. "Chickamauga and Chattanooga National Military Park." *Tennessee Historical Quarterly* 23, no. 1 (Mar. 1964): 3–23.

Long, E. B. *The Civil War Day by Day: An Almanac 1861–1865.* New York: Doubleday, 1971.

Lowe, William C. "'A Grand and Patriotic Pilgrimage': The Iowa Civil War Monuments Dedication Tour of 1906." *Annals of Iowa* 69, no. 1 (Winter 2010): 1–50.

Mackintosh, Barry. *C&O Canal: The Making of a Park.* Washington, D.C.: National Park Service, 1991.

———. *The National Historic Preservation Act and the National Park Service: A History.* Washington, D.C.: National Park Service, 1986.

Madison, James H. "Civil War Memories and 'Pardnership Forgittin', 1865–1913." *Indiana Magazine of History* 99, no. 3 (Sept. 2003): 198–230.

Martin, David G. *The Campaign of Shiloh, March–April, 1862.* New York: Fairfax Press, 1987.

Marvel, William. *Andersonville: The Last Depot.* Chapel Hill: Univ. of North Carolina Press, 1994.

———. *A Place Called Appomattox.* Chapel Hill: Univ. of North Carolina Press, 2000.

McDonough, James L. *Nashville: The Western Confederacy's Final Gamble.* Knoxville: Univ. of Tennessee Press, 2004.

McDonough, James L., and Thomas L. Connelly. *Five Tragic Hours: The Battle of Franklin.* Knoxville: Univ. of Tennessee Press, 1983.

McKeever, Kermit. *Where People and Nature Meet: A History of the West Virginia State Parks.* Charleston, WVa.: Pictorial Histories, 1988.

McPherson, James M. *Battle Cry of Freedom: The Civil War Era.* New York: Oxford Univ. Press, 1988.

Meader, J. Faith. *Fort Pulaski National Monument Administrative History.* Atlanta: National Park Service Southeast Region, 2003.

Meyer, Roy W. *Everyone's Country Estate: A History of Minnesota's State Parks.* St. Paul: Minnesota Historical Society Press, 1991.

Millett, Allan R., Peter Maslowski, and William B. Feis. *For the Common Defense: A Military History of the United States from 1607–2012.* New York: Free Press, 2012.

Morris, Stephen A. "American Battlefield Protection Program: Evolving Relationships." *CRM: Cultural Resource Management* 14, no. 4 (1991): 10–11.

Moss, George D. *The Rise of Modern America.* Upper Saddle River, N.J.: Prentice Hall, 1995.

Moyer, Teresa S., and Paul A. Shackel. *The Making of Harpers Ferry National Historical Park: A Devil, Two Rivers, and a Dream.* Lanham, Md.: Altamira Press, 2008.

Murray, Jennifer M. "'Far Above Our Poor Power to Add or Detract': National Park Service Administration of the Gettysburg Battlefield, 1933–1938." *Civil War History* 55, no. 1 (Mar. 2009): 56–81.

————. *On a Great Battlefield: The Making, Management, and Memory of Gettysburg National Military Park, 1933–2012.* Knoxville: Univ. of Tennessee Press, 2014.

Murtagh, William J. *Keeping Time: The History and Theory of Preservation in America.* New York: Wiley, 2005.

Musicant, Ivan. *Empire by Default: The Spanish-American War and the Dawn of the American Century.* New York: Henry Holt, 1998.

Myers, Richard. *The Vicksburg National Cemetery: An Administrative History.* Washington, D.C.: National Park Service, 1968.

Naftali, Timothy. *George H. W. Bush.* New York: Times Books, 2007.

"National American Indian Heritage Month." *CRM Bulletin* 13, no. 5 (1990): 16.

Neff, John R. *Honoring the Civil War Dead: Commemoration and the Problem of Reconciliation.* Lawrence: Univ. Press of Kansas, 2005.

Nelson, Danyelle A. "No Place for Women: Interpreting Civil War Battlefields." *CRM: Cultural Resource Management* 20, no. 3 (1997): 59.

Nelson, David J. "Florida Crackers and Yankee Tourists: The Civilian Conservation Corps, the Florida Park Service and the Emergence of Modern Florida Tourism." Ph.D. diss., Florida State Univ., 2008.

Nelson, Megan Kate. *Ruin Nation: Destruction and the American Civil War.* Athens: Univ. of Georgia Press, 2012.

Nevin, David. *The Road to Shiloh: Early Battles in the West.* Alexandria: Time-Life Books, 1983.

Noe, Kenneth W. *Perryville: This Grand Havoc of Battle.* Lexington: Univ. Press of Kentucky, 2001.

Owen, Lorrie K., ed. *Dictionary of Ohio Historic Places.* 2 vols. Minneapolis: Somerset, 1999.

Paige, John C. *The Civilian Conservation Corps and the National Park Service, 1933–1942: An Administrative History.* Washington, D.C.: National Park Service, 1985.

Paige, John C., and Jerome A. Greene. *Administrative History of Chickamauga and Chattanooga National Military Park.* Denver: National Park Service, 1983.

Painter, Nell Irvin. *Standing at Armageddon: The United States, 1877–1919.* New York: W. W. Norton, 1987.

Panhorst, Michael W. "'The First of Our Hundred Battle Monuments': Civil War Battle-field Monuments Built by Active-Duty Soldiers During the Civil War." *Southern Cultures* 20, no. 4 (Winter 2014): 22–43.

———. "Lest We Forget: Monuments and Memorial Sculpture in National Military Parks on Civil War Battlefields, 1861–1917." Ph.D. diss., Univ. of Delaware, 1988.

———. *The Memorial Art and Architecture of Vicksburg National Military Park.* Kent, Ohio: Kent State Univ. Press, 2015.

Patterson, James T. *Grand Expectations: The United States 1945–1974.* New York: Oxford Univ. Press, 1996.

———. *Restless Giant: The United States from Watergate to Bush v. Gore.* York: Oxford Univ. Press, 2007.

"Pecos National Historical Park—Glorieta Battlefield Trail Progress." *Hallowed Ground* 8, no. 4 (Winter 2007): 38.

Peterson, Gloria. *Administrative History: Fort Donelson National Military Park, Dover, Tennessee.* Washington, D.C.: National Park Service, 1968.

Piehler, G. Kurt. *Remembering War the American Way.* Washington, D.C.: Smithsonian Institution Press, 1995.

Pitcaithley, Dwight T. "The American Civil War and the Preservation of Memory." *CRM: Cultural Resources Management* 25, no. 4 (2002): 5–9.

Pollock, Robert R. "The Battle of Wilson's Creek in History and Memory." Master's thesis, Missouri State Univ., 2008.

Posner, Gerald. *Killing the Dream: James Earl Ray and the Assassination of Martin Luther King, Jr.* New York: Random House, 1998.

"Preserving Kentucky Battlefields." *Hallowed Ground* 11, no. 1 (Spring 2010): 26–35.

"Protecting Battlefields." *CRM Bulletin* 13, no. 5 (1990): 1–2.

Reardon, Carol. *Pickett's Charge in History and Memory.* Chapel Hill: Univ. of North Carolina Press, 1997.

Richardson, Heather Cox. *West from Appomattox: The Reconstruction of America After the Civil War.* New Haven, Conn.: Yale Univ. Press, 2008.

Riggins, Van L. *A History of Fort Donelson National Military Park Tennessee.* Washington, D.C.: National Park Service, 1958.

Robertson, William G. *The Staff Ride.* Washington, D.C.: Center of Military History, 1987.

Robison, Dan M. "The Carter House, Focus of the Battle of Nashville." *Tennessee Historical Quarterly* 22, no. 1 (Mar. 1963): 3–21.

Salmond, John A. *The Civilian Conservation Corps, 1933–1942: A New Deal Case Study.* Durham, N.C.: Duke Univ. Press, 1967.

"Saving Richmond's Battlefields—Gaines' Mill." *Hallowed Ground* 13, no. 2 (Summer 2012): 10–11.

Schroeder, Patrick A. *The Confederate Cemetery at Appomattox.* Lynchburg, Va.: Schroeder Publications, 1999.

———, ed. *Tarheels: Five Points in the Record of North Carolina in the Great War of 1861–65.* Lynchburg, Va.: Schroeder, 2000.

Sellars, Richard W. "The Granite Orchards of Gettysburg." *History News* 41, no. 4 (July–Aug. 1986): 22–23.

———. "The National Park System and the Historic American Past: A Brief Overview and Reflection." *George Wright Forum* 24, no. 1 (2007): 8–22.

———. "Pilgrim Places: Civil War Battlefields, Historic Preservation, and America's First National Military Parks, 1863–1900." *CRM: The Journal of Heritage Stewardship* 2, no. 1 (Winter 2005): 22–52.

———. *Pilgrim Places: Civil War Battlefields, Historic Preservation, and America's First National Military Parks, 1863–1900.* Fort Washington, Pa.: Eastern National, 2005.

———. "Vigil of Silence: The Civil War Memorials." *History News* 41, no. 4 (July—Aug. 1986): 19–21.

Serrano, Richard A. *Last of the Blue and Gray: Old Men, Stolen Glory, and the Mystery that Outlived the Civil War.* Washington, D.C.: Smithsonian, 2013.

Shea, William L., and Earl J. Hess. *Pea Ridge: Civil War Campaign in the West.* Chapel Hill: Univ. of North Carolina Press, 1992.

Shedd, Charles E. *A History of Shiloh National Military Park, Tennessee.* Washington, D.C.: Government Printing Office, 1954.

Sloane, David Charles. *The Last Great Necessity: Cemeteries in American History.* Baltimore: Johns Hopkins Univ. Press, 1991.

Smith, Jean Edward. *FDR.* New York: Random House, 2007.

Smith, Timothy B. "Black Soldiers and the CCC at Shiloh National Military Park." *CRM: The Journal of Heritage Stewardship* 3, no. 2 (Summer 2006): 73–84.

———. *Champion Hill: Decisive Battle for Vicksburg.* New York: Savas Beatie, 2004.

———. "A Chattanooga Plan: The Gateway City's Critical Role in Civil War Battlefield Preservation." In *The Chattanooga Campaign*, edited by Steven E. Woodworth and Charles D. Grear, 203–15. Carbondale: Southern Illinois Univ. Press, 2012.

———. *A Chickamauga Memorial: The Establishment of America's First Civil War National Military Park.* Knoxville: Univ. of Tennessee Press, 2009.

———. *Corinth 1862: Siege, Battle, Occupation.* Lawrence: Univ. of Kansas Press, 2012.

———. "DeLong Rice: Shiloh's Poet Preservationist." *Tennessee Historical Quarterly* 63, no. 2 (2004): 128–43.

———. *The Golden Age of Battlefield Preservation: The Decade of the 1890s and the Establishment of America's First Five Military Parks.* Knoxville: Univ. of Tennessee Press, 2008.

———. "'The Handsomest Cemetery in the South': Shiloh National Cemetery." *West Tennessee Historical Society Papers* 56 (2002): 1–16.

———. "Henry Van Ness Boynton and Chickamauga: The Pillars of the Modern Military Park Movement." In *The Chickamauga Campaign*, edited by Steven E. Woodworth, 165–87. Carbondale: Southern Illinois Univ. Press, 2010.

———. *The Mississippi Secession Convention: Delegates and Deliberations in Politics and War, 1861–1865*. Jackson: Univ. Press of Mississippi, 2014.

———. "The Politics of Battlefield Preservation: David B. Henderson and the National Military Parks." *Annals of Iowa* 66, nos. 3 and 4 (Summer/Fall 2007): 293–320.

———. *Rethinking Shiloh: Myth and Memory*. Knoxville: Univ. of Tennessee Press, 2013.

———. "*Shiloh: Portrait of a Battle*: Fifty Years Later." *Tennessee Historical Quarterly* 65, no. 2 (Summer 2006): 147–61.

———. "Shiloh's False Hero." *Civil War Times* 47, no. 6 (Dec. 2008): 28–35.

———. *This Great Battlefield of Shiloh: History, Memory, and the Establishment of a Civil War National Military Park*. Knoxville: Univ. of Tennessee Press, 2004.

———. *The Untold Story of Shiloh: The Battle and the Battlefield*. Knoxville: Univ. of Tennessee Press, 2006.

Snell, Charles W., and Sharon A. Brown. *Antietam National Battlefield and National Cemetery*. Washington, D.C.: National Park Service, 1986.

Spielvogel, J. Christian. *Interpreting Sacred Ground: The Rhetoric of National Civil War Parks and Battlefields*. Tuscaloosa: Univ. of Alabama Press, 2013.

Stampp, Kenneth M. *The Imperiled Union: Essays on the Background of the Civil War*. New York: Oxford Univ. Press, 1980.

Stauffer, William H. "There's No General Rule about Position of Feet on Equestrian Statues." *Civil War Times* 2 (July 1960): 6.

Stephens, Rachel. "The Battle of Shiloh Cyclorama: A Biased Commemoration." *Montage* 2 (2008): 103–16.

Stipe, Robert E., ed. *A Richer Heritage: Historic Preservation in the Twenty-first Century*. Chapel Hill: Univ. of North Carolina Press, 2003.

Stone, Richard D., and Mary M. Graham. "Selective Civil War Battlefield Preservation as a Method of Marketing the Southern 'Lost Cause,'" *Charm*, 2007, 221–27.

Styles, Sean M. *Stones River National Battlefield Historic Resource Study*. Atlanta: National Park Service Southeast Region, 2004.

Timmons, Carlin, and Sandy Pusey. "Fort Sumter National Monument's New Facility at Liberty Square." *CRM: Cultural Resources Management* 25, no. 4 (2002): 40–41.

Toplin, Robert Brent, ed. *Ken Burns's The Civil War: Historians Respond*. New York: Oxford Univ. Press, 1996.

Townsend, Jan. "Catalyst for Battlefield Preservation: The Civil War Sites Advisory Commission Study." *CRM: Cultural Resources Management* 20, no. 5 (1997): 7–10.

Tucker, Glenn. *Chickamauga: Bloody Battle in the West*. Indianapolis: Bobbs-Merrill, 1961.

Tyler, Norman, Ted J. Ligabel, and Ilene R. Tyler. *Historic Preservation: An Introduction to Its History, Principles, and Practice*. 2nd ed. New York: Norton, 2009.

"Unprecedented Mansfield Preservation." *Hallowed Ground* 15, no. 2 (Summer 2014): 8.

Unrau, Harlan D. *Administrative History: Gettysburg National Military Park and National Cemetery*. Denver: National Park Service, 1991.

Unrau, Harlan D., and George F. Williss. *Administrative History: Expansion of the National Park Service in the 1930s.* Washington, D.C.: National Park Service, 1983.

Upchurch, Thomas Adams. *Legislating Racism: The Billion Dollar Congress and the Birth of Jim Crow.* Lexington: Univ. Press of Kentucky, 2004.

Wade, Gregory L. "Nashville's Fort Negley Opens to the Public." *Civil War News,* Jan. 2005.

Wagner, Margaret E., Gary W. Gallagher, and Paul Finkelman, eds. *Library of Congress Civil War Desk Reference.* New York: Simon and Shuster, 2002.

Waldbauer, Richard, and Sherry Hutt. "The Antiquities Act of 1906 at Its Centennial." *CRM: The Journal of Heritage Stewardship* 3, no. 1 (Winter 2006): 36–48.

Waldrep, Christopher. *Vicksburg's Long Shadow: The Civil War Legacy of Race and Remembrance.* New York: Rowman and Littlefield, 2005.

Wallace, Lee A., Jr., and Martin R. Conway. *A History of Petersburg Battlefield.* Washington, D.C.: National Park Service, 1983.

"Walmart Controversy Fully Resolved." *Hallowed Ground* 15, no. 1 (Spring 2014): 14–15.

Ward, Geoffrey C., Ric Burns, and Ken Burns. *The Civil War: An Illustrated History.* New York: Knopf, 1990.

Weeks, Jim. *Gettysburg: Memory, Market, and an American Shrine.* Princeton, N.J.: Princeton Univ. Press, 2003.

Weigley, Russell F. *The American Way of War: A History of United States Military Strategy and Policy.* New York: Macmillan, 1973.

Welch, Paul D. *Archeology at Shiloh Indian Mounds, 1899–1999.* Tuscaloosa: Univ. of Alabama Press, 2006.

Wickham, Chris. *The Inheritance of Rome: Illuminating the Dark Ages, 400–1000.* New York: Viking, 2009.

Wiener, Jon. "Civil War, Cold War, Civil Rights: The Civil War Centennial in Context, 1960–1965." In *The Memory of the Civil War in American Culture,* edited by Alice Fahs and Joan Waugh, 237–57. Chapel Hill: Univ. of North Carolina Press, 2004.

Willett, Ann Wilson. "A History of Stones River National Military Park." Master's thesis, Middle Tennessee State College, 1958.

Wills, Gary. *Lincoln at Gettysburg: The Words that Remade America.* New York: Simon and Shuster, 1992.

Winschel, Terrence J. "Stephen D. Lee and the Making of an American Shrine." *Journal of Mississippi History* 63, no. 1 (2001): 17–32.

Wittenberg, Eric J. *The Battle of Monroe's Crossroads and the Civil War's Final Campaign.* El Dorado Hills, Calif.: Savas Beatie, 2006.

Woodward, C. Vann. *The Strange Career of Jim Crow.* 3rd ed. New York: Oxford Univ. Press, 1989.

Zeller, Bob. "The Birth of the Modern Battlefield Preservation Movement." *Hallowed Ground* 13, no. 2 (Summer 2012): 6–7.

Zenzen, Joan M. *Battling for Manassas: The Fifty-Year Preservation Struggle at Manassas National Battlefield Park.* Univ. Park: Pennsylvania State Univ. Press, 1998.

Websites

Arizona State Parks. http://azstateparks.com.

Civil War Trust. http://www.civilwar.org.

Franklin's Charge. http://www.franklinscharge.com.

Gettysburg Foundation. http://www.gettysburgfoundation.org.

Georgia Department of Natural Resources, State Parks and Historic Sites. http://gastateparks.org.

Harrell, Frank. http://nps-vip.net.

Harrison County Parks. http://www.harrisoncountyparks.com.

Historic Staunton River Foundation and Staunton River Battlefield State Park. http://www.stauntonriverbattlefield.org.

Kansas Historical Society. http://kshs.org.

Missouri State Parks. http://mostateparks.com.

National Park Service. http://www.nps.gov.

Resaca Battlefield Historical Site Park. http://www.resacabattlefield.org.

Tennessee GenWeb. http://tngenweb.org.

Personal Communication

Berthelot, Raymond. Jan. 13 and 14, 2011.

Fraering, Michael. July 27, 2010.

Hamilton, James. June 4, 2014.

Lacy, Rob. July 1, 2014.

McKinney, Zeb. Jan. 25, 2006.

Ogden, Jim. Oct. 20, 2003.

Phillips, Alvin. July 28, 2010.

Rogness, Diane. May 22 and 30, 2014.

Winschel, Terry. Aug. 18, 2004 and Sept. 19, 2014.

Index

Numbers in **boldface** refer to illustrations.